FANTASTIC EARTH FACTS

FANTASTIC EARTH FACTS

Miles Kelly

First published in 2017 by Miles Kelly Publishing Ltd
Harding's Barn, Bardfield End Green, Thaxted, Essex, CM6 3PX, UK

2 4 6 8 10 9 7 5 3 1

Publishing Director Belinda Gallagher
Creative Director Jo Cowan
Editors Carly Blake, Fran Bromage, Rosie Neave, Sarah Parkin, Claire Philip
Editorial Assistant Lauren White
Cover Designer Simon Lee
Designers Kayleigh Allen, John Christopher, Jo Cowan, Joe Jones, Sally Lace, Simon Lee, Sophie Pelham, Andrea Slane, Elaine Wilkinson
Image Manager Liberty Newton
Production Elizabeth Collins, Caroline Kelly
Reprographics Stephan Davis, Jennifer Cozens, Thom Allaway
Assets Lorraine King

ISBN 978-1-78617-334-8

Printed in China

British Library Cataloguing-in-Publication Data
A catalogue record for this book is available from the British Library

Made with paper from a sustainable forest

www.mileskelly.net

Contents

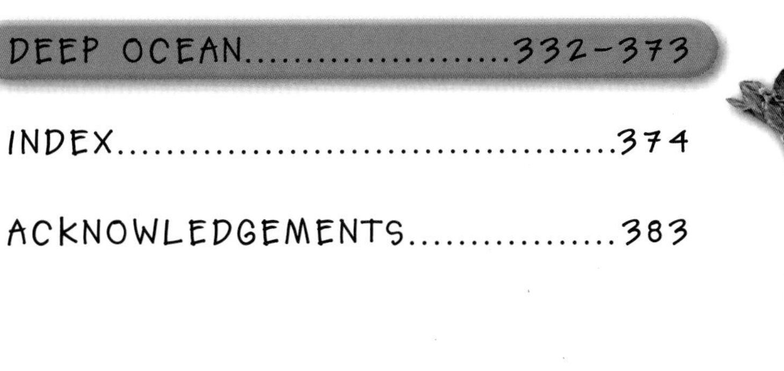

PLANET EARTH

EXTREME EARTH

ROCKS AND MINERALS

VOLCANOES

WEATHER

RAINFORESTS

FOSSILS

POLAR LANDS

PLANET EARTH

1 The Earth is a huge ball of rock moving through space at nearly 3000 metres per second. It weighs 6000 million, million, million tonnes. Up to two-thirds of the Earth's rocky surface is covered by water – this makes the seas and oceans. Rock that is not covered by water makes the land. Surrounding the Earth is a layer of gases called the atmosphere (air). This reaches about 700 kilometres from the Earth's surface – then space begins.

▶ Mercury, the planet nearest to the Sun, is small and hot. Venus and Earth are rocky and cooler.

Venus

Mercury

Sun

OCEANS

DEEP OCEAN

Where did Earth come from?

2 The Earth came from a cloud in space. Scientists think the Earth formed from a huge cloud of gas and dust around 4500 million years ago. A star near the cloud exploded, making the cloud spin. As the cloud spun around, gases gathered at its centre and formed the Sun. Dust whizzed around the Sun and stuck together to form lumps of rock. In time the rocks crashed into each other to make the planets. The Earth is one of these planets.

▶ Clouds of gas and dust are made by the remains of old stars that have exploded or simply stopped shining. It is here that new stars and their planets form.

3 At first the Earth was very hot. As the rocks crashed together they warmed each other up. Later, as the Earth formed, the rocks inside it melted. The new Earth was a ball of liquid rock with a thin, solid shell.

Moon
Earth

In a spin

6 The Earth is like a huge spinning top. It continues to spin because it was formed from a spinning cloud of gas and dust. It does not spin straight up like a top but leans a little to one side. The Earth takes 24 hours to spin around once. We call this period of time a day.

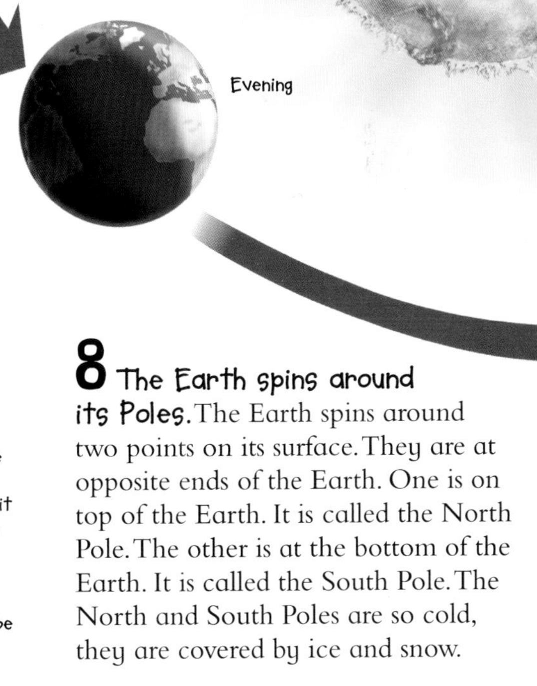

7 The Earth's spinning makes day and night. Each part of the Earth spins towards the Sun, and then away from it every day. When a part of the Earth is facing the Sun it is day-time there. When that part is facing away from the Sun it is night-time. Is the Earth facing the Sun or facing away from it where you are?

◀ If you were in space and looked at the Earth from the side, it would appear to move from left to right. If you looked down on Earth from the North Pole, it would seem to be moving anticlockwise.

8 The Earth spins around its Poles. The Earth spins around two points on its surface. They are at opposite ends of the Earth. One is on top of the Earth. It is called the North Pole. The other is at the bottom of the Earth. It is called the South Pole. The North and South Poles are so cold, they are covered by ice and snow.

4 Huge numbers of large rocks called meteorites crashed into the Earth. They made round hollows on the surface. These hollows are called craters. The Moon was hit with rocks at the same time. Look at the Moon with binoculars – you can see the craters that were made long ago.

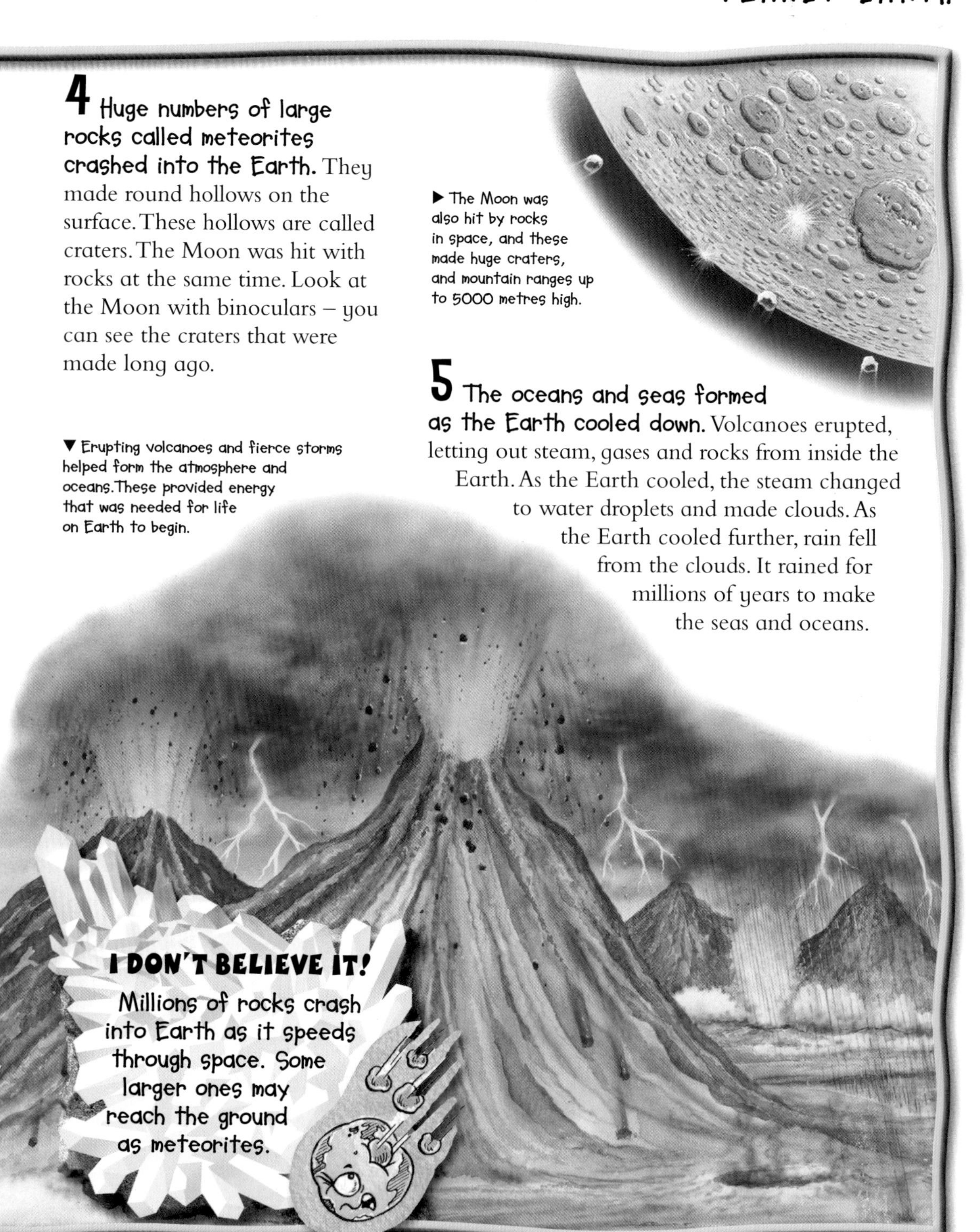

▶ The Moon was also hit by rocks in space, and these made huge craters, and mountain ranges up to 5000 metres high.

5 The oceans and seas formed as the Earth cooled down. Volcanoes erupted, letting out steam, gases and rocks from inside the Earth. As the Earth cooled, the steam changed to water droplets and made clouds. As the Earth cooled further, rain fell from the clouds. It rained for millions of years to make the seas and oceans.

▼ Erupting volcanoes and fierce storms helped form the atmosphere and oceans. These provided energy that was needed for life on Earth to begin.

I DON'T BELIEVE IT!

Millions of rocks crash into Earth as it speeds through space. Some larger ones may reach the ground as meteorites.

Massive mountains

10 The youngest mountains on Earth are the highest. Highest of all is Mount Everest, which formed 15 million years ago. Young mountains have jagged peaks because softer rocks on the mountain top are broken down by the weather. These pointy peaks are made from harder rocks that take longer to break down. In time, even these hard rocks are worn away. This makes an older mountain shorter and gives its top a rounded shape.

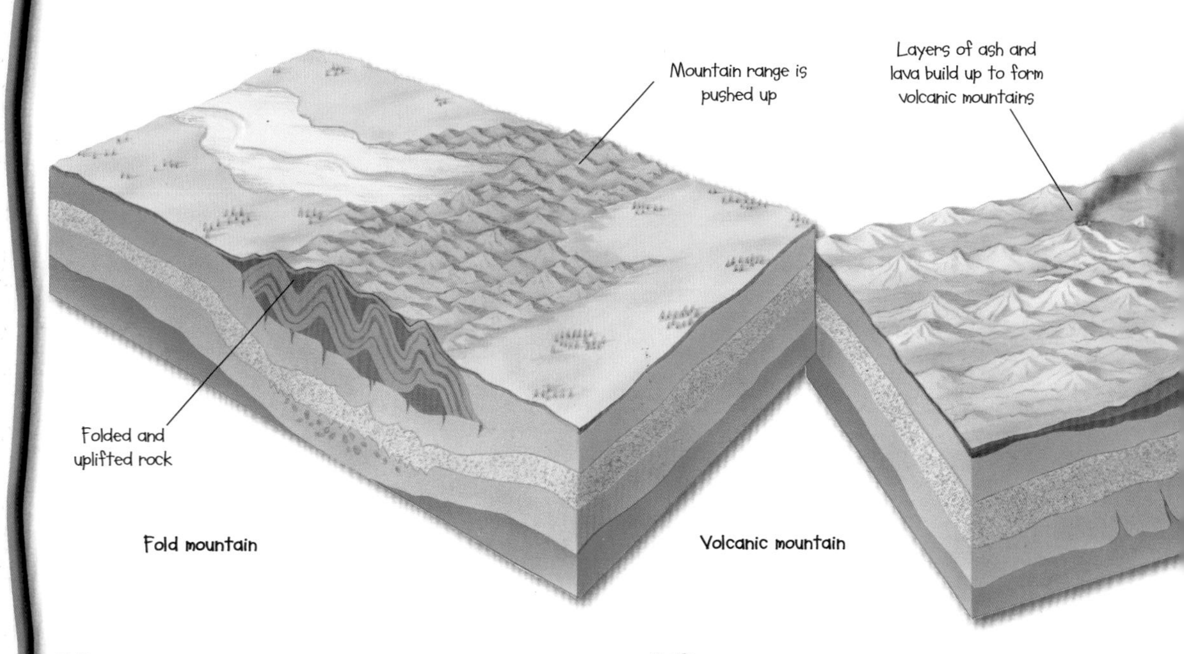

11 When plates in the Earth's crust crash together, mountains are formed. When two continental plates crash together, the crust at the edge of the plates crumples and folds, pushing up ranges of mountains. The Himalayan Mountains in Asia formed in this way.

12 Some of the Earth's highest mountains are volcanoes. These are formed when molten rock (lava) erupts through the Earth's crust. As the lava cools, it forms a rocky layer. With each new eruption, another layer is added.

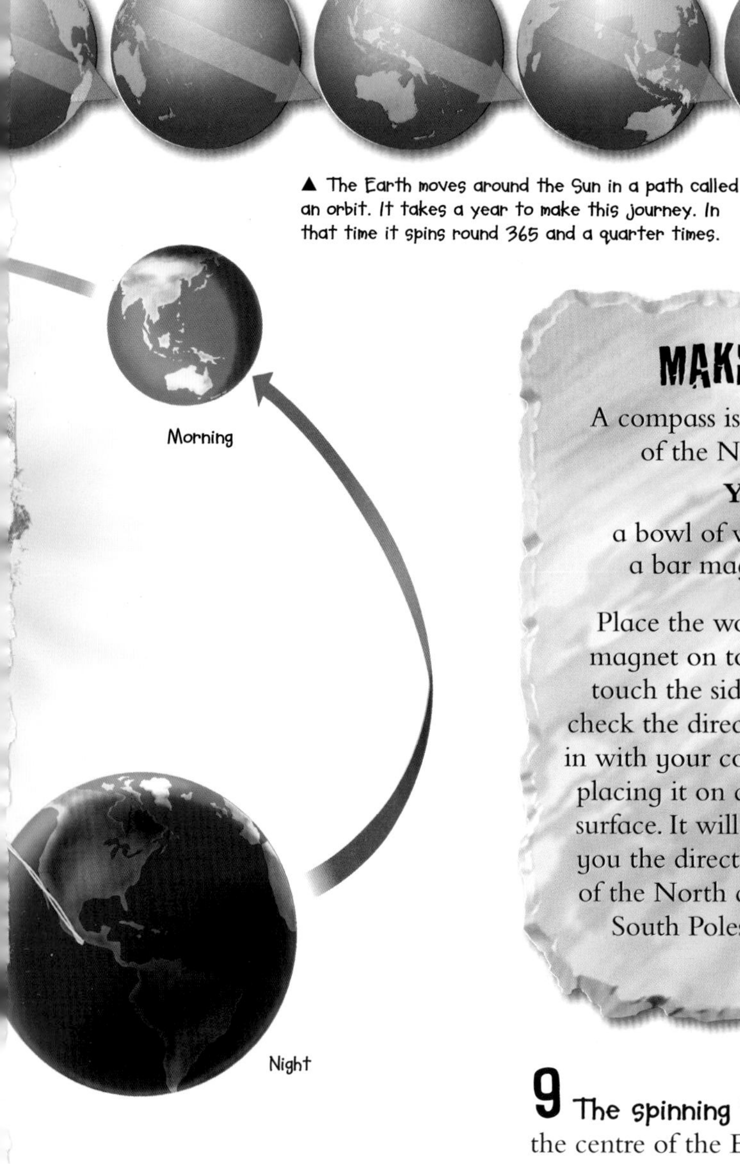

▲ The Earth moves around the Sun in a path called an orbit. It takes a year to make this journey. In that time it spins round 365 and a quarter times.

▲ As one part of the Earth turns into sunlight, another part turns into darkness. It is morning when a part turns into sunlight, and evening when it turns into darkness.

MAKE A COMPASS

A compass is used to find the direction of the North and South Poles.

You will need:

a bowl of water
a piece of wood
a bar magnet
a real compass

Place the wood in the water with the magnet on top. Make sure they do not touch the sides. When the wood is still, check the direction the magnet is pointing in with your compass, by placing it on a flat surface. It will tell you the direction of the North and South Poles.

9 The spinning Earth acts like a magnet. At the centre of the Earth is liquid iron. As the Earth spins, it makes the iron behave like a magnet with a North and South Pole. These act on the magnet in a compass to make the needle point to the North and South Poles.

Rivers and lakes

14 A mighty river can start from a spring. This is a place where water flows from the ground. Rain soaks into the ground, through the soil and rock, until it gushes out on the side of a hill. The trickle of water from a spring is called a stream. Many streams join together to make a river.

15 Water wears rocks down to make a waterfall. When a river flows off a layer of hard rock onto softer rock, it wears the softer rock away. The rocks and pebbles in the water grind the soft rock away to make a cliff face. At the bottom of the waterfall they make a deep pool called a plunge pool.

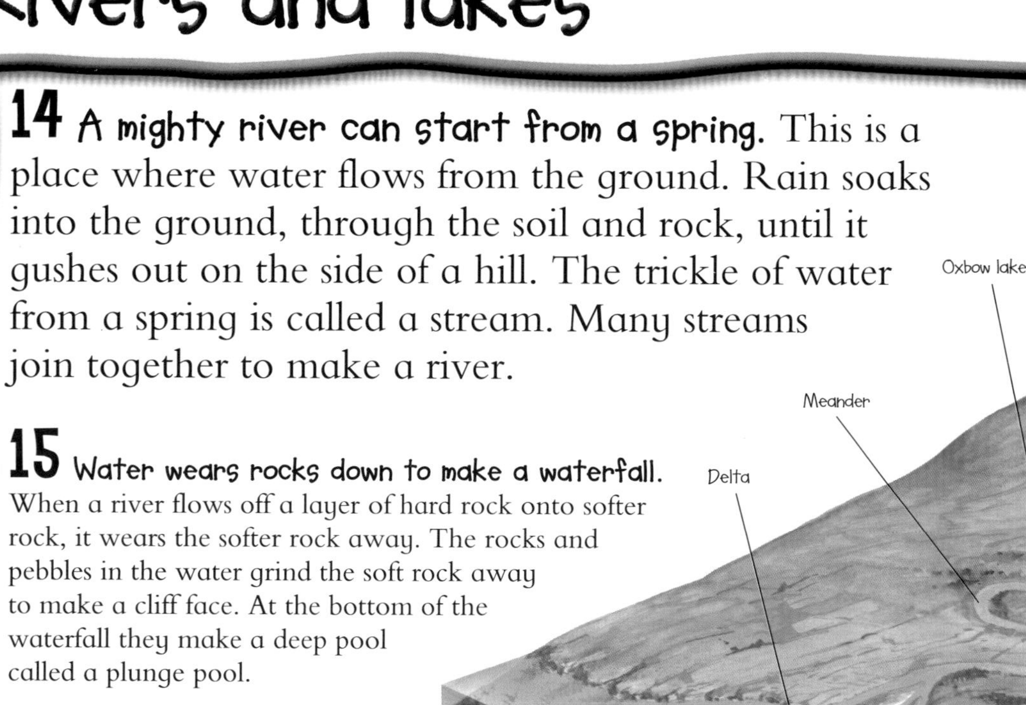

▶ High in the mountains, streams join to form the headwater of a river. From here the river flows through the mountains then more slowly across the plains to the sea.

16 A river changes as it flows to the sea. Rivers begin in hills and mountains. They are narrow and flow quickly there. When the river flows through flatter land it becomes wider and slow-moving. It makes loops called meanders which may separate and form oxbow lakes. Where the river meets the sea is the river mouth. It may be a wide channel called an estuary or a group of sandy islands called a delta.

◀ Waterfalls may only be a few centimetres high, or come crashing over a cliff with a massive drop. Angel Falls in Venezuela form the highest falls in the world. One of the drops is an amazing 807 metres.

▲ Mountains are the tallest things on Earth. A good example of a young mountain range are the Himalayas, with their sharp, jagged peaks.

MAKE FOLD MOUNTAINS

Put a towel on a table top. Place one hand at either end of the towel. Push your hands together slowly and watch miniature fold mountains form.

Active volcano

Block forced down

Block forced up

Fault

Molten rock

Block mountain

13 The movement of the Earth's crust can make blocks of rock pop up to make mountains. When the plates in the crust push together, they make heat, which softens the rock, letting it fold. Farther away from this heat, cooler rock snaps when it is pushed. The snapped rock makes huge cracks called faults in the crust. When a block of rock between two faults is pushed by the rest of the crust, it rises to form a block mountain.

▲ It takes millions of years for mountains to form and the process is happening all the time. A group of mountains is called a range. The biggest ranges are the Alps in Europe, the Andes in South America, the Rockies in North America and the highest of all – the Himalayas in Asia.

The planet of life

20 There are millions of different kinds of life forms on Earth. So far, life has not been found anywhere else. Living things survive here because it is warm, there is water and the air contains oxygen. If we discover other planets with these conditions, there may be life on them too.

21 Many living things on the Earth are tiny. They are so small that we cannot see them. A whale shark is the largest fish on the planet, yet it feeds on tiny shrimp-like creatures. These in turn feed on even smaller plant-like organisms called plankton,which make food from sunlight and sea water. Microscopic bacteria are found in the soil and even on your skin.

▲ Despite being the biggest fish in the oceans, the mighty whale shark feeds on tiny shrimplike creatures and plankton (right).

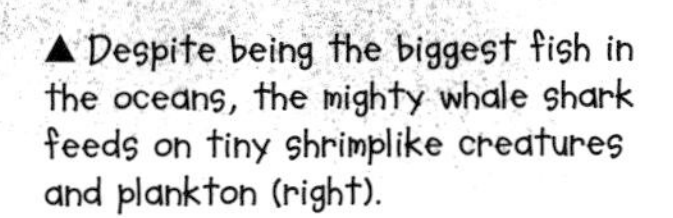

22 Animals cannot live without plants. A plant makes food from sunlight, water, air and minerals in the soil. Animals cannot make their own food so many of them eat plants. Others survive by eating the plant-eaters. If plants died out, all the animals would die too.

◀ This caterpillar eats as much plant-life as possible before beginning its change to a butterfly.

17 Lakes form in hollows in the ground. The hollows may be left when glaciers melt or when plates in the crust split open. Some lakes form when a landslide makes a dam across a river.

▲ A landslide has fallen into the river and blocked the flow of water to make a lake.

▼ A volcano can sometimes form in a lake inside a crater.

18 A lake can form in the crater of a volcano. A few crater lakes have formed in craters left by meteorites that hit Earth long ago.

▼ Most lakes are just blue but some are green, pink, red or even white. The Laguna Colorado in Chile is red due to tiny organisms (creatures) that live in the water.

19 Some lake water may be brightly coloured. The colours are made by tiny organisms called algae or by minerals dissolved in the water.

EXTREME EARTH

26 The Earth is a planet of extremes. At the North and South Poles, freezing temperatures reach as low as -40°C. Meanwhile, hot water gushes out from the seabed at over 400°C. Explorers trek to the tops of mountains many kilometres high, and into deep caves thousands of metres underground. Rainforests are drenched by torrential rain every day, while deserts remain dry for years on end. The Earth also regularly explodes, rumbles, roars and shakes with wild weather, giant waves, earthquakes and volcanoes.

23 The air can be full of animals. On a warm day, midges and gnats form clouds close to the ground. In spring and autumn flocks of birds fly to different parts of the world to nest. On summer evenings bats hunt for midges flying in the air.

24 The surface of the ground is home to many small animals. Mice scurry through the grass. Larger animals such as deer hide in bushes. The elephant is the largest land animal. It does not need to hide because few animals would attack it.

25 If you dig into the ground you can find animals living there. The earthworm is a common creature found in the soil. It feeds on rotting plants that it pulls into the soil. Earthworms are eaten by moles that dig their way underground.

I DON'T BELIEVE IT!

The star-nosed mole has feelers on the end of its nose. It uses them to find food.

Climbing high

27 The Earth is covered with a thick layer of rock, or 'crust'. In some places, sections of crust have squeezed together, forcing their way upwards to make mountains. Mountains often form in a long line or group, called a mountain range. High up, it is cold and windy. This means that the tops of mountains are very icy, snowy and stormy.

Mount Everest 8848 metres (Asia)

Mount Kilimanjaro 5895 metres (Africa)

Mount Cook 3754 metres (Oceania)

28 Mount Everest is the world's highest mountain. It's on the border between Nepal and China, in the Himalayas mountain range. It is about 8848 metres high. The first people to climb to the top of Everest were Edmund Hillary and Tenzing Norgay, on 29 May, 1953.

▼ Mount Everest is so high that climbers have to climb it over several days, stopping at camps along the way.

29 The highest mountain on Earth isn't the hardest to climb. Another peak, K2, is much tougher for mountaineers. At 8611 metres, it's the world's second-highest mountain. Its steep slopes and swirling storms make it incredibly dangerous. Fewer than 300 people have ever climbed it, and over 65 have died in the attempt.

▲ Edmund Hillary (left) and Tenzing Norgay, photographed in 1953, the year they became the first to climb Mount Everest. Hillary died in 2008.

▼ A wave crashes ashore on rocks at Cape Arago, Oregon, USA, throwing up a huge fountain of spray. Heavy waves can sink boats, smash buildings and sweep people off the shore.

Violent volcanoes

32 A volcano is a place where hot, liquid rock (magma) bursts out of the Earth. At the Earth's surface, magma is called lava. Red-hot lava can be seen flowing or shooting out of a volcano. After a volcano erupts, the lava cools into solid rock. These rocky layers build the volcano higher and higher with each eruption.

33 The biggest eruptions happen when pressure builds up underground. The magma pushes up and up, but the crust on top stops it from escaping. The ground bulges and swells, until at last the magma bursts out in a huge explosion. This happened at Mount St Helens in Washington State, USA in 1980. The explosion was so huge, it blew away half the mountain!

▼ When first erupted, the temperature of lava is between 700 and 1300 degrees Centigrade.

Mount Aconcagua 6959 metres (South America)

Mount McKinley 6194 metres (North America)

Mount Blanc 4807 metres (Europe)

◀ This diagram shows a height comparison of the highest mountains by continent.

I DON'T BELIEVE IT!

Mountains seem big to us, but they're very small compared to the whole planet. If the world was shrunk to the size of a football, it would feel totally smooth.

30 Most mountains are shaped like big humps – but a cliff is a sheer drop. The east face of Great Trango, a mountain in Pakistan, is 1340 metres high, making it the tallest vertical cliff in the world. There's another giant cliff on Mount Thor in Canada, with a drop of 1250 metres. If a pebble fell off one of these cliffs, it would take more than 15 seconds to reach the bottom!

31 Some people don't just climb to the tops of high mountains – they live there! The town of Wenzhuan in Tibet, China, is the highest in the world. It is in the Himalayas, 5100 metres up – that's over 5 kilometres above sea level! The highest capital city is La Paz, in the Andes in Bolivia, South America.

▼ The city of La Paz in Bolivia is situated in the Andes mountains. It has an altitude (height) of around 3600 metres.

34 The biggest volcanic eruption ever recorded was the eruption of Mount Tambora in Indonesia in 1815. The eruption was heard on the island of Sumatra, over 2000 kilometres away. Ash from the eruption filled the sky and blocked out sunlight all around the Earth. It made the weather very cold, and people called 1816 'the year without a summer'.

▲ Mount Etna in Italy is a large, active volcano. It's fertile slopes are used by farmers to grow crops.

▲ The island of Surtsey today, more than 40 years after it appeared out of the sea.

35 Volcanoes can be killers. Victims can be burned by hot lava, hit by flying rocks, suffocated under hot ash or poisoned by gas. After the eruption, ash can mix with rainwater to make fast-flowing mud that can drown whole towns. People are in danger from eruptions because there are many towns and farms close to volcanoes. This is partly because volcanic ash helps to make the land fertile for growing crops.

36 A volcano can build a brand-new island! In 1963, smoke and steam began to billow out of the sea near Iceland. A volcano was erupting on the seabed. As the lava and ash piled up, it built a new island. The island was named Surtsey. Gradually, moss, grass and trees began to grow, and birds and insects began to live there.

VINEGAR VOLCANO MODEL

You will need:

Vinegar Bicarbonate of soda Red food colouring Sand Tray Jug Plastic bottle

Put a tablespoon of bicarbonate of soda in the plastic bottle. Stand the bottle on a tray and make a cone of sand around it. Put a few drops of red food colouring in half a cup of vinegar. Tip the vinegar into a jug then pour it into the bottle. In a few moments the volcano should erupt with red, frothy 'lava'.

Hot springs and fountains

37 There are natural hot baths and showers all over the world. You might think water outdoors is cold, but in some places, water meets hot rock under the ground and gets heated up. It sometimes even boils. The hot water can then make a lake or spring – or even shoot out of the ground like a fountain, forming a geyser.

▲ A mudpot, like this one in Myvatn Geothermal Area in Iceland, is a pool of hot, bubbling mud. Some mudpots are boiling hot. Others bubble as hot gases burst up through them.

38 Besides geysers, the Earth's hot water can form amazing thermal (hot) springs and pools. They often occur in places where there are lots of volcanoes, such as New Zealand and Japan. Some thermal pools are famous for their beautiful colours. These are caused by millions of bacteria (tiny living things) that live in the very hot water.

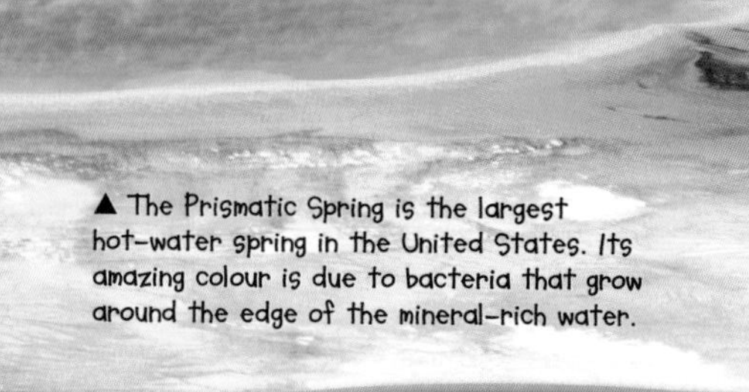

▲ The Prismatic Spring is the largest hot-water spring in the United States. Its amazing colour is due to bacteria that grow around the edge of the mineral-rich water.

39 You shouldn't stand too close to a geyser – even if nothing's happening! A geyser is a hole in the ground that suddenly shoots out hot water and steam. Under the hole there is a water-filled chamber. Hot rock beneath it heats the water until it rises back to the surface and erupts in a giant jet of water and steam.

40 Old Faithful is one of the world's most famous geysers. Found in Yellowstone National Park USA, it gets its name because it erupts on average once every 94 minutes. Its jet of steam and water can reach 55 metres high – as high as a 15-storey building.

▶ Strokkur (Icelandic for 'churn') is a geyser in Iceland. It erupts regularly, every 5–10 minutes, and can shoot water up to 25 metres in the air.

41 Soap helps geysers to erupt. People discovered this when they tried to use hot water pools and geysers to wash their clothes in. Soap disturbs the cold water in the chamber, helping the hot water to burst through.

I DON'T BELIEVE IT!

Japanese macaque monkeys use thermal springs as hot baths! They live in the mountains of Japan where winters are very cold. They climb into the natural hot pools to keep themselves warm.

▼ When rainwater seeps into the earth, it can be heated by hot rocks underground before rising back up to the surface as hot springs, pools and geysers.

Rainfall adds to groundwater

Geyser

Hot spring

Cold water travels down

Water is heated by hot rocks

Heated water starts to move upwards

Heat from Earth's interior

Rivers and waterfalls

42 The Earth is laced with thousands of rivers. Rivers are channels of water that flow towards the sea. They allow the rain that falls on the land to drain away. Rivers also provide people and animals with drinking water and a place to wash, swim and fish. A waterfall is a place where a river flows over a rocky ledge and pours down to a lower level.

43 The world's longest river is the Nile, in Africa. It starts in the area near Lake Victoria and flows north to Egypt, where it opens into the Mediterranean Sea. The journey covers nearly 6700 kilometres, and about 3470 cubic metres of water flows out of the Nile every second. The Nile provides water, a transport route, and fishing for millions of people. If it wasn't for the Nile, the civilization of ancient Egypt could not have existed.

44 Although the Nile is the longest river, the Amazon is the biggest. The Amazon flows from west to east across South America, and empties into the Atlantic Ocean. It carries 58 times as much water as the Nile, and about 200,000 cubic metres flow out of it each second. In some places, the Amazon is an amazing 60 kilometres wide.

◀ This aerial photo of the River Amazon shows how it twists and loops as it flows through the Amazon rainforest in South America.

▶ At Angel Falls, the world's highest waterfall, the water spreads out into a misty spray as it plunges down the cliff.

◀ Part of the Grand Canyon, with the Colorado River visible at the bottom of a deep gorge.

45 Angel Falls in Venezuela is the world's highest waterfall, spilling over a drop 979 metres high. It flows off the side of a very high, flat-topped mountain. Although it's the world's highest waterfall, it's not the biggest. Many waterfalls are much wider and carry more water – including Niagara Falls in North America and Victoria Falls in Africa.

46 Rivers can cut through solid rock. Over thousands of years, as a river flows, it wears away the rock around it. If the stone is quite soft, the river can carve a deep, steep-sided valley, or gorge. The Grand Canyon in Arizona, USA, is a massive gorge cut by the Colorado River. It is about 450 kilometres long, and in areas it is up to 29 kilometres wide and 1.8 kilometres deep.

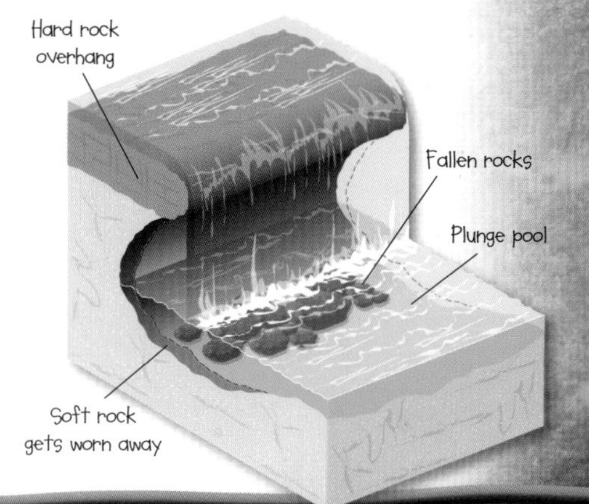

◀ A waterfall forms where a river flows from hard rock onto softer rock. The softer rock is worn away faster, while the overhanging ledge of hard rock gradually crumbles away. Over time, the waterfall retreats, or moves upstream.

Record-breaking lakes

47 The Caspian Sea in central Asia is actually the world's biggest lake! It covers 378,000 square kilometres. It isn't connected to true seas and oceans, but because it's so big, and is salty like the sea, some experts say it isn't a proper lake, either. The world's biggest freshwater (non-salty) lake is Lake Superior, in the USA and Canada.

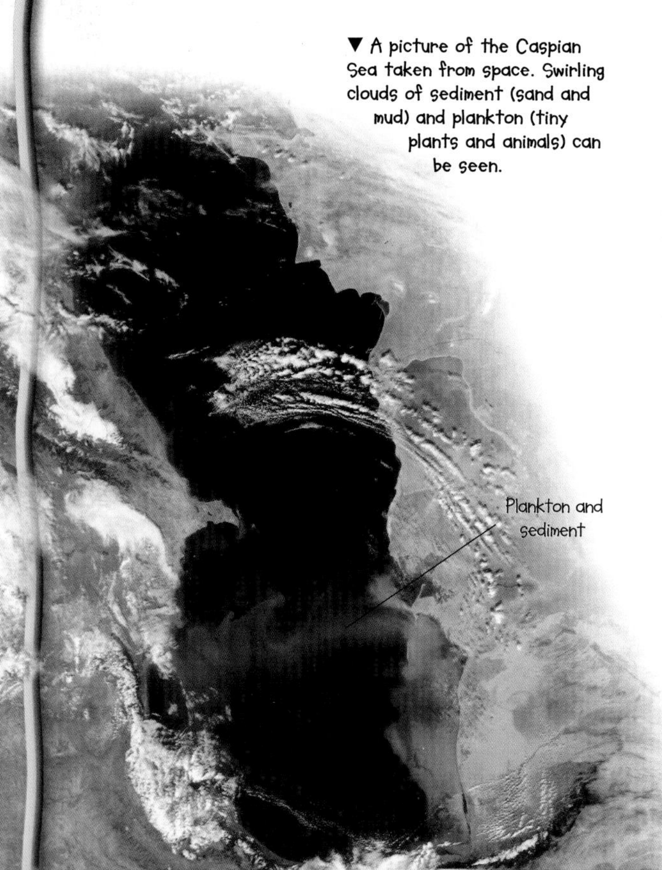

▼ A picture of the Caspian Sea taken from space. Swirling clouds of sediment (sand and mud) and plankton (tiny plants and animals) can be seen.

48 The Dead Sea in Israel is another lake that is referred to as a sea. At 400 metres below sea level, it is the lowest lake in the world. The Dead Sea is very salty because no rivers flow out of it. All the salts and minerals that are washed into it remain there as the water evaporates in the Sun's heat. In fact the Dead Sea is nine times saltier than the real sea. It gets its name because no fish or other animals can live in such salty water.

49 The world's deepest lake is Lake Baikal in Russia. At its deepest point, it's 1700 metres deep. Because of this, it contains far more water than any other lake in the world. Twenty percent of all the unfrozen freshwater on Earth is in Lake Baikal.

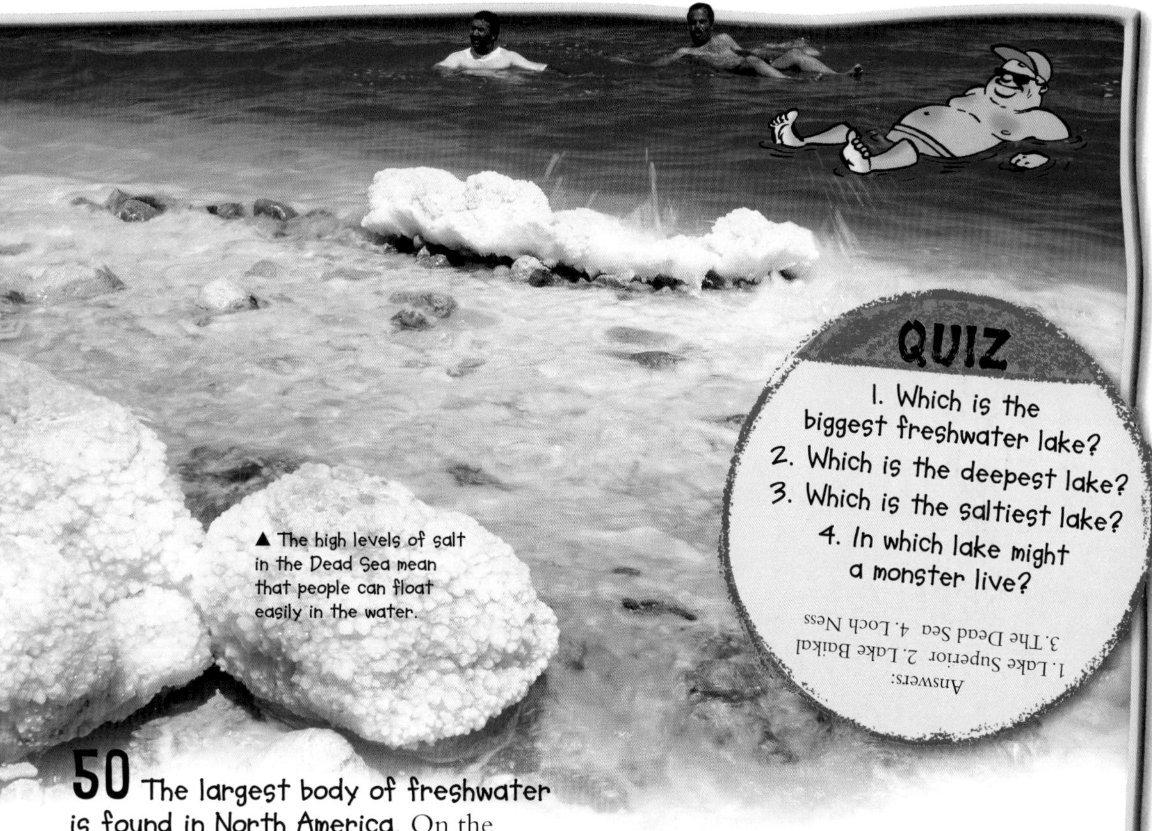

▲ The high levels of salt in the Dead Sea mean that people can float easily in the water.

QUIZ

1. Which is the biggest freshwater lake?
2. Which is the deepest lake?
3. Which is the saltiest lake?
4. In which lake might a monster live?

Answers:
1. Lake Superior 2. Lake Baikal
3. The Dead Sea 4. Loch Ness

50 The largest body of freshwater is found in North America. On the border between the United States and Canada are the Great Lakes. They contain one-fifth of the world's freshwater – a staggering 22.8 quadrillion litres!

51 Many lakes around the world are believed to be home to mysterious monsters. According to legend, a monster that looks similar to a plesiosaur lives in Loch Ness in Scotland, UK. Plesiosaurs were prehistoric water reptiles that lived at the same time as the dinosaurs. Scientists think they became extinct (died out) 65 million years ago. However some people believe they may still live in Loch Ness.

◀ The five Great Lakes are situated in the USA and Canada. The biggest is Lake Superior, followed by Huron, Michigan, Erie and Ontario.

Going underground

52 Humans have climbed the world's highest mountains – but many underground caves are still unexplored. Caves are usually formed by water flowing through cracks underground. The water slowly dissolves certain types of rock, such as limestone. Over thousands of years, it can hollow out deep shafts, tunnels and even huge underground chambers.

▼ Cavers explore one of the many interconnected passageways in Mammoth Cave in Kentucky, U.S.A.

53 A cave in Malaysia contains the world's biggest single underground chamber. The Sarawak chamber measures 600 metres long, 400 metres wide and at least 80 metres high. You could line up eight Boeing 747 aircraft, nose to tail, along its length – and still have space to spare.

54 The world's longest cave system is Mammoth Cave in Kentucky, USA. It has at least 570 kilometres of passageways – but explorers keep discovering more. Some experts think that only a small part of the whole cave has been explored.

▼ Caves form over thousands of years as water flows through cracks in underground rocks.

1. Rainwater seeps into cracks in rocks

2. Water dissolves rock, forming channels

3. Over time, large cave systems develop

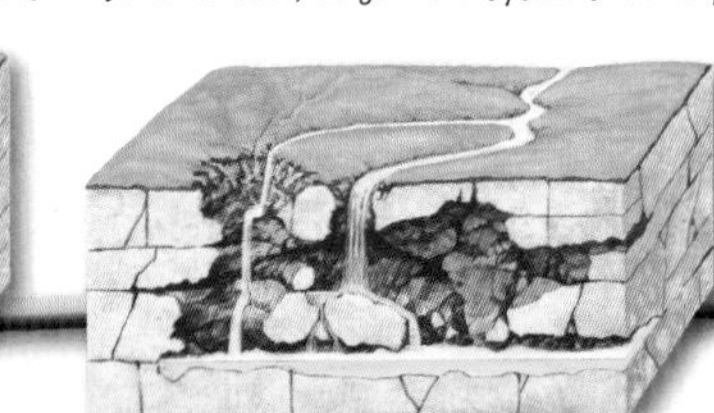

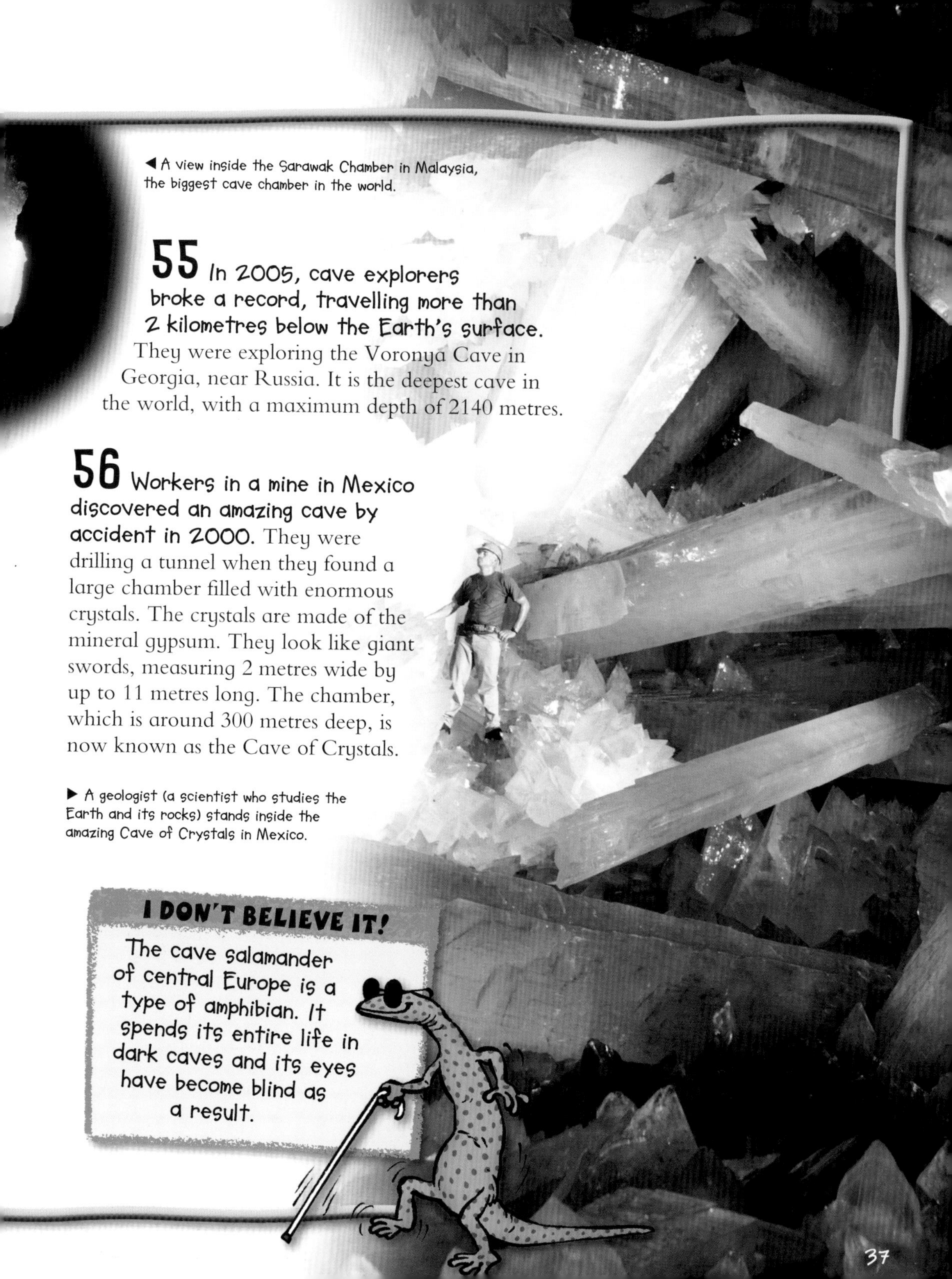

◀ A view inside the Sarawak Chamber in Malaysia, the biggest cave chamber in the world.

55 **In 2005, cave explorers broke a record, travelling more than 2 kilometres below the Earth's surface.** They were exploring the Voronya Cave in Georgia, near Russia. It is the deepest cave in the world, with a maximum depth of 2140 metres.

56 **Workers in a mine in Mexico discovered an amazing cave by accident in 2000.** They were drilling a tunnel when they found a large chamber filled with enormous crystals. The crystals are made of the mineral gypsum. They look like giant swords, measuring 2 metres wide by up to 11 metres long. The chamber, which is around 300 metres deep, is now known as the Cave of Crystals.

▶ A geologist (a scientist who studies the Earth and its rocks) stands inside the amazing Cave of Crystals in Mexico.

I DON'T BELIEVE IT!

The cave salamander of central Europe is a type of amphibian. It spends its entire life in dark caves and its eyes have become blind as a result.

Extreme earthquakes

57 An earthquake happens when the Earth's crust moves suddenly. The crust trembles, cracks, or lurches up and down. Earthquakes can be disastrous. They make houses fall down, tear roads apart and destroy bridges. They can also cause tsunamis.

58 Earthquakes happen because the Earth's crust is like a jigsaw. It is made up of several huge pieces called tectonic plates. The plates fit together quite neatly, covering the Earth. However they can squeeze and push against each other. Sometimes, this pushing makes the plates slip and move suddenly, causing an earthquake.

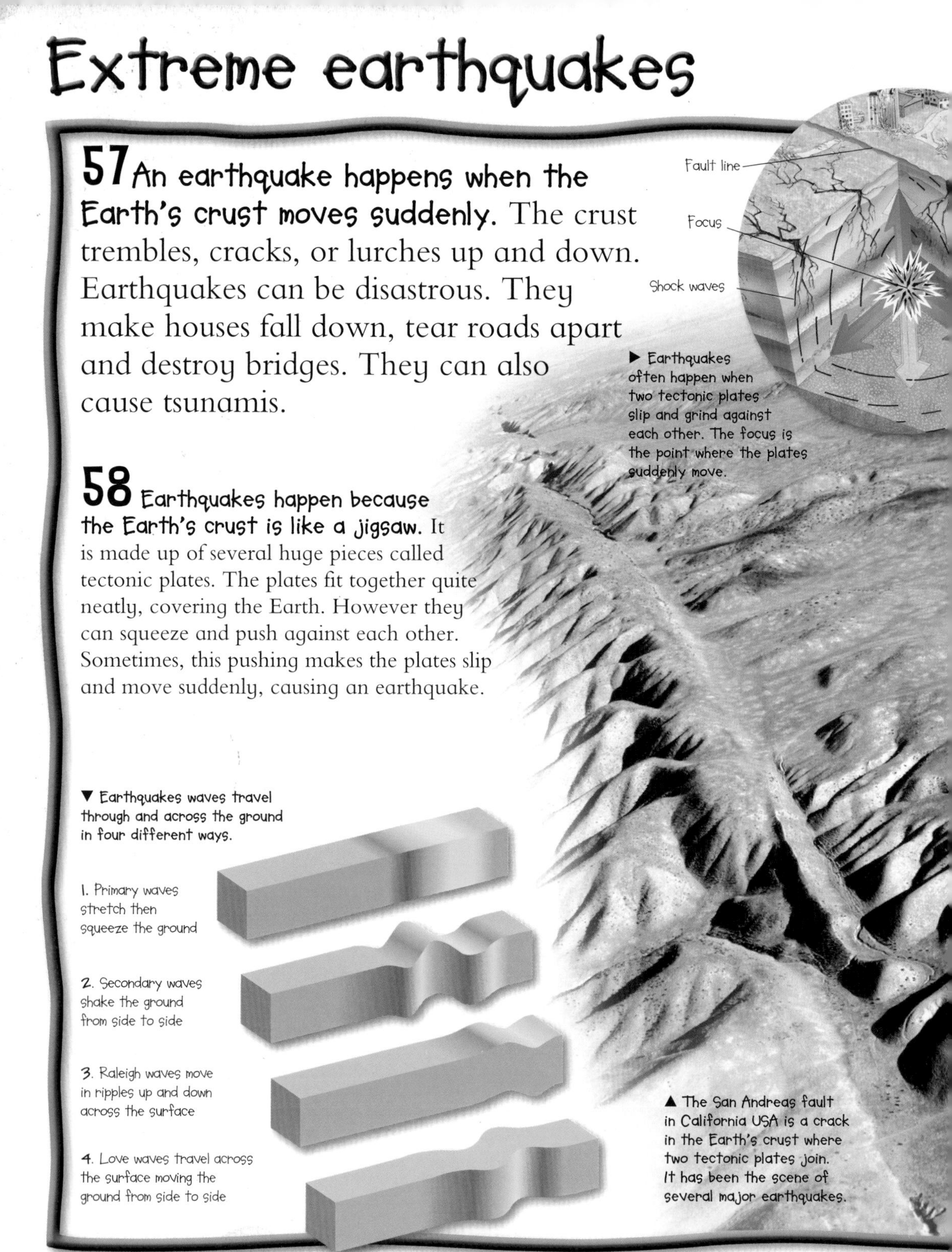

▶ Earthquakes often happen when two tectonic plates slip and grind against each other. The focus is the point where the plates suddenly move.

▼ Earthquakes waves travel through and across the ground in four different ways.

▲ The San Andreas fault in California USA is a crack in the Earth's crust where two tectonic plates join. It has been the scene of several major earthquakes.

▶ Damage caused by an earthquake in Kobe, Japan, 1995. It measured 7.2 on the Richter Scale and killed more than 6000 people.

59 Earthquakes can flatten whole cities and kill thousands. One of the deadliest earthquakes ever hit the city of Tangshan, China in 1976. Most of the city's buildings were destroyed, and at least 240,000 people died. In 2003, an earthquake destroyed the ancient city of Bam in Iran. Over 70 percent of its buildings fell down and around 30,000 people were killed.

I DON'T BELIEVE IT!

Since ancient times, people have noticed animals behaving strangely just before earthquakes. Dogs and cats can get agitated, and herds of cattle have been known to run away.

60 Scientists measure earthquakes using the Richter scale. It records the amount of energy that an earthquake releases. The biggest quakes are not always the most dangerous – it depends where they happen. In a big city, a quake measuring 4 or 5 on the scale could do more damage than a quake measuring 8 or 9 in the countryside.

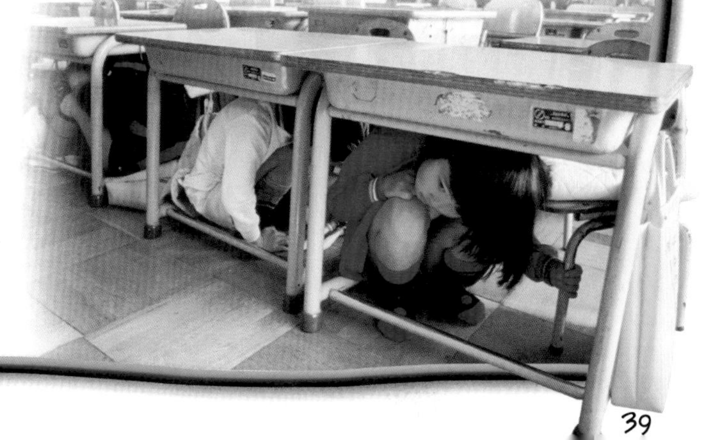

▼ As there are a lot of earthquakes in Japan, school children regularly practise what to do if an earthquake strikes.

61 There are things you can do to stay safer during an earthquake. For example, if you are outside, you should keep away from buildings and power lines. If you are indoors, you should shelter under a strong table. Some places also have quake-proof buildings.

Terrifying tsunamis

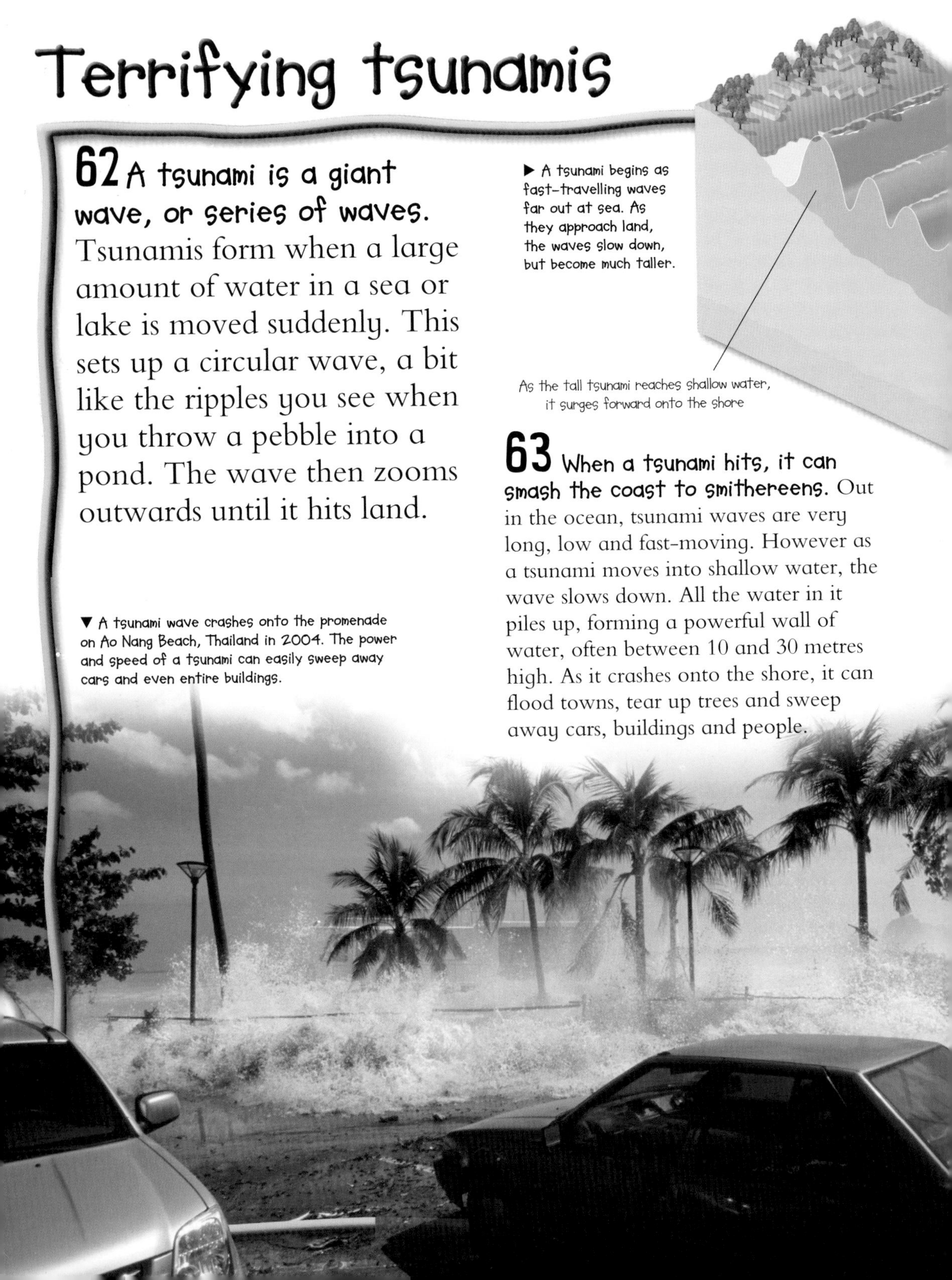

62 A tsunami is a giant wave, or series of waves. Tsunamis form when a large amount of water in a sea or lake is moved suddenly. This sets up a circular wave, a bit like the ripples you see when you throw a pebble into a pond. The wave then zooms outwards until it hits land.

▶ A tsunami begins as fast-travelling waves far out at sea. As they approach land, the waves slow down, but become much taller.

As the tall tsunami reaches shallow water, it surges forward onto the shore

63 When a tsunami hits, it can smash the coast to smithereens. Out in the ocean, tsunami waves are very long, low and fast-moving. However as a tsunami moves into shallow water, the wave slows down. All the water in it piles up, forming a powerful wall of water, often between 10 and 30 metres high. As it crashes onto the shore, it can flood towns, tear up trees and sweep away cars, buildings and people.

▼ A tsunami wave crashes onto the promenade on Ao Nang Beach, Thailand in 2004. The power and speed of a tsunami can easily sweep away cars and even entire buildings.

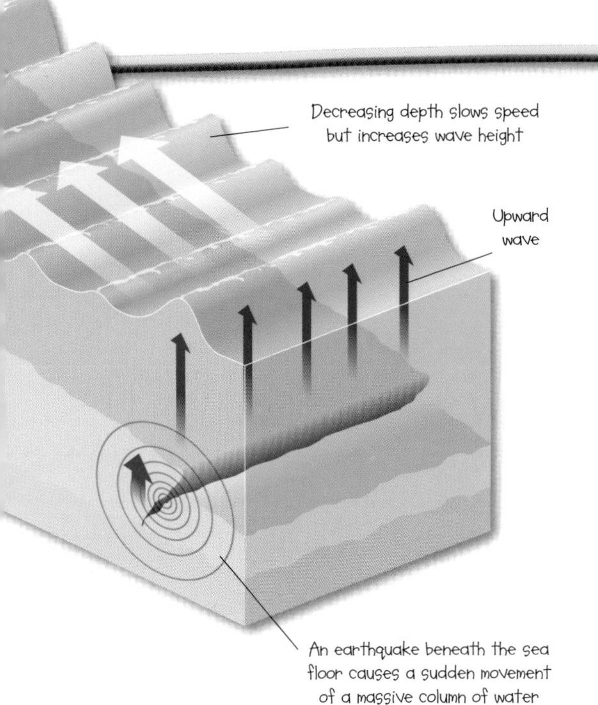

65 The tallest tsunami was higher than a skyscraper. It occurred at Lituya Bay, in Alaska, USA, in 1958. An earthquake triggered a landslide, and rock and soil plunged into the sea. A giant tsunami, over 500 metres high, zoomed down the bay. Luckily, there were no towns there, but the wave stripped the coast of trees. A giant tsunami such as this is sometimes called a mega tsunami.

64 Most tsunamis are caused by earthquakes under the sea. A section of seabed shifts suddenly and the water above it is jolted upwards. Tsunamis can also happen when a landslide or volcanic eruption throws a large amount of rock into the sea, pushing the water aside. This happened when Krakatau, a volcano in Indonesia, erupted in 1883. The tsunamis it caused killed 36,000 people.

66 A tsunami in the Indian Ocean in 2004 was the deadliest ever recorded. It was caused by a huge undersea earthquake near the coast of Indonesia. Tsunami waves spread across the ocean and swamped coasts in Indonesia, Thailand, Sri Lanka, India and the Maldive Islands. Around 230,000 people were killed.

▼ The town of Kalutara in Sri Lanka, shown in satellite images before (left) and after (right) being swamped by the deadly 2004 tsunami.

Dry deserts

67 Deserts occur in places where it's hard for rain to reach. Most rain comes from clouds that form over the sea and blow onto the land. If there's a big mountain range, the clouds never reach the other side. An area called a rainshadow desert forms. Deserts also form in the middle of continents. The land there is so far from the sea, rainclouds rarely reach it.

▲ The Namib Desert in the southwest of Africa contains some of the biggest sand dunes in the world.

QUIZ

Which of these things would be useful if you were lost in the desert?

1. Mirror
2. Woolly blanket
3. Swimming costume
4. Umbrella

Answers:
1, 2 and 4.
You should not wear swimming gear in case of sunburn

68 The world's biggest desert used to be a swamp! The Sahara takes up most of northern Africa. It is made up of 9 million square kilometres of dry sand, pebbles and boulders. There are some oases too, where freshwater springs flow out of the ground. Animal bones and objects left by ancient peoples show that around 6000 years ago, the Sahara was green and swampy. Lots of hippos, crocodiles and humans lived there.

▼ These sand piles show the relative sizes of the world's biggest deserts.

Kalahari Desert
520,000 km²

Gobi Desert
1,040,000 km²

Arabian Desert
1,300,000 km²

Australian deserts
3,800,000 km²

Sahara
9,269,000 km²

70 Deserts aren't always hot. The hottest temperature ever recorded was 57.8°C in Libya. However, deserts can be cold, too. The average temperature in the Atacama Desert, South America is only about 10°C. In the Gobi Desert in Asia, winter temperatures can drop to –40°C. All deserts can be cold at night, as there are no clouds to stop heat escaping.

▲ Desert roses aren't plants. They occur when desert minerals, such as gypsum, combine with sand to form crystals.

▶ Sand dunes form in different shapes and patterns, depending on the type of wind and sand in the desert. The blue arrows indicate the wind direction.

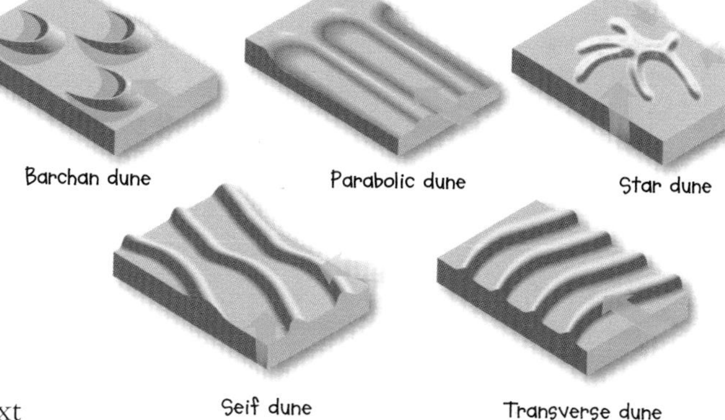

69 The world's driest desert is the Aatacama Desert in Chile, South America. This desert is right next to the sea! It formed because in South America, rainclouds blow from east to west. They drop their rain on the Amazon rainforest, but cannot get past the Andes mountains. On the other side of the Andes, next to the Pacific Ocean, is the Atacama Desert. It is so dry that people who died there 9000 years ago have been preserved as mummies.

71 Even in dry deserts, there is water if you know where to look. Desert plants, such as cactuses store water in their stems, leaves or spines. When rain does fall, it seeps into the ground and stays there. Desert people and animals chew desert plants or dig into the ground to find enough water.

▶ An oasis is a freshwater spring in a desert. Oases form when water stored deep underground meets a barrier of rock that it can't soak through, and rises to the desert surface.

The ends of the Earth

72 The Earth is round, but it has two 'ends' – the North Pole and the South Pole. The Earth is constantly spinning around an imaginary line called the axis. At the ends of this axis are the poles. Here, it is always cold, because the poles are so far from the Sun.

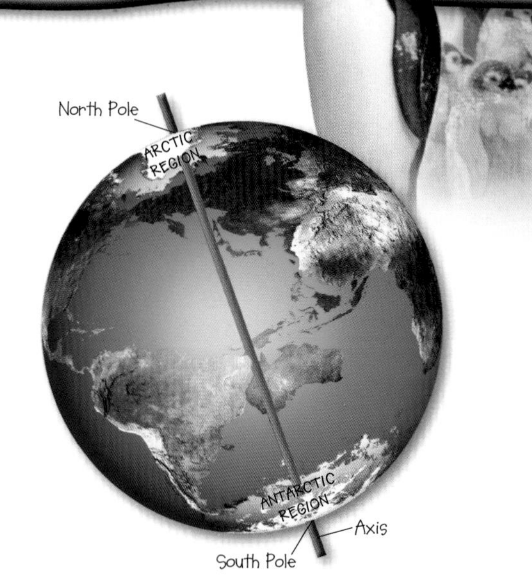

▲ The position of the poles means they receive little heat from the Sun.

73 At the North Pole, the average temperature is –20°C. At the South pole, it's much colder – about –50°C. It's hard for humans to survive in this cold. Water droplets in your breath would freeze on your face. If you were to touch something made of metal with your bare hand, it would freeze onto your skin and stick there.

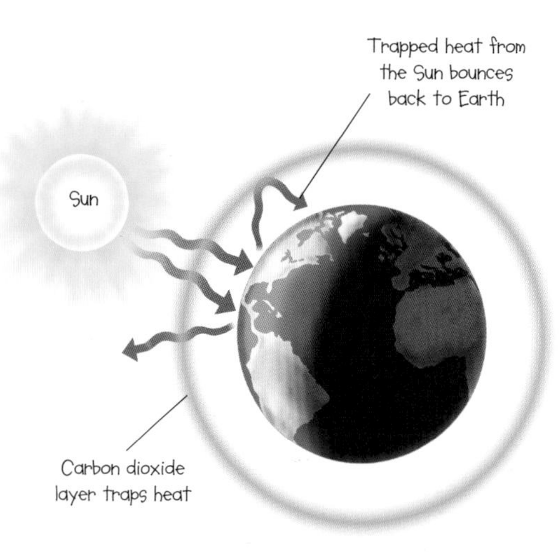

74 The area around the North Pole is called the Arctic. Parts of Europe, Asia and North America reach into the Arctic, but most of it is actually the Arctic Ocean. Many animals live in the Arctic. Polar bears and seals live on the ice and Arctic foxes, Arctic hares and snowy owls live on the land. The sea around the pole is mainly frozen. Scientists have found the ice is melting because of global warming. This is happening because pollution in the air is trapping heat close to the Earth, making it warm up.

◀ Pollution in the form of carbon dioxide gas traps heat from the Sun, making the Earth warm up. This is one reason that the polar ice is melting.

▲ There are several different species (types) of penguins living in Antarctica. These emperor penguins and their chicks are the largest species.

75 The Antarctic is mostly made up of a huge continent, called Antarctica. Much of it is covered in a layer of solid ice up to 4.7 kilometres thick. The Antarctic is colder than the Arctic because its thick ice and mountains make it very high, and the air is colder higher up. Because Antarctica is so big, the seas around it cannot warm it very much. Little wildlife lives here, but it is home to lots of penguins.

I DON'T BELIEVE IT!

Explorers at the poles sometimes lose body parts. If they let their fingers, toes or nose get too cold, they can get frostbite. Blood stops flowing to these parts, and they can turn black and fall off.

76 Explorers didn't make it to the poles until the 20th century. US explorer Robert Peary and his team reached the North Pole in 1909. Soon afterwards, two explorers raced to reach the South Pole. Norwegian Roald Amundsen arrived first, in December 1911. British explorer Robert Scott arrived one month later – but he and his men died on their way home.

◀ There are no towns or cities in Antarctica as it's so cold, but people do go there to explore and to study nature. They sometimes use snowmobiles to travel around on the snow and ice.

Glaciers and icebergs

77 About two percent of the water in the world is permanently frozen as ice. The ice is found at the chilly polar regions, and on high mountains where the air is freezing cold. On steep slopes, the ice creeps downhill, like a very slow river. This kind of ice 'river' is called a glacier. On high mountains, glaciers flow downhill until they reach warmer air and start to melt. At the poles, many glaciers flow into the sea.

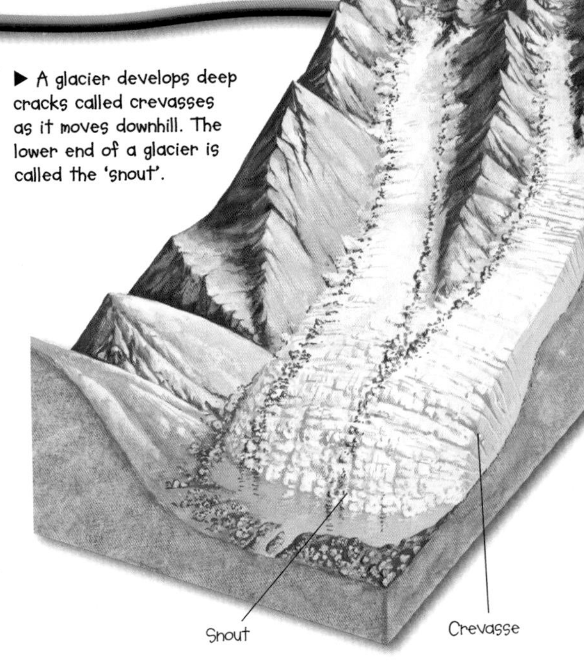

▶ A glacier develops deep cracks called crevasses as it moves downhill. The lower end of a glacier is called the 'snout'.

78 One of the world's biggest glaciers, not including the ice at the poles, is the Siachen Glacier in the Himalayas. It is 78 kilometres long and, in places, its ice is over 100 metres thick. India and Pakistan have been fighting a war over who the glacier belongs to since 1984. It has been home to hundreds of soldiers for more than 20 years.

▼ Instead of melting on the way down a mountain, this glacier in Prince William Sound, Alaska is flowing into a fjord.

79 Glaciers have shaped the Earth. As a glacier flows down a mountain, the heavy ice pushes and scrapes at the soil and rocks. This carves a huge, U-shaped valley, known as a glacial valley. 20,000 years ago, when the Earth was in an Ice Age, glaciers covered much more of the land than they do now. Since then, many have melted, revealing their glacial valleys.

81 Icebergs exist because of glaciers. At the poles, glaciers flow downhill to the sea. There, the ice is slowly pushed out into the water, where it starts to float. Every so often, a large chunk of the glacier breaks off and floats away into the sea. This is an iceberg and it drifts until it melts.

80 Icebergs are a problem for ships. As an iceberg floats, only about one-tenth of it sticks up out of the sea. The rest is below the surface. Many icebergs have odd, lumpy shapes. This means that a ship can bump into the underwater part of an iceberg, even if the part above water looks far away. Icebergs have damaged and sunk many ships, including the famous ocean liner *Titanic* in 1912.

▼ These penguins are on an iceberg in the Southern Ocean, close to Antarctica. A huge mass of ice can be seen below the water's surface.

MAKE AN ICEBERG

You will need:

Plastic container Clear bowl Water

1. Fill the container with water and put it in the freezer.
2. When frozen, remove your 'iceberg' from the container.
3. Fill the clear bowl with water and place your iceberg in it.
4. Look through the side to see how much of your iceberg is underwater, and what shape it makes.

Amazing oceans

82 About 70 percent of the Earth's surface is covered by ocean. The oceans cover about 361 million square kilometres and they are all connected. The average depth of the ocean is 3750 metres. Over 90 percent of the Earth's species (types) of living things live in the oceans.

84 If you were sitting at the bottom of the deep ocean, you'd be squashed flat. At great depths, the weight of all the water above presses from all sides. At the bottom of Challenger Deep, the water pressure is more than 1000 times stronger than at the surface. It's cold, too – only just above freezing point. People can only go there inside specially built diving machines with thick walls that can resist the pressure and cold.

▶ The *Trieste*, which made the deepest deep-sea dive ever in 1960, was made of a large tank full of gasoline to give buoyancy, with a small round passenger chamber fixed underneath.

83 The deepest point in all the world's oceans is called Challenger Deep. It is in the Mariana Trench in the Pacific Ocean and is 10,923 metres deep – almost 11 kilometres. A tower of 3500 elephants, one on top of the next, could stand in it without touching the surface. In 1960, two explorers, Jacques Piccard and Don Walsh, visited the bottom of Challenger Deep in a diving vessel called *Trieste*.

Oceanic crust
Deep-sea trench
Ocean ridge
Underwater volcano

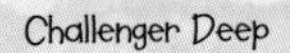

▶ This map shows the ridges, trenches, plains and mountains within the world's oceans, as well as those on land.

85 One of the world's most extreme environments is found under the sea. At hydrothermal vents, incredibly hot water bubbles out from inside the Earth at temperatures of up to 400°C. Around the hot vents live unusual creatures such as giant tubeworms and sea spiders, and tiny bacteria that feed on the minerals dissolved in the hot water. Hydrothermal vents were only discovered in 1977.

86 Sea level – the height of the sea – is about the same all over the world. It changes over time, as the Earth's temperature varies. About 20,000 years ago, during the Ice Age, the sea level was 130 metres lower than it is now. At the moment, the sea level is rising because global warming is making ice melt at the poles.

▼ A cross-section of the seabed. It usually slopes gently away from the shore, then drops steeply down to a flat plain.

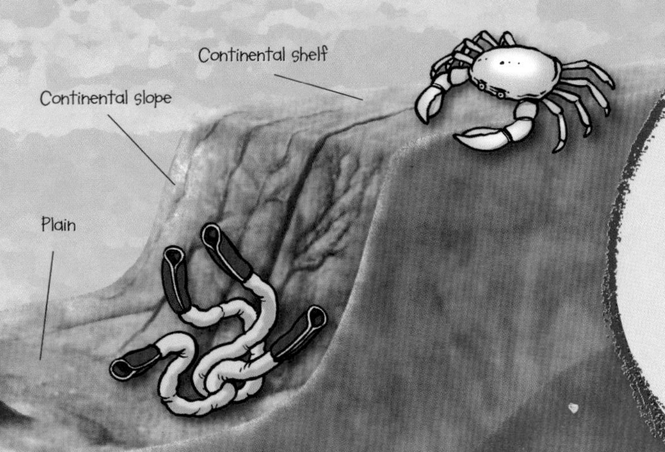

TRUE OR FALSE?

1. Challenger Deep is deeper than Mount Everest is tall.
2. The water at the bottom of the sea is always very cold.
3. Sea creatures bigger than blue whales could exist.

Answers:
1. True – Everest is only 8848 m high 2. False – the water can be hot around hydrothermal vents
3. True – the sea is so big, it could contain species unknown to science

87 It may seem like bad weather, but we need rain. Rain happens because the Sun's heat makes water in the sea evaporate. It turns into a gas, rises into the air and forms clouds. The clouds then blow over the land. They cool down, turn back into water, and fall as rain. If this didn't happen, there would be no life on Earth – all living things need water to survive.

88 In rainforests it rains almost every day. Rainforests are found in the warm tropical parts of the Earth, near the Equator. The hot sunshine makes lots of water evaporate and fall as rain. A lot of the rain that falls on a rainforest never touches the ground. It collects on the treetops, then evaporates into the air, before falling as rain again.

▲ Heavy rain is accompanied by big, black clouds.

89 The world's rainiest place is Meghalaya, an area of north-east India. Some towns there, such as Cherrapunji and Mawsynram, get around 11,500 millimetres of rain a year. If the rain didn't drain away or evaporate, it would be 11.5 metres deep after one year!

MAKE A RAIN GAUGE

You will need:

Jar or food container with a flat base and straight sides Ruler Notebook

1. Find a good place to put your container, in a shady spot, away from buildings.
2. Dig a small hole in the ground to fit it into, or put stones around it to hold it in place.
3. Each day at the same time, measure the depth of the water then empty your container.
4. Record your results in a notebook to keep

▼ Water continually rises from the sea into the air, falls on the land as rain, then flows back to the sea. This is called the water cycle.

91 It doesn't really rain cats and dogs – but there have been reports of red rain, and showers of frogs, fish and crabs. Frogs and toads were reported falling in Minneapolis, USA in 1901. It has rained fish in Singapore, and crabs in the UK. These strange showers probably happen when tornadoes or strong winds sweep up water containing living creatures, which then fall to the ground.

▼ A rickshaw driver and passenger travel through monsoon floods in India. When rains are heavy, streets turn to rivers and people's homes may be washed away.

90 A monsoon is a very rainy season. Monsoons happen in parts of Asia, especially India, in late summer. The land gets very hot and heats the air above it. The hot air rises, and this sucks in damp, cloudy air from the sea. The clouds rush over the land. When they meet the Himalayan mountains, they rise and get colder. This creates lots of rain, especially in northern India.

Lightning strikes

92 Lightning is a giant spark of electricity. It happens when tiny droplets of water and ice swirl around inside a stormcloud. This makes the cloud develop a strong electrical charge. Eventually, a spark jumps between the base of the cloud and the ground. This allows electricity to flow, releasing the electrical charge. We see the spark as a flash or 'bolt' of lightning.

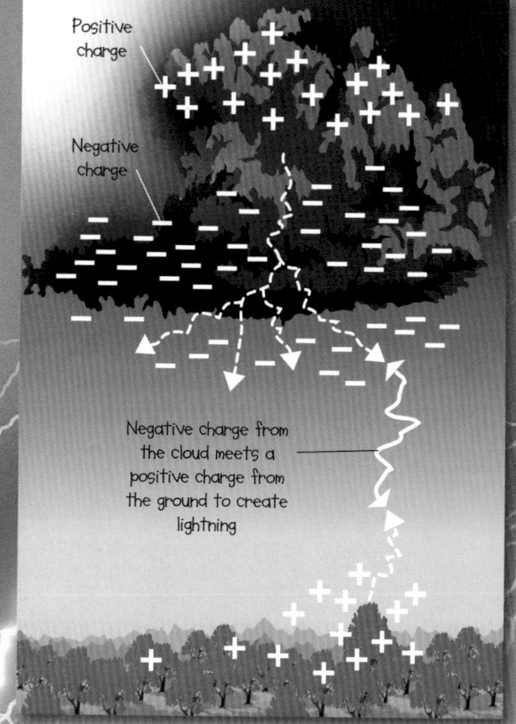

▲ During a thunderstorm, negative electrical charge builds up at the base of a cloud, while the ground has a positive charge. A lightning spark jumps between them to release the charge.

I DON'T BELIEVE IT!

At any one time, there are around 2000 thunderstorms happening on Earth. Lightning strikes somewhere in the world about 100 times every second.

93 Thunder and lightning go together. In fact, thunder is the sound of lightning. When a lightning bolt jumps through the air, it is very hot. It can reach a temperature of 30,000°C. It heats the air around it very quickly. Heat makes air expand (get bigger). It expands so suddenly that it pushes against the air around it, and creates a shock wave. The wave travels through the air and our ears detect it as a loud boom.

94 Long ago, people used to think lightning was a punishment sent by their gods. However, from the 1500s, scientists began learning about electricity and how it worked. Around 1750, US scientist Benjamin Franklin found that lightning was a kind of electricity. He invented the lightning conductor to protect buildings from lightning damage. It is a metal pole that can be fixed to tall buildings. If lightning strikes, the electrical charge runs down the pole and down a metal wire, then flows safely into the ground.

95 It is quite rare for lightning to strike people, and most of those who are struck, survive. However, lightning does kill over 2000 people around the world each year.

▼ Fulgarites occur when lightning strikes sand. The high temperature makes the sand melt. It eventually cools into hollow tubes.

◀ You can clearly see the lightning conductor on the spire of this cathedral in Liverpool, UK.

96 Lightning can make glass. Glass is made by heating up sand. When lightning strikes in a sandy desert or on a sandy beach, this happens naturally. At the place where the lightning hits the ground, it creates a tubelike tunnel of glass in the sand. These natural glass tubes are called fulgurites.

Hammered by hail

97 Hail doesn't happen often – but it can be one of the scariest kinds of weather. When it hails, balls of hard, heavy ice fall out of the sky. Hailstones are usually small, about the size of peas. However, they can be bigger – marble-sized, egg-sized or even tennis-ball-sized. Sometimes they're big enough to crush crops, smash car windows or even kill people.

▼ A man shows off scars on his back – the result of being hit by hailstones while riding a bicycle.

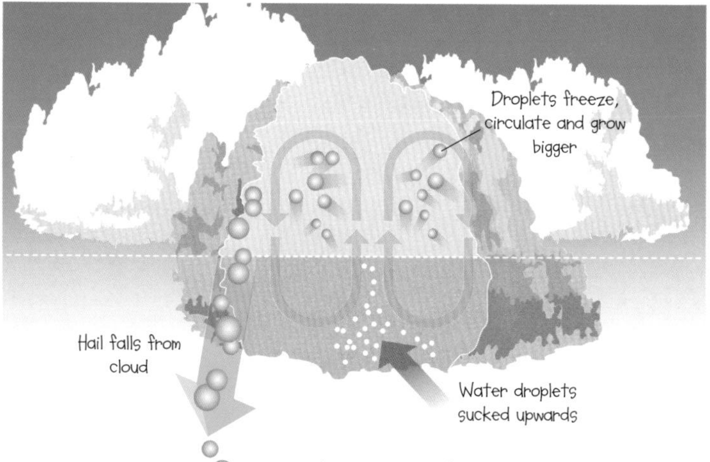

▲ Hailstones only form inside thunderclouds. Eventually they become too heavy, and fall to the ground as lumps of ice.

98 A hailstone needs a seed. Hailstones form inside thunderclouds when very cold water droplets freeze onto a tiny object – the 'seed'. It could be a speck of dust or a plant seed carried into the sky by the wind. The tiny hailstone is then tossed around by strong winds inside the cloud. More and more layers of ice build up around it, until it is so heavy that it falls to the ground.

99 The biggest hailstone ever recorded was the size of a melon! This giant hailstone fell in Aurora, Nebraska, USA in 2003. It measured 18 centimetres across. The biggest hailstones are usually 'aggregate' hailstones. They are made of smaller hailstones that have clumped together before falling to the ground.

▲ The largest hailstone on record is shown here at actual size. It fell in Nebraska, USA in 2003.

I DON'T BELIEVE IT!

Hail usually only falls for a few minutes. However, a hailstorm in Kansas, USA in 1959 went on for over an hour. It covered the ground with a layer of hailstones 46 centimetres deep!

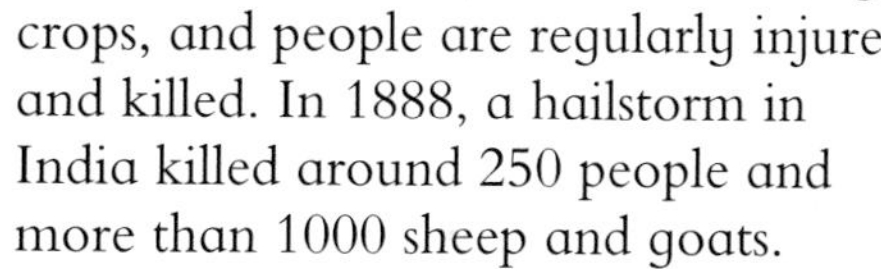

101 The world's worst hailstorms happen in Northern India and Bangladesh. Hailstones often destroy crops, and people are regularly injured and killed. In 1888, a hailstorm in India killed around 250 people and more than 1000 sheep and goats.

100 Sometimes a hailstone forms around a living thing. A farmer in Quebec, Canada reported finding a frog inside a hailstone in 1864. In 1894, a hailstone with a turtle inside was reported to have fallen on Bovina, Mississippi, USA. Smaller creatures such as spiders and flies are often trapped inside hailstones.

▶ People in Mexico City, Mexico, shovel hailstones after a huge hailstorm on 3 August, 2006.

Extreme snow and ice

102 An ice storm isn't stormy – but it is dangerous. Cold rain falls onto freezing cold surfaces. The rain freezes solid, forming a thick layer of ice on the ground, trees and other objects. Ice storms cause 'black ice'– invisible ice on roads that causes accidents. Ice-laden trees fall down, breaking power lines and cutting off roads.

◀ Overburdened by the weight of ice from an ice storm, this tree has collapsed across a road.

▲ An avalanche thunders downhill in Silverton, Colorado, USA. This avalanche was started deliberately by dropping explosives, in order to make the mountains safer for visitors.

103 An avalanche is a massive pile of snow crashing down a mountainside. Avalanches can happen whenever lots of snow piles up at the top of a slope. They can be deadly if the snow lands on top of mountain walkers or skiers. Sometimes, big avalanches bury whole houses or even whole villages.

104 A blizzard, or snowstorm, is even more dangerous than an ice storm. If you get caught outdoors in a blizzard, it's very easy to get lost. Falling snow fills the air, making it impossible to see. Thick snowdrifts build up, making it hard to walk or drive. People have lost their way and died in blizzards, just a short distance from safety.

▲ Ice can form beautiful crystal patterns as it freezes across a window or car windscreen.

QUIZ

Which of these things could help you survive if you were lost in the snow?

1. Woolly hat
2. Magazine
3. Chocolate
4. Torch
5. Metal camping plate

Answer:
All of them!

105 **If you get stuck in a blizzard or avalanche, a hole in the snow can keep you warm.** Snow is a great insulator. as heat does not flow through it very well. If you curl up inside a hole dug in the snow, it traps the heat from your body and keeps it close to you. Many people have survived blizzards by making snow holes.

▼ A man uses a reindeer sledge to collect remains of a woolly mammoth discovered buried in ice.

106 **We put food in a freezer to keep it fresh – and the same thing happens in nature.** Snow and ice can stop dead bodies from rotting away. Woolly mammoths that lived 10,000 years ago have been dug out of the ice in northern Russia, perfectly preserved. In 1991, the body of a 5000-year-old man was found in the ice in mountains in Austria. He was nicknamed Ötzi the Iceman.

Twisting tornadoes

107 Tornadoes are also called twisters. A tornado is an incredibly powerful windstorm that twists around in a swirling 'vortex' shape. It forms a narrow funnel or tube, stretching from the clouds to the ground. Tornadoes often look dark because of all the dirt, dust and broken objects that they pick up as they travel across the land.

108 You can sometimes tell when a tornado is coming, because the sky turns green. Tornadoes usually develop from thunderclouds. Scientists are not sure exactly how they form. They think that as warm, damp air rises, drier, colder air is pulled in and begins to swirl around it. This creates a spinning tube of wind that moves along the ground. A tornado can travel at up to 80 kilometres an hour.

◀ Tornadoes often form where a front, or mass, of cold air meets warm air. They spin around each other and form a funnel shape.

109 Tornadoes contain some of the fastest winds on the planet. Wind inside a tornado can move at up to 500 kilometres an hour. This powerful wind can cause terrible damage. Tornadoes smash buildings, tear off roofs, make bridges collapse, and suck out doors and windows. They can pick up people, animals and cars, and carry them through the air. In 2006, a tornado in Missouri, USA picked up 19-year-old Matt Suter and carried him nearly 400 metres. He survived with only cuts and bruises.

TORNADO IN A BOTTLE

You will need:
Two plastic drinks bottles the same size
Water Sticky tape

1. Fill one of the bottles almost full with water.
2. Position the second bottle upside-down on top of the first, so that their necks join together. Tape them together firmly.
3. Turn both bottles over and swirl them around in a circle as fast as you can.
4. When you hold them still, you should see a tornado shape as the water forms a vortex.

▲ A large, terrifying tornado snakes down to the ground from the base of a big thundercloud.

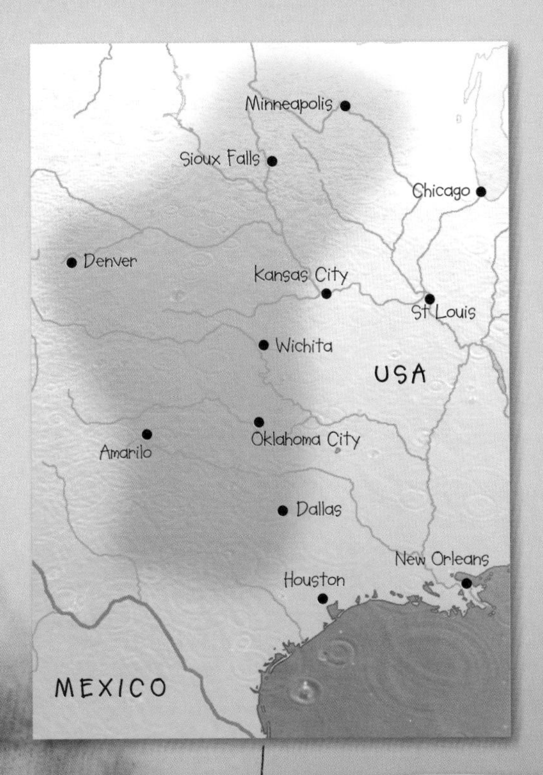

110 Damaging tornadoes happen most often in Tornado Alley. This is an area which stretches across the middle of the USA, between the states of Texas and Illinois. Tornadoes are most common there in the tornado season, from April to August. The Great Tri-State Tornado of 1925 was one of the worst ever. It roared through Missouri, Illionois and Indiana, travelling 350 kilometres. It destroyed 15,000 homes and killed 695 people.

◀ The shaded area on this map shows the part of the USA known as Tornado Alley, where tornadoes are most common.

111 Sometimes, tornadoes occur in deserts, or over the sea. In sandy deserts, small tornadoes pick up sand and carry it along in a whirling tower. They are called sand devils or dust devils. Tornadoes over the sea can suck up water in the same way, and carry it for long distances. They are known as waterspouts.

Howling hurricanes

▲ A man struggles through the high winds of Hurricane Andrew that hit the USA in 1992. Only Hurricane Katrina in 2005 has been more destructive.

112 A hurricane is a huge, swirling mass of stormclouds. Hurricanes form over the ocean, but often travel onto land where they cause floods and destroy whole towns. A typical hurricane is about 500 kilometres wide. In the middle is a small, circular area with no clouds in it, about 70 kilometres wide. This is called the 'eye' of the hurricane.

113 Hurricanes begin in the tropics where the ocean is warm. The ocean surface has to be about 27°C or warmer for a hurricane to start. Warm, wet air rises, forming rainclouds. These begin to swirl in a spiral, caused by the spinning Earth. If the winds reach 118 kilometres an hour, the storm is called a hurricane. Hurricane winds can be as fast as 240 kilometres an hour.

114 The word 'hurricane' is only used to describe storms in the Atlantic Ocean. The scientific name for this type of storm is a tropical cyclone. The same type of storm in the Indian Ocean is known as a cyclone, and in the Pacific Ocean it is called a typhoon.

I DON'T BELIEVE IT!

Surrounding the eye of the hurricane is the eyewall. This is a mass of severe thunderstorms where most of the worst weather occurs.

115 Most hurricanes rage harmlessly over the ocean. If they hit land, less powerful, slow-moving hurricanes can cause more damage than stronger hurricanes, which die out more quickly.

▲ A satellite view from space showing a hurricane swirling across the Gulf of Mexico.

116 Hurricanes and other tropical cyclones can cause terrible disasters. When Hurricane Katrina struck the southern coast of the USA in August 2005, it damaged many cities on the coasts of Mississippi and Louisiana. In New Orleans, huge waves broke through the flood barriers and more than 80 percent of the city was flooded. The hurricane killed over 1800 people and caused damage costing over $80 billion. The Bhola cyclone, which hit Bangladesh in 1970, killed over 300,000 people.

117 Scientists think hurricanes are getting worse. Global warming means that the Earth's temperature is rising, so the seas are getting warmer. This means that more hurricanes are likely. Hurricanes are also becoming bigger and more powerful, as there is more heat energy to fuel them.

▼ These buildings near Lake Pontchartrain, Louisiana, USA, were destroyed by Hurricane Katrina in 2005.

Water, water everywhere

118 A flood happens when water overflows and covers what is normally land. Floods can be caused by rivers overflowing their banks after heavy rain. The sea can also flood the land with large waves or tsunamis. Floods can be useful – some rivers flood every year in the rainy season, bringing water and mud that make farmland moist and fertile. However, most floods are bad news.

▲ A satellite image of the River Nile in Egypt flowing into the Mediterranean Sea. The green triangular area is the Nile Delta. The Nile used to flood each summer, spreading fertile silt across the land. These floods are now controlled by the Aswan Dam in southern Egypt.

▼ A woman carries a precious pot of clean drinking water through dirty floodwaters during a flood in Bangladesh in 1998.

119 Floods can cause death and destruction. When floodwater flows into houses, it fills them with mud, rubbish and sewage (smelly waste from drains and toilets). It ruins electrical appliances, carpets and furniture. After a flood, homes have to be completely cleaned out and repaired – costing huge amounts of money. Even worse, fast-flowing floodwater can sweep away people, cars and even buildings.

▲ Heavy floods hit many parts of England in the summer of 2007. This aerial photo shows Tewkesbury in Gloucestershire.

120 Floods often cause water shortages. Although there's water everywhere, it's dirty and not safe to drink. The dirty water can fill up water supply pipes and water treatment works. They can't supply clean water, and the taps have to be switched off. During bad floods, the emergency services have to deliver water in bottles or tanks, so that people have enough clean water to drink.

I DON'T BELIEVE IT!

The Bible tells of a great flood that covered the world in water. Some scientists think flood stories may be based on flooding that happened around 10,000 years ago, as sea levels rose when ice melted after the last Ice Age.

121 More floods are coming. Because of global warming, the Earth is heating up. In some areas, this means more water will evaporate into the air, causing more clouds and more rain. Global warming also means higher sea levels, so more areas of land are at risk of being flooded.

▼ This car was caught in a flash flood (a sudden, unexpected flood) in Texas, USA. Flash floods can wash entire towns away.

Disastrous droughts

122 A drought is a shortage of rainfall that leaves the land dry. Deserts hardly ever get rain, and are dry and dusty all the time. A drought happens when a place gets much less rain than usual. Scientists don't always know why weather patterns change. However, this can be caused by changes in the oceans. Every few years, a change in sea temperatures in the Pacific, called El Niño, affects weather around the world and causes droughts.

▲ During drought conditions, water is precious. Without it people, animals and plants will die.

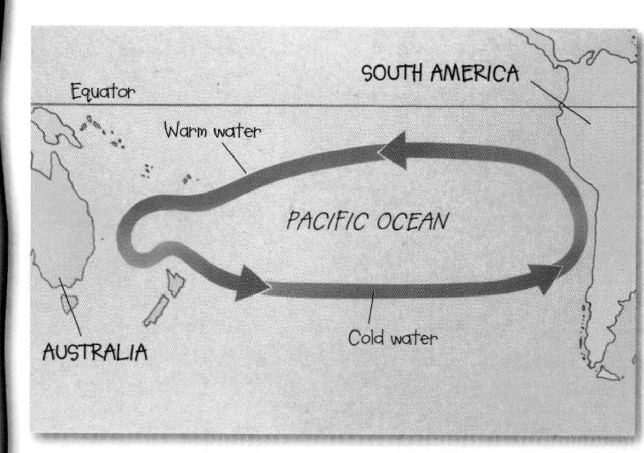

▲ El Niño is a warming of surface ocean waters in the eastern Pacific that can lead to flooding and drought around the world.

123 Droughts are disastrous for people, animals and plants. A shortage of rain means crops can't grow properly, and herds of animals can't get enough drinking water. So people face food and water shortages. Dried-out grass and trees can easily catch fire, and loose dust can blow up into blinding dust storms. Droughts can also cause wars, when people are forced to leave their lands and flock into other areas.

▲ Part of the Murray River in southern Australia, usually flowing with water, lies empty during a drought.

125 Droughts have always happened. They are mentioned in many ancient books, such as the Bible and the writings of the ancient Mesopotamians, who lived in the area around what is now Iraq. However, scientists think that today, global warming is making some droughts worse. As the world gets warmer, weather patterns are changing. Some areas, such as eastern Australia, are now having worse droughts than they used to.

124 The 'Dust Bowl' was a great drought disaster that hit the USA in the 1930s. Several years of drought dried out farm soil in the central states of the USA, such as Oklahoma and Kansas. It blew away in huge dust storms, and farmers could not grow their crops. Hundreds of thousands of people had to leave the area. Many trekked west in search of new lives and jobs.

TRUE OR FALSE?

1. Droughts make forest fires more likely.
2. The Dust Bowl is a volcano in the USA.
3. El Niño is a temperature change in the Indian Ocean.

Answers:
1. True. Droughts make forests drier so they burn more easily 2. False. The Dust Bowl was a drought 3. Fasle. El Niño is in the Pacific Ocean

◄ A massive dust storm about to engulf a farm during the Dust Bowl years. Caused by drought conditions, these storms devastated the American prairies.

VOLCANOES

126 A volcano is an opening on the Earth's surface where molten (liquid) rock emerges from underground. When a volcano erupts, magma (molten rock below the Earth's surface) is expelled. Sometimes it is spewed out as lava – in flowing rivers or as spectacular lava fountains, or sometimes towering clouds of ash are blasted into the air. As lava solidifies and ash is compressed, new rock may form. Volcanoes have shaped much of the Earth's surface.

▼ This is Karymsky, a volcano in eastern Russia. Its perfect cone has been built up from layers of erupted ash and lava.

Around the world

127 Volcanoes happen because the Earth is hot inside. The surface is cool, but it gets hotter the deeper you go into the Earth. Under the crust, magma is under so much pressure that it is almost solid. Sometimes the pressure is released by the shifting of the crust and the magma melts. Then it can bubble up through the cracks in the crust as volcanoes.

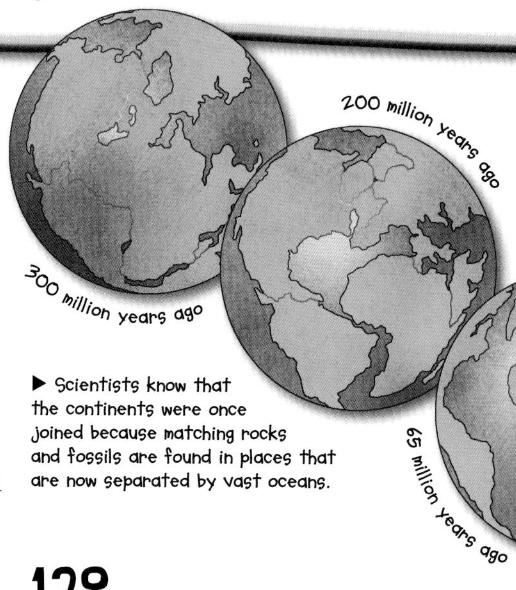

▶ Scientists know that the continents were once joined because matching rocks and fossils are found in places that are now separated by vast oceans.

128 The Earth's crust is cracked into giant pieces called tectonic plates. There are about 60 plates, and the seven largest are thousands of kilometres across. Tectonic plates move slowly across the Earth's surface. This movement, called continental drift, has caused the continents to move apart over millions of years.

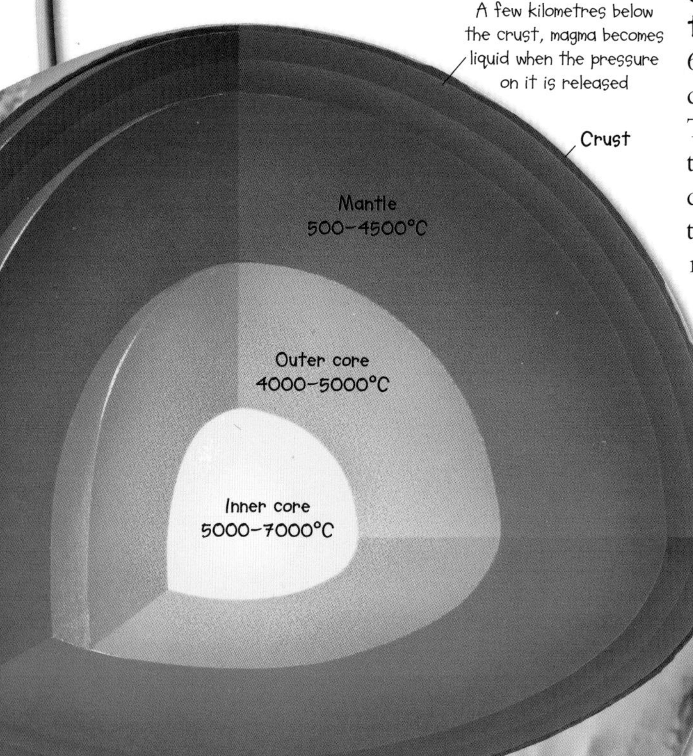

◀ The internal structure of the Earth. The centre of the Earth – the inner core – is solid even though it is intensely hot. This is because it is under extreme pressure.

I DON'T BELIEVE IT!

Tectonic plates move at about the same speed as your fingernails grow. That is just a few centimetres each year.

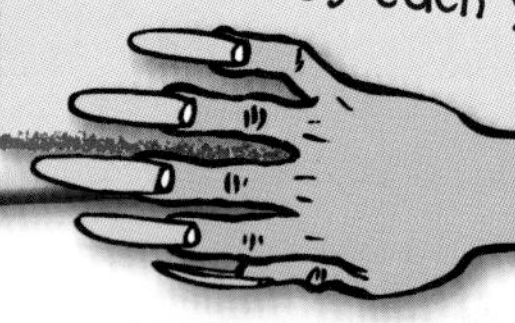

129 About 250 million years ago there was just one continent, known as Pangaea. The movement of tectonics plates broke Pangaea apart and moved the land around to form the continents we recognize today.

130 Most volcanoes erupt along plate boundaries. These are the cracks separating tectonic plates. On a world map of plate boundaries (below) you can see there are often rows of volcanoes along boundaries.

131 Volcanoes also happen at 'hot spots'. These are places where especially hot magma being driven upwards in the mantle, burns through the middle of a plate to form volcanoes. The most famous hot-spot volcanoes are those of the Hawaiian islands.

▼ Most active volcanoes occur along the 'Ring of Fire' (tinted red). Five volcanoes from around the world are highlighted on the map below.

Plate boundaries

132 Tectonic plates meet at plate boundaries. The plates on either side of a boundary are moving at different speeds and in different directions. There are three types of plate boundary – constructive, destructive and transform.

133 In some places, tectonic plates move away from each other. The boundaries between these plates are known as constructive boundaries. As the plates move apart, magma moves up from below into the gap and cools, forming new crust.

▶ At Thingvellir in Iceland, giant cracks in the landscape show the position of a constructive plate boundary.

Plates move apart

Mantle

Magma erupts through the gap

▲ Constructive boundaries often occur in the middle of oceans, forming ocean ridges.

134 Some volcanoes occur along constructive boundaries. Most constructive boundaries are under the ocean, so volcanic activity here usually goes unnoticed. The Mid-Atlantic Ridge is an undersea constructive boundary and the volcanic islands of the Azores, off Portugal, have formed

135 **In other places tectonic plates move towards each other.** The boundaries between these plates are called destructive boundaries. One of the plates often dips below the other and is destroyed as it moves into the mantle below. This is called subduction.

▼ Here, an oceanic plate dips below a continental plate. The thinner oceanic plate is pushed down into the mantle.

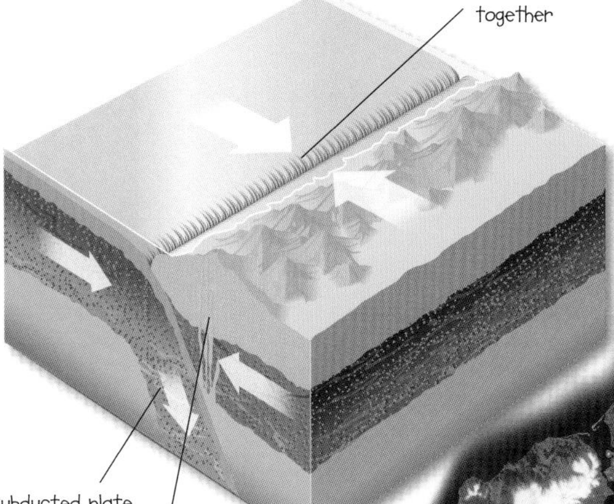

Plates move together

Subducted plate melts into mantle

A volcano has formed along the edge of the overlying plate

136 **Some volcanoes form on destructive plate boundaries.** As one plate is forced down, magma may force its way up through the plate above. If it melts through the surface, it erupts as a violent volcano. The volcanoes of the Andes, South America, have formed over a subduction zone.

I DON'T BELIEVE IT!

The Mid-Atlantic Ridge stretches 14,000 kilometres along the sea floor under the Atlantic Ocean.

▲ The Aleutian Islands, off Alaska, are volcanic islands, formed along a destructive plate boundary.

Parts of a volcano

137 Material erupted from a volcano can build up to form a mountain. Beneath the surface is a system of pipes and chambers that supply the volcano with magma from below the crust.

139 A magma chamber is a store of molten rock under a volcano. As magma moves through cracks in the Earth's crust, it collects in huge reservoirs underground. Magma chambers are usually 1–10 kilometres underground. Some volcanoes have several magma chambers.

138 Magma rises up through a conduit. This is a giant pipe that leads from the magma chamber to the surface. Usually there is one main conduit that leads to the summit of a volcano. The hole at the top of the conduit is called a vent. There are often side vents on a volcano's slopes that have branched off the main conduit.

◀ The mountain on the surface is only the tip of a volcano. Chambers and pipes deep underground store and feed magma to the volcano.

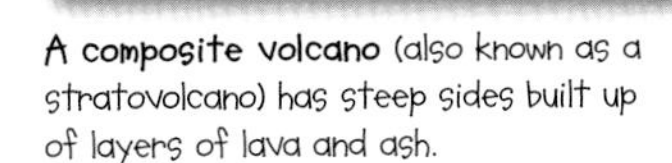

A **composite volcano** (also known as a stratovolcano) has steep sides built up of layers of lava and ash.

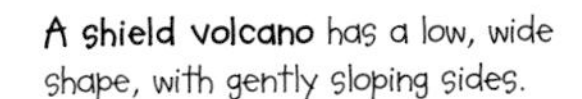

A **shield volcano** has a low, wide shape, with gently sloping sides.

▶ Volcanoes come in different shapes and sizes. Here are three common examples.

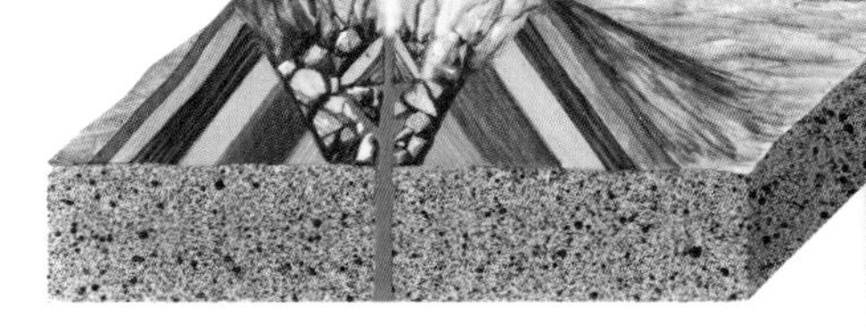

A **caldera** is a huge crater left after an old eruption. New cones often grow again inside.

140 A crater can form around the vent of a volcano. As magma is blasted out during an eruption, the material forms a rim around the top of the vent. Sometimes several vents may be erupting into the same crater. A crater can fill with lava during an eruption. When this forms a pool it is known as a lava lake.

141 Lakes can form in the craters of dormant (inactive) volcanoes. When a volcano stops erupting and cools down, its crater can slowly fill with rain water, creating a lake. Crater lakes also form in calderas – huge craters that form when a volcano collapses into its empty magma chamber.

▼ Crater Lake in Oregon, USA. It formed in the caldera of Mount Mazama and is around 9 kilometres across.

QUIZ

Which of these are parts of a volcano?

1. Conduit
2. Bed chamber
3. Side vent
4. Ventricle
5. Crater

Answers:
Only 1, 3 and 5 are parts of a volcano

Eruptions

▲ A cross-section of an erupting volcano. Eruptions create large ash clouds and lava flows, although these rarely happen at the same time.

142 At any time, about 20 volcanoes are erupting around the world. On average, 60 volcanoes erupt each year. Eruptions can go on for just a few days or for years on end. A single eruption can spew out millions of tonnes of material.

143 An eruption happens when magma swells beneath the Earth's surface. Magma is a mixture of molten rock and other materials, including dissolved water and gases. As magma rises, the pressure on it lessens. This allows the dissolved gas and water to form bubbles. This makes the magma swell quickly, causing an eruption.

▲ The island of Stromboli, Italy, is an active volcano that erupts almost continuously.

144 As well as lava and hot gases, explosive eruptions throw out pieces of solid magma. As the volcano erupts, the pieces of rock are blasted into billions of fragments called pyroclasts. These fragments mainly form vast clouds of ash during an eruption.

GASES IN MAGMA

You will need:
bottle of fizzy drink

Shake the bottle of fizzy drink a little, but not too much, and put it in the sink. As you gradually open the cap, watch the drink in the bottle closely. Bubbles of gas will form, rush upwards and force the drink out of the bottle. The gas stays dissolved in the drink until the pressure on the drink is released. This is the same as what happens when the pressure on magma is released.

145 A volcano can be active or dormant. An active volcano is one that is erupting now or seems likely to erupt. Some scientists define an active volcano as one that has erupted in the last 10,000 years. A dormant volcano is one that is not active at the moment, but might become so in the future.

146 Volcanoes that seem unlikely to erupt again are described as extinct. Some say that a volcano that has not erupted in the last 10,000 years is extinct. But experts cannot always be sure that a volcano will never erupt again.

▶ Sugar Loaf Mountain in Brazil is a volcanic plug – the solidified core of an extinct volcano.

Lava

◀ A slow-moving lava flow engulfs a road. A person could walk away from a lava flow like this without any danger.

147 Lava is liquid rock ejected from a volcano. Some lava is very runny and flows downhill quickly. Another type is thick and gooey and flows very slowly. The temperature, consistency and thickness of lava affect the way it is erupted.

148 A lava flow is a river of lava. Thin, runny lava can flow downhill at speeds up to 100 kilometres an hour. Lava flows follow the natural contours of the land. They can reach many kilometres from the volcano before the lava cools and stops. Lava often spreads out to form lava fields.

TRUE OR FALSE?

1. Aa lava is fast flowing.
2. Igneous rock is made when lava cools down.
3. A shortcrust bomb is made from lava.

Answers:
1. True – aa lava is thick, slow-moving lava
2. True – all igneous rocks are formed when magma, lava or ash cools
3. False – but a breadcrust bomb is

▼ Sometimes lava keeps flowing below the surface through a 'lava tunnel', under a solidified crust.

149 When lava or magma cools, it forms rock. This kind of rock is called igneous rock. Basalt – a dark-coloured rock – is one common type of igneous rock. Over time, lava flows build up on top of each other forming deep layers of igneous rock.

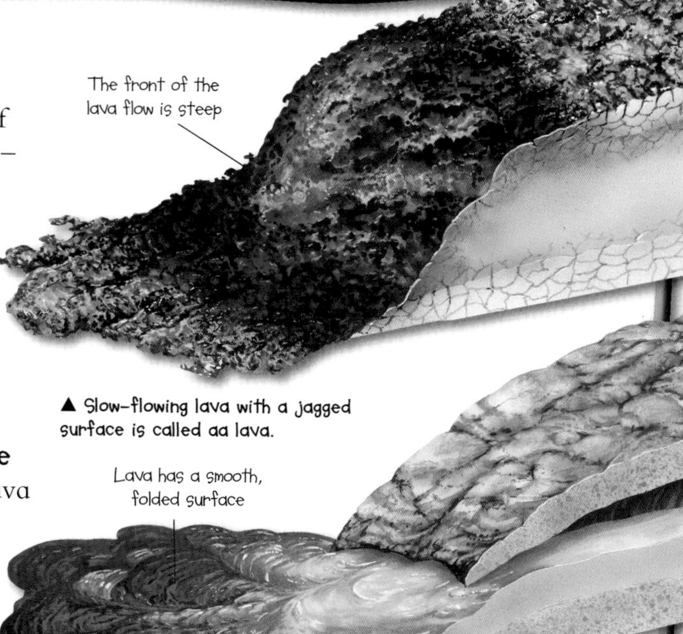

▲ Slow-flowing lava with a jagged surface is called aa lava.

▲ Fast-flowing lava, called pahoehoe lava, cools to form smooth, rope-like rock.

150 Pahoehoe and aa are the two main types of lava. Thick lava that flows slowly cools to form jagged blocks. This is called aa (say ah) lava. Fast-flowing, runny lava cools to form rock with a smooth surface. This is called pahoehoe (say pa-hoey-hoey) lava.

Pele's tears

▶ Pele's tears are tiny lava bombs often produced in Hawaiian eruptions.

Breadcrust bomb

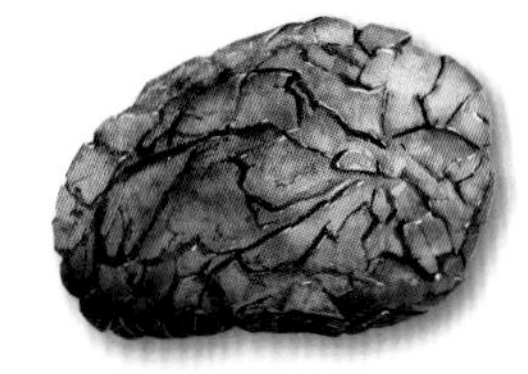

Spindle bomb

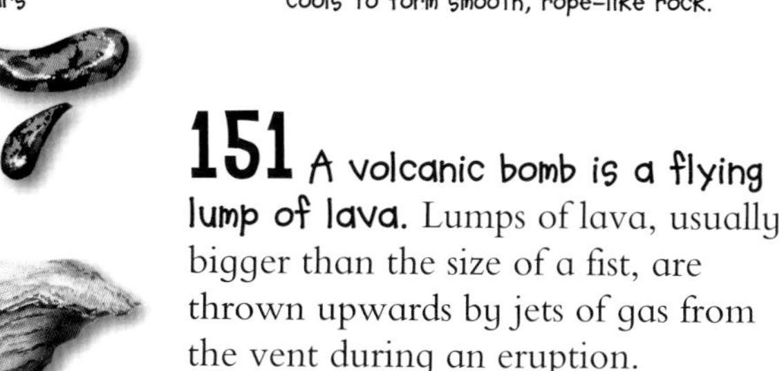

Cowpat bomb

Ribbon bomb

151 A volcanic bomb is a flying lump of lava. Lumps of lava, usually bigger than the size of a fist, are thrown upwards by jets of gas from the vent during an eruption. Sometimes the outside of a bomb solidifies while it is in the air and splits open when it lands. This is called a breadcrust bomb. If the bomb is still soft when it lands, the bomb splats like a cowpat.

◀ Lumps of lava blasted into the air by a volcano form different shapes in the air.

Volcanic ash

152 Volcanic ash is made up of tiny bits of rock. Close up, pieces of ash look like tiny shards of glass. Sometimes, frothy lumps of lava are blasted out with the ash. They cool to form pumice rock, which looks like honeycomb.

▶ Pumice rock is full of holes making it very light.

153 Towering clouds of ash form during explosive eruptions. Hot gases rush out of a volcano's vent at hundreds of metres a second, firing ash thousands of metres into the air. It billows upwards and outwards in an eruption column. These towering ash clouds can reach more than 50 kilometres into the sky.

MAKE A MODEL VOLCANO

You will need:

vinegar plastic bottle bicarbonate of soda jug red food colouring tray sand

Put a tablespoon of bicarbonate of soda in the bottle. Stand the bottle on a tray and make a cone of sand around it. Put a few drops of red food colouring in half a cup of vinegar. Use the jug to pour the vinegar into the bottle. The volcano should erupt with red frothy lava!

▶ Ash is blasted into the sky from the crater of Mount St Helens, USA.

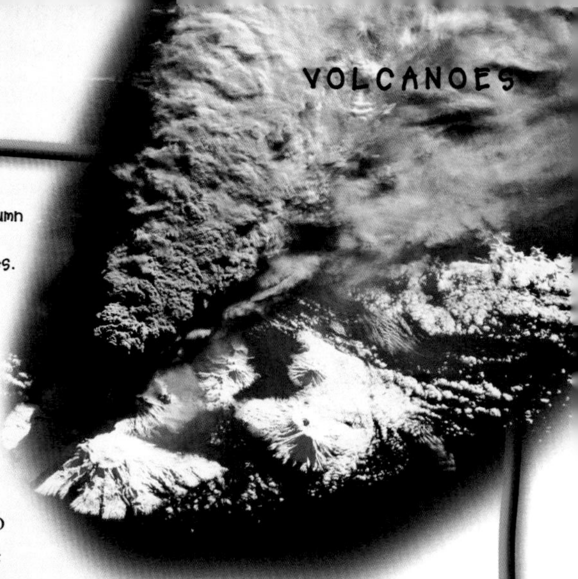

▶ When the wind blows an ash column sideways, it creates an ash plume that can can stretch for kilometres.

154 **Volcanic ash can travel thousands of kilometres.** Ash that is carried high into the atmosphere can be blown great distances before it finally falls. Near the volcano, the fallen ash builds up in layers and over time compresses to form a type of rock called tuff.

155 **Ash sometimes forms red-hot avalanches.** If part of an eruption column collapses, it turns into an avalanche of ash, rock and hot gases, which flows down the side of a volcano. This kind of avalanche is called a pyroclastic flow. Pyroclastic flows can also be set off when the side of a steep volcano collapses.

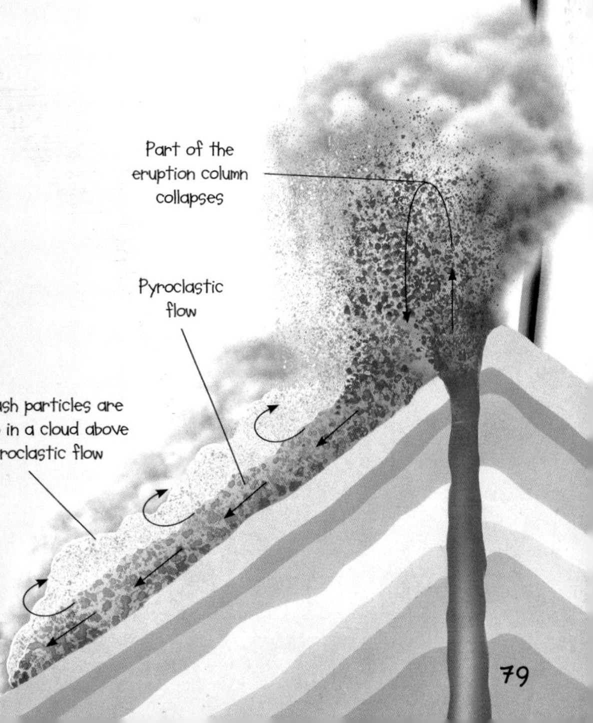

156 **Pyroclastic flows can travel long distances.** They can reach speeds up to 700 kilometres an hour and they can even flow up and over hills that are in their way. Their super-heated gases and swirling ash destroy everything in their path.

▶ A pyroclastic flow is a mixture of ash, pumice and hot gases, which flows down the side of a volcano.

Gentle and explosive

157 **When you think of an eruption, you probably imagine lava flowing out of a crater.** Lava is produced in relatively gentle eruptions. An explosive eruption produces lots of ash and may even blast the mountain apart!

◀ The volcano of Kilauea on Hawaii's Big Island erupts quite gently. Lava fountains like this are common in Hawaiian eruptions.

158 **Runny magma produces gentle eruptions.** Bubbles of gas rise easily through runny magma and escape from the volcano with little build-up of pressure. So lava flows gently from the volcano's vent. Gentle eruptions occur over hot spots and constructive plate boundaries.

159 **Gentle eruptions produce lots of lava.** Rivers of lava often flow from side vents as well as the main vent, down the mountainside. If there is a lot of gas in the magma, lava is blasted upwards in towering lava fountains.

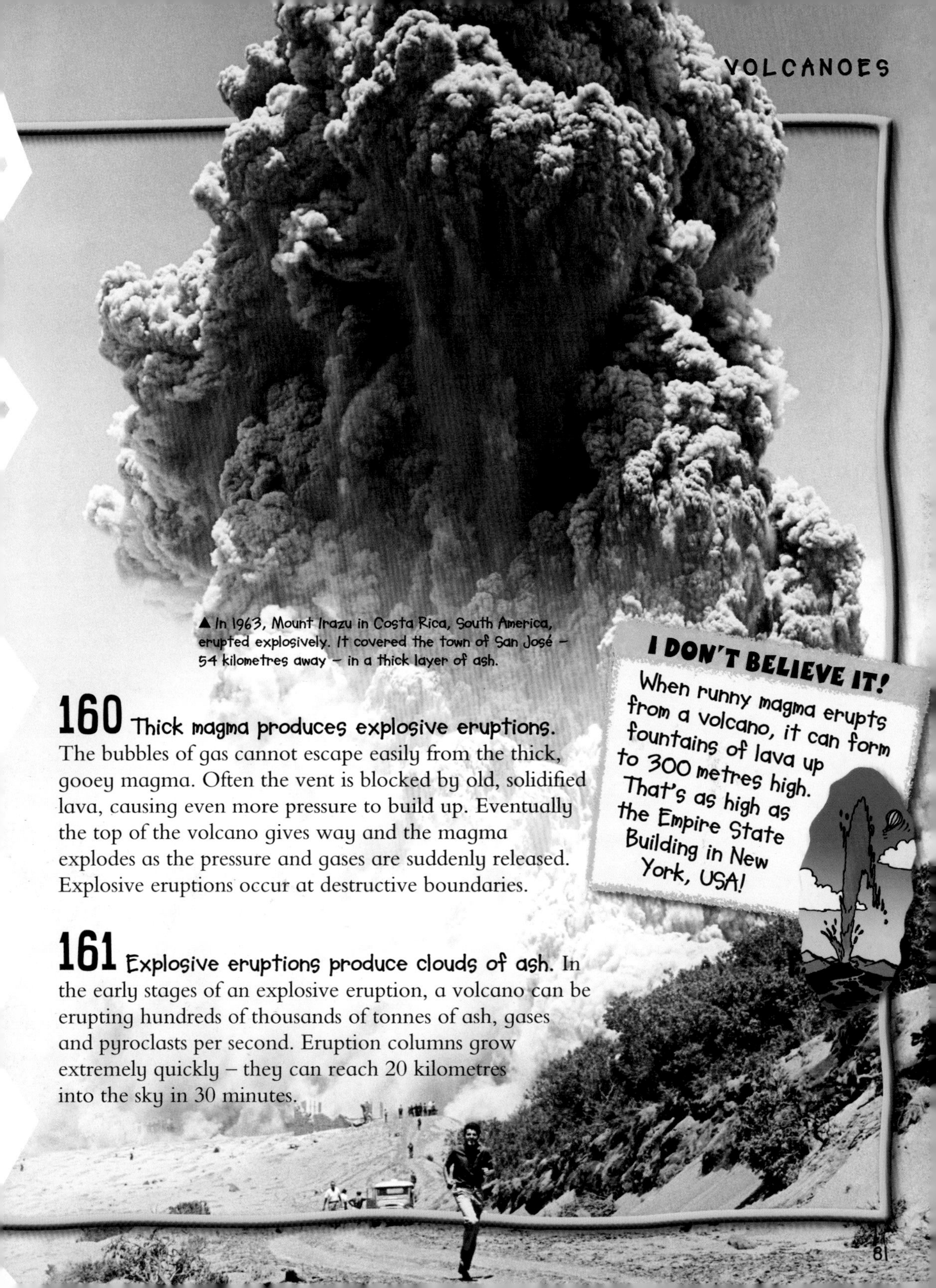

▲ In 1963, Mount Irazu in Costa Rica, South America, erupted explosively. It covered the town of San José – 54 kilometres away – in a thick layer of ash.

160 **Thick magma produces explosive eruptions.** The bubbles of gas cannot escape easily from the thick, gooey magma. Often the vent is blocked by old, solidified lava, causing even more pressure to build up. Eventually the top of the volcano gives way and the magma explodes as the pressure and gases are suddenly released. Explosive eruptions occur at destructive boundaries.

161 **Explosive eruptions produce clouds of ash.** In the early stages of an explosive eruption, a volcano can be erupting hundreds of thousands of tonnes of ash, gases and pyroclasts per second. Eruption columns grow extremely quickly – they can reach 20 kilometres into the sky in 30 minutes.

I DON'T BELIEVE IT!

When runny magma erupts from a volcano, it can form fountains of lava up to 300 metres high. That's as high as the Empire State Building in New York, USA!

Volcanic features

162 Volcanic activity creates features on the landscape. The heat in rocks in regions of volcanic activity cause features such as fumaroles, geysers, hot springs and boiling mud pools. These features can be seen in places where there are no actual volcanoes.

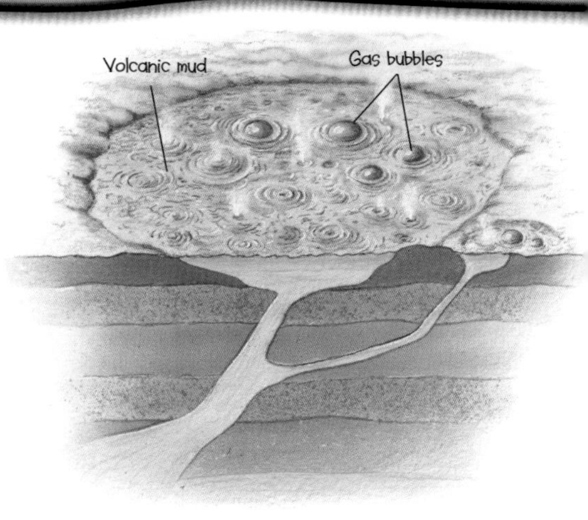

▲ A volcanic mud pool (or mudpot) forms where steam and hot gas bubble up through mud on the surface.

▼ Iceland's Blue Lagoon geothermal spa. Seawater is heated deep underground and it emerges as hot springs at the surface, rich in minerals. The nearby geothermal power station uses the heat to produce electricity.

163 Fumaroles are steaming holes in the ground. They form where groundwater (water under the ground) comes into contact with hot rock or magma and turns to steam. The steam rises through cracks, and vents at the surface as a fumarole. Gases, such as sulphur dioxide, are also emitted.

QUIZ

1. What makes the mud in a mud pool boil?
2. What does the word 'geyser' mean in Icelandic?
3. What is the most famous geyser?

Answers:
1. Steam and hot gas bubble up through surface mud 2. 'Geyser' is Icelandic for 'gush' 3. Old Faithful, Yellowstone National Park

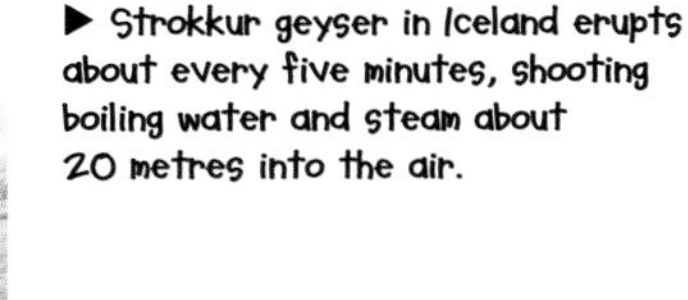

▶ Strokkur geyser in Iceland erupts about every five minutes, shooting boiling water and steam about 20 metres into the air.

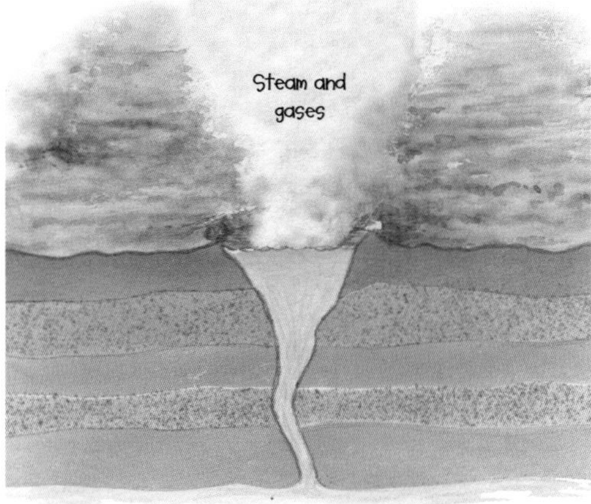

▲ A fumarole is a hole that emits steam and sulphurous gases. Yellow sulphur crystals often form around the hole.

164 The word 'geyser' comes from Iceland. It is derived from the Icelandic word for 'gush'. The most famous geyser is Old Faithful in Yellowstone National Park, USA. It is called Old Faithful because every hour or so it produces a hot-water fountain 35 metres high.

165 A geyser is a fountain of boiling water and steam. Geysers form when groundwater is heated deep below the ground under pressure. The hot water moves up through rock layers to the surface to find a place to escape. When it starts to bubble up, releasing the pressure, a jet of super-heated water and steam blasts from a hole in the ground for a few seconds.

Hazards of a volcano

166 Volcanic eruptions can be extremely dangerous to anyone living in their vicinity. The main hazards are lava flows, pyroclastic flows, ash and side effects such as mudflows. In the past, volcanoes have killed thousands of people, destroying homes, and even whole villages and towns.

167 Lava flows are very destructive. They can knock down buildings, bury objects and they set light to anything that will burn. However, most lava flows creep along slower than walking pace, and people can normally run or drive away from the danger of an approaching lava flow.

▼ A lava flow creeps along, engulfing and incinerating palm trees on Hawaii.

▲ This aerial view shows the paths of the pyroclastic flows that swept down Mount Unzen, Japan.

168 The deadliest volcano hazards are pyroclastic flows. Temperatures inside these high-speed avalanches of searing hot ash, gas and rock reach hundreds of degrees Celsius. When a pyroclastic flow hits objects, such as trees or houses, the blast flattens them, and the heat burns them to a cinder.

169 Pyroclastic flows can travel as fast as a jet plane. Anyone caught in a pyroclastic flow cannot survive the heat. In 1991, hundreds of observers and journalists gathered at Mount Unzen, Japan, as it began to erupt. Forty-two of them were killed by a pyroclastic flow.

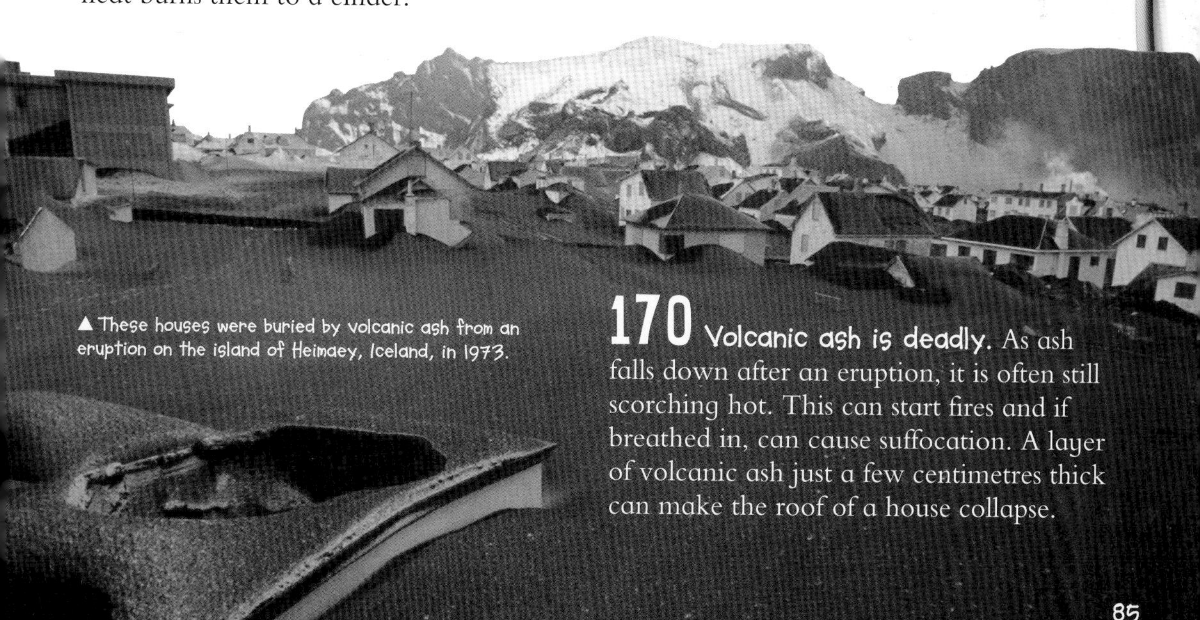

▲ These houses were buried by volcanic ash from an eruption on the island of Heimaey, Iceland, in 1973.

170 Volcanic ash is deadly. As ash falls down after an eruption, it is often still scorching hot. This can start fires and if breathed in, can cause suffocation. A layer of volcanic ash just a few centimetres thick can make the roof of a house collapse.

Side effects

171 Volcanoes can set off floods, mudflows and tsunamis. It is not just the material expelled by volcanoes, such as lava, bombs, ash and pyroclastic flows, which is dangerous. Eruptions can also cause hazardous side effects, which are just as deadly.

172 A volcanic mudflow is a river of ash and water. Mudflows are also called lahars. Some occur when hot ash falls on snow and ice on the upper slopes of volcanoes. Ash mixes with the meltwater and flows downhill. Others form from heavy rain falling on the ash deposits. When a mudflow stops flowing it sets solid like concrete.

QUIZ

1. What is a lahar?
2. What town was buried by a mudflow in 1985?
3. What happens to tsunami waves as they hit shallow water?

Answers:
1. Lahar is another name for a volcanic mudflow 2. Armero in Colombia, South America 3. They increase in size and become closer together

▲ Near the crater of Mount Ruapehu in New Zealand, a mudflow, or lahar, begins to flow down the slopes. The flow formed after an eruption in 2007.

173 The town of Armero, Colombia, was devastated by a mudflow. In 1985, the volcano Nevado del Ruiz erupted. It was not a large eruption, but ash melted snow on the summit, setting off a mudflow. It rushed down a river valley and swept through Armero. Practically the entire population of 22,000 died.

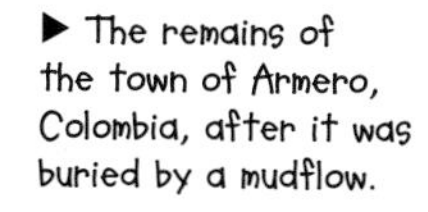

▶ The remains of the town of Armero, Colombia, after it was buried by a mudflow.

174 Volcanoes can cause floods. Landslides set off by eruptions can fall into lakes, causing floods in rivers below. In Iceland, volcanoes sometimes erupt under the ice cap. The eruptions melt huge volumes of ice, setting off vast floods that sweep out to sea.

175 Explosive eruptions can set off tsunamis. A tsunami is a huge wave that travels across the sea and causes floods on any coasts it hits. The eruption of the volcanic island of Krakatoa, Indonesia, in 1883, set off tsunamis that travelled thousands of kilometres around the world.

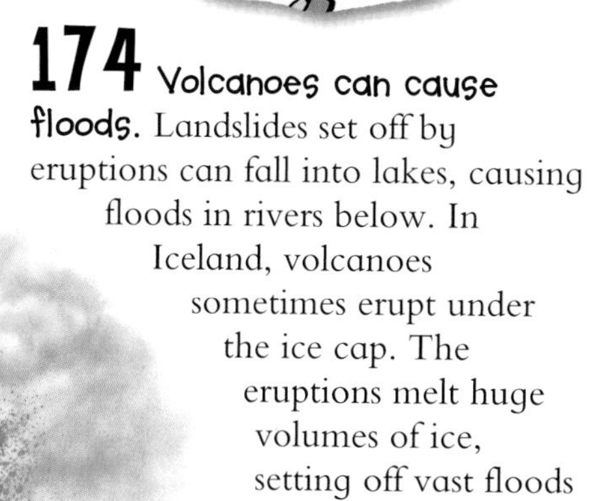

▼ When Krakatoa erupted, nearby islands were swamped by tsunamis set off by pyroclastic flows entering the sea.

Using volcanoes

▲ Wairakei power station in New Zealand is located on a field of geothermal activity. The pipes carry water heated by underground rocks.

QUIZ

1. What type of energy comes from the natural heat from the Earth?
2. What mineral is mined around volcanoes?
3. Why is volcanic soil good for growing crops?

Answers:
1. Geothermal energy 2. Sulphur 3. Because it is rich in minerals

176 Millions of people live near active volcanoes. About one in ten of all the people in the world could be in danger from eruptions. However, people living near volcanoes can benefit from them – heat from volcanoes can be turned into electricity and the soil is good for farming.

177 Volcanoes are sources of energy. The rocks around them are normally extremely hot. Heat energy from the Earth, called geothermal energy, can be collected and used for heating and to generate electricity. At geothermal power stations, water is pumped down into the ground where it is heated, creating hot water and steam. The hot water is used to heat homes and the steam to drive turbines and generators.

178 Sulphur is mined from around volcanoes. This yellow mineral is an important raw material for the chemical industries. Sulphur crystals are common around the vents of volcanoes and hot springs because magma gives off sulphurous gases. Sulphur is also extracted from volcanic rocks.

180 Many people believe water filtered through volcanic rock is good for your health. Natural sources of water in volcanic regions are rich in minerals including calcium and magnesium, which are good for growth and general health. A lot of mineral water is bottled at its source and exported for sale.

▶ In 2006, 20,000 people were evacuated due to the eruption of Mayon, the most active volcano in the Phillipines.

179 Volcanic soil is good for farming. Soil is normally made up of broken-down rock. Near volcanoes, soil is made up of eroded lava or ash and is rich in the minerals that plants need to grow. Mayon, a volcano in the Phillipines, regularly erupts explosively, but the land around Mayon is still farmed.

◀ A miner collects pieces of sulphur at a crater in Indonesia. Huge deposits of sulphur can build up around a volcano's crater.

Volcano science

181 The science of volcanoes is called volcanology. Scientists called volcanologists study the structure of volcanoes, causes of eruptions, old lava flows and how ash travels in the air. They also monitor volcanoes to try to predict future eruptions.

▲ A volcanologist measures the levels of different gases coming from a fumarole.

▼ In 1994, the Dante II robot was lowered into the hot crater of Mount Spurr, Alaska. It collected gas and water samples and recorded video pictures.

182 Volcanologists analyze volcanic gases. The main gases emitted by volcanoes are steam, sulphur dioxide and carbon dioxide. The volume and proportion of gases coming from a volcano's vent indicates what magma is doing underground. An increase in sulphur dioxide shows that fresh magma may be near the surface and an eruption could happen soon.

TRUE OR FALSE?

1. More sulphur dioxide coming from a volcano means there could be an eruption.
2. Tiltmeters measure earthquakes.
3. Volcanologists wear silver suits to absorb the heat.

Answers:
1. True 2. False
3. False

183 Earthquakes show that magma is moving. Volcanologists set up earthquake-detecting instruments called seismographs on volcanoes. If earthquakes become more frequent, an eruption may be about to happen. Tiltmeters are used to detect if the ground is bulging. This shows if magma is building up underneath.

184 Volcanologists study old lava flows. Evidence of previous eruptions is a good guide to what might happen in the future. Old lava flows and ashfall on and around a volcano show the frequency and size of past eruptions. This gives a good indication of the areas that might be affected by future eruptions.

▼ Heat-reflecting silver suits protect volcanologists measuring the temperature of lava at Fournaise volcano, Reunion Island.

185 Volcanologists wear protective clothes. Hot rocks, lava flows, bombs, falling ash and poisonous gases make active volcanoes dangerous places to be. When they visit volcanoes, volcanologists wear sturdy boots, hard hats and heat-resistant gloves. In very dangerous areas they also wear heat-reflecting overalls and gas masks.

Fighting volcanoes

186 People cannot stop volcanoes from erupting. However, we can reduce the damage that volcanoes cause by stopping or diverting lava and mudflows away from cities and towns. Injury and death can also be prevented by predicting eruptions accurately.

I DON'T BELIEVE IT!

Islanders of Heimaey pumped a total of 6.3 million cubic metres of sea water (enough to fill 2000 Olympic-sized swimming pools) onto the lava to stop it.

187 A lava flow was stopped with sea water. In 1973, an eruption on the island of Heimaey, Iceland, sent lava flows heading towards the island's harbour where its fishing fleet was moored. Islanders pumped sea water onto the lava for months. Eventually it was stopped and the harbour was saved.

▼ The towering lava flows destroyed many houses on the island of Heimaey, Iceland, during the eruption in 1973.

◀ During the eruption of Mount Etna, Italy, in 1983, bulldozers piled up rock in banks to channel a lava flow away from houses.

188 Mudflows can be reduced with dams. Deadly mudflows are fast-flowing and dense with ash and heavy debris. Special dams, called sabo dams, slow mudflows by trapping the ash and debris and letting the water flow harmlessly away.

189 There are various ways to reduce the damage of lava flows. In the past people have built walls and dug channels to divert flows. Bombs have also been dropped on lava flows to make them spread out and slow down, as used on Mount Etna in 1992.

▼ Sabo dams on the slopes of Sakurajima volcano in Japan are designed to slow mudflows.

190 Preparation saves lives. People living in danger zones near active volcanoes have a plan of action in case of eruption. Local authorities should also communicate with volcanologists and the emergency services when an eruption threatens so that people can be evacuated in good time.

Mount St Helens

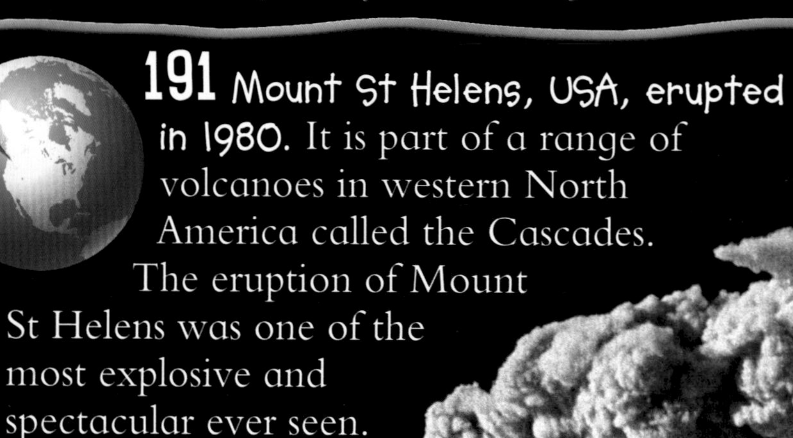

191 Mount St Helens, USA, erupted in 1980. It is part of a range of volcanoes in western North America called the Cascades. The eruption of Mount St Helens was one of the most explosive and spectacular ever seen.

▲ Mount St Helens before the 1980 eruption. The bulge that grew on the north side is clearly visible.

192 Mount St Helens bulged outwards before the blast. The eruption began in March 1980 with a cloud of ash that grew to 6000 metres tall. In April, the north side of the volcano began bulging outwards. Gradually the bulge grew, showing that magma was building up underneath.

► Ash blasting from the vent of Mount St Helens during the eruption. The cloud grew more than 20 kilometres high.

▶ The scars of the devastating mudflows and pyroclastic flows can still be seen in this satellite image taken in 1997.

193 The bulge collapsed on 18 May. The pressure on the magma was released suddenly and the volcano exploded sideways. A pyroclastic flow hurtled across the landscape at more than 300 kilometres an hour. It flattened millions of trees, some 32 kilometres away. Landslides of rock, mixed with water, snow and ice, caused mudflows that travelled up to 30 kilometres away.

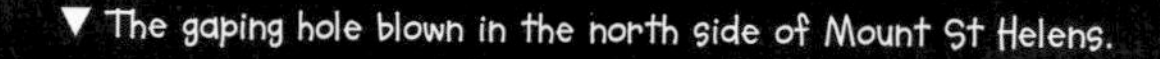

▼ The gaping hole blown in the north side of Mount St Helens.

194 Fifty-seven people were killed at Mount St Helens. They were forestry workers, volcanologists, campers and tourists. Most victims thought they were a safe distance away from the volcano. However, nobody expected the devastating sideways blast.

I DON'T BELIEVE IT!

Local man Harry Truman refused to leave his home near Mount St Helens despite warnings. The lodge he lived in was buried in the eruption.

195 Mount St Helens is rebuilding itself. About 300 metres was blown off the top of the volcano in the 1980 eruption. Since then, a new lava dome (heap of solidified lava) has grown inside the crater – a sign that one day Mount St Helens will erupt again.

Mount Pinatubo

196 Mount Pinatubo erupted violently in June 1991. It is a stratovolcano in the Philippines, close to the city of Manila. Its 1991 eruption was the most devastating of the 20th century.

I DON'T BELIEVE IT!

Two months before the main eruption, scientists were recording hundreds of small earthquakes every day in the surrounding area.

197 Mount Pinatubo had been dormant for 600 years. The first signs of an eruption were explosions of steam from the summit. Volcanologists from the Philippines and USA quickly set up an observatory at the nearby Clark Air Base to monitor the activity. They set up instruments on the volcano that showed magma was on the move below.

198 An exclusion zone was set up around the volcano. At first, the zone extended 10 kilometres from the volcano. This was steadily increased to 30 kilometres. In total, 58,000 people were evacuated, which saved many lives.

▼ A truck races to escape a boiling pyroclastic flow rolling down from Mount Pinatubo.

▲ Ash fell far from the eruption column of Mount Pinatubo, smothering local villages and countryside.

200 Heavy rains caused devastating mudflows. A typhoon hit the Philippines as Mount Pinatubo erupted, bringing days of torrential rain. The rain set off huge mudflows that swept away thousands of homes and 100 square kilometres of valuable farmland. More mudflows followed as the heavy rains returned in the following years.

199 Mount Pinatubo erupted with giant explosions. An ash cloud rose 40 kilometres into the sky and pyroclastic flows reached up to 20 kilometres from the volcano. They deposited ash and debris tens of metres deep along their route. Ash in the air made it dark in the middle of the day and gases from the eruption spread around the Earth. This caused temperatures to fall by 0.5°C for several months.

▶ A false-colour satellite image taken after Pinatubo's eruption shows mudflows in red and the large crater (centre) left after the eruption.

Mount Vesuvius

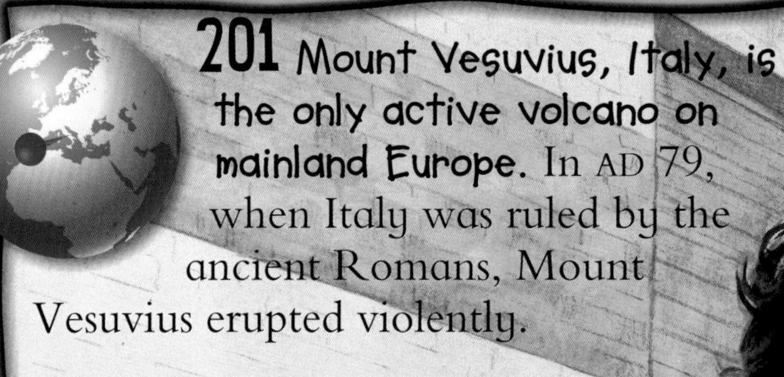

201 Mount Vesuvius, Italy, is the only active volcano on mainland Europe. In AD 79, when Italy was ruled by the ancient Romans, Mount Vesuvius erupted violently.

202 The eruption was seen by a Roman called Pliny the Younger. Pliny wrote letters describing the ash cloud – he said it looked like a giant pine tree. His uncle, Pliny the Elder, went to help people escape, but was killed by falling ash. Today, explosive eruptions are called Plinian eruptions after Pliny.

▶ Ash and pyroclasts raining down from Vesuvius would have caused complete panic in the streets of Pompeii.

203 The city of Pompeii was completely buried by ash. Pompeii lay 15 kilometres south of Mount Vesuvius. Ash and pumice rained down on the city, filling the streets and making buildings collapse.

I DON'T BELIEVE IT!

Before AD 79, Mount Vesuvius had not erupted for 800 years. The Romans did not realize it was a volcano or that there was any danger.

▲ The last major eruption of Mount Vesuvius happened in 1944. Two villages on the slopes were hit by lava flows.

204 People had little time to escape. Thousands died as they ran through the streets, suffocated by the hot, choking ash. Since excavations started in the 1750s, archaeologists digging through the layers of ash have uncovered the remains of people and animals.

205 Mount Vesuvius is still a dangerous volcano. It has erupted dozens of times since AD 79. Nearby towns and villages have been regularly destroyed by eruptions, yet millions of people still live close to the volcano.

Volcanoes at sea

206 Many islands are the tops of volcanoes. Volcanic islands grow over hotspots and other regions of volcanic activity under the sea. There are hundreds of hidden undersea volcanoes that have not broke the ocean's surface yet. These are called seamounts.

▲ Anak Krakatoa is a new island in Indonesia that first appeared out of the sea in 1927. It has grown in the place of the island of Krakatoa.

207 Underwater eruptions produce pillow lava. As lava is exposed to cold sea water, it cools quickly, forming round humps of lava that look like pillows piled on top of each other. Pillow lava also forms when lava flows reach the sea.

TRUE OR FALSE?

1. Mauna Kea is the world's tallest mountain.
2. More Hawaiian islands will form in the future.
3. Surtsey island is near Fiji.

Answers:
1. True – from the sea floor, Mauna Kea is slightly taller than Mount Everest 2. True – as the tectonic plate moves over the hotspot more, more islands will form 3. False – Surtsey is near Iceland. The island that formed in 2006 is near Fiji

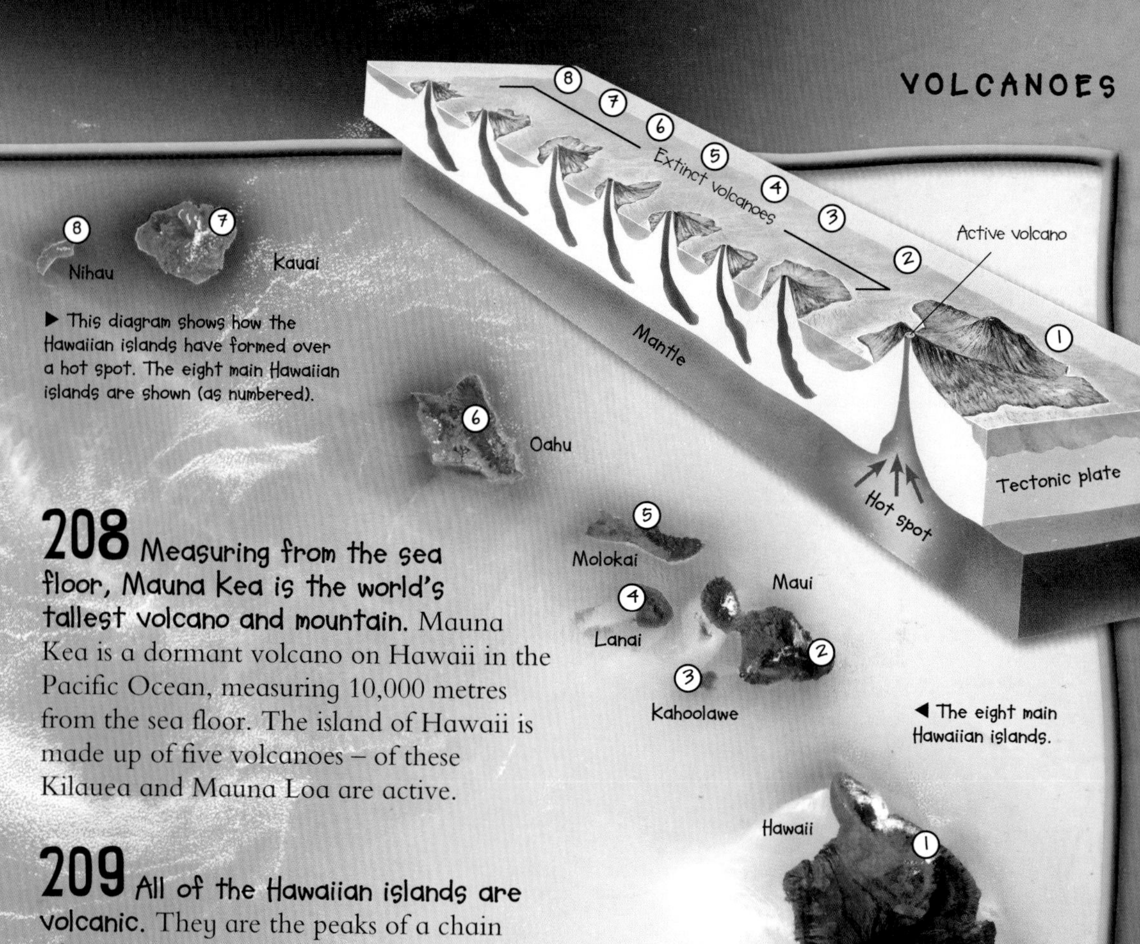

▶ This diagram shows how the Hawaiian islands have formed over a hot spot. The eight main Hawaiian islands are shown (as numbered).

◀ The eight main Hawaiian islands.

208 Measuring from the sea floor, Mauna Kea is the world's tallest volcano and mountain. Mauna Kea is a dormant volcano on Hawaii in the Pacific Ocean, measuring 10,000 metres from the sea floor. The island of Hawaii is made up of five volcanoes – of these Kilauea and Mauna Loa are active.

209 All of the Hawaiian islands are volcanic. They are the peaks of a chain of undersea volcanoes that have grown over a hot spot in the centre of the Pacific plate. New islands have formed over millions of years as the plate has moved and more will form in the future.

210 In 1963, a new island appeared near Iceland. At first, a cloud of steam and ash rose from the sea. Ten days later, an island one kilometre across and 90 metres high had built up. The new island was named Surtsey. More recently in 2006, sailor Fredrik Fransson came across a newly forming island off Fiji in the Pacific Ocean.

◀ A new volcanic island in the Pacific Ocean (left). Fredrik Fransson on board his yacht sails through a floating 'raft' of pumice (far left) erupted from the volcanic island.

The biggest volcanoes

211 Eruptions of the biggest volcanoes affect the whole planet. Ash and gases are blasted over 50 kilometres into the atmosphere. Winds that blow at high altitude spread the ash and gas for thousands of kilometres – sometimes right around the world.

VEI 8 – Mega-colossal
Ash column height 25 km +
Volume erupted 1000 km^3

VEI 7 – Super-colossal
Ash column height 25 km +
Volume erupted 100 km^3

VEI 6 – Colossal
Ash column height 25 km +
Volume erupted 10 km^3

VEI 5 – Paroxysmal
Ash column height 25 km +
Volume erupted 1 km^3

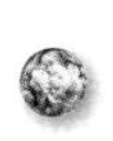

VEI 4 – Cataclysmic
Ash column height 10–25 km
Volume erupted 100,000,000 m^3

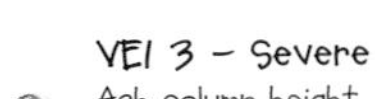

VEI 3 – Severe
Ash column height 3–15 km
Volume erupted 10,000,000 m^3

VEI 2 – Explosive
Ash column height 1–5 km
Volume erupted 1,000,000 m^3

VEI 1 – Gentle
Ash column height 100–1000 m
Volume erupted 10,000 m^3

▲ The Volcanic Explosivity Index. Each stage represents a ten-fold increase in explosivity.

212 The power of an eruption is measured on the VEI scale. VEI stands for Volcanic Explosivity Index and it is based on the amount of material erupted and the height of the ash column. Each stage on the scale has a name – 1 is a 'gentle' eruption and 8 is a 'mega-colossal' eruption. The eruption of Mount St. Helens had a VEI of 5 and that of Mount Vesuvius in AD 79 had a VEI of 4.

213 The biggest eruption in historical time had a VEI of 7. In 1815 the Indonesian volcano Tambora erupted. Ash spread around the world. It blocked sunlight and caused temperatures to fall and crops to fail. The following year, 1816, is known as 'the year without a summer' because of the cold weather. Over 90,000 people were killed by the eruption.

▲ An artist's impression of the eruption of Krakatoa in 1883 (main image). Most of the island was destroyed during the eruption (above right).

214 The island of Krakatoa was destroyed in an eruption. Krakatoa was a volcanic island in Indonesia. In 1883 it erupted in a series of huge explosions that blew the island apart. The eruption caused tsunamis that devastated nearby islands and coasts. Today, a new volcano – Anak Krakatoa (meaning 'child of Krakatoa') – is growing in the sea where Krakatoa once stood.

215 The eruption of Toba had a VEI of 8. Toba in Indonesia erupted about 74,000 years ago. Volcanologists think it was the biggest eruption in the last two million years. Its effects may have nearly wiped out the human population. Eruptions of this massive scale are called super eruptions.

◀ The 100-kilometre-long Lake Toba fills the caldera left by the super-eruption of Toba.

QUIZ

1. What does VEI stand for?
2. What does the name Anak Krakatoa mean?
3. Which volcanic eruption had a VEI of 8?

Answers:
1. Volcanic Explosivity Index 2. Child of Krakatoa 3. Toba, 74,000 years ago

Past and future

216 The Earth was once covered by volcanoes. When the Earth formed 4500 billion years ago, its surface was molten. It gradually cooled and a crust formed. At this time the Earth's surface was covered with millions of volcanoes.

▼ The young planet Earth was a fiery ball of molten rock.

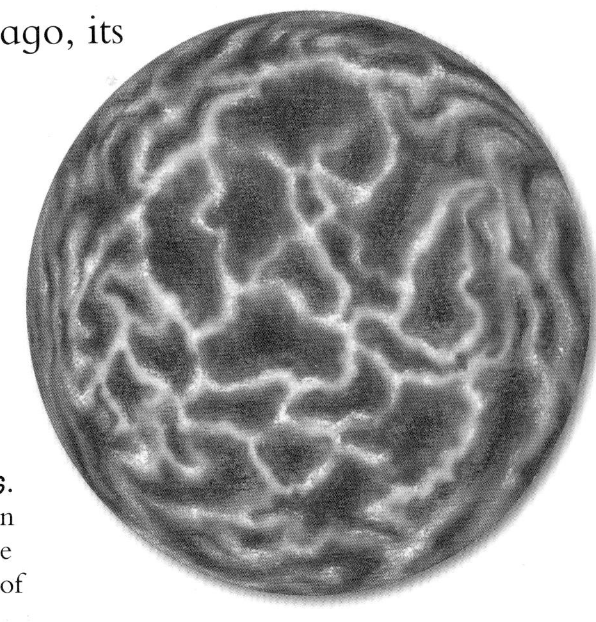

217 A VEI 8 eruption happens roughly once every 100,000 years. That is what volcanologists think as an average. A VEI 8 eruption would wipe out many countries and kill off much of the world's human population.

I DON'T BELIEVE IT!

There are volcanoes on Io, one of Jupiter's moons. They erupt giant fountains of sulphur that make the surface appear yellow.

218 We do not know when the next super-volcano will erupt. Super-eruptions are at the highest end (and beyond) of the VEI scale. The last super-eruption was Toba 74,000 years ago. The next one could happen in tens of thousands of years, more than a million years or even much sooner!

219 Yellowstone National Park, USA, could erupt soon! Yellowstone is over a hot spot in the crust. It is the site of a caldera that is 60 kilometres across. There were VEI 8 eruptions here two million, 1.3 million and 640,000 years ago. That means another one is due.

▼ Tourists flock to Yellowstone National Park to see the volcanic features, such as the Old Faithful geyser. The park lies on the site of a super-volcano.

▶ Olympus Mons on Mars photographed from overhead by a space probe.

220 Other planets have volcanoes too. Astronomers have discovered more than 1000 volcanoes on Venus, but all are extinct. Mars has the largest volcano in the Solar System, called Olympus Mons, which is 24 kilometres high.

Myths and legends

221 People once thought eruptions were the work of gods. Until scientists began to understand volcanoes, nobody knew how or why they erupted. People were scared by eruptions and thought that they meant the gods were angry.

▶ The word 'volcano' originates from Vulcan, the Roman god of fire.

222 Vulcan was the Roman god of fire. Roman legend says that Vulcan lived on the island of Vulcano, near Sicily. He was blacksmith to the gods, forging their weapons. Fire and smoke from Vulcano were thought to be caused by Vulcan hammering hot metal in his forge.

223 Mount Fuji in Japan is a sacred mountain. For hundreds of years, Japanese people have made pilgrimages to its summit. Mount Fuji is one of the world's most beautiful volcanoes, with a perfect snow-capped cone and lakes around its lower slopes. It appears many times in Japanese art and photography and is also shown on Japanese currency.

224 Pele is the Hawaiian goddess of volcanoes. Hawaiians believe that Pele lives on Kilauea on Hawaii. Drop-shaped pieces of volcanic glass erupted from Hawaiian voclanoes are known as Pele's tears and thin strands of the same material are called Pele's hair.

▼ The perfect cone of Mount Fuji. The mountain is sacred for many Japanese people.

▲ Pele, the Hawaiian goddess of volcanoes is also goddess of fire and lightning.

QUIZ

1. What was Vulcan the Roman god of?
2. Where was the goddess Pele thought to live?
3. What did the gods turn Popocatépetl and his princess into?

Answers:
1. Fire 2. Kilauea on Hawaii 3. Mountains

225 A warrior was named after the Mexican volcano Popocatépetl. In Aztec folklore, the warrior Popocatépetl fell in love with a princess. They wanted to marry but the princess's father would only agree if Popocatépetl went to battle for him. He was away for such a long time that the princess thought he was dead, so she drank poison and died. When Popocatépetl returned, he held the princess in his arms and it is said the gods turned them both into mountains. Popocatépetl made fire because of his anger.

226 Rain, sunshine, snow and storms are all types of weather. These help us decide what clothes we wear, what food we eat, and what kind of life we lead. Weather also affects how animals and plants survive. Different types of weather are caused by what is happening in the atmosphere, the air above our heads. In some parts of the world, the weather changes every day, in others, it is nearly always the same.

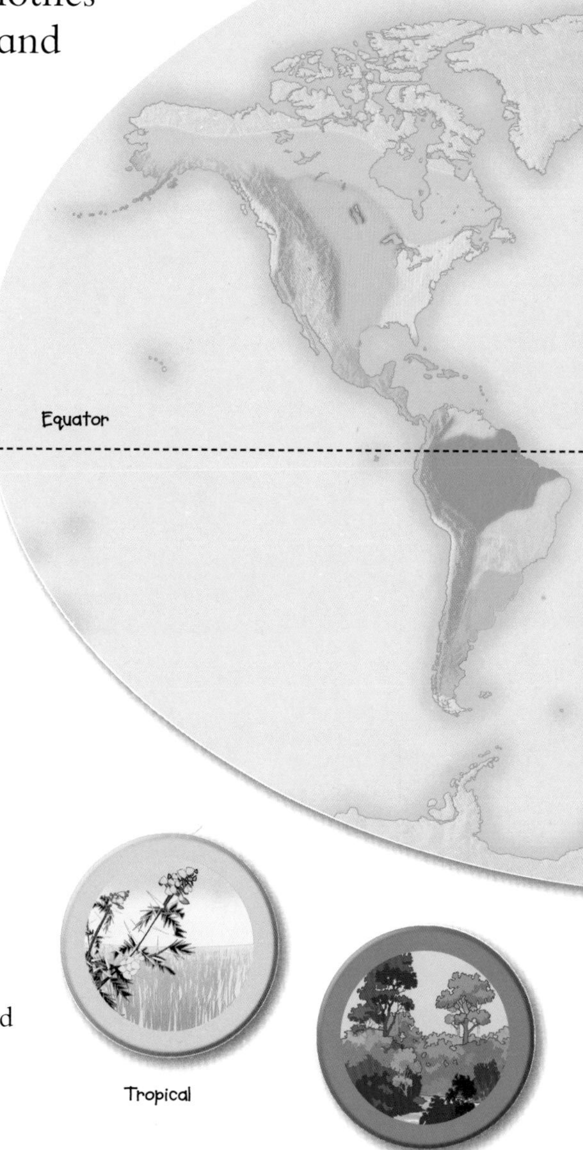

227 Tropical, temperate and polar are all types of climate. Climate is the name we give to patterns of weather over a period of time. Near the Equator, the weather is mostly hot and steamy. We call this a tropical climate. Near the North and South Poles, ice lies on the ground year-round and there are biting-cold blizzards. This is a polar climate. Most of the world has a temperate climate, with a mix of cold and warm seasons.

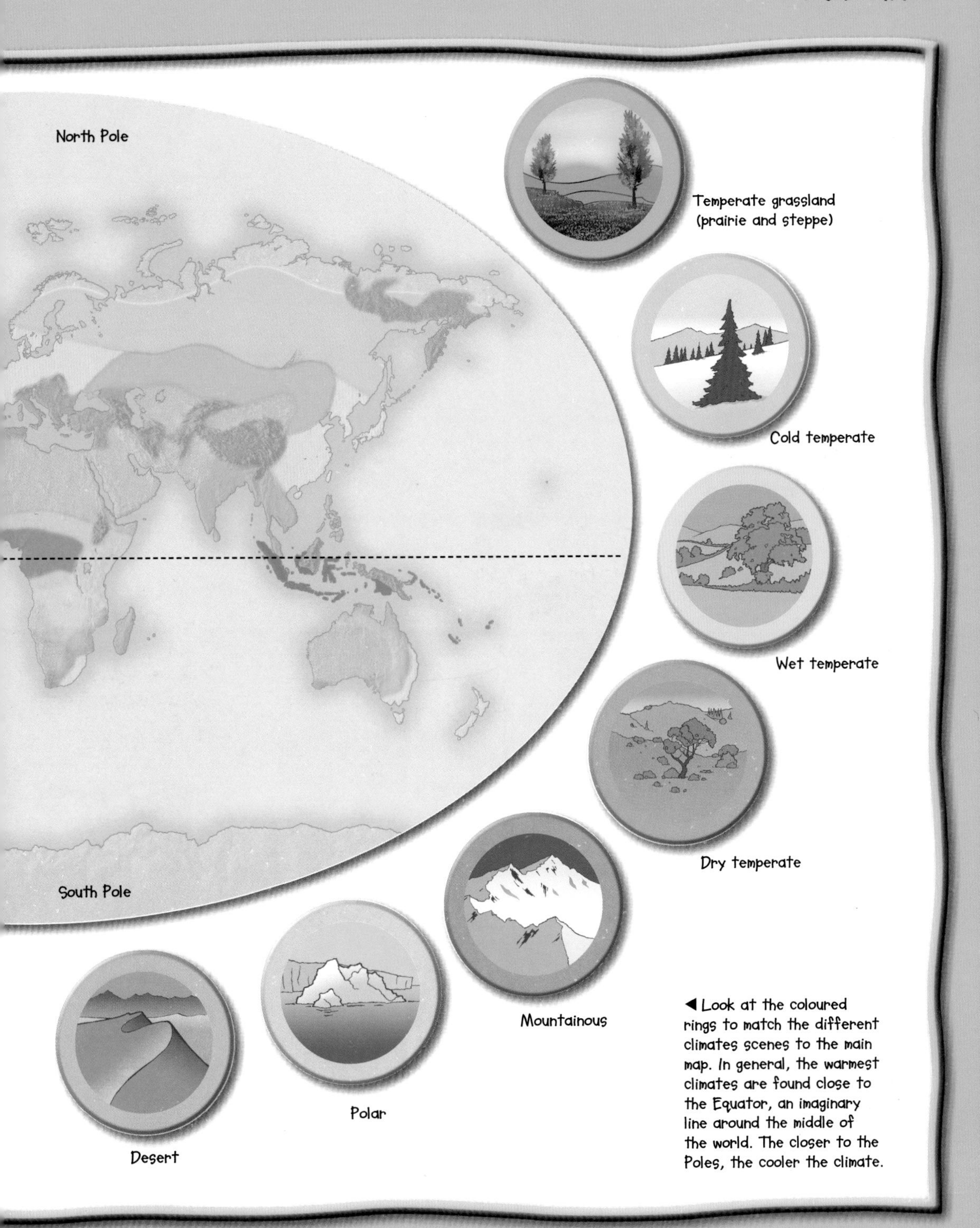

◀ Look at the coloured rings to match the different climates scenes to the main map. In general, the warmest climates are found close to the Equator, an imaginary line around the middle of the world. The closer to the Poles, the cooler the climate.

The four seasons

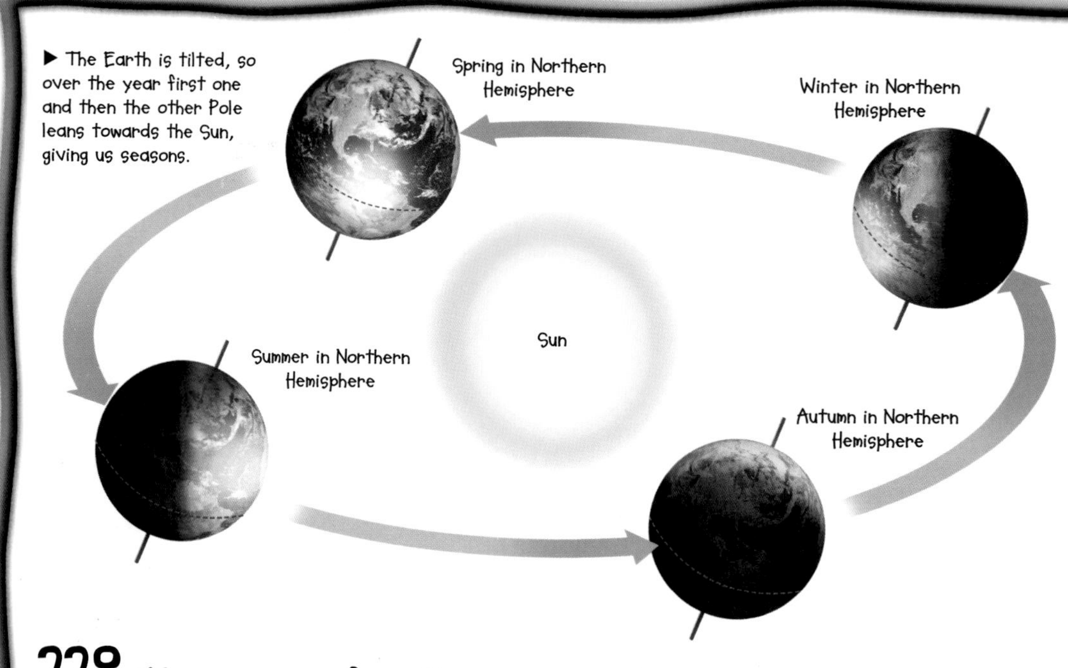

▶ The Earth is tilted, so over the year first one and then the other Pole leans towards the Sun, giving us seasons.

228 The reason for the seasons lies in space. Our planet Earth plots a path through space that takes it around the Sun. This path, or orbit, takes one year. In June, for example, the North Pole leans towards the Sun. The Sun heats the northern half of Earth and there is summer.

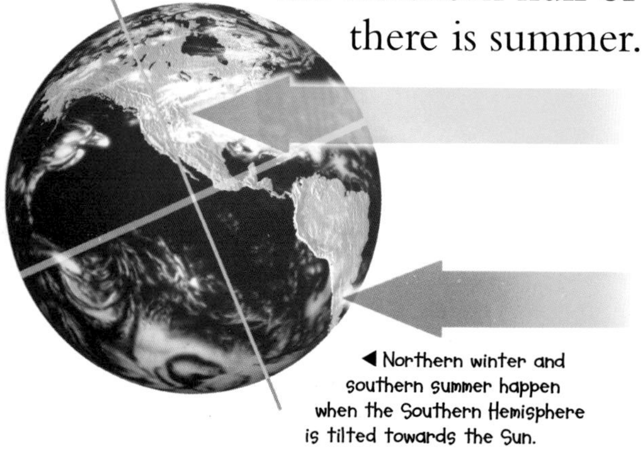

◀ Northern winter and southern summer happen when the Southern Hemisphere is tilted towards the Sun.

229 When it is summer in Argentina, it is winter in Canada. In December, the South Pole leans towards the Sun. Places in the southern half of the world, such as Argentina, have summer. At the same time, places in the northern half, such as Canada, have winter.

230 A day can last 21 hours!

Night and day happen because Earth is spinning as it circles the Sun. At the height of summer, places near the North Pole are so tilted towards the Sun that it is light almost all day long. In Stockholm, Sweden, Midsummer's Eve lasts 21 hours because the Sun disappears below the horizon for only three hours.

▲ At the North Pole, the Sun never disappears below the horizon at Midsummer's Day.

▼ Deciduous trees like these lose their leaves in autumn, but evergreens keep their leaves all year round.

I DON'T BELIEVE IT!

When the Sun shines all day in the far north, there is 24-hour night in the far south.

231 Forests change colour in the autumn.

Autumn comes between summer and winter. Trees prepare for the cold winter months ahead by losing their leaves. First, though, they suck back the precious green chlorophyll, or dye, in their leaves, making them turn glorious shades of red, orange and brown.

Fewer seasons

232 Monsoons are winds that carry heavy rains. The rains fall in the tropics in summer during the hot, rainy season. The Sun warms up the sea, which causes huge banks of cloud to form. Monsoons then blow these clouds towards land. Once the rains hit the continent, they can pour for weeks.

▶ When the rains are especially heavy, they cause chaos. Streets turn to rivers and sometimes people's homes are even washed away.

I DON'T BELIEVE IT !

In parts of monsoon India, over 26,000 millimetres of rain have fallen in a single year!

233 Monsoons happen mainly in Asia. However, there are some parts of the Americas that are close to the Equator that also have a season that is very rainy. Winds can carry such heavy rain clouds that there are flash floods in the deserts of the southwestern United States. The floods happen because the land has been baked hard during the dry season.

234 Many parts of the tropics have two seasons, not four. They are the parts of the world closest to the Equator, an imaginary line around the middle of the Earth. Here it is always hot, as these places are constantly facing the Sun. However, the movement of the Earth affects the position of a great band of cloud. In June, the tropical areas north of the Equator have the strongest heat and the heaviest rain storms. In December, it is the turn of the areas south of the Equator.

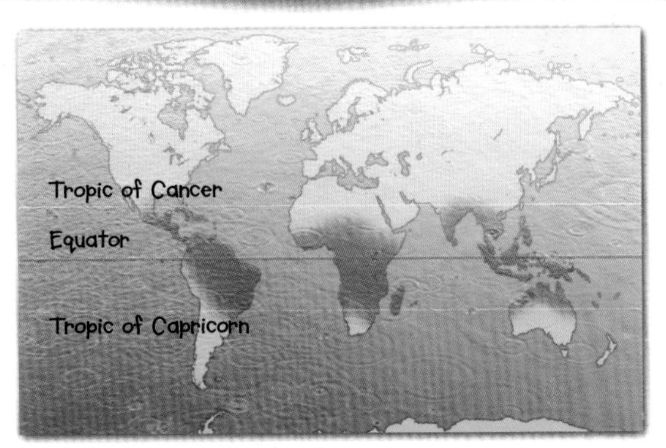

▲ The tropics lie either side of the Equator, between lines of latitude called the Tropic of Cancer and the Tropic of Capricorn.

235 In a tropical rainforest, you need your umbrella every day! Rainforests have rainy weather all year round – but there is still a wet and a dry season. It is just that the wet season is even wetter!

▼ Daily rainfall feeds the lush rainforest vegetation.

What a scorcher!

236 All our heat comes from the Sun. The Sun is a star, a super-hot ball of burning gases. It gives off heat rays that travel 150 million kilometres through space to our planet. Over the journey, the rays cool down, but they can still scorch the Earth.

QUIZ

1. How many seasons are there in the tropics?
2. On which continent do most monsoons occur?
3. Where is the hottest recorded place in the world?
4. Is El Niño a wind or a current?

Answers:
1. Two 2. Asia
3. Al Aziziyah in Libya 4. A current

237 The Sahara is the sunniest place. This North African desert once had 4300 hours of sunshine in a year! People who live there, such as the Tuareg Arabs, cover their skin to avoid being sunburnt.

238 The hottest place on Earth is Al Aziziyah in Libya. It is 58°C in the shade – hot enough to fry an egg!

▶ Desert peoples wear headdresses to protect their skin and eyes from the sun and sand.

▼ A mirage is just a trick of the light. It can make us see something that is not really there.

239 The Sun can trick your eyes. Sometimes, as sunlight passes through our atmosphere, it hits layers of air at different temperatures. When this happens, the air bends the light and can trick our eyes into seeing something that is not there. This is a mirage. For example, what looks like a pool of water might really be part of the sky reflected on to the land.

240 Too much sun brings drought. Clear skies and sunshine are not always good news. Without rain crops wither, and people and their animals go hungry.

▲ The 'Dust Bowl' was caused by strong winds and dust storms. These destroyed huge areas of land.

241 One terrible drought made a 'Dust Bowl'. Settlers in the American Mid-West were ruined by a long drought during the 1930s. As crops died, there were no roots to hold the soil together. The dry earth turned to dust and some farms simply blew away!

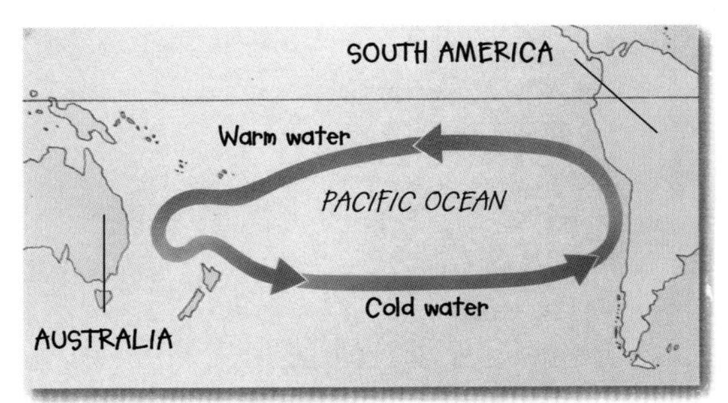

▲ El Niño has been known to cause violent weather conditions. It returns on average every four years.

242 A sea current can set forests alight. All sorts of things affect our weather and climate. The movements of a sea current called El Niño have been blamed for causing terrible droughts – which led to unstoppable forest fires.

Our atmosphere

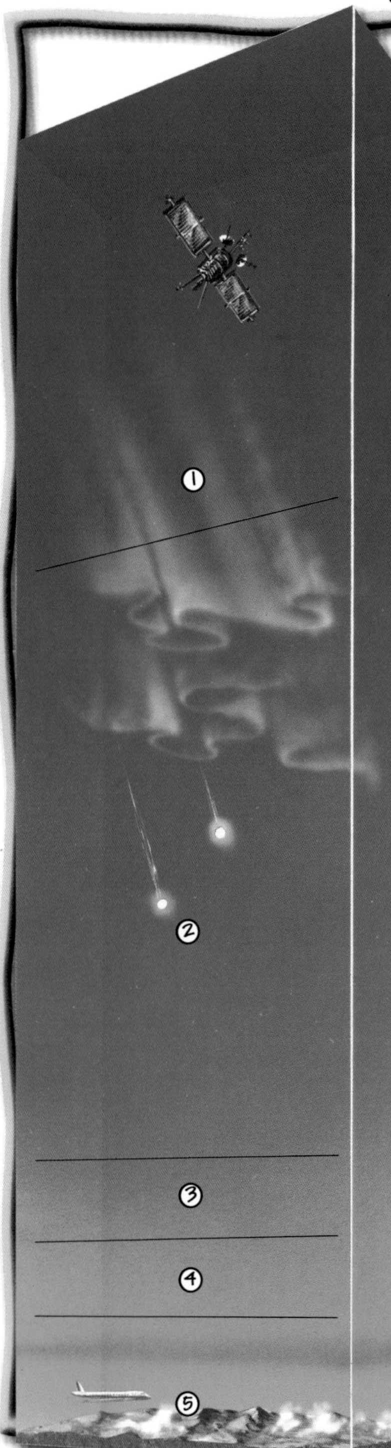

243 Our planet is wrapped in a blanket of air. We call this blanket the atmosphere. It stretches hundreds of kilometres above our heads. The blanket keeps in heat, especially at night when part of the planet faces away from the Sun. During the day, the blanket becomes a sunscreen instead. Without an atmosphere, there would be no weather.

244 Most weather happens in the troposphere. This is the layer of atmosphere that stretches from the ground to around 10 kilometres above your head. The higher in the troposphere you go, the cooler the air. Because of this, clouds are most likely to form here. Clouds with flattened tops show just where the troposphere meets the next layer, the stratosphere.

KEY

1. Exosphere 190 to 960 kilometres
2. Thermosphere 80 to 190 kilometres
3. Mesosphere 50 to 80 kilometres
4. Stratosphere 10 to 50 kilometres
5. Troposphere 0 to 10 kilometres

◀ The atmosphere stretches right into space. Scientists have split it into five layers, or spheres, such as the troposphere.

245 Air just cannot keep still. Tiny particles in air, called molecules, are always bumping into each other! The more they smash into each other, the greater the air pressure. Generally, there are more smashes lower in the troposphere, because the pull of gravity makes the molecules fall towards the Earth's surface. The higher you go, the lower the air pressure, and the less oxygen there is in the air.

▶ At high altitudes there is less oxygen. That is why mountaineers often wear breathing equipment.

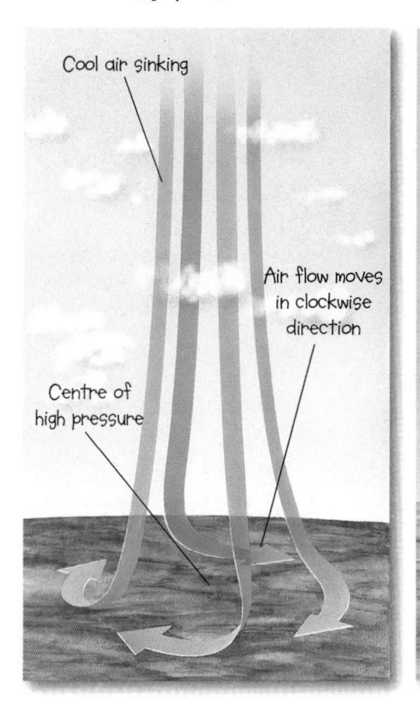

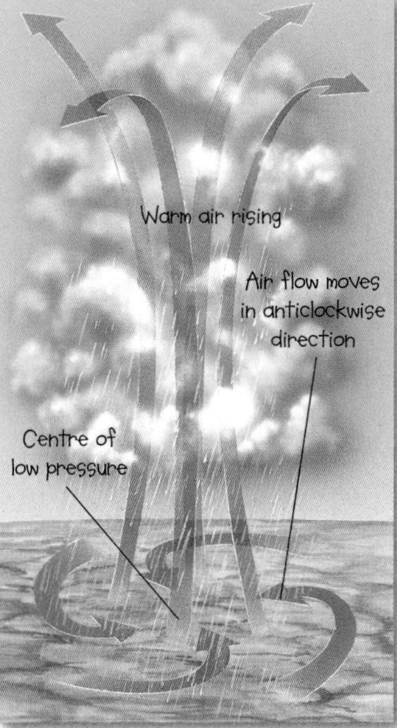

246 Warmth makes air move. When heat from the Sun warms the molecules in air, they move faster and spread out more. This makes the air lighter, so it rises in the sky, creating low pressure. As it gets higher, the air cools. The molecules slow down and become heavier again, so they start to sink back to Earth.

◀ A high pressure weather system gives us warmer weather, while low pressure gives us cooler more unsettled weather.

Clouds and rain

247 Rain comes from the sea. As the Sun heats the surface of the ocean, some seawater turns into water vapour and rises into the air. As it rises, it cools and turns back into water droplets. Lots of water droplets make clouds. The droplets join together to make bigger and bigger drops that eventually fall as rain. Some rain is soaked up by the land, but a lot finds its way back to the sea. This is called the water cycle.

RAIN GAUGE

You will need:

jam jar waterproof marker pen
ruler notebook pen

Put the jar outside. At the same time each day, mark the rainwater level on the jar with your pen. At the end of a week, empty the jar. Measure and record how much rain fell each day and over the whole week.

248 Some mountains are so tall that their summits (peaks) are hidden by cloud. Really huge mountains even affect the weather. When moving air hits a mountain slope it is forced upwards. As it travels up, the temperature drops, and clouds form.

◀ Warm, rising air may be forced up the side of a mountain. At a certain level, lower temperatures make the water form clouds.

▼ The water cycle involves all the water on Earth. Water vapour rises from lakes, rivers and the sea to form clouds in the atmosphere.

▼ Virga happens when rain reaches a layer of dry air. The rain droplets turn back into water vapour in mid-air, and seem to disappear.

249 Some rain never reaches the ground. The raindrops turn back into water vapour because they hit a layer of super-dry air. You can actually see the drops falling like a curtain from the cloud, but the curtain stops in mid-air. This type of weather is called virga.

250 Clouds gobble up heat and keep the Earth's temperature regular. From each 2-metre-square patch of land, clouds can remove the equivalent energy created by a 60-Watt lightbulb.

Not just fluffy

251 Clouds come in all shapes and sizes. To help recognize them, scientists split them into ten basic types. The type depends on what the cloud looks like and where it forms in the sky. Cirrus clouds look like wisps of smoke. They form high in the troposphere and rarely mean rain. Stratus clouds form in flat layers and may produce drizzle or a sprinkling of snow. All types of cumulus clouds bring rain. Some are huge cauliflower shapes. They look soft and fluffy – but would feel soggy to touch.

Cumulonimbus clouds give heavy rain showers

▶ The main classes of cloud – cirrus, cumulus and stratus – were named in the 1800s. An amateur British weather scientist called Luke Howard identified the different types.

252 Not all clouds produce rain. Cumulus humilis clouds are the smallest heap-shaped clouds. In the sky, they look like lumpy, cotton wool sausages! They are too small to produce rain, but they can grow into much bigger, rain-carrying cumulus clouds. The biggest cumulus clouds, cumulus congestus, bring heavy showers.

Cumulus clouds bring rain

Cirrus clouds occur at great heights from the ground

Contrails are the white streaks created by planes

254 Not all clouds are made by nature. Contrails are streaky clouds that a plane leaves behind it as it flies. They are made of water vapour that comes from the plane's engines. The second it hits the cold air, the vapour turns into ice crystals, leaving a trail of white snow cloud.

Cirrostratus

253 Sometimes the sky is filled with white patches of cloud that look like shimmering fish scales. These are called mackerel skies. It takes lots of gusty wind to break the cloud into these little patches, and so mackerel skies are usually a sign of changeable weather.

MIX AND MATCH

Can you match the names of these five types of clouds to their meanings?

1. Altostratus
2. Cirrus
3. Cumulonimbus
4. Cumulus
5. Stratus

a. heap
b. layer
c. high + layer
d. wisp
e. heap + rain

Answers:
1.C 2.D 3.E
4.A 5.B

Stratus clouds can bring drizzle or appear as fog

Flood warning

255 Too much rain brings floods. There are two different types of floods. Flash floods happen after a short burst of heavy rainfall, usually caused by thunderstorms. Broadscale flooding happens when rain falls steadily over a wide area – for weeks or months – without stopping. When this happens, rivers slowly fill and eventually burst their banks. Tropical storms, such as hurricanes, can also lead to broadscale flooding.

▲ Flooding can cause great damage to buildings and the countryside.

256 There can be floods in the desert. When a lot of rain falls very quickly on to land that has been baked dry, it cannot soak in. Instead, it sits on the surface, causing flash floods.

◀ A desert flash flood can create streams of muddy brown water. After the water level falls, vegetation bursts into life.

257 There really was a Great Flood. The Bible tells of a terrible flood, and how a man called Noah was saved. Recently, explorers found the first real evidence of the Flood – a sunken beach 140 metres below the surface of the Black Sea. There are ruins of houses, dating back to 5600 BC. Stories of a huge flood in ancient times do not appear only in the Bible – the Babylonians and Greeks told of one, too.

▲ In the Bible story, Noah survived the Great Flood by building a huge wooden boat called an ark.

258 Mud can flood. When rain mixes with earth it makes mud. On bare mountainsides, there are no tree roots to hold the soil together. An avalanche of mud can slide off the mountain. The worst ever mudslide happened after flooding in Colombia, South America in 1985. It buried 23,000 people from the town of Armero.

I DON'T BELIEVE IT!

The ancient Egyptians had a story to explain the yearly flooding of the Nile. They said the goddess Isis filled the river with tears, as she cried for her lost husband.

▼ Mudslides can devastate whole towns and villages, as the flow of mud covers everything it meets.

Deep freeze

259 Snow is made of tiny ice crystals. When air temperatures are very cold – around 0°C – the water droplets in the clouds freeze to make tiny ice crystals. Sometimes, individual crystals fall, but usually they clump together into snowflakes.

261 Black ice is not really black. Drizzle or rain turns to ice when it touches freezing-cold ground. This 'black' ice is see-through, and hard to spot against a road's dark tarmac. It is also terribly slippery – like a deadly ice rink.

I DON'T BELIEVE IT!

Antarctica is the coldest place on Earth. Temperatures of –89.2°C have been recorded there.

▲ Falling snow is made worse by strong winds, which can form deep drifts.

260 No two snowflakes are the same. This is because snowflakes are made up of ice crystals, and every ice crystal is as unique as your fingerprint. Most crystals look like six-pointed stars, but they come in other shapes too.

▶ Ice crystals seen under a microscope. A snowflake that is several centimetres across will be made up of lots of crystals like these.

▶ An avalanche gathers speed as it thunders down the mountainside.

262 Avalanches are like giant snowballs. They happen after lots of snow falls on a mountain. The slightest movement or sudden noise can jolt the pile of snow and start it moving down the slope. As it crashes down, the avalanche picks up extra snow and can end up large enough to bury whole towns.

▲ Antarctica is a frozen wilderness. The ice piles up to form amazing shapes, like this arch.

263 Marksmen shoot at snowy mountains. One way to prevent deadly avalanches is to stop too much snow from building up. In mountain areas, marksmen set off mini avalanches on purpose. They make sure people are out of the danger zone, then fire guns to trigger a snowslide.

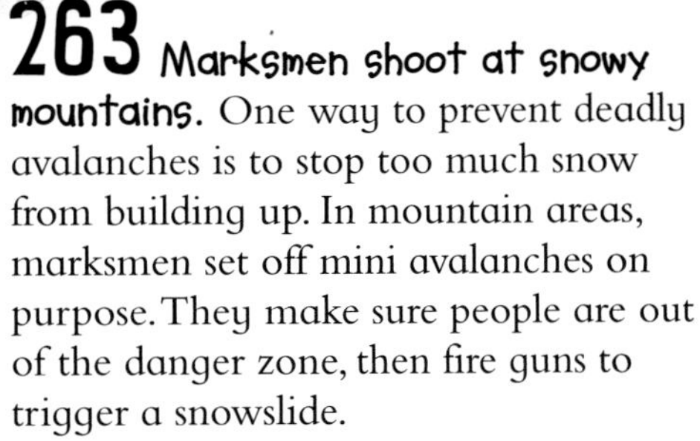

264 Ice can stay frozen for millions of years. At the North and South Poles, the weather never warms up enough for the ice to thaw. When fresh snow falls, it presses down on the snow already there, forming thick sheets. Some ice may not have melted for a million years or more.

When the wind blows

265 Wind is moving air. Winds blow because air is constantly moving from areas of high pressure to areas of low pressure. The bigger the difference in temperature between the two areas, the faster the wind blows.

▶ These trees have been forced into strange shapes by the wind.

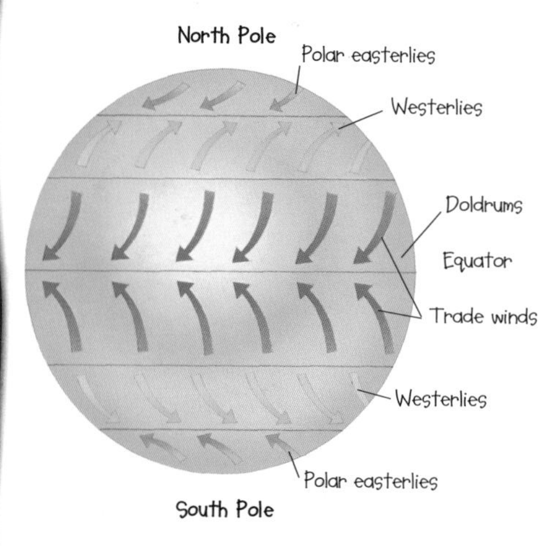

▲ This map shows the pattern of the world's main winds.

266 Winds have names. World wind patterns are called global winds. The most famous are the trade winds that blow towards the Equator. There are also well-known local winds, such as the cold, dry mistral that blows down to southern France, or the hot, dry sirroco that blows north of the Sahara.

267 Trade winds blow one way north of the Equator, and another way in the south. Trade winds blow in the tropics, where air is moving to an area of low pressure at the Equator. Their name comes from their importance to traders, when goods travelled by sailing ship.

QUIZ

1. At what temperature does water freeze?
2. What does the Beaufort Scale measure?
3. What are the mistral and sirroco?
4. How many sides does an ice crystal usually have?

Answers:
1. 0°C 2. Wind strength
3. Local winds 4. Six

268 You can tell how windy it is by looking at the leaves on a tree. Wind ranges from light breezes to hurricanes. Its strength is measured on the Beaufort Scale, named after the Irish admiral who devised it. The scale ranges from Force 0, meaning total calm, to Force 12, which is a hurricane.

Force 0: Calm
Force 1: Light air
Force 2: Light breeze
Force 3: Gentle breeze
Force 4: Moderate breeze
Force 5: Fresh breeze
Force 6: Strong breeze
Force 7: Near gale
Force 8: Gale
Force 9: Strong gale
Force 10: Storm
Force 11: Violent storm
Force 12: Hurricane

▶ The Beaufort Scale.

▶ Turbines convert the wind's energy into electrical energy.

269 Wind can turn on your TV. People can harness the energy of the wind to make electricity for our homes. Tall turbines are positioned in windy spots. As the wind turns the turbine, the movement powers a generator and produces electrical energy.

270 Wind can make you mad! The Föhn wind, which blows across Switzerland, Austria and Bavaria in southern Germany, brings with it changeable weather. This has been blamed for road accidents and even bouts of madness!

Thunderbolts and lightning

271 Thunderstorms are most likely in summer. Hot weather creates warm, moist air that rises and forms towering cumulonimbus clouds. Inside each cloud, water droplets and ice crystals bang about, building up positive and negative electrical charges. Electricity flows between the charges, creating a flash that heats the air around it. Lightning is so hot that it makes the air expand, making a loud noise or thunderclap.

▼ Cloud-to-cloud lightning is called sheet lightning, while lightning travelling from the cloud to the ground is called fork lightning.

272 Lightning comes in different colours. If there is rain in the thundercloud, the lightning looks red; if there's hail, it looks blue. Lightning can also be yellow or white.

▼ Lightning conductors absorb the shock and protect tall buildings.

▶ Dramatic lightning flashes light up the sky.

273 Tall buildings are protected from lightning. Church steeples and other tall structures are often struck by bolts of lightning. This could damage the building, or give electric shocks to people inside, so lightning conductors are placed on the roof. These channel the lightning safely away.

274 A person can survive a lightning strike. Lightning is very dangerous and can give a big enough shock to kill you. However, an American park ranger called Roy Sullivan survived being struck seven times.

HOW CLOSE?

Lightning and thunder happen at the same time, but light travels faster than sound. Count the seconds between the flash and the clap and divide them by three. This is how many kilometres away the storm is.

275 Hailstones can be as big as melons! These chunks of ice can fall from thunderclouds. The biggest ever fell in Gopaljang, Bangladesh, in 1986 and weighed 1 kilogram each!

▼ A sudden hail storm can leave the ground littered with small chunks of ice.

Eye of the hurricane

276 Some winds travel at speeds of more than 120 kilometres an hour. Violent tropical storms happen when strong winds blow into an area of low pressure and start spinning very fast. They develop over warm seas and pick up speed until they reach land, where there is no more moist sea air to feed them. Such storms bring torrential rain.

I DON'T BELIEVE IT!

Tropical storms are called different names. Hurricanes develop over the Atlantic, typhoons over the Pacific, and cyclones over the Indian Ocean.

▼ A Hurricane Hunter heads into the storm.

277 The centre of a hurricane is calm and still. This part is called the 'eye'. As the eye of the storm passes over, there is a pause in the terrifying rains and wind.

▲ This satellite photograph of a hurricane shows how the storm whirls around a central, still 'eye'.

278 Hurricane Hunters fly close to the eye of a hurricane. These are special weather planes that fly into the storm in order to take measurements. It is a dangerous job for the pilots, but the information they gather helps to predict the hurricane's path – and saves lives.

▲ A hurricane brings battering rain and massive waves.

279 **Hurricanes have names.** One of the worst hurricanes was Hurricane Andrew, which battered the coast of Florida in 1992. Perhaps there is a hurricane named after you!

280 **Hurricanes whip up wild waves.** As the storm races over the ocean, the winds create giant waves. These hit the shore as a huge sea surge. In 1961, the sea surge following Hurricane Hattie washed away Belize City in South America.

281 **Typhoons saved the Japanese from Genghis Khan.** The 13th-century Mongol leader made two attempts to invade Japan – and both times, a terrible typhoon battered his fleet and saved the Japanese!

► A typhoon prevented Genghis Khan's navy from invading Japan.

Wild whirling winds

282 Tornadoes spin at speeds of 480 kilometres an hour! These whirling columns of wind, also known as twisters, are some of the most destructive storms on Earth. They form in strong thunderstorms, when the back part of the thundercloud starts spinning. The spinning air forms a funnel that reaches down towards the Earth. When it touches the ground, it becomes a tornado.

► A tornado can cause great damage to anything in its path.

283 A tornado can be strong enough to lift a train! The spinning tornado whizzes along the ground like an enormous, high-speed vacuum cleaner, sucking up everything in its path. It rips the roofs off houses, and even tosses buildings into the air. In the 1930s, a twister in Minnesota, USA, threw a train carriage full of people more than eight metres through the air!

284 Tornados can happen anywhere in the world. They are especially active in the United States from Texas up through Oklahoma, Kansas, Nebraska and Dakota. Here, warm, moist air from the Gulf of Mexico meets cold air from the north, which causes storms to form.

▲ Tornadoes are powerful storms that can cause severe damage.

285 A pillar of whirling water can rise out of a lake or the sea. Waterspouts are spiralling columns of water that can be sucked up by a tornado as it forms over a lake or the sea. They tend to spin more slowly than tornadoes, because water is much heavier than air.

I DON'T BELIEVE IT!

Loch Ness in Scotland is famous for sightings of a monster nicknamed Nessie. Perhaps people who have seen Nessie were really seeing a waterspout.

▲ Waterspouts can suck up fish living in a lake!

▼ A whirling storm of sand in the desert.

286 Dust devils are desert tornadoes. They shift tonnes of sand and cause terrible damage – they can strip the paintwork from a car in seconds!

Pretty lights

287 Rainbows are made up of seven colours. They are caused by sunlight passing through falling raindrops. The water acts like a glass prism, splitting the light. White light is made up of seven colours – red, orange, yellow, green, blue, indigo and violet – so these are the colours, from top to bottom, that make up the rainbow.

REMEMBER IT!

Richard Of York Gave Battle In Vain

The first letter of every word of this rhyme gives the first letter of each colour of the rainbow – as it appears in the sky:

Red Orange Yellow Green Blue Indigo Violet

288 Two rainbows can appear at once. The top rainbow is a reflection of the bottom one, so its colours appear the opposite way round, with the violet band at the top and red at the bottom.

289 Some rainbows appear at night. They happen when falling raindrops split moonlight, rather than sunlight. This sort of rainbow is called a moonbow.

▲ Although a fogbow is colourless, its inner edge may appear slightly blue and its outer edge slightly red.

290 It is not just angels that wear halos! When you look at the Sun or Moon through a curtain of ice crystals, they seem to be surrounded by a glowing ring of light called a halo.

291 Three suns can appear in our sky! 'Mock suns' are two bright spots that appear on either side of the Sun. They often happen at the same time as a halo, and have the same cause – light passing through ice crystals in the air.

▼ An aurora – the most dazzling natural light show on Earth!

292 Some rainbows are just white. Fogbows happen when sunlight passes through a patch of fog. The water droplets in the fog are too small to work like prisms, so the arching bow is white or colourless.

▲ A halo looks like a circle of light surrounding the Sun or Moon.

▲ Mock suns are also known as parhelia or sundogs.

293 Auroras are curtains of lights in the sky. They happen in the far north or south of the world when particles from the Sun smash into molecules in the air – at speeds of 1600 kilometres an hour. The lights may be blue, red or yellow.

Made for weather

294 Camels can go for two weeks without a drink. They are adapted to life in a hot, dry climate. Camels do not sweat until their body temperature hits 40°C, which helps them to save water. Their humps are fat stores, which are used for energy when food and drink is scarce.

▼ These animals have adapted to life in very dry climates. However, they live in different deserts around the world.

295 Lizards lose salt through their noses. Most animals get rid of excess salt in their urine, but lizards, such as iguanas and geckos, live in dry parts of the world. They need to lose as little water from their bodies as possible.

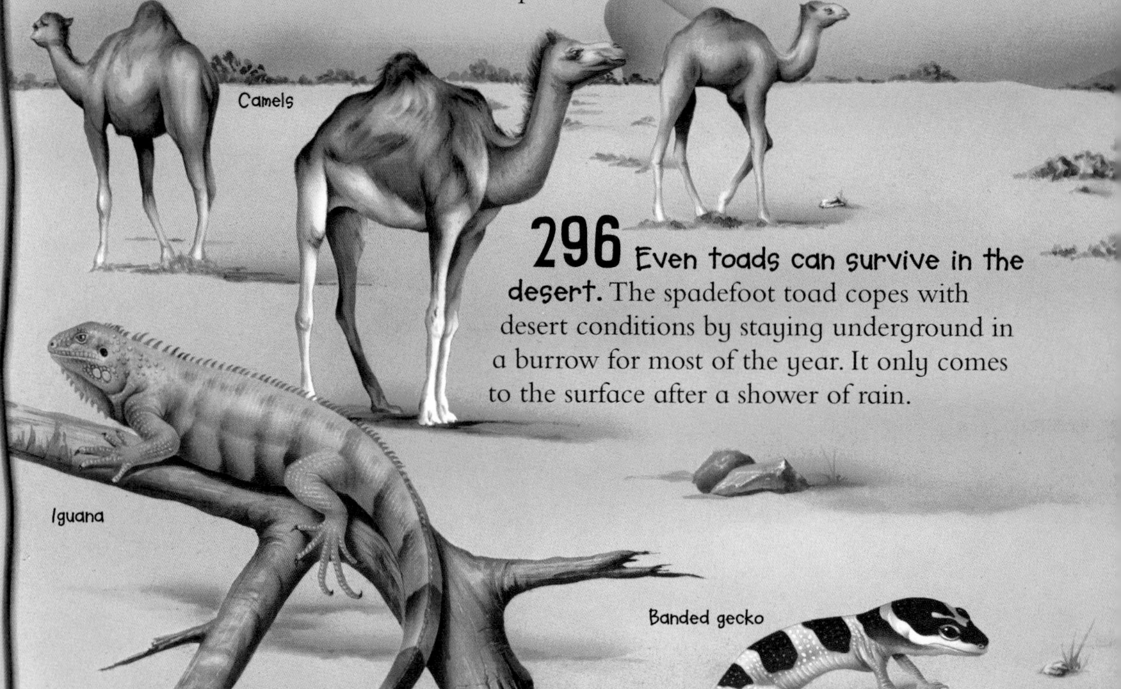

Camels

296 Even toads can survive in the desert. The spadefoot toad copes with desert conditions by staying underground in a burrow for most of the year. It only comes to the surface after a shower of rain.

Iguana

Banded gecko

QUIZ

Rearrange the letters to find the names of four plants that can cope with a very dry climate.

1. ROAGAUS SACCUT
2. OBABBA ETRE
3. YLPCIRK REAP
4. SCUYTPALUE

Answers:
1. Saguaro cactus 2. Baobab tree
3. Prickly pear 4. Eucalyptus

Spadefoot toad

▶ Beneath its gleaming-white fur, the polar bear's skin is black to absorb heat from the Sun.

297 **Polar bears have black skin.** These bears have all sorts of special ways to survive the polar climate. Plenty of body fat and thick fur keeps them snug and warm, while their black skin soaks up as much warmth from the Sun as possible.

298 **Acorn woodpeckers store nuts for winter.** Animals in temperate climates have to be prepared if they are to survive the cold winter months. Acorn woodpeckers turn tree trunks into larders. During autumn, when acorns are ripe, the birds collect as many as they can, storing them in holes that they bore into a tree.

▶ Storing acorns helps this woodpecker survive the cold winter months.

Weather myths

299 People once thought the Sun was a god. The sun god was often considered to be the most important god of all, because he brought light and warmth and ripened crops. The ancient Egyptians built pyramids that pointed up to their sun god, Re, while the Aztecs believed that their sun god, Huitzilpochtli, had even shown them where to build their capital city.

300 The Vikings thought a god brought thunder. Thor was the god of war and thunder, worshipped across what is now Scandinavia. The Vikings pictured Thor as a red-bearded giant. He carried a hammer that produced bolts of lightning. Our day, Thursday, is named in Thor's honour.

◀ In Scandinavian mythology, Thor was the god of thunder.

▲ The Egyptian sun god, Re, was often shown with the head of a falcon.

301 Hurricanes are named after a god. The Mayan people lived in Central America, the part of the world that is most affected by hurricanes. Their creator god was called Huracan.

302 Totem poles honoured the Thunderbird. Certain tribes of Native American Indians built tall, painted totem poles, carved in the image of the Thunderbird. They wanted to keep the spirit happy, because they thought it brought rain to feed the plants.

▶ A Native American Indian totem pole depicting the spirit of the Thunderbird.

303 People once danced for rain. In hot places such as Africa, people developed dances to bring rain. These were performed by the village shaman (religious woman or man), using wooden instruments such as bullroarers. Sometimes water was sprinkled on the ground. Rain dances are still performed in some countries today.

◀ Shamans wore a special costume for their rain dance.

MAKE A BULLROARER

You will need:

wooden ruler string

Ask an adult to drill a hole in one end of the ruler. Thread through the string, and knot it, to stop it slipping through the hole. In an open space, whirl the instrument above your head to create a wind noise!

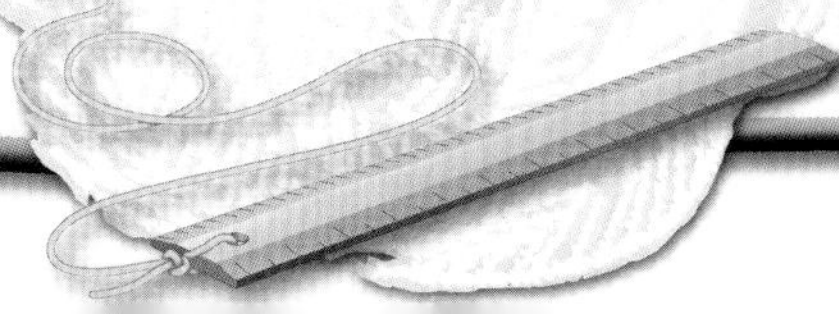

Rain or shine?

304 Seaweed can tell us if rain is on the way. Long ago, people looked to nature for clues about the weather. One traditional way of forecasting was to hang up strands of seaweed. If the seaweed stayed slimy, the air was damp and rain was likely. If the seaweed shrivelled up, the weather would be dry.

◀ Kelp picks up any moisture in the air, so it is a good way of telling how damp the atmosphere is.

I DON'T BELIEVE IT!

People used to say that cows lay down when rain was coming – but there is no truth in it! They lie down whether rain is on the way or not!

305 'Red sky at night is the sailor's delight'. This is one of the most famous pieces of weather lore and means that a glorious sunset is followed by a fine morning. The saying is also known as 'shepherd's delight'. There is no evidence that the saying is true, though.

306 Groundhogs tell the weather when they wake. Of course, they don't really, but in parts of the USA, Groundhog Day is a huge celebration. On 2 February, people gather to see the groundhog come out. If you see the creature's shadow, it means there are six more weeks of cold to come.

Groundhog

▼ A blood-red sunset is delightful to look at, but it can't help a sailor to predict the next day's weather.

▲ The Moon is clearly visible in a cloudless night sky. Its light casts a silvery glow over the Earth.

307 'Clear moon, frost soon'. This old saying does have some truth in it. If there are few clouds in the sky, the view of the Moon will be clear – and there will also be no blanket of cloud to keep in the Earth's heat. That makes a frost more likely – during the colder months, at least.

308 The earliest weather records are over 3000 years old. They were found on a piece of tortoiseshell and had been written down by Chinese weather watchers. The inscriptions describe when it rained or snowed and how windy it was.

◀ Records of ancient weather were scratched on to this piece of shell.

Instruments and inventors

309 The Tower of Winds was built 2000 years ago. It was an eight-sided building and is the first known weather station. It had a wind vane on the roof and a water clock inside.

310 The first barometer was made by one of Galileo's students. Barometers measure air pressure. The first person to describe air pressure – and to make an instrument for measuring it – was an Italian, Evangelista Torricelli. He had studied under the great scientist Galileo. Torricelli made his barometer in 1643.

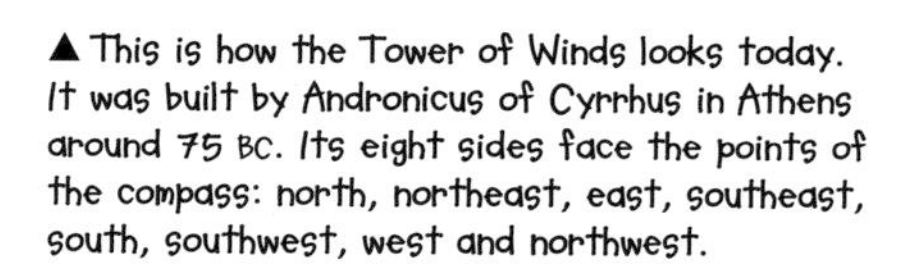

▲ This is how the Tower of Winds looks today. It was built by Andronicus of Cyrrhus in Athens around 75 BC. Its eight sides face the points of the compass: north, northeast, east, southeast, south, southwest, west and northwest.

◀ Torricelli took a bowl of mercury and placed it under the open end of a glass tube, also filled with mercury. It was the weight, or pressure, of air on the mercury in the bowl that stopped the mercury in the tube from falling.

311 Weather cocks have a special meaning. They have four pointers that show the directions of north, south, east and west. The cockerel at the top swivels so that its head always shows the direction of the wind.

▶ Weather cocks are often placed on top of church steeples.

312 A weather house really can predict the weather. It is a type of hygrometer – an instrument that detects how much moisture is in the air. If there is lots, the rainy-day character comes out of the door!

▶ Weather houses have two figures. One comes out when the air is damp and the other when the air is dry.

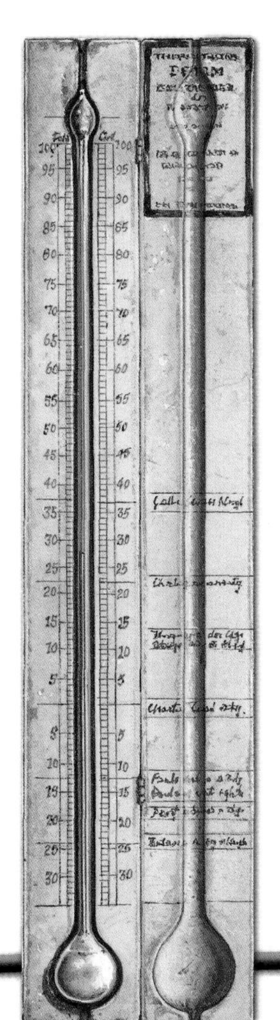

◀ This early thermometer shows both the Fahrenheit and the Celsius temperature scales.

313 Fahrenheit made the first thermometer in 1714. Thermometers are instruments that measure temperature. Gabriel Daniel Fahrenheit invented the thermometer using a blob of mercury sealed in an airtight tube. The Fahrenheit scale for measuring heat was named after him. The Centigrade scale was introduced in 1742 by the Swedish scientist Anders Celsius.

QUIZ

1. What is another name for the liquid metal, mercury?
2. What does an anemometer measure?
3. What does a wind vane measure?
4. On the Fahrenheit scale, at what temperature does water freeze?

Answers:
1. Quicksilver 2. Wind speed
3. Wind direction 4. 32°F

World of weather

314 Working out what the weather will be like is called forecasting. By looking at changes in the atmosphere, and comparing them to weather patterns of the past, forecasters can make an accurate guess at what the weather will be tomorrow, the next day, or even further ahead than that. But even forecasters get it wrong sometimes!

315 The first national weather offices appeared in the 1800s. This was when people realized that science could explain how weather worked – and save people from disasters. The first network of weather stations was set up in France, in 1855. This was after the scientist Le Verrier showed how a French warship, sunk in a storm, could have been saved. Le Verrier explained how the path of the storm could have been tracked, and the ship sailed to safety.

A cold front is shown by a blue triangle

A warm front is shown by a red semi-circle

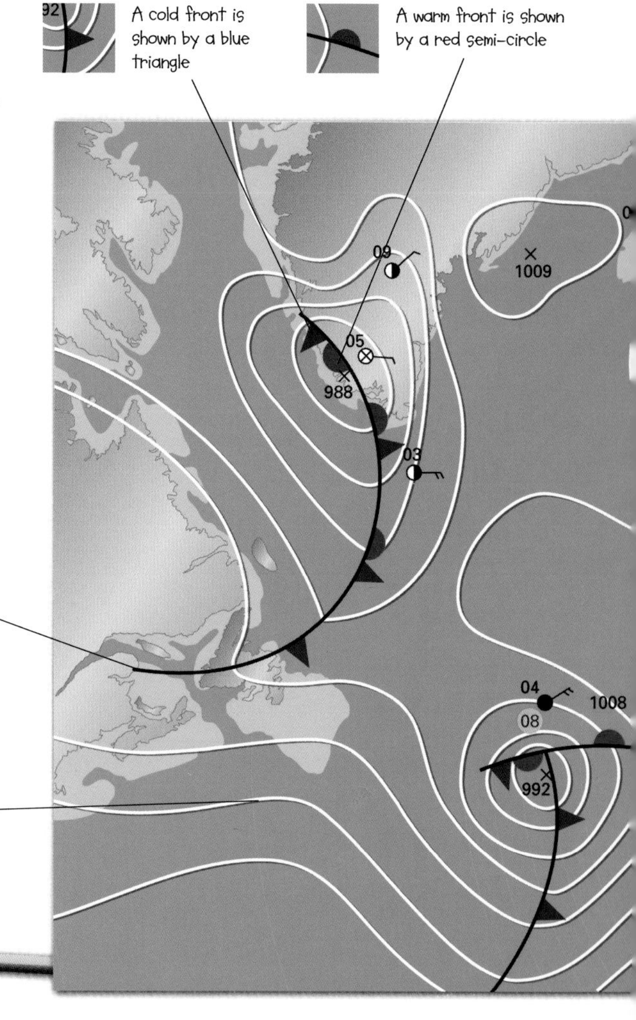

Look for the black lines with red semi-circles and blue triangles – they represent an occluded front, where a cold front meets a warm front

These white lines are isobars – they connect places where air pressure is the same

WEATHER SYMBOLS

Learn how to represent the weather on your own synoptic charts. Here are some of the basic symbols to get you started. You may come across them in newspapers or while watching television. Can you guess what they mean?

316 Nations need to share weather data. By 1865, nearly 60 weather stations across Europe were swapping information. These early weather scientists, or meteorologists, realized that they needed to present their information using symbols that they could all understand. To this day, meteorologists plot their findings on maps called synoptic charts. They use lines called isobars to show which areas have the same air pressure. The Internet makes it easier for meteorologists to access information.

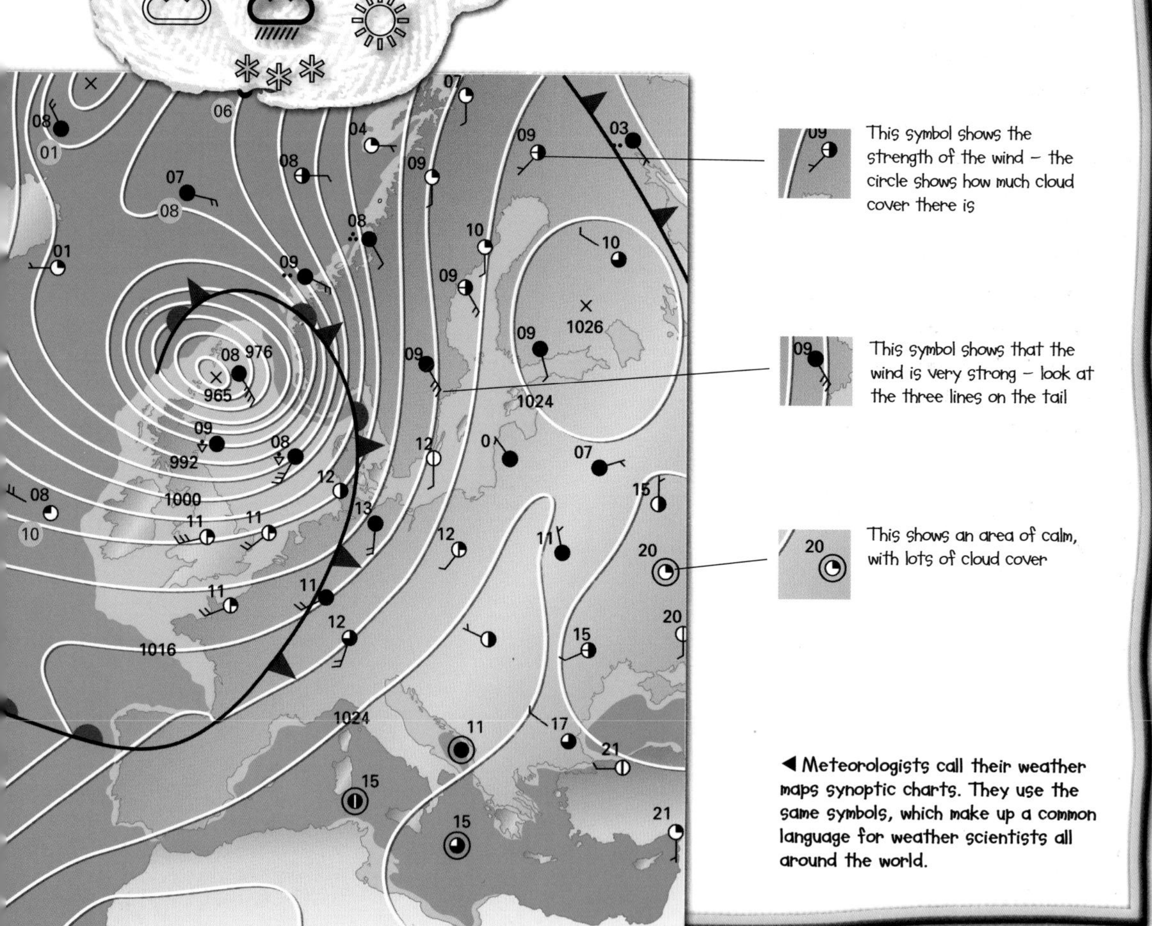

This symbol shows the strength of the wind – the circle shows how much cloud cover there is

This symbol shows that the wind is very strong – look at the three lines on the tail

This shows an area of calm, with lots of cloud cover

◀ Meteorologists call their weather maps synoptic charts. They use the same symbols, which make up a common language for weather scientists all around the world.

Weather watch

317 Balloons can tell us about the weather. Weather balloons are hot-air balloons that are sent high into the atmosphere. As they rise, onboard equipment takes readings. These find out air pressure, and how moist, or humid, the air is, as well as how warm. The findings are radioed back to meteorologists on the ground, using a system called radiosonde. Hundreds of balloons are launched around the world every day.

▶ A weather balloon carries its scientific instruments high into the atmosphere.

318 Some planes hound the weather. Weather planes provide more atmospheric measurements than balloons can. *Snoopy* is the name of one of the British weather planes. The instruments are carried on its long, pointy nose, so they can test the air ahead of the plane.

▼ Snoopy's long nose carries all the equipment needed to monitor the weather.

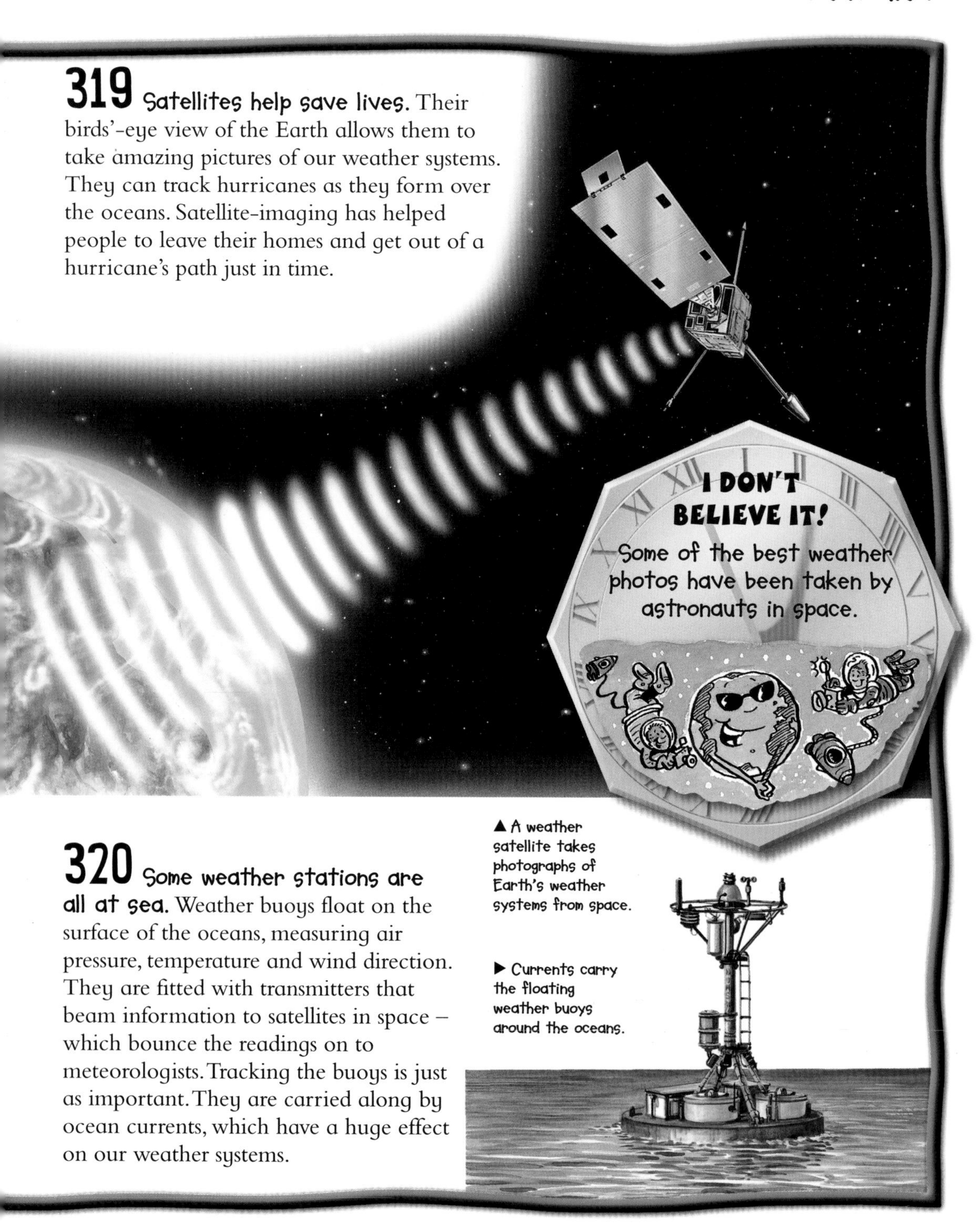

319 Satellites help save lives. Their birds'-eye view of the Earth allows them to take amazing pictures of our weather systems. They can track hurricanes as they form over the oceans. Satellite-imaging has helped people to leave their homes and get out of a hurricane's path just in time.

▲ A weather satellite takes photographs of Earth's weather systems from space.

320 Some weather stations are all at sea. Weather buoys float on the surface of the oceans, measuring air pressure, temperature and wind direction. They are fitted with transmitters that beam information to satellites in space – which bounce the readings on to meteorologists. Tracking the buoys is just as important. They are carried along by ocean currents, which have a huge effect on our weather systems.

▶ Currents carry the floating weather buoys around the oceans.

Changing climate

321 Climate change destroyed the dinosaurs – but no one can agree on what caused it. The best explanation is that a huge piece of space rock, called a meteorite, smashed into Earth. It threw up a giant cloud of dust that blocked out the Sun, plunging the world into cold and dark.

▼ Could a meteorite have crashed to Earth and changed the climate? A meteorite crater found in the Gulf of Mexico dates to 65 million years ago – exactly the time that the dinosaurs died out. Perhaps the impact changed the warm climate the dinosaurs were so used to.

322 Greenland used to be green! This island lies in the Arctic Ocean and is mostly covered by a huge ice sheet. Even in Viking times, Greenland was cold, but Viking settlers built at least two farming colonies there. These died out around the 1400s, after the climate cooled.

◀ Vikings settled on Greenland's coastline. Inland areas were covered in ice.

323 A volcano can change the climate! Big volcanic explosions can create dust that blots out the Sun, just as a meteorite impact can. Dust from the 1815 eruption of a volcano called Tambora did this. This made many crops fail around the world and many people starved.

◀ Like all plants, rainforest trees take in carbon dioxide and give out oxygen. As rainforests are destroyed, the amount of carbon dioxide in the atmosphere increases.

324 Tree-felling is affecting our weather. In areas of Southeast Asia and South America, rainforests are being cleared for farming. When the trees are burned, the fires release carbon dioxide – a greenhouse gas which helps to blanket the Earth and keep in the heat. Unfortunately, high levels of carbon dioxide raise the temperature too much.

325 Air temperatures are rising. Scientists think the average world temperature may increase by around 1.5°C this century. This may not sound like much, but the extra warmth will mean more storms, including hurricanes and tornadoes, and more droughts, too.

QUIZ

1. What may have caused the death of the dinosaurs?
2. Which settlers once lived along the coast of Greenland?
3. Which gas do plants take in?

Answers:
1. Meteorite impact 2. Vikings
3. Carbon dioxide

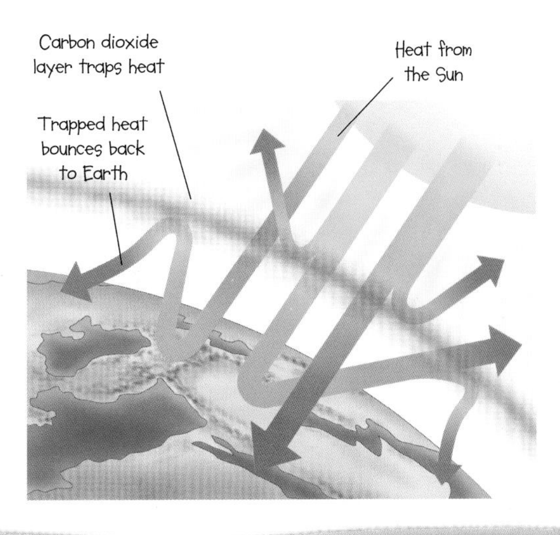

▶ Too much carbon dioxide in the atmosphere creates a 'greenhouse effect'. Just as glass traps heat, so does carbon dioxide. This means more storms and droughts.

326 Rocks and minerals form our planet, so they are all around us. Minerals are the building blocks of rocks. They are formed inorganically, meaning no living thing helps to create them. Rocks are aggregates (combinations) of particles from one or more minerals. Rocks and minerals make up much of the Earth and we couldn't live without them. We use them for building, cleaning, art – we even eat them.

▲ The Marble Cathedral or grotto (cave), under Lake General Carrera, on the borders of Chile and Patagonia. The marble was formed by intense heat from other kinds of rocks and then worn away (eroded) into these beautiful shapes by the constant movement of the water.

The rock cycle

327 There are layers inside the Earth. The first is the crust (the solid outer shell), which is between 6 and 70 kilometres thick. Under this is the mantle – a layer of hot rock that is around 2500 kilometres thick. The uppermost layers of the mantle are fused to the crust. Beneath these layers is an outer core of liquid metal and an inner core – a solid ball of hot iron.

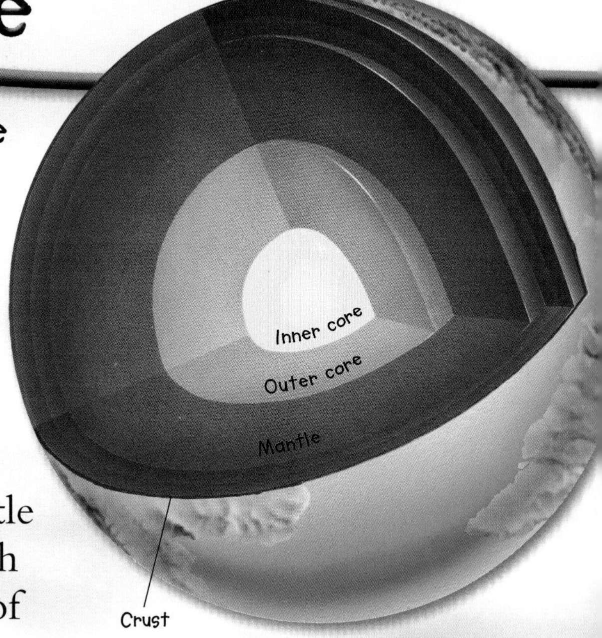

Inner core
Outer core
Mantle
Crust

▲ Under the crust and mantle are layers of liquid metal and, in the centre, a solid ball of sizzling iron.

Weathering of rocks at surface
Erosion and transport
Laying down of sediment
Burial and becoming more compact under pressure
SEDIMENTARY ROCK
Deep burial and metamorphism (changing structure)

► The rock cycle is the long, slow journey of rocks down from the surface and then up again. Rocks are often changed during this process.

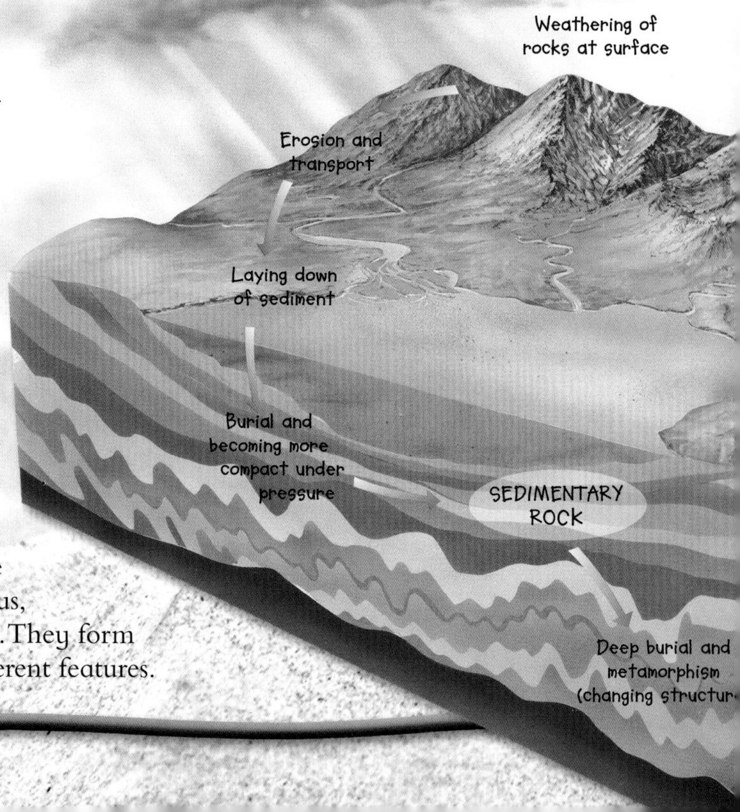

328 All rock goes through a cycle over millions of years. During the rock cycle rocks form deep in the Earth, move and sometimes change, go up to the surface and eventually return below the ground. There are three kinds of rock – igneous, sedimentary and metamorphic. They form in different ways and have different features.

329 Rocks can go around the cycle in lots of ways. Igneous rocks were once molten (liquid), and have hardened beneath or above the surface. Metamorphic rock forms when rock is changed by heat, pressure or a combination of the two. Sedimentary rocks are formed when sediment – small particles of rock – becomes buried.

I DON'T BELIEVE IT!

The outer rock layer of the Earth is made of seven main segments (plates). Over time, these plates have moved across the surface of the Earth at a rate of between 5 and 15 centimetres a year, creating volcanoes, mountains and oceans.

330 Exposed rock is eroded (worn away) over time. This is a process in which tiny pieces (particles) of rock are loosened and transported as a result of gravity, wind, water or ice. Gradually these particles may become buried under more rock particles, forming sediment. If the sediment is buried deep enough to reach the mantle it will be heated by magma (hot molten rock), which may melt or bake it. Uplift and erosion can then expose them again.

IGNEOUS ROCK

Magma forms crystals as it cools

METAMORPHIC ROCK

Melting to form magma

Formed in fire

331 Rock that forms when hot molten rock (magma or lava) cools and hardens is called igneous rock. Igneous rock is divided into two types, extrusive and intrusive, depending on where it forms.

◀ When the pressure in the magma chamber is high enough, the volcano erupts and spews out its lava with incredible force.

332 Igneous rock is known as 'extrusive' if it forms above Earth's surface. This can happen if it erupts or flows from a volcano as lava. Sometimes lava settles, sealing the volcano until pressure builds for another eruption. Extrusive rock can form over thousands or even millions of years. As extrusive rock cools, its fine grains grow into larger crystals.

333 Intrusive rock cools and solidifies inside the Earth's crust below the surface. It only becomes visible when the rocks above it wear away. Granite and dolerite are two examples of intrusive rock.

QUIZ

1. What is igneous rock before it hardens?
2. Where does 'extrusive' rock form?
3. How were the columns at the Giant's Causeway formed?

Answers:
1. Molten rock, or magma
2. Above ground 3. They formed as lava cooled and shrank

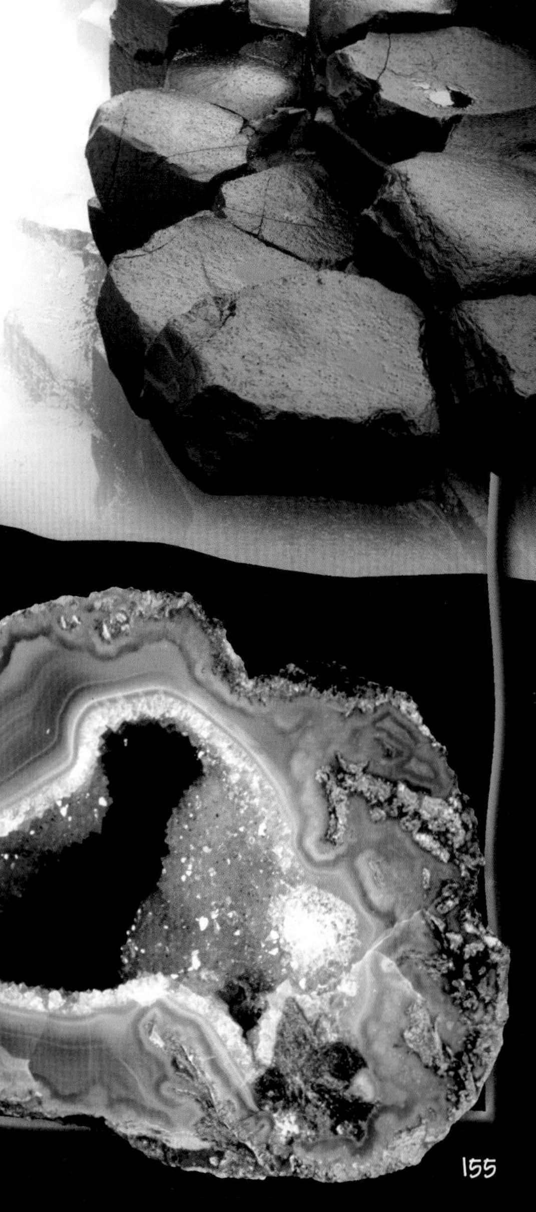

▶ An ancient volcanic eruption formed the Giant's Causeway, which consists of around 40,000 columns of basalt that interlock like a giant jigsaw.

334 The most common type of igneous rock is basalt, which often cools in hexagonal columns. At the Giant's Causeway in Northern Ireland, thousands of these columns were created as lava cooled and shrank over millions of years. Legend says that the columns, some as much as 2 metres in height, are stepping stones for giants to walk across the sea.

335 Sometimes gas creates holes in rock. Crystals form inside the holes, creating geodes – dull-looking stones from the outside, lined with brilliant crystals on the inside. Geodes are often sold cut in half and polished to reveal their glittering insides.

▶ Geodes are rock cavities with crystal formations or circular bands inside them.

Incredible igneous

▼ Volcanic ash settled over the dead of Pompeii. Over time the bodies rotted away leaving cavities in the ash. The scientists who uncovered these filled them with plaster to create casts of the victims' bodies.

336 The igneous rock, basalt, is so durable that it was used to pave the ancient Roman city of Pompeii. However, in AD 79 the nearby volcano Vesuvius erupted, covering the town with fresh ash. Buildings, streets and many people were buried and lay untouched for centuries.

▼ Pumice is frothy lava turned solid. It is widely used to make lightweight concrete.

337 Pumice is solidified lava. It is so light it will float until water soaks into it. It has tiny holes with sharp edges all over it, making it ideal for rubbing down rough surfaces and cleaning skin. Stonewashed jeans are treated with ground-up pumice.

338 Granite has a high content of the mineral quartz. This makes it very tough so it is often used for construction. It can be seen in many famous buildings, such as parts of London's Tower Bridge and some of the ancient Egyptian pyramids and obelisks.

▲ Curling is an event at the Winter Olympics. Teams slide granite stones towards a target.

339 The sport of curling uses granite stones. Teams slide large, heavy, polished granite discs along ice towards a target. Two sweepers with brooms brush the ice to make the stone go in the direction that they want.

◀ Ancient Egyptian obelisks such as this have survived for thousands of years because granite is so tough it takes ages to erode.

TRUE OR FALSE?

1. Pumice is one of the heaviest types of rock.
2. Granite is often used in building because it is so strong.
3. In tennis, players pass granite stones to one another.

Answers:
1. False, it is very light
2. True
3. False, granite stones are used in curling

340 Igneous rock is crushed to make aggregate. This is the material used for the foundations of roads and railways. It forms a strong, stable base on top of which the road surface can be laid. You can sometimes see it as the layer underneath the tarmac when roads are being repaired.

Lots of layers

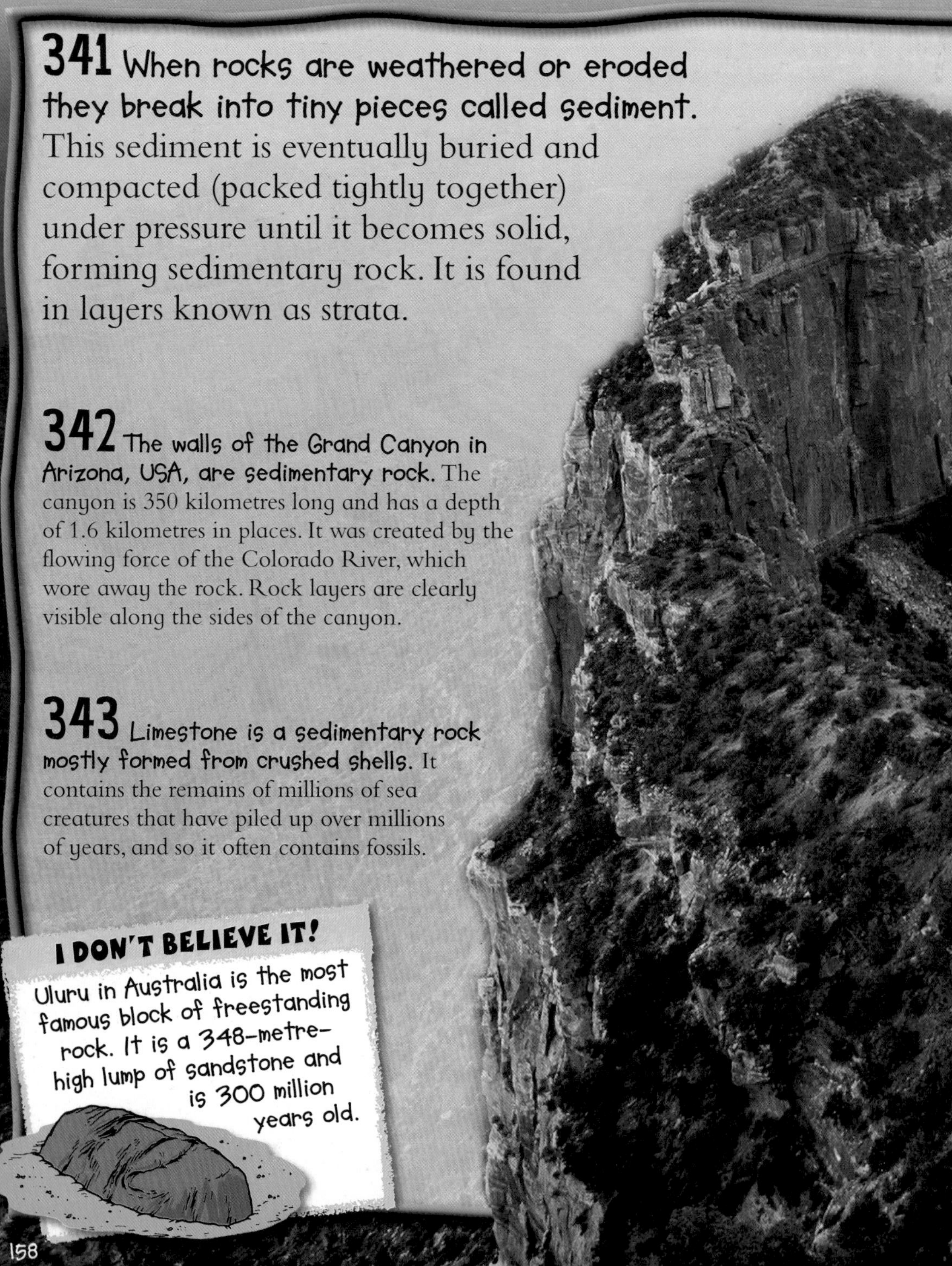

341 When rocks are weathered or eroded they break into tiny pieces called sediment. This sediment is eventually buried and compacted (packed tightly together) under pressure until it becomes solid, forming sedimentary rock. It is found in layers known as strata.

342 The walls of the Grand Canyon in Arizona, USA, are sedimentary rock. The canyon is 350 kilometres long and has a depth of 1.6 kilometres in places. It was created by the flowing force of the Colorado River, which wore away the rock. Rock layers are clearly visible along the sides of the canyon.

343 Limestone is a sedimentary rock mostly formed from crushed shells. It contains the remains of millions of sea creatures that have piled up over millions of years, and so it often contains fossils.

I DON'T BELIEVE IT!

Uluru in Australia is the most famous block of freestanding rock. It is a 348-metre-high lump of sandstone and is 300 million years old.

344 Some sedimentary rocks are formed when saline (salt) water evaporates. This can happen when a bay or gulf is cut off from the sea and starts to dry up. These mineral-rich rocks are known as evaporites and include gypsum, rock salt (halite) and potash.

345 Coal is a sedimentary rock formed over millions of years. Vegetation from swampy forests died and rotted away. As the water dried out, the vegetation became first peat and eventually coal. Both peat and coal can be mined and burned as fuel.

◀ The Grand Canyon was formed by two billion years of erosion from the Colorado River exposing countless layers of sedimentary rock.

Super sedimentary

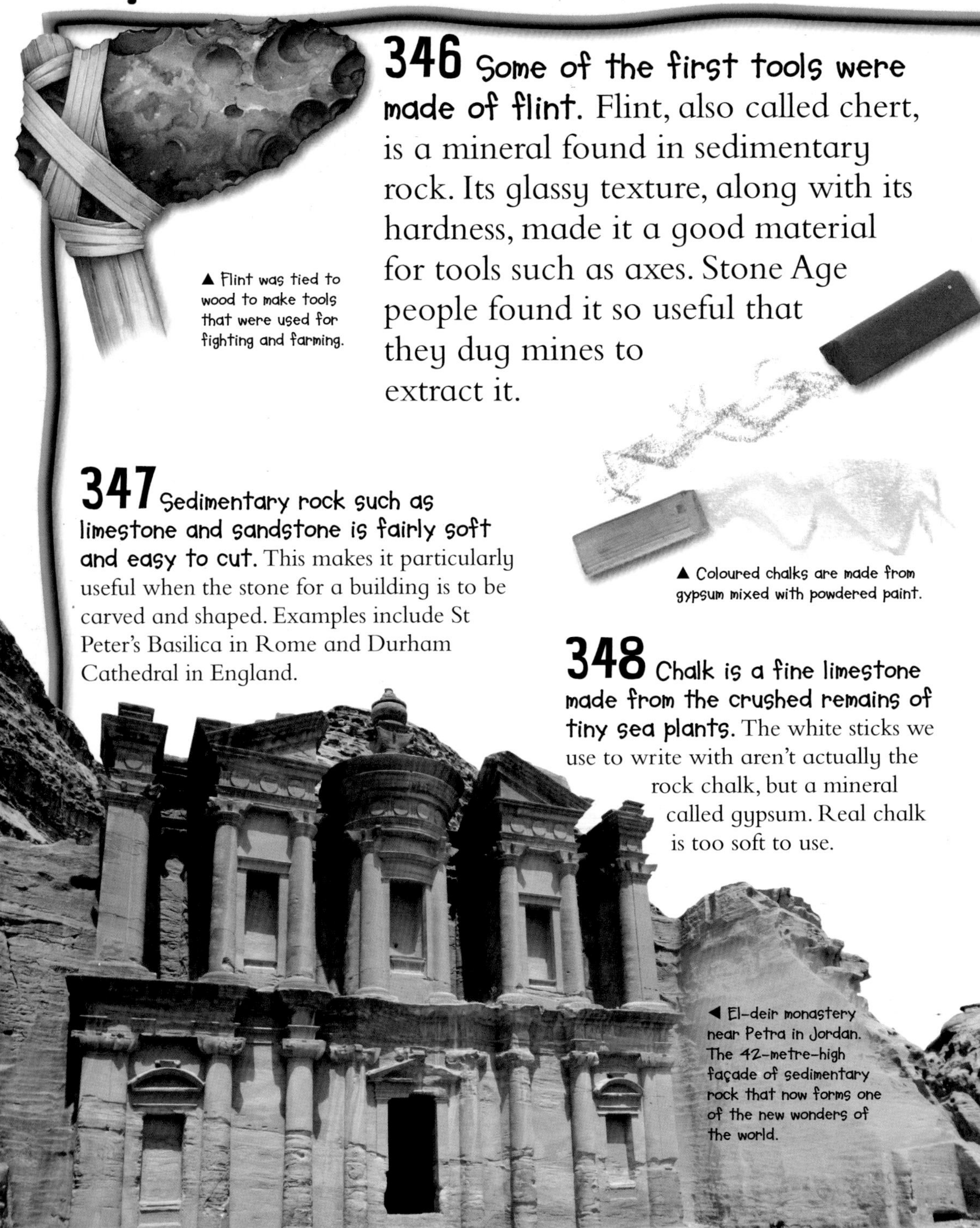

346 Some of the first tools were made of flint. Flint, also called chert, is a mineral found in sedimentary rock. Its glassy texture, along with its hardness, made it a good material for tools such as axes. Stone Age people found it so useful that they dug mines to extract it.

▲ Flint was tied to wood to make tools that were used for fighting and farming.

347 Sedimentary rock such as limestone and sandstone is fairly soft and easy to cut. This makes it particularly useful when the stone for a building is to be carved and shaped. Examples include St Peter's Basilica in Rome and Durham Cathedral in England.

▲ Coloured chalks are made from gypsum mixed with powdered paint.

348 Chalk is a fine limestone made from the crushed remains of tiny sea plants. The white sticks we use to write with aren't actually the rock chalk, but a mineral called gypsum. Real chalk is too soft to use.

◀ El-deir monastery near Petra in Jordan. The 42-metre-high façade of sedimentary rock that now forms one of the new wonders of the world.

349 Stalactites are an amazing feature of some limestone caves. A stalactite develops when a drop of water evaporates, leaving behind a mineral deposit of calcite. If this keeps happening, a spike of mineral starts to 'grow' as more water drips down. Stalactites only grow a few millimetres a year.

GROW YOUR OWN STALACTITE

Make sure you ask an adult to help you. Dissolve some Epsom salts (magnesium sulphate) in two jars of hot water. Drape string between the two jars with each end in the liquid, holding it in place with a paper clip. Leave for a few days and a stalactite should start to form on the string.

350 Sometimes the minerals falling from a stalactite collect on the cave floor and start to 'grow' up, making a stalagmite. Eventually the two might meet and join, forming a column. A good way to remember the difference between stalactites and stalagmites is: Watch out! If stalactites grow down, stalag*mites might* grow up.

▼ Stalactites are formed by slow dripping water, just like icicles, except the water has evaporated leaving its minerals behind. The shapes made when stalactites and stalagmites join into pillars have been called 'organ pipes' and 'hanging curtains'.

The rock that changes

351 Metamorphic rock is rock that has been changed by heat or pressure (or both) into a new form deep underground. Pressure from movement of the Earth's crust, the weight of the rocks above and heat from magma cause metamorphic changes. Most of these happen at temperatures of 200–500°C. The rock does not melt – that would make igneous rock – but it is altered.

352 The appearance and texture of rock changes as a result of heat and pressure. Crystals break down and form, and a rock's chemical structure can change as its minerals react together. If the change is made under pressure, the rock crystals grow flat and form layers. If shale is compressed it forms slate.

▼ Slate forms when fine clay settles in layers and is then compressed and heated.

1. Bands of shale form solid layers

Shale

2. Movement creates curves

Slate

▼ Part of a slate landscape on Valencia Island off the coast of Ireland. This useful rock has been quarried and mined for thousands of years.

353 Sometimes rocks don't stop changing. For example, over centuries shale becomes slate, which looks the same as shale but is far harder and is more likely to split into sheets. However, if slate is then heated and squeezed it will be transformed again into phyllite, then schist and finally gneiss. This is the incredibly hard rock that forms the Alps.

I DON'T BELIEVE IT!

Gneiss found in northern Canada is the world's oldest rock. It was created under the volcanoes that made the first landmasses around four billion years ago.

▼ The Alps is a long mountain range stretching from east to west across Europe, formed about 40–20 million years ago.

354 Eclogite is one of the rarest, but most interesting, metamorphic rocks. It is full of crystals and minerals so it is very coarse-grained. Eclogite is green and often studded with red garnets, and sometimes even diamonds. It forms deep in the Earth's mantle, reaching the surface through volcanoes.

▼ No other rock contains as many interesting crystals and minerals as eclogite, which is formed by extremely high pressures and temperatures.

Marvellous metamorphic

355 The metamorphic rock marble is used in building. It is especially good for curved buildings, such as the Taj Mahal in India. The dome is made of white marble and seems to change colour through the day. It took 20,000 workers 22 years to finish the temple and the surrounding buildings in 1648.

▼ The Taj Mahal is an intricately carved, symmetrical tomb made of white marble. It is now a World Heritage Site.

QUIZ

1. Which type of rock can be used to make roofing tiles?
2. What do the Inuit people use serpentinite for?
3. What is the Taj Mahal made from?

Answers:
1. Slate 2. Carving sculptures
3. Marble

▶ Marble can be cut in any direction and has been used by artists for thousands of years.

356 Marble was a favourite material of Greek and Roman sculptors. Pure marble only contains one mineral – calcite – so it is not formed in bands. This means it is smooth and can be easily carved, so it is perfect for creating complex shapes. The best-known marble comes from Italy.

358 **Some Inuit people of the Arctic carve sculptures using the metamorphic rock serpentinite.** It has the dark greens, browns and blacks of snakeskin, which is how it got its name (serpent means snake).

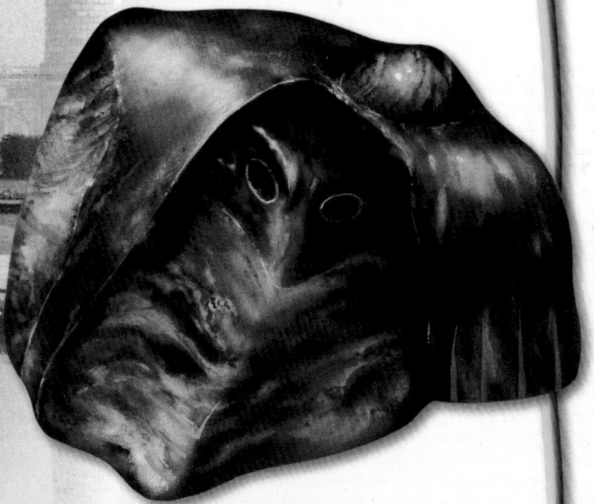

▼ The Inuit travel for days to reach supplies of serpentinite, which they carve into beautiful shapes such as this bird.

▼ Slate is light, hard and easy to shape, so it is an ideal material for roofing tiles where its colours add to the beauty of the building.

357 **Slate is a very different kind of metamorphic rock.** It is light but hard, water-resistant and can be split into thin sheets, so it is an ideal material for roofing tiles. It is also used to make smooth, flat bases for snooker tables.

359 Meteoroids, asteroids and comets are all rocky objects flying through space. Around 1000 meteoroids, which are the smallest types, land on Earth each year as meteorites. The largest meteorite fell onto Namibia, Africa, around 80,000 years ago. Known as the Hoba meteorite, it is thought to weigh over 60 tonnes and is the biggest naturally-made piece of iron on Earth's surface.

▶ The Moon's surface is covered with craters blasted out by asteroids and comets. The craters are preserved by the lack of atmosphere.

360 Some meteorites have smashed huge craters in the Earth. One rock that hit Vredefort, South Africa, is estimated to be more than 10 kilometres wide and blasted a crater 250 kilometres across. Another, at Meteor Crater in Arizona, USA, blasted out 175 million tons of rock in an explosion about 150 times as powerful as the atomic bombs dropped on Japan during World War II.

361 Small grains of space rock can burn up upon entering Earth's atmosphere. When this happens, they look like streaks of light flying through the night sky. Meteoroids heading towards Earth heat up and some turn into balls of fire. We call these shooting stars. The lumps of rock that land on the Earth are called meteorites. More than 30,000 have been found.

◀ Comets leave a trail of dust and ice. If these

362 **Tests on rocks from the Moon show the oldest date back 4.5 billion years.** The most ancient rocks on Earth are younger, at 4 billion years. We can study lunar rock because it has been collected by space missions and some small amounts have fallen to Earth as meteorites. All Moon rock is igneous.

▶ The six Apollo Moon-landing missions collected 2415 samples of Moon rock. It has high levels of a mineral called anorthite.

I DON'T BELIEVE IT!

Some scientists believe the dinosaurs were wiped out by a meteorite fall that threw up so much dust it blocked out the sun and changed the climate.

Time capsules

363 Fossils are time capsules buried in rock. They form when a dead animal or plant is buried in sediment, which slowly turns into rock. Sometimes the plant or animal dissolves, leaving a gap of the same shape. This gap is then filled by minerals that create a perfect replica in the mould.

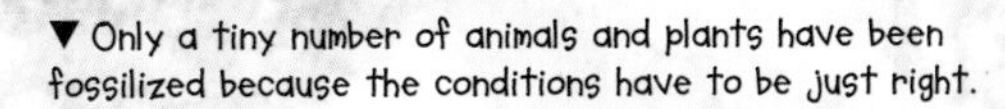

▼ Only a tiny number of animals and plants have been fossilized because the conditions have to be just right.

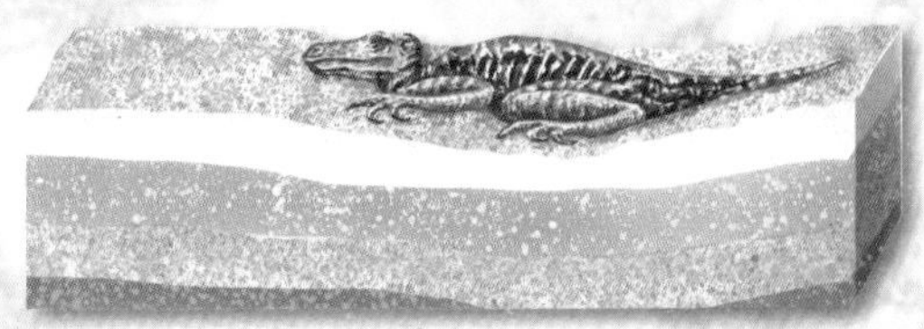

1. The animal dies and its soft parts rot or are eaten

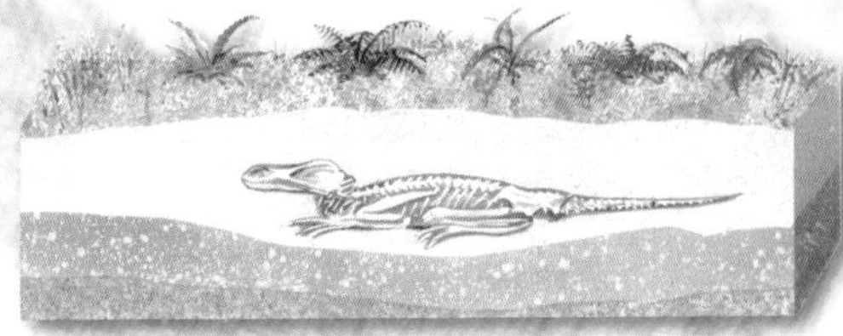

2. It is covered by sediment, slowing its decay

3. More layers form and the skeleton is replaced by minerals

4. The upper rocks wear away and the fossil is exposed

364 More animals have become extinct (died out) than are living today and we only know about them from fossils. For example, no one has ever seen a living dinosaur, but through fossils we have learned about the many types of these reptiles that ruled the earth for 175 million years.

I DON'T BELIEVE IT!

Not all fossils are stone. Tree sap hardens into amber, and sometimes insects and tiny animals become trapped in sap. When the sap hardens, the animal is preserved inside the amber forever.

365 The study of fossils is called palaeontology. One of its first experts was Georges Cuvier (1769–1832). He could work out what a prehistoric animal looked like from studying its fossils and comparing them with the anatomies of living animals, and proved that there were animals alive in the past that are now extinct.

366 **Fossils can tell us the age of rocks.** If scientists can identify a fossilized animal or plant, they will be able to identify the time period in which it lived, so the rock that the fossil has been found in must also date from that period.

367 **Sometimes footprints, burrows and animal droppings are fossilized.** These 'trace fossils' are created when mud or sand fills cavities before they are washed away. Scientists can work out the size and speed of dinosaurs from trace fossils of their footprints.

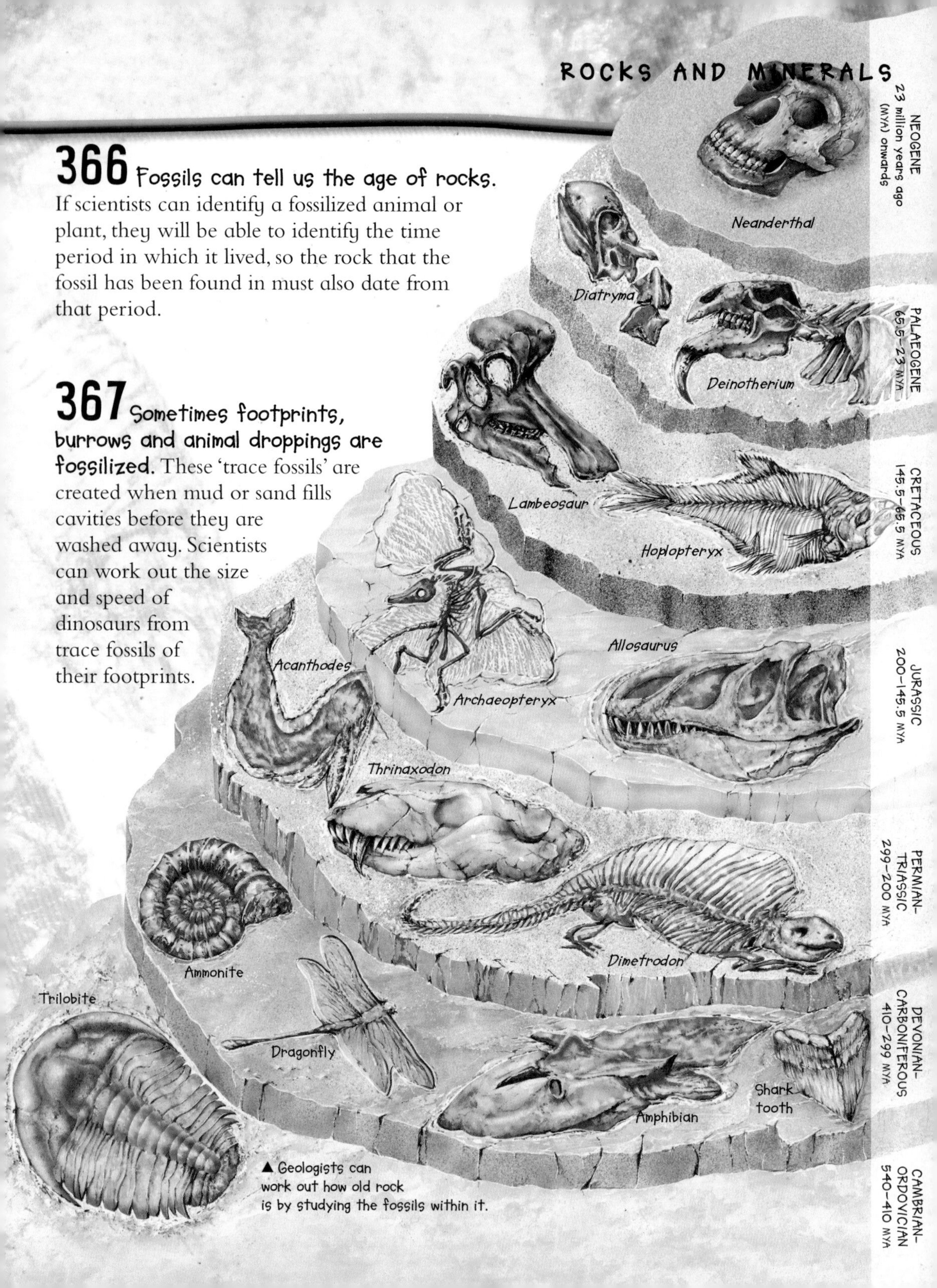

▲ Geologists can work out how old rock is by studying the fossils within it.

The changing landscape

368 Rocks form our landscape but they are slowly changing all the time. They are always being pulled down by gravity, but rocks can also be pushed up from below or worn down in different ways. Many things affect how fast rock is broken down, but it happens to all exposed rock eventually.

369 When movement wears down rocks it is known as erosion. This might be a pebble being ground down as it rolls down a river or glacier, or the top of a hill on a beauty spot being pounded by the feet of countless visitors.

370 When rocks break down without moving it is known as weathering. This can be because of rain, frost, sun or wind. Flowing water wears rock away, which is often how valleys form. If the water falls inside a crack and then freezes and expands, it can shatter the rock. This is called frost damage.

371 Even wind can break down rock, as the movement of small particles in the air slowly wears it away. This happens faster in deserts where the sand and dust carried by the wind rub at the rock.

▶ Sometimes the lower rock of a cliff face is eroded, leaving an overhang.

372 On the coast, breakwaters (strong walls) are sometimes put up to protect against sea erosion. The current, along with powerful waves, breaks up rock and moves vast amounts of sand. Some beaches would disappear without the protection of breakwaters.

373 Pollution can damage buildings made from rock. During the Industrial Revolution in the 18th century, people noticed that buildings crumbled more in towns where lots of coal was being burnt. Minerals in the rock were being eaten away by acid in the atmosphere created by the burning coal. Acid rain is still a big problem today, damaging many buildings worldwide.

▲ The strange landscape of Monument Valley in Arizona, USA, was formed as tiny particles of sand and dust carried by the wind wore away the softer rock, leaving landforms known as 'buttes'.

What are minerals?

374 Minerals are natural substances that form crystals. There are over 4000 different minerals but only about 30 are found all over the world. Quartz and feldspar are two of the most common types of mineral.

▼ Crystal shapes are set by the arrangement of atoms and molecules inside the mineral.

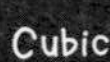

Cubic

Tetragonal

Orthorhombic

Monoclinic

375 A mineral is a chemical compound (a combination of two or more substances) or element (a single fundamental substance). Rocks are made from minerals. Limestone is made mainly of the mineral calcite (calcium carbonate), and granite contains quartz, mica and feldspar.

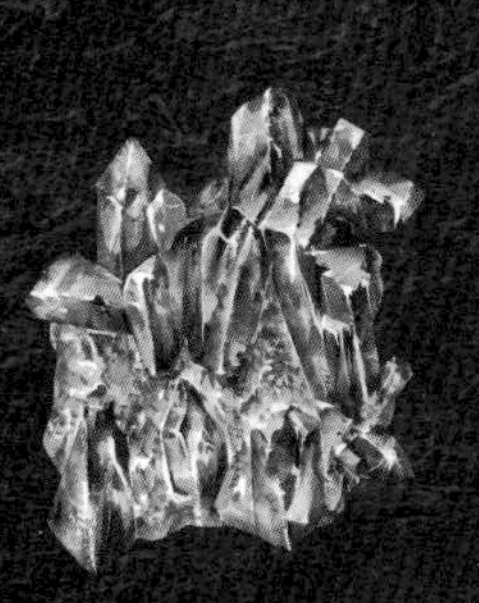

Triclinic

Hexagonal

Trigonal

376 Minerals form crystals. They can do this in several ways. Some are formed as hot molten magma cools. Others come from water (the white powder left when water evaporates is a mineral deposit). Crystals can also be formed when minerals are altered by heat or pressure.

377 Crystals have seven basic shapes. Some just look like a jumble of different surfaces and angles. They have flat, often shiny faces and sharp edges.

378 The tiny grains you can see in most rocks are actually minerals, often forced together. Large crystals form in cracks and holes in rocks, where they have space to grow. The deeper the rock, the longer it generally takes to reach the surface, and the more time the crystal has to grow.

379 Some minerals are so valuable that they are mined. This might mean scraping them from the ground, or blowing up the rocks that hold them. Minerals buried deep underground are reached by drilling down and digging tunnels. People have mined minerals for thousands of years.

▶ Miners have to follow the direction of the mineral-rich band in the seam of rock.

Mineral detectives

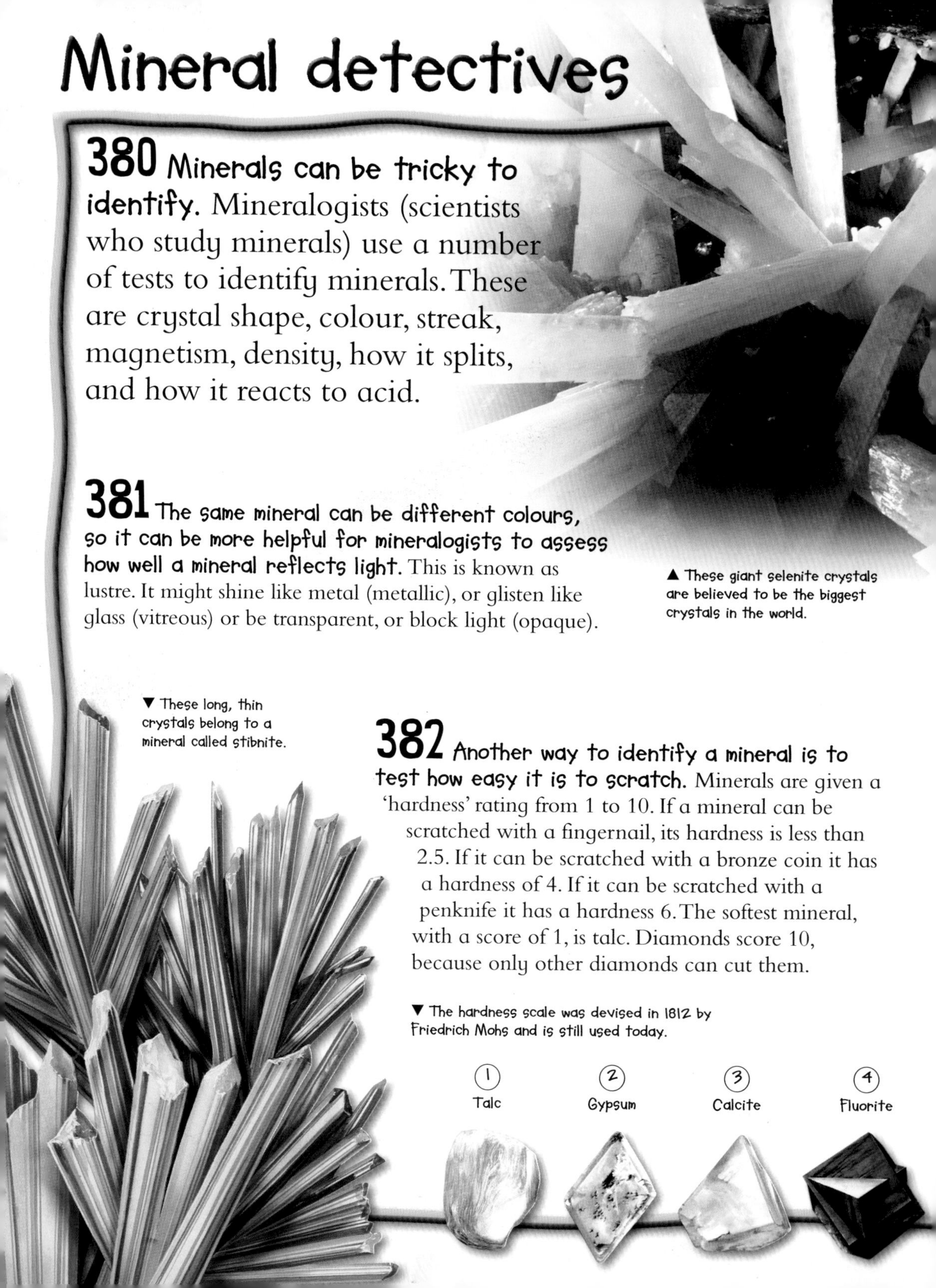

380 Minerals can be tricky to identify. Mineralogists (scientists who study minerals) use a number of tests to identify minerals. These are crystal shape, colour, streak, magnetism, density, how it splits, and how it reacts to acid.

381 The same mineral can be different colours, so it can be more helpful for mineralogists to assess how well a mineral reflects light. This is known as lustre. It might shine like metal (metallic), or glisten like glass (vitreous) or be transparent, or block light (opaque).

▲ These giant selenite crystals are believed to be the biggest crystals in the world.

▼ These long, thin crystals belong to a mineral called stibnite.

382 Another way to identify a mineral is to test how easy it is to scratch. Minerals are given a 'hardness' rating from 1 to 10. If a mineral can be scratched with a fingernail, its hardness is less than 2.5. If it can be scratched with a bronze coin it has a hardness of 4. If it can be scratched with a penknife it has a hardness 6. The softest mineral, with a score of 1, is talc. Diamonds score 10, because only other diamonds can cut them.

▼ The hardness scale was devised in 1812 by Friedrich Mohs and is still used today.

383 The way crystals split is known as cleavage. They break along lines of weakness, known as cleavage planes. Some, such as mica, break into flat sheets or flakes. Others split in two planes like a square rod – orthoclase feldspar does this. Galena breaks in three planes so that the face looks like steps.

▶ Some mica crystals can be split into wafer-like sheets that are so thin they can become almost transparent.

384 The real mineral colour test is the streak test. When the mineral is rubbed against the back of a white porcelain tile it will always mark the tile with the same colour. For example quartz can be purple, green, red, yellow or black, but it leaves a white streak on tiles.

▶ The most common mineral on Earth's land surface, quartz, is usually colourless or white, but it can be many colours.

GET A REACTION

A group of minerals called carbonates all react to acid. You can test this by dropping a rock into vinegar. If the rock has carbonates in it, it will fizz and bubble. Try this with a lump of chalk or limestone, as their main ingredient is calcite. The fizzing is carbon dioxide gas being released as the mineral dissolves.

Brilliant colours

385 The caves of Lascaux in France are decorated with nearly 2000 figures painted onto the walls by cave dwellers nearly 17,000 years ago. They painted horses, stags, bison and huge bulls using ground-down minerals.

I DON'T BELIEVE IT!

Elizabethan women painted their faces with a paste called ceruse (made with the mineral cerussite). They also used the metal mineral mercury sulphide as blush for their cheeks, but unfortunately it made their hair fall out.

◀ Charcoal is just burnt wood, so there was a plenty of it around for Stone Age artists.

386 Minerals were used for thousands of years to make pigments. At first, earth colours were used, but they were not very bright. Gradually people discovered how to make brilliant blues and greens and the new pigments were traded over long distances. Today most pigments are synthetic (man-made).

◀ The Lascaux cave paintings are one of only a few surviving examples of prehistoric art.

▶ One word for a deep but bright blue is azure, taken from the pigment azurite.

387 Pigments need to have a binding agent to hold them in place. Otherwise they just turn back to powder after any water has evaporated. One natural binding agent is egg yolk (the yellow part of the egg).

▶ Artists have long prized the intense blue made from the semi-precious stone lapis lazuli.

388 Chalk was the first substance to be used as white pigment, while earth colours were made with iron minerals. A copper compound called azurite made a beautiful blue, bettered only by the rarer and more expensive lapis lazuli. The mineral pigment terra verte was used to make green paint, and was so common around Verona, Italy, that it was also known as Verona Green.

▲ Made from a copper compound, green malachite has been in use as a pigment since the Bronze Age in Egypt.

389 Ancient Egyptian beauties used mineral make-up! Women of the time used green malachite, along with the black minerals galena or lead sulphide, for eye make-up. Other minerals were used for beauty treatments, and the mineral jasper was used to cure eye infections.

▶ The abundant minerals found or traded by the ancient Egyptians were used for make-up and body decoration.

Metal minerals

390 Most minerals are mixtures known as compounds. However, there are about 20 'native elements' that rarely mix and are mostly pure. Most of these are metals and without them our world would be very different.

391 Metals are mined, quarried or dredged up. At this point they are known as ore, the word for rock containing metals. The ore is heated beyond its melting point (this is called smelting), and the precious metal is poured out as a liquid and put in a mould to set.

392 Silver has long featured in jewellery but it is also used in the electronics industry. It is found as small specks or thin wiry shapes in igneous rock. Today, silver is less valuable than gold, but in the past it has been rarer than gold, and so more valuable. It goes dull and black very quickly so it has to be polished to make it shiny.

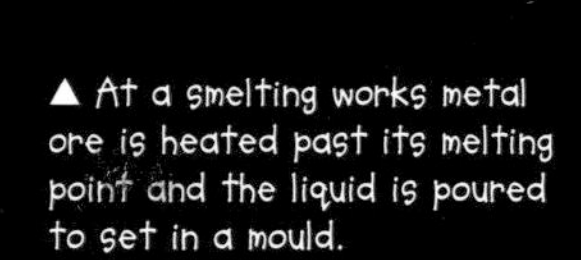

▲ At a smelting works metal ore is heated past its melting point and the liquid is poured to set in a mould.

▶ With its red-gold colour, copper makes one of the most distinctive metals, and is found in many minerals.

393 **Aluminium is quite a common metal – it makes up 8 percent of the weight of the Earth's crust.** It is found in about 270 minerals but is mainly extracted from the ore bauxite. It is light but strong, and is used to make vehicles such as cars and planes as well as many other things. Aluminium isn't magnetic, unlike iron.

▲ ▶ Bauxite ore produces aluminium, a strong but light metal that is ideal for forming the body of vehicles such as planes.

▶ Bronze is the most popular material for metal sculptures. This bronze and marble sculpture is *The Thinker* by Rodin.

394 **Metals can be mixed together to make alloys.** One of the most important alloys in our history is bronze, a blend of copper and tin. Copper is soft, so wasn't useful for tools or containers as it didn't stay sharp or in shape. Adding tin made it harder and allowed people to make swords, armour, ploughs and cooking pots.

395 **Platinum is one of the rarest metals.** It is 30 times more scarce than gold and is usually found as fine grains. Most platinum is found in two parts of the world – Russia and South Africa. It is used in jewellery, laboratories and in catalytic converters (devices used to reduce damaging substances in car emissions). Some coins were made from it in the past.

Panning for gold

◀ Gold panners scoop up the riverbed and shake their pans to see if any pieces of gold are hidden in the rocks and mud.

396 Gold is one of the most valuable materials. It has been used as money and as jewellery and decoration for centuries. One of the reasons that it is so precious is that it is very hard to find. Gold is a pure element – it rarely mixes with other minerals.

397 Gold forms in igneous and sedimentary rocks. It is sometimes found in lumps known as nuggets, but more commonly as tiny specks. People still pan for gold today, filtering gravel and sand in the hope that they will find some heavier gold grains in their sieve.

TRUE OR FALSE?

1. The mineral pyrite is worth the same as gold.
2. Gold is often used in jewellery.
3. Gold was only recently discovered.

Answers:
1. False 2. True
3. False, it has been used since ancient times

◀ Gold sometimes forms in veins of quartz that are then extracted and smelted.

398 The ancient Egyptians decorated their temples with gold. The Turin Papyrus, drawn in 1160 BC, shows a gold mine in the Egyptian desert. Gold is good to work with as it can be softened and shaped relatively easily. It is also very strong and polishes well.

◀ 'Bling' is the slang term for flashy jewellery with lots of gold in it, as worn here by the rapper Slick Rick.

▲ Tutankhamun's death mask was made of solid gold decorated with semi-precious stones and glass. It weighs 10 kilograms.

399 When lots of people travel to an area where gold has been found it is called a gold rush. Gold rushes occurred in Roman times and during the Spanish conquest of the Americas. In the 19th century whole towns were founded in America, Brazil and Australia when gold-panners moved in and started their search.

400 Some minerals look like gold. Known as 'fool's gold', pyrite and chalcopyrite have often been mistaken for the real thing because they resemble it so closely. Both are harder than real gold.

▶ Fool's gold can still be useful – it makes sparks when struck and was used in early firearms.

Special effects

401 A firework display is a big mineral burn-up. The colours depend on which mineral is used. For example, celestite burns red, while greens are from barite, tourmaline burns yellow and copper burns blue. Firework makers mix minerals into compounds to create new colours. Flashes and shower effects are made with aluminium. The smell from fireworks is actually the mineral sulphur burning.

◀ The blues in a firework display are produced by copper minerals being burnt.

402 Ultraviolet (UV) light makes some minerals glow fantastic colours that are completely different to their dull appearance in daylight. This is called fluorescence after the best example, fluorite. This mineral shines blue or green in UV light, probably because it has traces of radioactive uranium.

I DON'T BELIEVE IT!

In 1602, alchemists (early chemists) discovered how to make minerals glow. At first they thought they had discovered a magic way to turn metals to gold.

403 Gypsum can be dried into a powder. This powder forms the base for many plasters (such as plaster of Paris) and cements. It is also used in fertilizers and paper.

▲ Fluorite shines in UV light and it also glows when gently heated.

▶ Coal mining is dangerous because the seams of coal are deep under the ground.

▲ Coal can be treated so that it burns without producing smoke.

404 **Fossil fuels such as coal, oil and gas are made from minerals found in the remains of plants that lived millions of years ago.** They are used to get energy because they burn well. Coal is solid, and mostly made up of the element carbon.

405 **Kaolin is named after Kao-ling hill in China, where it has been quarried for 1400 years.** Made from the mineral kaolinite, it is a soft, white and fine-grained clay used to make porcelain. It has many uses – it is also found in some light bulbs, medicines and glossy paper.

▶ This kaolin (china clay) mine is in St Austell, Cornwall, UK.

A mineral meal

Cheese is an excellent source of the mineral apatite

406 Our bodies need minerals to stay healthy. The mineral apatite helps to form teeth and bones (its chemical name is calcium phosphate). We get it from dairy foods such as cheese.

407 We need iron in our blood. It is found in red meat and eggs. Potassium keeps our muscles working (bananas are full of it). Zinc helps us fight diseases and heal cuts – it is found in meat and beans.

▶ People have mined salt for thousands of years. Salt was once so valuable that Roman soldiers were paid with it.

408 The most commonly used mineral is salt. Also known as table salt and rock salt, its chemical name is halite, or sodium chloride. Salt forms where salty water evaporates. Thick layers of it can be found in some sedimentary rock. Some salt is mined underground. Shafts are dug and the salt is loosened with an explosion and then removed.

Eggs are a source of iron

Pulses such as beans provide zinc

Bananas are an excellent source of potassium

▲ The minerals we need to keep our bodies healthy come from the foods we eat. This is one reason why it is so important to eat a varied diet.

409 **Your body is like a machine, and it needs minerals to function.** In total, about four percent of your body is made up of minerals. This includes small amounts of manganese, copper, iodine, cobalt, fluoride, selenium and many others.

410 **Plants take minerals from the soil as part of the mix of nutrients they need to live.** Minerals used by plants include sulphides, sulphates, calcium and magnesium. They are taken up through the roots.

▶ Calcite defines point 3 on the hardness scale. It forms as sharply pointed or flattened six-sided crystals.

QUIZ

1. Which fruit is packed with potassium?
2. What is the most commonly used mineral?
3. Red meat and eggs provide us with which mineral?

Answers:
1. Bananas 2. Salt 3. Iron

411 **Have you ever noticed the cream-coloured 'fur' that collects in kettles?** It is actually a form of calcite, one of the most common minerals in the world. It dissolves in water and then gets left behind. Calcite is the main ingredient in limestone, marble and chalk.

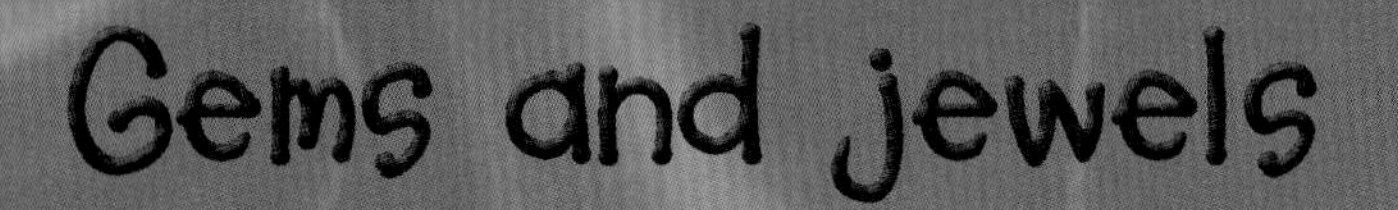

Gems and jewels

412 Gemstones are crystals of natural minerals that shine or sparkle in beautiful colours. They are very popular set in jewellery such as rings, earrings, necklaces and bracelets. They look dull when they are dug up in rocks, but then they are cut to shape and polished to sparkle.

413 The mineral corundum forms blue sapphires and red rubies. These are two of the most precious gemstones. Corundum is very hard (second only to diamonds) and is used to make emery boards that people use to file their nails. It is colourless when pure and is made red by tiny amounts of chromium, or blue by the presence of iron and titanium.

◀ One of the British Crown Jewels, the Imperial State Crown contains diamonds, pearls, sapphires, emeralds and rubies.

I DON'T BELIEVE IT!

Gems are given a carat rating, which refers to their weight (a carat is about one-fifth of a gram). The word carat comes from the ancient Greek practise of weighing gems using carab tree seeds.

▼ Ruby is regarded as the king of gemstones because of its rich red colouring and its strength.

▶ Everybody has a birthstone and some people like to wear their own special gem.

414 One of the earliest highly prized gems was emerald. The Egyptians sent slaves to work in the desert mining these green gems. The Inca of South America regarded them as sacred and decorated their golden statues and jewellery with them.

January
Garnet

February
Amethyst

March
Aquamarine

April
Diamond

May
Emerald

June
Pearl

July
Ruby

August
Peridot

September
Sapphire

October
Opal

November
Topaz

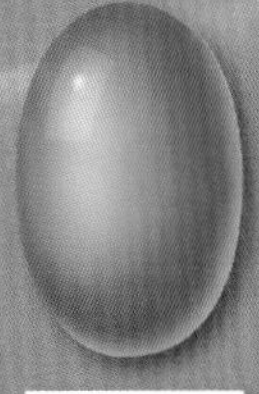

December
Turquoise

415 Some gemstones are identified with certain months. For example, May is emerald and October is opal. There are even meanings given to gemstones, such as peace for amethyst and energy for topaz.

416 There are 130 different gemstones, of which the rarest are diamonds, emeralds, rubies and sapphires. Dealers describe gemstones using the four Cs: clarity, colour, cut and carat (weight). The largest stones are usually the most valuable.

Diamonds are forever

◀ Large machinery is used to uncover diamond-rich gravel at this coastal diamond mine in Namibia, Africa.

417 Diamonds are the hardest known mineral. They are named after the Greek word for indestructible, *adamas*. They are the toughest known material, scoring 10 on the mineral hardness scale. They are used in jewellery, and also in industry for cutting and drilling through dense materials such as rock.

418 Most diamonds are mined from a rock called kimberlite. They form deep in the Earth, up to 200 kilometres below the surface, under high pressure and at temperatures between 900 and 1300°C. Some diamond mine tunnels have to be cooled for people to work in because they are heated by the Earth's magma.

◀ The Millennium Star diamond is one of the most famous in the world. It took three years to cut it into this perfect pear shape using lasers.

◀ This diamond-bearing rock formed deep in the Earth and was brought up by an erupting volcano.

TRUE OR FALSE?

1. Diamonds are very soft.
2. Volcanic eruptions can bring diamonds to the Earth's surface.
3. Aluminium is formed when diamonds are heated to very high temperatures.

Answers:
1. False, diamonds are extremely hard 2. True 3. False, graphite is formed in these conditions

▶ This 18th-century skull is studded with 8601 diamonds to create a piece of art that has been valued at £50 million.

419 **When they are cut and polished, diamonds sparkle beautifully.** This makes them very popular for jewellery, but it wasn't until the Middle Ages that jewellers cut and polished diamonds and discovered their amazing brilliance.

420 **If diamonds are heated above 900°C they become graphite, the mineral that is mixed with clay to form the 'lead' in pencils.** It gets its name from the Greek word for writing, *graphein*. Graphite is a soft and very stable mineral and it is also used for lots of things from tennis rackets to steel making and nuclear power stations.

▶ Diamonds mean glamour, so movie stars such as Elizabeth Taylor (1932–2011) (shown here at the 42nd Annual Academy Awards in 1970) spend huge amounts of money on them.

How to be a geologist

421 Geology is the study of the Earth including its rocks and minerals. Some people do it as a hobby, others as a job. Geologists might be called in to help plan where to build roads and houses or to look for precious gems or minerals. Many are employed helping to search for valuable resources such as metals, gas and oil.

STUDYING ROCKS

Study a piece of rock through a magnifier. How many colours can you find? You might find it's made of tiny grains with shiny surfaces – crystals. Try to find any tiny dark flecks of mica, or glassy grains of quartz. Look for evidence of sea creatures – you might be looking at the fossil of something that swam in the oceans millions of years ago.

422 If you want to collect rocks, fossils and minerals you must have permission from the landowner and go with an adult. You need a notepad, map, guidebook, magnifier, gloves, boots and maybe a helmet. Carry a digital camera so you can take pictures of what you find.

▼ Geologists study how rocks form and measure how much they move as the Earth changes.

423 Don't collect from cliffs and quarry walls as they can be dangerous. Only use a hammer if you've been shown how. You can just collect information, noted down or photographed. Wrap any specimens in newspaper or other material to stop them getting damaged.

424 Beaches are great places to hunt for rocks and fossils. Fossils can be exposed as the wind and waves wash away soil and loose rock. You could start by studying pebbles. Different colours probably indicate different minerals. Some rocks may have been in the same place for centuries, others could have come in on the tide that day. You can also look at the rock strata of cliffs.

▲ A geologist picks up a piece of molten rock from a lava flow. The study of volcanoes is called volcanology.

425 Geology really started about 250 years ago with James Hutton (1726–97). Hutton showed that rivers wash away rocks and even eventually whole hills and mountains. He also noticed that rocks were formed from crystals and could be changed by the Earth's heat. He was one of the first people to show that our planet was far older than had been thought. We now know it is about 4.6 billion years old and has been through many stages and changes.

◀ In Hutton's time many people believed that all rocks formed in the sea. His idea that they came from deep in the Earth was thought very strange at first.

FOSSILS

426 Without fossils, we would know nothing about prehistoric life. Fossils are the remains of animals and plants that died a very long time ago and became preserved in rocks. These remains are our 'window on the past'. They show us the amazing variety of life that thrived and then disappeared over millions of years of Earth's history.

▲ A preserved rhinoceros skeleton gradually emerges from ten-million-year-old rocks at a fossil excavation or 'dig' in Nebraska, USA. Removing the remains is just the first part of recreating how this great beast looked, lived and died.

What are fossils?

427 Fossils are the preserved remains of once-living things, such as bones, teeth and claws. Usually the remains were buried in sediments – layers of tiny particles such as sand, silt or mud. Very slowly, the layers and the remains inside them turned into solid rock.

428 In general it takes at least 10,000 years, but usually millions, for fossils to form. So the remains of living things that are a few hundred or thousand years old, such as the bandage-wrapped mummies of pharaohs in ancient Egypt, are not true fossils.

▲ A seed cone fossil of the extinct plant *Williamsonia*.

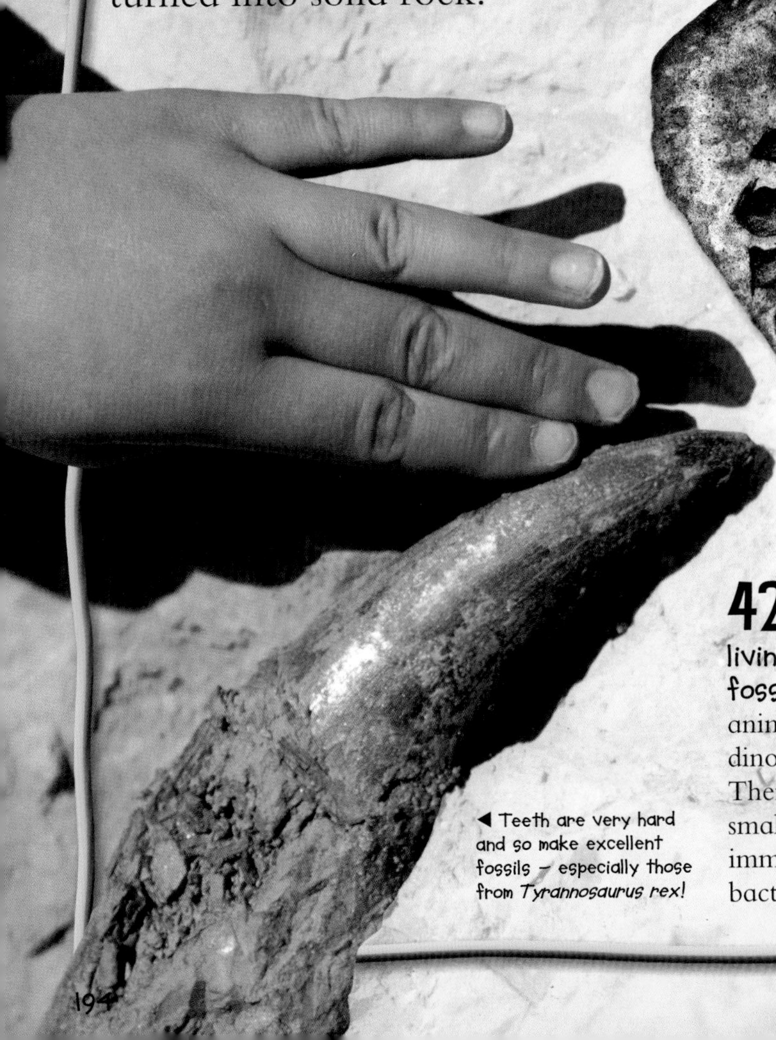

429 Many kinds of once-living things have formed fossils. They include all kinds of animals from enormous whales and dinosaurs to tiny flies and beetles. There are fossils of plants too, from small mosses and flowers to immense trees. Even microscopic bacteria have been preserved.

◀ Teeth are very hard and so make excellent fossils – especially those from *Tyrannosaurus rex*!

▶ It is unusual for thin, delicate bones, such as those of the bat *Icaronycteris*, to fossilize.

430 **In most cases, fossils formed from the hard parts of living things that did not rot away soon after death.** As well as bones, teeth and claws these include shells, scales and the bark, roots, cones and seeds of plants.

431 **Much more rarely, soft parts have been preserved as fossils, such as flower petals and worm bodies.** Where this has happened, it gives a fascinating glimpse into how these ancient life-forms looked and lived.

▼ The tube worms' soft bodies soon decayed but their hard, coiled tubes were preserved in the seabed mud.

QUIZ

Which of these are true fossils?
A. A bird called the dodo, which died out over 300 years ago
B. Two-thousand-year-old pots and vases from ancient Rome
C. The first shellfish that appeared in the sea over 500 million years ago

Answer:
C is a true fossil.
The others are much too recent.

Fossils in myth and legend

432 Centuries ago, the word 'fossil' was used for anything dug out of the ground. This included strange-shaped rocks, crystals and gold nuggets. However 'fossil' gradually came to mean the remains of once-living plants or animals.

▲ Fossilized *Gryphea* oyster shells were known as 'devil's toenails' due to their curved shape.

433 Long ago, some people regarded fossils as rocks and stones that had been specially shaped by gods to resemble animal teeth, tree bark and similar items. People believed this could be to show the gods' great powers and to test the faith of believers.

► It was once believed that ammonites (prehistoric sea creatures) were snakes that had turned to stone. This ammonite fossil has had a snake's head carved on it.

I DON'T BELIEVE IT!

The ancient Greeks likened ammonite fossils to coiled goat horns, believing them to be sacred because they associated them with the horned god, Jupiter Ammon.

434 In some parts of the world, fossils were seen as the remains of animals that perished in a terrible catastrophe. An example was the Great Flood as described in the Bible. A man named Noah managed to save many creatures by building an ark, but most perished in the rising waters.

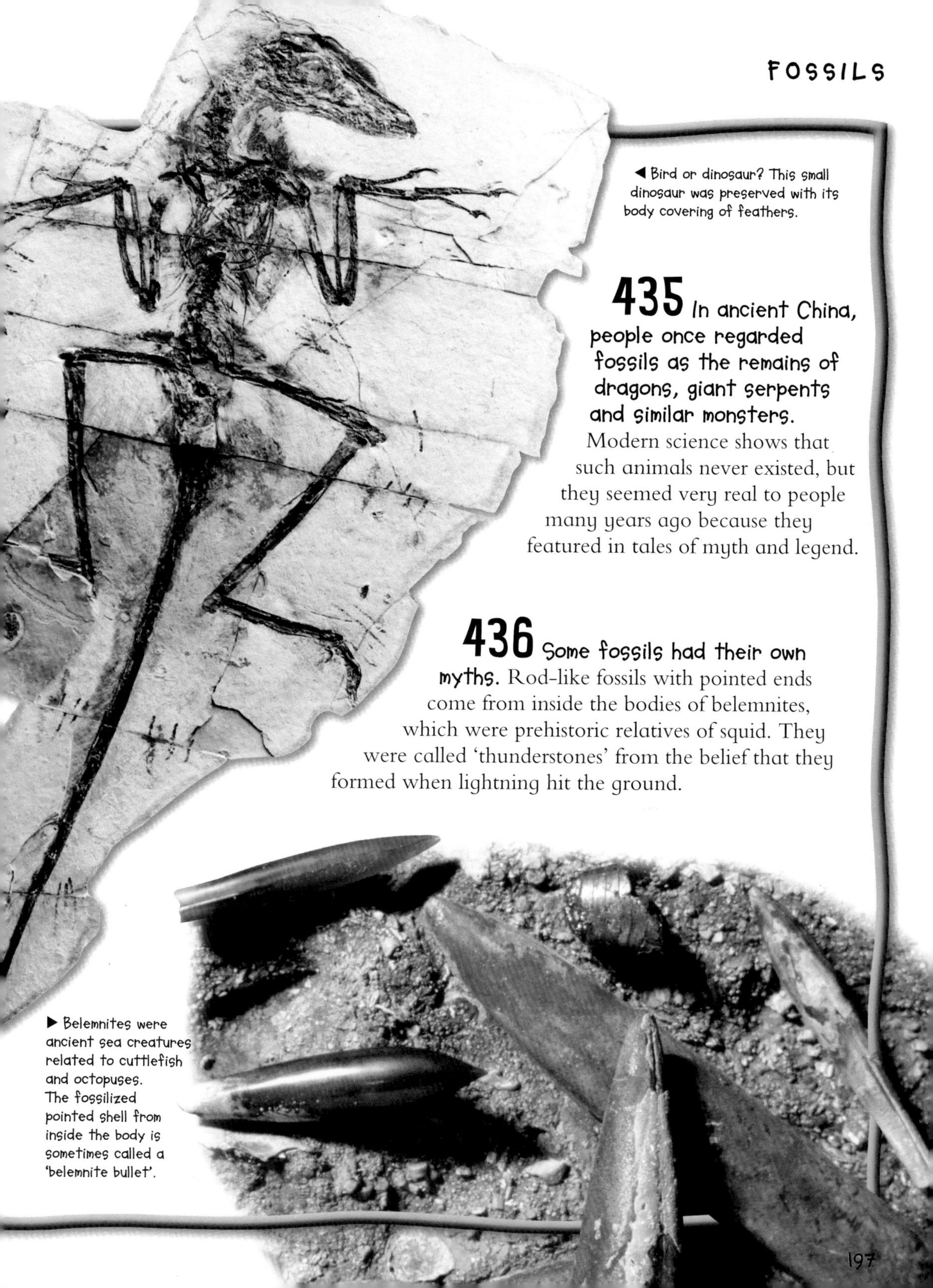

◀ Bird or dinosaur? This small dinosaur was preserved with its body covering of feathers.

435 In ancient China, people once regarded fossils as the remains of dragons, giant serpents and similar monsters. Modern science shows that such animals never existed, but they seemed very real to people many years ago because they featured in tales of myth and legend.

436 Some fossils had their own myths. Rod-like fossils with pointed ends come from inside the bodies of belemnites, which were prehistoric relatives of squid. They were called 'thunderstones' from the belief that they formed when lightning hit the ground.

▶ Belemnites were ancient sea creatures related to cuttlefish and octopuses. The fossilized pointed shell from inside the body is sometimes called a 'belemnite bullet'.

Fossils get scientific

437 People turned to science to explain fossils. Danish geologist (rock expert) Nicolas Steno (1638–1686) noticed that objects called 'tongue stones' looked similar to the teeth of living sharks. He wondered if the teeth of ancient sharks had turned to stone.

▶ Nicolas Steno made sketches of the strange, pointed 'rocks' he found, and saw that they were similar in shape to the teeth of living sharks.

438 French scientist Georges Cuvier (1769–1832) showed that fossils of elephants were similar to those living today. He suggested they had become extinct – died out forever. This caused a great stir. Most people at that time believed God created animals and plants and would never let any of them die out.

▶ Cuvier recognized several extinct elephants including the woolly mammoth (right).

I DON'T BELIEVE IT!

Before scientists could explain how fossils formed, bones of huge animals such as dinosaurs were thought to be from human giants – some more than 5 metres tall!

439 **In the 1820s, English doctor Gideon Mantell (1790–1852) found some huge fossil teeth similar to those of the iguana lizard, but bigger.** He called the beast they came from *Iguanodon*. This was the first dinosaur to be named. Soon the search was on for fossils of more dinosaurs and other extinct animals.

440 **In 1859, English naturalist Charles Darwin (1809–1882) published his book *On The Origin of Species*.** In it, Darwin suggested that species (kinds) of living things that could not succeed in the struggle for survival died out or changed into new kinds, leaving fossils on the way.

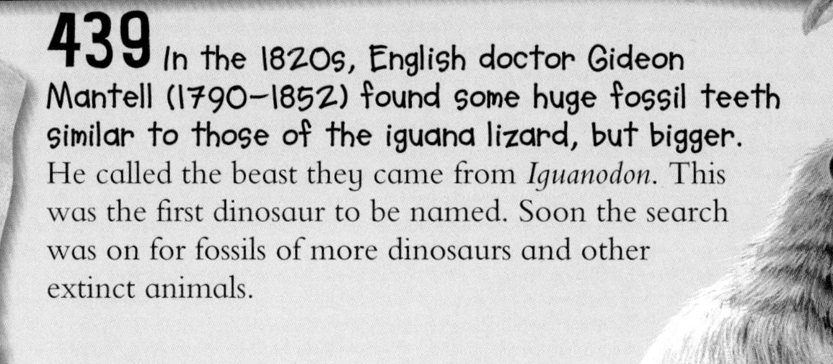

◀ Darwin examined fossils of the giant sloth *Megatherium* and wrote: "Existing animals have a close relation in form to extinct species."

441 **During the 1800s, palaeontology became a new and important branch of science.** This is the study of prehistoric life and it relies greatly on fossils of all kinds.

How fossils form

▼ All living things die. Those living in water, such as this ichthyosaur, are more likely to leave fossils than those on land.

442 When a living thing dies, its flesh and other soft parts start to rot. Sometimes they are eaten by scavenging creatures such as worms and insects. The harder parts, such as teeth and bones, rot more slowly and last longer.

443 Fossil formation usually begins like this, and very often in water. Sediments tend to settle on dead animals and plants in ponds, lakes, rivers and seas. This is the main reason why most fossils are of plants and animals that lived in water or somehow got washed into water.

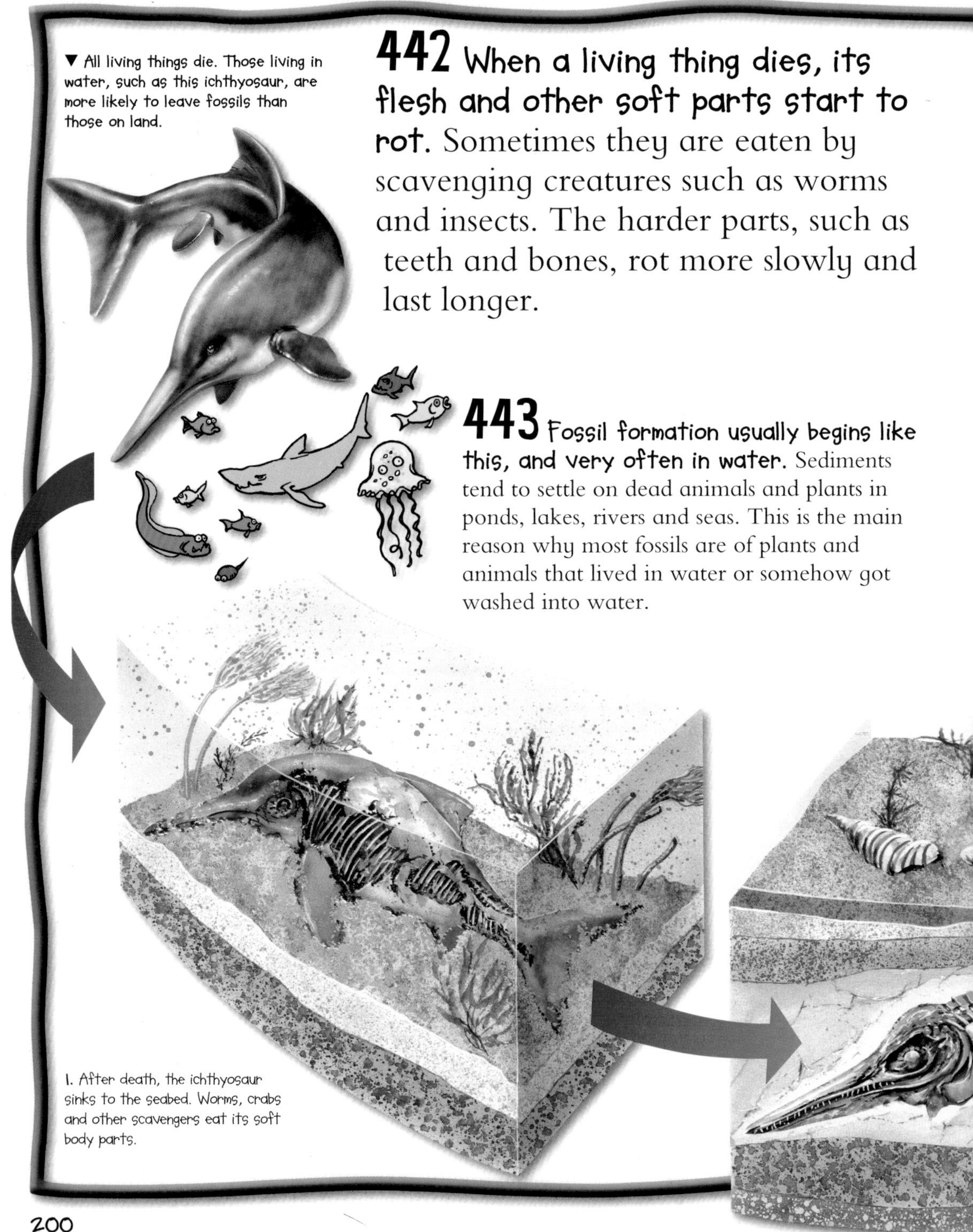

1. After death, the ichthyosaur sinks to the seabed. Worms, crabs and other scavengers eat its soft body parts.

START SOME FOSSILS

You will need:
small stones glass mixing jug
sand water

Imagine the stones are 'bones' of an ancient creature. They get washed into a river – put them in the jug and half-fill with water. Then the 'bones' are covered by sediment – sprinkle in the sand.

444 **Over time, more sediment layers settle on top of the remains.** As they are covered deeper, further rotting or scavenging is less likely.

445 **Water trickles into the sediments and once-living remains.** The water contains dissolved substances such as minerals and salts. Gradually, these replace the once-living parts and turn them and the sediments into solid rock. This is called permineralization.

446 **Most living things rot away soon after death, so the chances of anything becoming a fossil are slim.** Also, sedimentary rock layers change over time, becoming heated and bent, which can destroy fossils in them. The chances of anyone finding a fossil are even tinier. This is why the record of fossils in rocks represents only a tiny proportion of prehistoric life.

2. Sediments cover the hard body parts, such as bones and teeth, which gradually turn into solid rock.

3. Millions of years later the upper rock layers wear away and the fossil remains are exposed.

Mould and cast fossils

447 **Due to the way fossils form, they are almost always found in sedimentary rocks such as sandstone, limestone, chalk, shale and slate.** Other kinds of rocks, such as igneous rocks that cool from red-hot, runny lava erupted from volcanoes, do not contain fossils.

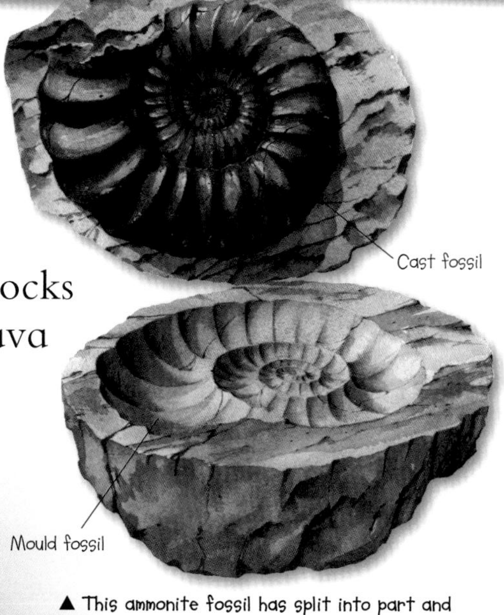

▼ Ammonites were fierce hunting animals related to squid. They died out with the dinosaurs 65 million years ago.

▲ This ammonite fossil has split into part and counterpart, with a mould and cast fossil inside.

448 **As the bits and pieces of sediments become solid rock, the once-living remains within them may not.** They are dissolved by water and gradually washed away. The result is a hole in the rock the same shape as the remains, called a mould fossil.

449 **After more time, the hole or mould in the rock may fill with minerals deposited by water.** This produces a lump of stone that is different in make-up from the surrounding rocks, but is the same shape as the original remains. This is known as a cast fossil.

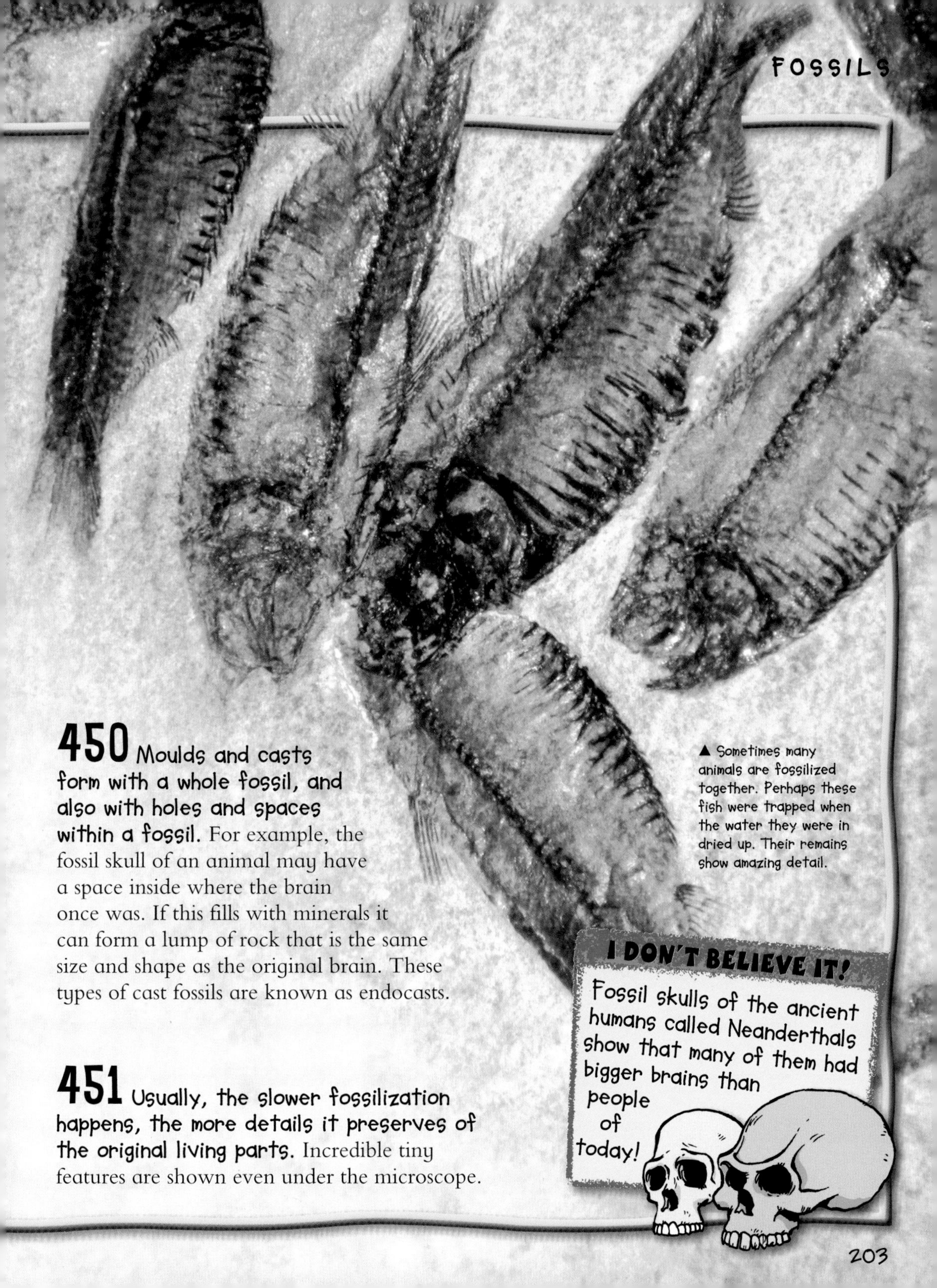

▲ Sometimes many animals are fossilized together. Perhaps these fish were trapped when the water they were in dried up. Their remains show amazing detail.

450 Moulds and casts form with a whole fossil, and also with holes and spaces within a fossil. For example, the fossil skull of an animal may have a space inside where the brain once was. If this fills with minerals it can form a lump of rock that is the same size and shape as the original brain. These types of cast fossils are known as endocasts.

451 Usually, the slower fossilization happens, the more details it preserves of the original living parts. Incredible tiny features are shown even under the microscope.

I DON'T BELIEVE IT!

Fossil skulls of the ancient humans called Neanderthals show that many of them had bigger brains than people of today!

Special preservation

▲ This frog dried out before its flesh could rot away, leaving its mummified remains.

452 Once-living things can be preserved in many different ways. Mummification is when a dead plant or animal is left to dry out slowly. Some dinosaurs and animals have been preserved in this way in the windblown sands of deserts.

453 Amber is the sap (sticky resin) from prehistoric trees, especially conifers, that has been fossilized. If small creatures became trapped by the resin, they are preserved within it. Insects, spiders, frogs, and even leaves and seeds have all been preserved in this way.

◀ Amber preserves amazingly small details, even the delicate wings of this fly.

454 Natural pools of thick, sticky tar ooze up from the ground in some places such as forests and scrubland. Animals that become trapped sink into the tar pit and may be preserved – even huge creatures such as wolves, deer, bears, sabre-tooth cats and mammoths.

▶ In 1977, the perfectly preserved body of this baby mammoth was found thawing out in Siberia. The mammoth had been trapped in ice for thousands of years.

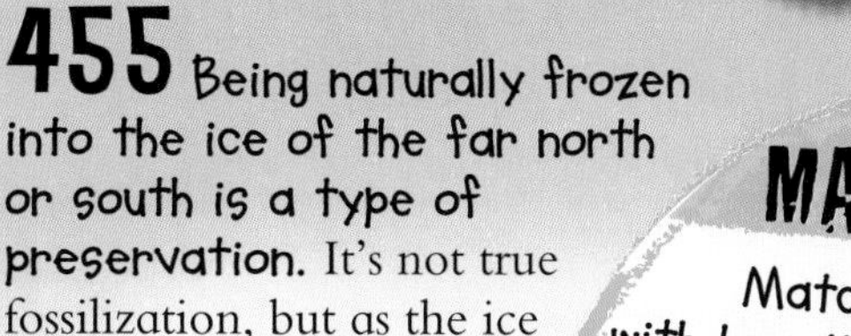

455 Being naturally frozen into the ice of the far north or south is a type of preservation. It's not true fossilization, but as the ice melts it reveals deep-frozen flowers, trees, mammoths and deer.

◀ Fossilized human footprints in southeastern Australia. The spacing of fossil footprints, called trackways, show how their makers walked and ran.

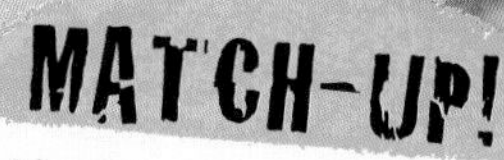

MATCH-UP!

Match the following with how they were preserved.

A. Desert-living dinosaur
B. Wolf in woodland
C. Tree-dwelling insect

1 Natural tar pit
2 Trapped in amber
3 Mummification.

Answers:
A3 B1 C2

456 Trace fossils are not actual body parts of once-living things. They are signs or 'traces' made by them, which then became fossilized. Examples include the footprints of animals, their burrows, egg shells, teeth marks and scratch marks, which can all turn to stone.

Fossils from jelly

457 Some rare and exciting fossils were not formed from the hard parts of living things. They were once soft creatures such as worms, jellyfish and anemones, preserved in unusual conditions.

458 Almost all living things need oxygen to survive. In some kinds of seabed mud, the water is still and brings no oxygen, so there is no life. If sea animals and plants end up here, maybe after an underwater mudslide, there are no living things to rot them in the usual way.

459 In oxygen-less conditions, dead, soft-bodied creatures and plants gradually undergo a strange type of fossilization into carbon films and impressions. These are like smears of oil or powder in the rock. They occur especially in sedimentary rocks called shales or mudstones.

◀ Jellyfish are soft and floppy, but they have on rare occasions left fossilized impressions in sand and mud.

◀ This fossil, called *Mawsonites*, may have been a jellyfish, the root-like holdfast of a seaweed or an animal's burrow network in the mud.

460 About 505 million years ago some seabed mud slid and slumped into deep, oxygen-free water. The black shale rocks that formed are at Burgess Pass in the Rocky Mountains of British Columbia, Canada.

QUIZ

1. Name a gas that most living things need to survive.
2. What type of rock is mudstone?
3. Of all the types of animals and plants that have ever lived, how many have died out?

Answers:
1. Oxygen 2. Sedimentary
3. 999 out of 1000

461 Burgess Shale fossils number many tens of thousands. They include the strangest kinds of creatures resembling worms, jellyfish and shrimps. Some are like no other animals ever known.

462 Rare fossils give a tiny glimpse into the myriad of creatures that thrived long ago, but are rarely preserved. They show that of all the kinds of animals and plants that have ever lived, more than 999 out of 1000 are long gone and extinct (died out).

▼ The Burgess Shale area is a World Heritage Site. It has yielded more than 60,000 fossils from the Cambrian Period, 582–488 million years ago.

Fossils and time

463 Fossils are studied by many kinds of scientists. Palaeontologists are general experts on fossils and prehistoric life. Palaeozoologists specialize in prehistoric creatures, and palaeobotanists in prehistoric plants. Geologists study rocks, soil and other substances that make up the Earth. All of these sciences allow us to work out the immense prehistory of the Earth.

464 Earth's existence is divided into enormous lengths of time called eons, which are split into eras, then periods, epochs and finally, stages. Each of these time divisions is marked by changes in the rocks formed at the time – and if the rocks are sedimentary, by the fossils they contain. The whole time span, from the formation of the Earth 4600 million years ago to today, is known as the geological time scale.

▼ Starting with the Cambrian Period (far right), this timeline shows 11 major time periods in Earth's history. It gives examples of some of the fossil animals and plants that have been found for each period. 'MYA' stands for 'millions of years ago'.

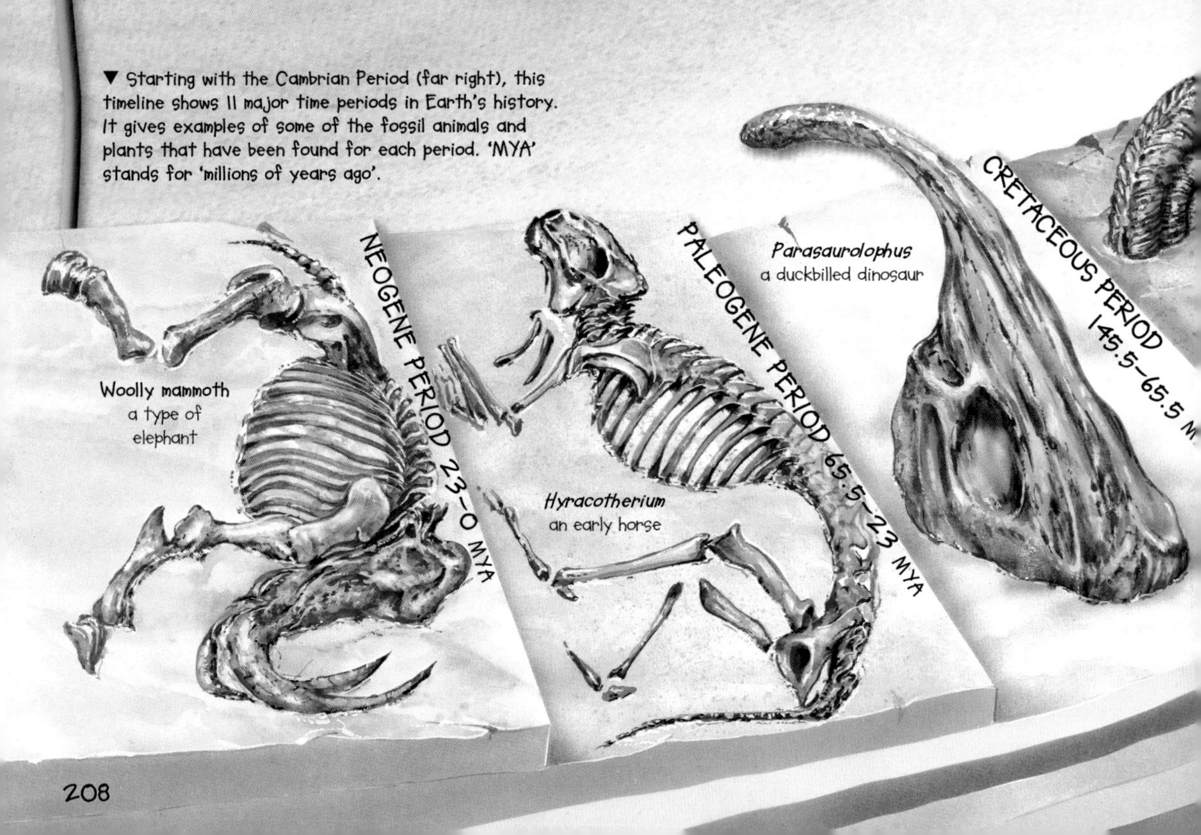

465 An example of a geological time division is the Cretaceous Period, from 145.5 to 65.5 million years ago. It is named after creta or *kreta*, a Latin word for chalk. Due to temperature, rainfall and other climate conditions, layers of chalk rocks formed. They contained fossils such as certain kinds of shellfish, the winged reptiles known as pterosaurs and many kinds of dinosaurs.

MAKE CHALK FOSSILS

You will need:
chalk sticks metal teaspoon

Chalk often contains fossil shellfish. Find pictures of long, thin examples, such as razorshells, mussels and belemnites. Use the spoon to scrape and carve the chalk sticks into shapes to make your own 'fossil' museum.

Working out dates

466 'Dating' a fossil means finding out how old it is. Usually, rocks found deeper in the ground are older than the rock layers above them, so any fossils they contain are also older. Sedimentary rock layers and their fossils have been compared to build up a picture of which fossilized plants and animals lived when.

I DON'T BELIEVE IT!

Thousands of kinds of ammonites lived from 400–65 million years ago, and some were more than 3 metres across!

▼ Different rock layers can be clearly seen in the Grand Canyon, USA. The layers have been revealed by the Colorado River as it winds its way through the canyon.

467 If a new fossil is found, it can be compared with this overall pattern to get an idea of its age. This is known as relative dating – finding the date of a fossil relative to other fossils of known ages.

▲ Some types of chalk rocks are almost entirely made of the fossils of small sea creatures.

468 Certain types of plants and animals were very common, survived for millions of years and left plenty of fossil remains. This makes them extremely useful for relative dating. They are known as marker, index, indicator, guide or zone fossils.

469 Most index fossils come from the sea, where preservation is more likely than on land. They include multi-legged trilobites, curly-shelled ammonites, ball-shaped echinoids (sea urchins) and net-like graptolites. On land, tough pollen grains and spores from plants are useful index fossils.

▶ Trilobites make good index fossils. Different kinds appeared and then died out between 530 million and about 250 million years ago.

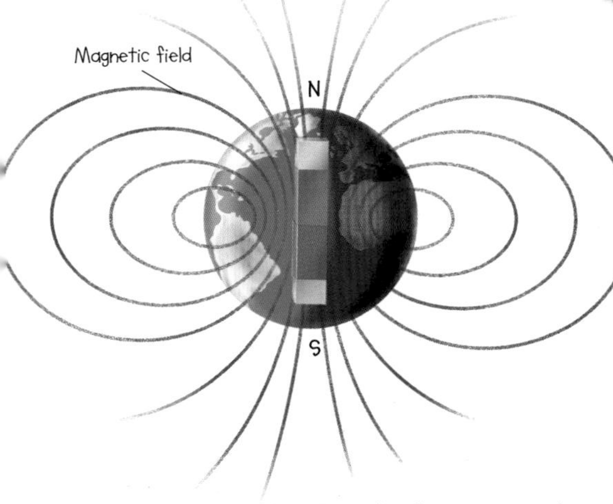

▲ Earth's magnetism has changed and even reversed over millions of years, helping to date fossils.

470 Earth's natural magnetic field changed many times through prehistory. When some kinds of igneous rocks formed by cooling, the magnetism was 'frozen' into them, known as palaeomagnetism. It can be dated by comparison with the whole pattern of magnetic changes through Earth's history.

How many years ago?

471 Relative dating, by comparing fossils with each other, shows if one fossil is older or younger than another. But how do we know the actual age of fossils in millions of years, known as absolute dating?

I DON'T BELIEVE IT!

The oldest fossils are believed to be tiny blob-like microbes similar to today's bacteria and blue-green algae (cyanobacteria). They are more than 3400 million years old.

472 The main kind of absolute dating is based on naturally occurring substances that give off tiny amounts of rays and particles, known as radioactivity. As they give off these weak forms of energy, the substances – known as radioisotopes – change or 'decay' slightly. The amounts of different radioisotopes in a fossil can be measured to show how long ago it formed. This is known as radiometric dating.

473 Several kinds of substances are used for radiometric dating. Each decays at a set rate, some slower than others. Very slow ones are useful for the oldest fossils, and the fastest ones for young fossils.

◀ The rocks of the Canadian Shield, a huge area of land in eastern and central Canada, have been dated to more than 2500 million years ago.

474 Radiocarbon dating is based on the change or decay of one form of carbon known as C14. It happens relatively fast and is useful for a time span up to 60,000 years ago. This helps with dating young fossils and with items such as deep-frozen mammoths.

475 In potassium-argon dating, the element potassium changes into argon very slowly, over billions of years. It's useful for rock layers formed just above or below fossils from billions of years ago to about 100,000 years ago. Rubidium-strontium and uranium-lead dating can reveal the age of even older rocks, almost back to when Earth began.

▼ Radiocarbon dating.

1. Woolly mammoth eats plants containing C14

2. Mammoth dies, no more C14 is taken in

3. Half of C14 decays every 5730 years

▼ Geologists measure tiny amounts of radioactivity in rocks and fossils using equipment such as Geiger counters.

Fossil-hunting takes off

476 From the early 19th century, fossil-hunting became more popular. Towns and cities as well as rich individuals began to establish museums and collections of the 'wonders of nature' with displays of stuffed animals, pinned insects, pressed flowers – and lots of fossils.

FOSSIL MATCH

Match the scientific names of these fossils with the places they were found.

A. Argentinosaurus (dinosaur)
B. Toxorhynchites mexicanus (mosquito in amber)
C. Proconsul africanus (ape-monkey)

1 Mexico, Central America
2 Argentina, South America
3 Africa

Answers:
A2 B1 C3

477 People began to earn a living by finding and selling fossils. One of the first was Mary Anning (1799–1847) of Lyme Regis, southern England. For many years she collected fossils from the seashore, where waves and storms regularly cracked open boulders and cliffs to reveal new finds. Mary discovered fossil fish, ichthyosaurs, plesiosaurs, pterosaurs and many other animals.

▶ As in Mary Anning's time, fossils still appear from the rocks at Lyme Regis.

478 **In 1881, the British Museum opened its display of natural history collections in London, which showed fossils and similar wonders from around the world.** Other great cities had similar museums and sent fossil-hunters to remote places for the most spectacular finds.

▲ By the 1860s many museums had fossils on display, such as this 'sea serpent' or mosasaur.

▼ Cope and Marsh found and described about 130 new kinds of dinosaurs.

479 **Between the 1870s and 1890s, two of the leading fossil-hunters were Americans Othniel Charles Marsh and Edward Drinker Cope.** Their teams tried to outdo each other to discover the most and best fossil dinosaurs, as well as other animals and plants too.

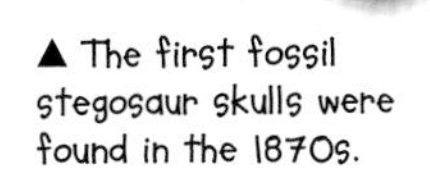

▲ The first fossil stegosaur skulls were found in the 1870s.

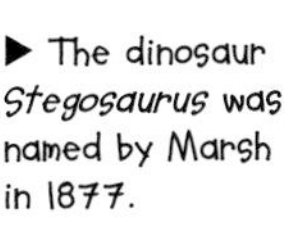

▶ The dinosaur *Stegosaurus* was named by Marsh in 1877.

480 **From the early 1900s fossil-hunting spread to Africa and then in the 1920s to Mongolia and China.** From the 1970s there were finds in South America and Australia. Today, fossil-hunters go all over the world in search of new discoveries.

Famous hot spots

481 Some places around the world have become famous for their fossils. These places are often in the news because of dinosaur remains. However, dinosaur finds are only some of the thousands of fossils being unearthed and studied.

▼ This map shows some of the most famous fossil sites around the world.

482 The Midwest 'Badlands' of North America has many famous fossil sites. At Dinosaur National Monument, on the border between Colorado and Utah, USA, the rocks date to almost 150 million years ago. Apart from dinosaur remains they also yield fossils of crocodiles, turtles, frogs, shellfish and plants.

◀ Dinosaur fossils at Dinosaur National Monument. This park opened in 1915 and receives over 350,000 visitors each year.

483 In northeast Brazil in South America there are limestone rocks about 110–90 million years old known as the Santana Formation. Detailed fossils include pterosaurs, reptiles, frogs, insects and plants. Some fossil fish were preserved with the remains of their last meals inside their bodies.

◀ This 100-million-year-old dragonfly is one of thousands from Brazil's Santana Formation rocks.

484 Some of the best European fossils come from limestone quarries around Solnhofen, southern Germany. There are dinosaurs, pterosaurs, the earliest known bird *Archaeopteryx*, fish, insects and soft-bodied jellyfish.

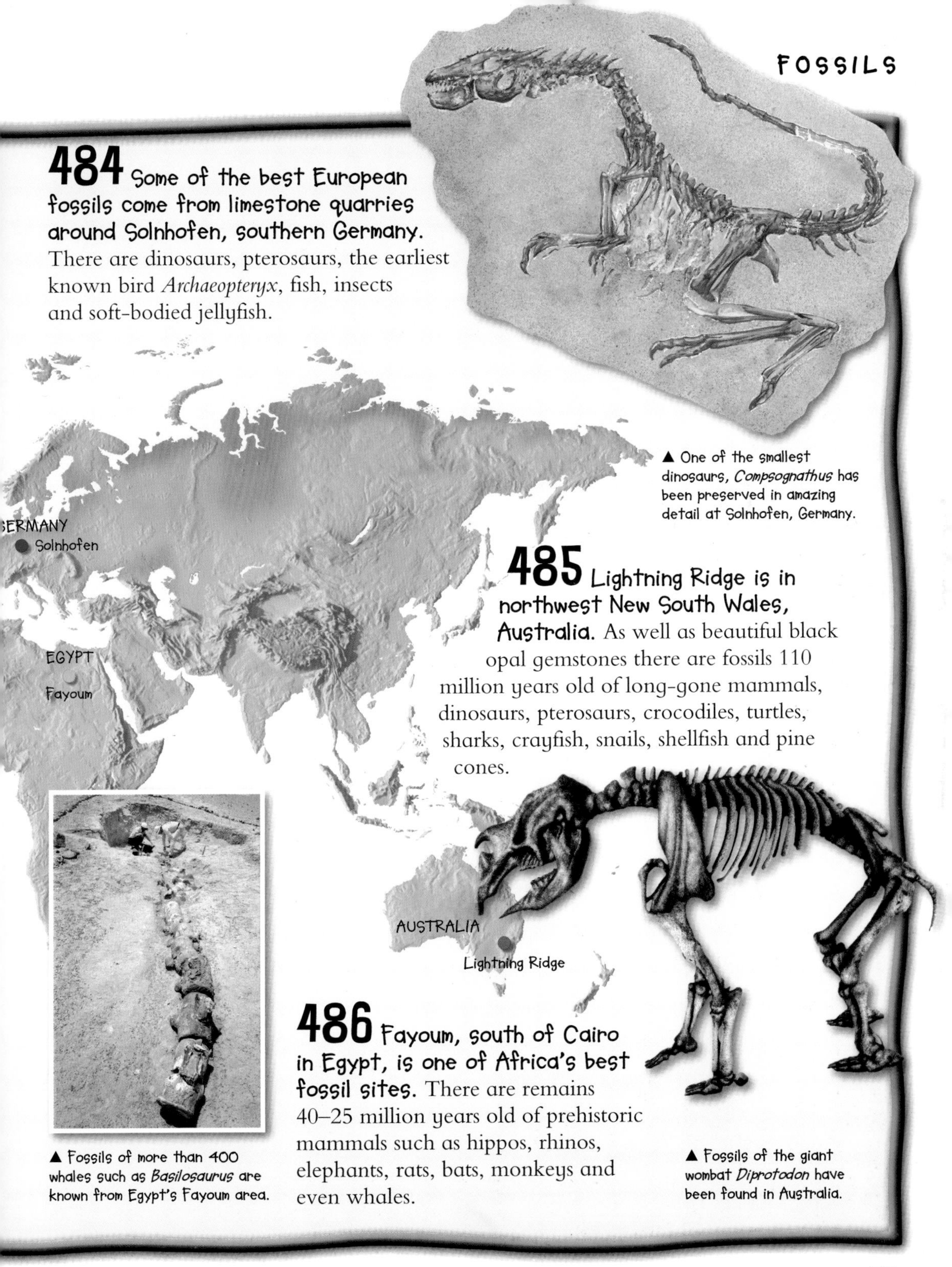

▲ One of the smallest dinosaurs, *Compsognathus* has been preserved in amazing detail at Solnhofen, Germany.

485 Lightning Ridge is in northwest New South Wales, Australia. As well as beautiful black opal gemstones there are fossils 110 million years old of long-gone mammals, dinosaurs, pterosaurs, crocodiles, turtles, sharks, crayfish, snails, shellfish and pine cones.

486 Fayoum, south of Cairo in Egypt, is one of Africa's best fossil sites. There are remains 40–25 million years old of prehistoric mammals such as hippos, rhinos, elephants, rats, bats, monkeys and even whales.

▲ Fossils of more than 400 whales such as *Basilosaurus* are known from Egypt's Fayoum area.

▲ Fossils of the giant wombat *Diprotodon* have been found in Australia.

Looking for fossils

487 Where do we find fossils? Fossil-hunters use many kinds of aids and clues to find the best sites. Geological maps show which kinds of rocks are found at or just under the surface. To contain fossils, these rocks need to be sedimentary, such as limestone.

PLAN A FOSSIL DIG

You will need:
pencil and notebook
pictures of fossil dig sites

You're in charge of a fossil-finding trip to a remote desert. Make a list of the equipment and supplies you think you'll need. Look through the pages of this book for clues. Once you have a list, draw a plan of your dig and decide who to take with you.

488 Fossil-hunters are careful to get permission to search a site. The landowner, land manager and local authorities must all agree on the search methods and the ownership of any finds. This avoids problems such as trespassing, criminal damage and 'fossil-rustling' (stealing).

▶ Palaeontologists sift through rocks and common fossils for signs of important specimens at Bromacker Quarry, Germany.

▶ Year after year sun, wind, rain and ice wear away rocks and reveal fossils at Dinosaur Provincial Park, Alberta, Canada.

489 Good places to look for fossils are where rocks are regularly broken apart and worn away by waves, wind, sun, ice and other weather. This is the process of erosion. It happens at cliffs, seashores, river banks and valleys, canyons and caves. It also happens where people dig quarries, mines, road and railway cuttings and building foundations.

490 Satellite images, aerial photographs, survey trips by plane, or even just walking around show the nature of the ground. Bare rocky areas are best, rather than areas covered with soil, plants and trees.

▶ This satellite photo of East Africa's Olduvai Gorge shows one of the world's best areas for prehistoric human fossils.

491 Fossil-hunters also follow a collector's code of guidelines. These show how to cause the least damage when digging, how to stay safe and how to restore the site afterwards. Find out more about this by logging on to the following web address: http://www.discoveringfossils.co.uk/fossil_hunting_guide.html

At the dig

492 Some people look for fossils in their spare time and if they find one it's a bonus. At an important site, scientists such as palaeontologists organize an excavation or 'dig' that can last for many months.

I DON'T BELIEVE IT!

A fossil leg bone from a huge dinosaur, being solid rock, can weigh more than one tonne!

493 The dig area is divided into squares called a grid, usually by string or strips of wood. This is used to record the positions of the finds. As the excavation continues, the workers make notes, take photographs, draw sketches and use many other recording methods.

▼ Palaeontologists dig up fossilized mammoth remains in California, USA. The valuable specimens are wrapped in layers of sacking and plaster before being moved.

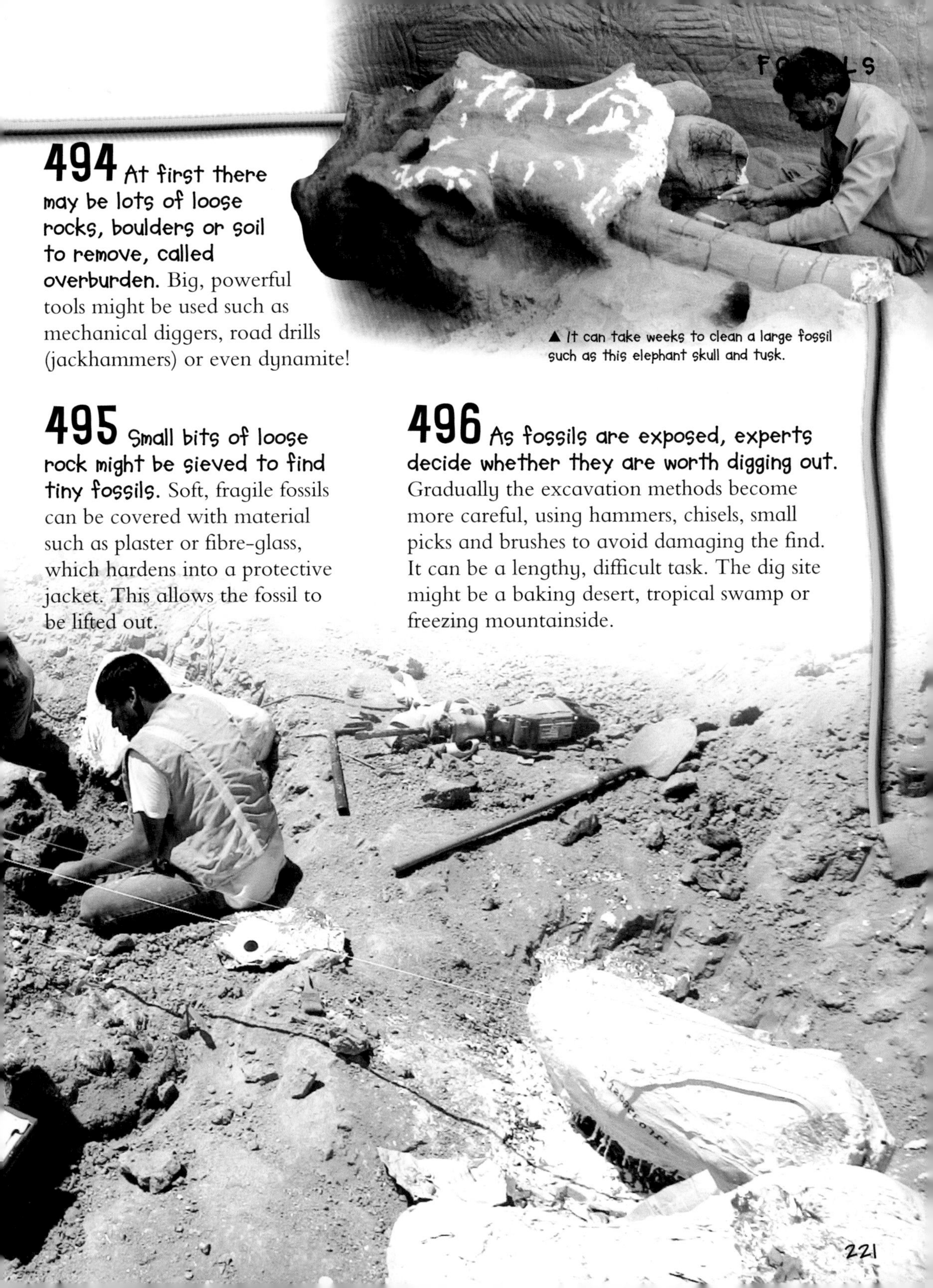

▲ It can take weeks to clean a large fossil such as this elephant skull and tusk.

494 At first there may be lots of loose rocks, boulders or soil to remove, called overburden. Big, powerful tools might be used such as mechanical diggers, road drills (jackhammers) or even dynamite!

495 Small bits of loose rock might be sieved to find tiny fossils. Soft, fragile fossils can be covered with material such as plaster or fibre-glass, which hardens into a protective jacket. This allows the fossil to be lifted out.

496 As fossils are exposed, experts decide whether they are worth digging out. Gradually the excavation methods become more careful, using hammers, chisels, small picks and brushes to avoid damaging the find. It can be a lengthy, difficult task. The dig site might be a baking desert, tropical swamp or freezing mountainside.

Cleaning up fossils

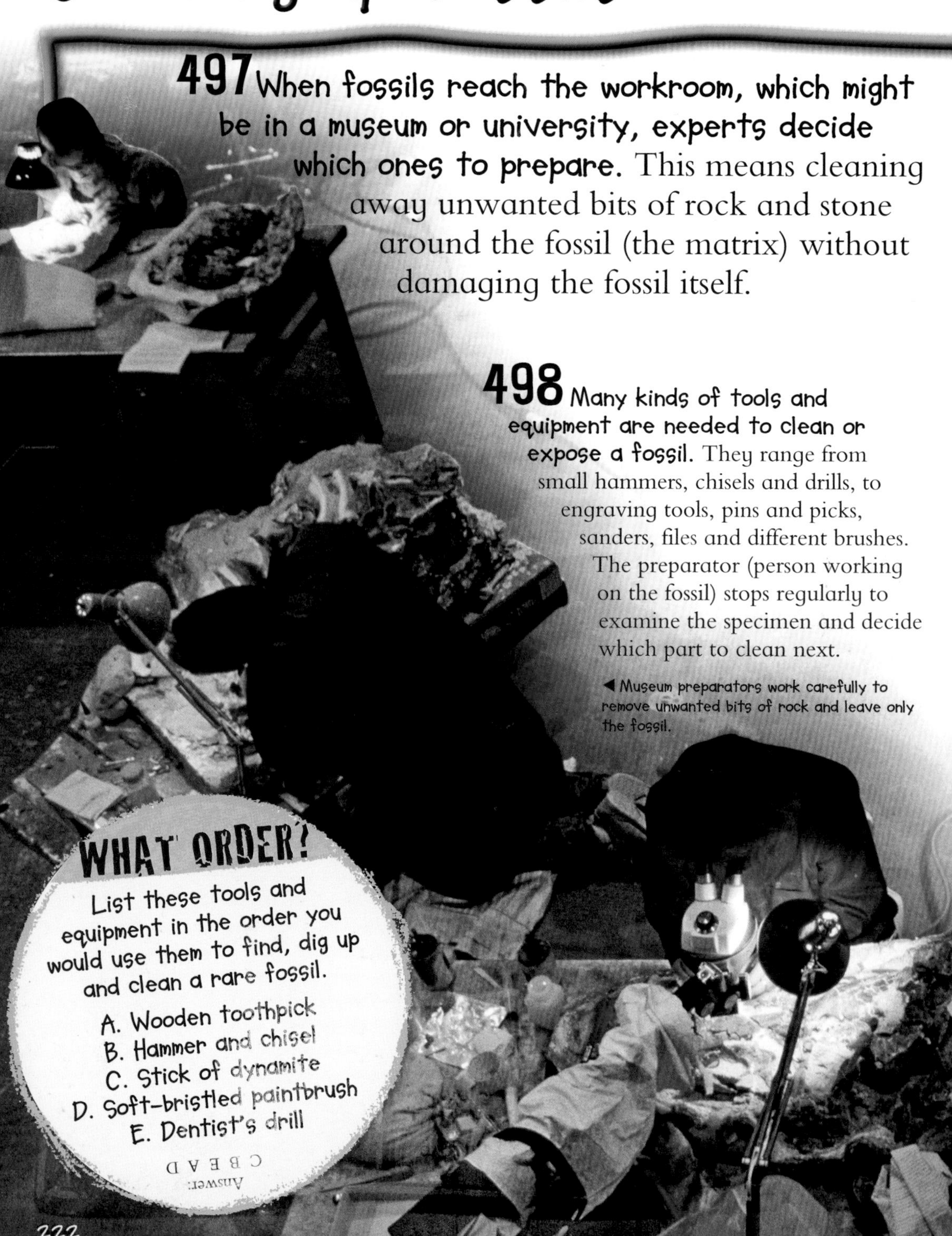

497 When fossils reach the workroom, which might be in a museum or university, experts decide which ones to prepare. This means cleaning away unwanted bits of rock and stone around the fossil (the matrix) without damaging the fossil itself.

498 Many kinds of tools and equipment are needed to clean or expose a fossil. They range from small hammers, chisels and drills, to engraving tools, pins and picks, sanders, files and different brushes. The preparator (person working on the fossil) stops regularly to examine the specimen and decide which part to clean next.

◀ Museum preparators work carefully to remove unwanted bits of rock and leave only the fossil.

WHAT ORDER?

List these tools and equipment in the order you would use them to find, dig up and clean a rare fossil.

A. Wooden toothpick
B. Hammer and chisel
C. Stick of dynamite
D. Soft-bristled paintbrush
E. Dentist's drill

Answer:
C B E A D

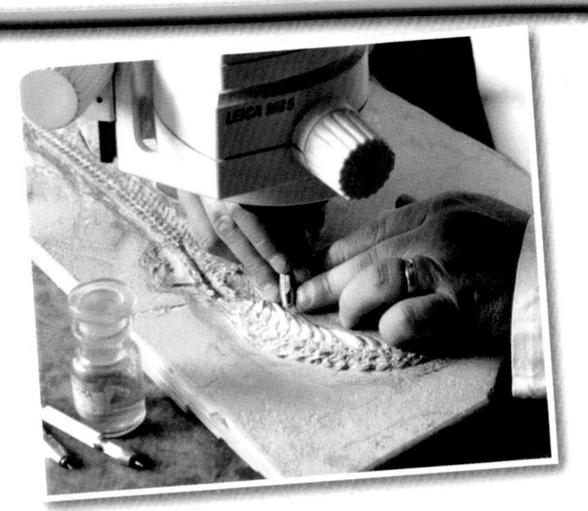

▲ The enlarged view through a stereo microscope shows lots of detail, to avoid scratching or chipping the specimen.

499 Microscopes are often used to show tiny details of a fossil during preparation. Usually this is a stereoscopic microscope with two eyepieces, like binoculars, mounted on a stand with the specimen beneath.

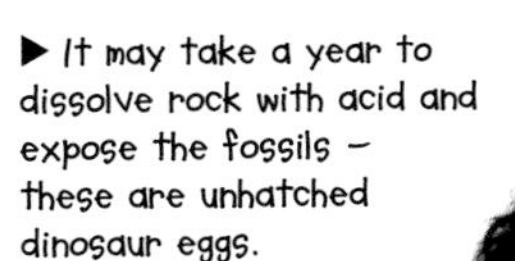

▶ It may take a year to dissolve rock with acid and expose the fossils – these are unhatched dinosaur eggs.

500 When the fossil is one type of rock and the matrix is another, preparators may use chemicals to expose the fossil. Different acids are tested on small parts of the matrix and fossil, to see if they dissolve the former but not the latter.

501 Very few animals or plants die neatly in one piece and are preserved whole. So it's incredibly rare to find a whole fossilized plant or animal with all the parts positioned as they were in life. Most fossils are bits and pieces that are crushed and distorted. Putting them back together is very difficult!

On display

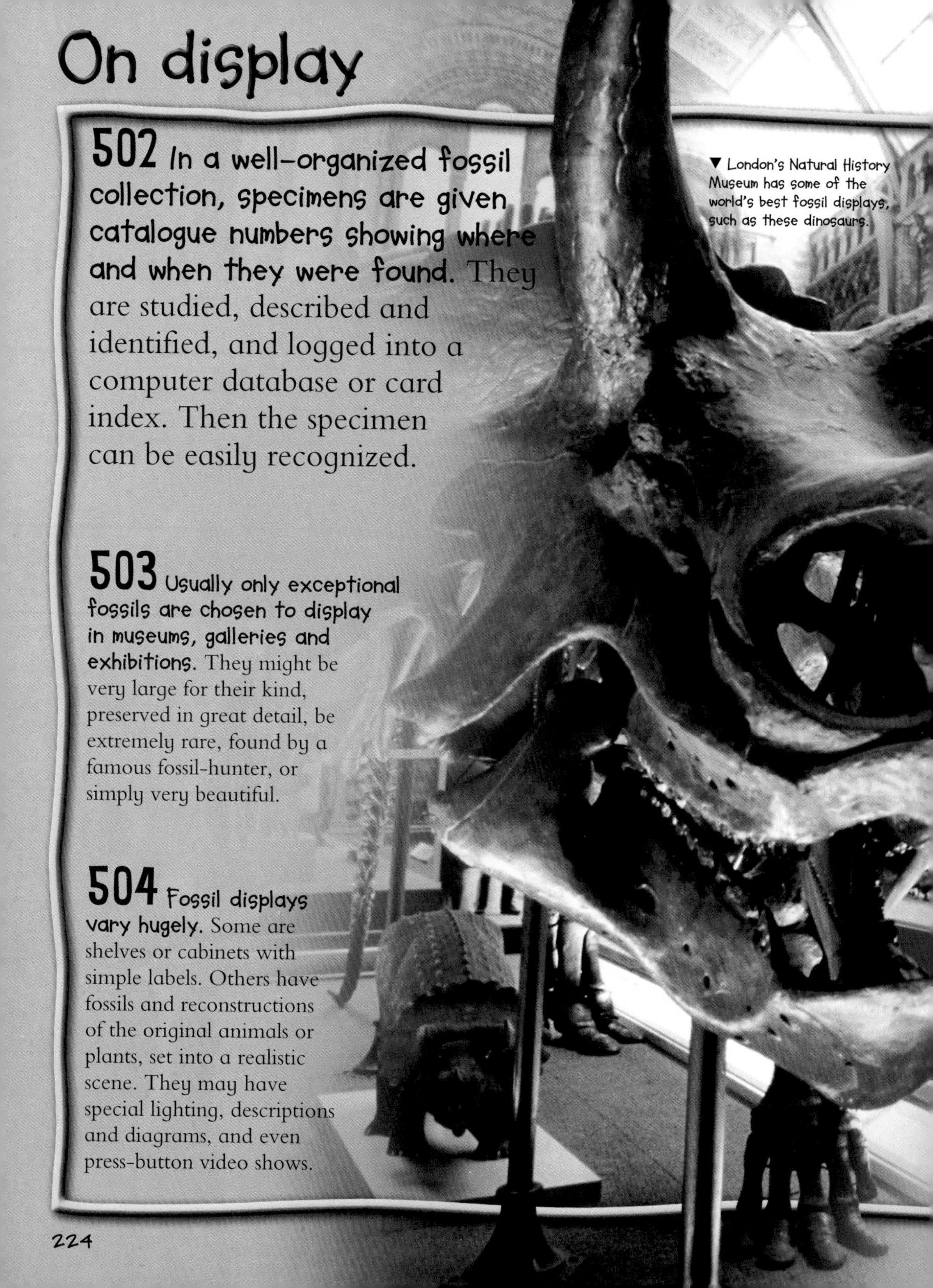

▼ London's Natural History Museum has some of the world's best fossil displays, such as these dinosaurs.

502 In a well-organized fossil collection, specimens are given catalogue numbers showing where and when they were found. They are studied, described and identified, and logged into a computer database or card index. Then the specimen can be easily recognized.

503 Usually only exceptional fossils are chosen to display in museums, galleries and exhibitions. They might be very large for their kind, preserved in great detail, be extremely rare, found by a famous fossil-hunter, or simply very beautiful.

504 Fossil displays vary hugely. Some are shelves or cabinets with simple labels. Others have fossils and reconstructions of the original animals or plants, set into a realistic scene. They may have special lighting, descriptions and diagrams, and even press-button video shows.

I DON'T BELIEVE IT!

In 2002, experts re-examined the fossil jaws of a tiny creature called *Rhyniognatha* found in 1919. They realized it was probably the earliest known insect, and that it was almost 400 million years old.

505 **Some fossils are so rare, delicate or valuable that they are not displayed – copies are.** Copies or replicas of very rare fossils might be sent to other museums so more people can study them.

506 **Copies are used for big creatures such as dinosaurs, whales and mammoths.** The original fossils are solid rock and can weigh many tonnes. Lightweight copies are easier and safer to put on a frame or hang by wires, to build up the animal in a lifelike position.

Fossils come alive!

507 One of the most exciting parts of fossil study is to reconstruct (rebuild) the original plant or animal. This needs a detailed knowledge of anatomy, or body structure. For example, fossils of prehistoric birds are compared to the same body parts of similar birds alive today. This is called comparative anatomy.

508 Tiny marks or 'scars' on fossil bones show where the animal's muscles attached in real life. These help to reveal muscle shapes and arrangements so experts can gradually put the flesh on the (fossil) bones.

Fossil bones
Faint scars on fossil bones can help scientists work out how and where muscles were attached

▲ This reconstruction of an ankylosaur, an armoured dinosaur, is being done head-first. The tail is still bare fossils of the bones.

509 We can see how a living creature walks, runs and jumps using the joints between its bones. If fossil bones have their joints preserved, their detailed shapes and designs show the range of motion and how the animal moved.

MULTI-COLOURED BIRD

You will need:
pictures of *Archaeopteryx* colour pens
tracing paper white paper

No one knows what colour the first bird *Archaeopteryx* was. Look at pictures of it in books and on web sites. See how its feather colours and patterns differ. Trace an outline of *Archaeopteryx* from a book and colour it to your own amazing design.

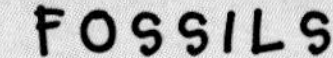

510 Gradually, soft parts such as the guts of an animal or the petals of a flower, can be guessed and added to the reconstruction. Again, experts use information from fossil relatives and living cousins.

511 The outward appearance of an animal might be known from fossils such as an outer shell, scaly skin, feathers or fur. However, fossils are not original living parts – they have changed to rock. So the colour of fossil skin is the colour of the type of rock, not the animal. Experts guess at colours and patterns for their reconstructions.

Trading, stealing, faking

512 Fossils are big business. Thousands of people work at digs, in workrooms and in museums, exhibitions and galleries. A find such as a new dinosaur can hit the news headlines and make the discoverer famous – and rich!

513 The biggest, most complete fossil *Tyrannosaurus rex* was found in 1990 near Faith, Dakota, by Sue Hendrickson. The dinosaur was nicknamed 'Sue' and there was a long legal dispute about who owned it. Finally it was sold to the Field Museum of Chicago for more than seven million dollars!

◀ Street traders offer fossils for sale in North Africa. There is no guarantee the fossils came from the local area.

I DON'T BELIEVE IT!

In 2008, a 7-metre-long fossil *Triceratops* dinosaur went on sale for £400,000 along with a fossil skull of a sabre-tooth cat for £35,000.

▶ Chinese palaeontologist Dong Zhiming with some smuggled dinosaur eggs. Every year police, customs and security staff uncover illegal collections such as this.

514 Real fossils, replicas and models are sold around the world by museums, shops, mail-order catalogues and on the Internet. Buyers range from leading museums to individuals who like the idea of a home fossil collection without the trouble of digging them up.

▼ Rare or unusual fossils, such as this ammonite shell showing detailed internal structure, can fetch huge sums of money at auction.

515 Stealing and faking fossils has been going on for centuries. In 1999 scientists announced a fossil creature called *Archaeoraptor* that seemed to be part-bird and part-dinosaur. *Archaeoraptor* showed how small meat-eating dinosaurs evolved into birds. However, further study revealed that the specimen was indeed part-dinosaur and part-bird, because it was a fake with separate fossils cleverly glued together.

Famous fossils

516 Many fossils and prehistoric sites around the world are massive attractions, visited by millions of people. The Petrified Forest National Park in Arizona, USA has hundreds of huge fossilized trees and smaller specimens of animals such as dinosaurs, dating from about 225 million years ago. It receives more than half a million visitors yearly.

▲ The coelacanth is known as a 'living fossil', meaning it is very similar to its long-extinct relatives.

517 The coelacanth fish was known only from fossils and thought to have been extinct for more than 60 million years. In 1938 a living coelacanth was caught off southeast Africa and more have been discovered since. Living things that are very similar to their prehistoric relatives are known as 'living fossils'.

▶ Thousands of fossil tree trunks and branches litter the ground at Arizona's Petrified Forest National Park.

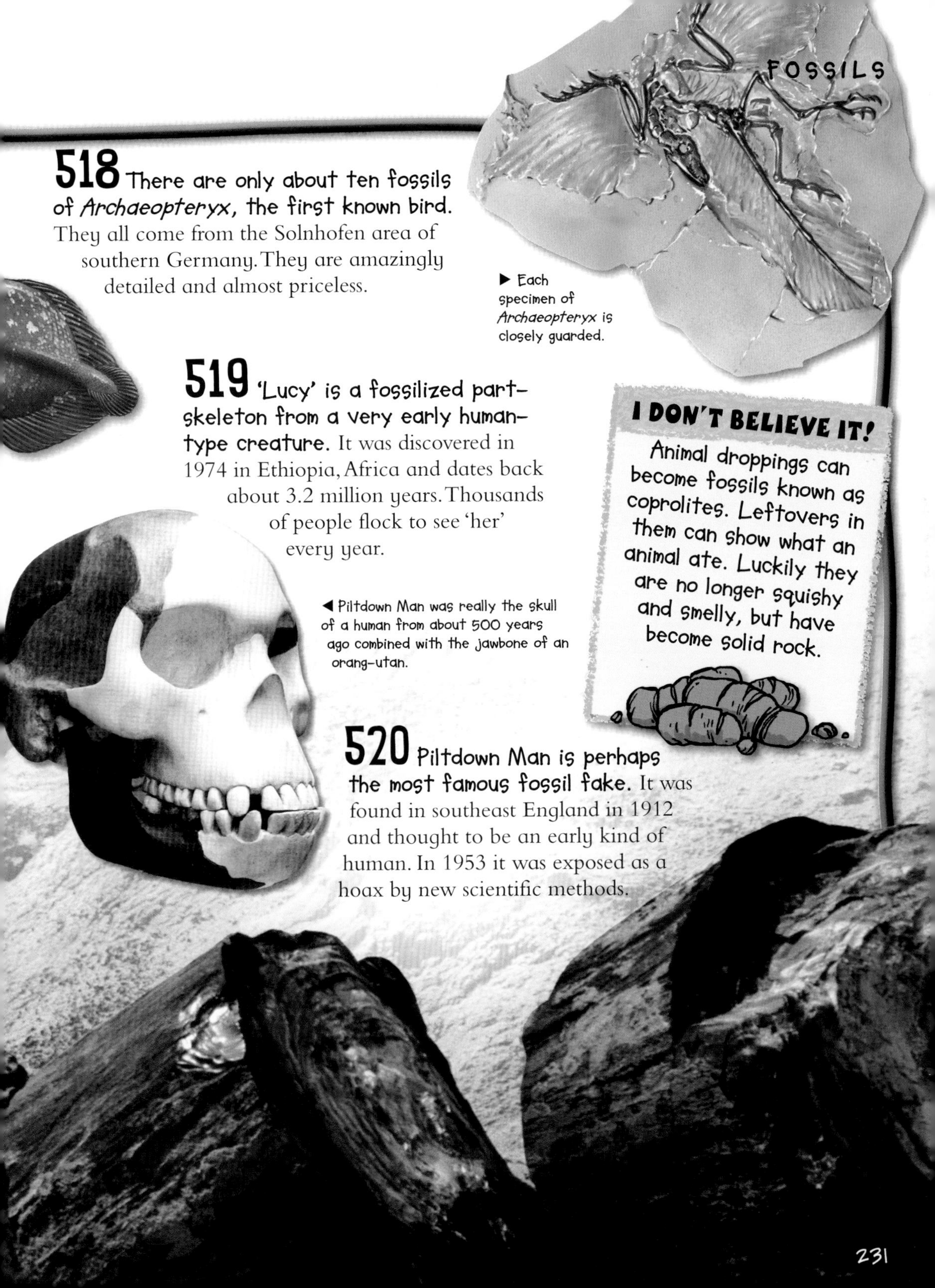

518 There are only about ten fossils of *Archaeopteryx*, the first known bird. They all come from the Solnhofen area of southern Germany. They are amazingly detailed and almost priceless.

▶ Each specimen of *Archaeopteryx* is closely guarded.

519 'Lucy' is a fossilized part-skeleton from a very early human-type creature. It was discovered in 1974 in Ethiopia, Africa and dates back about 3.2 million years. Thousands of people flock to see 'her' every year.

◀ Piltdown Man was really the skull of a human from about 500 years ago combined with the jawbone of an orang-utan.

I DON'T BELIEVE IT!

Animal droppings can become fossils known as coprolites. Leftovers in them can show what an animal ate. Luckily they are no longer squishy and smelly, but have become solid rock.

520 Piltdown Man is perhaps the most famous fossil fake. It was found in southeast England in 1912 and thought to be an early kind of human. In 1953 it was exposed as a hoax by new scientific methods.

Looking to the future

521 As fossil-hunting goes on around the world, scientific methods and equipment become more powerful every year. Ground-penetrating radar, X-rays and CT (computerized tomography) scanners can 'see' fossils inside solid rock.

▲ A CT scanner examines the fossil skull of an ancient type of otter.

522 As we improve ways to study fossils, old specimens are looked at again to see new details. The dinosaur *Oviraptor* or 'egg thief' was named because one of its fossils suggested it was stealing the eggs of another dinosaur. Then X-rays of similar eggs showed baby *Oviraptor*s inside. The 'egg thief' fossil was probably looking after its own eggs.

◄ This *Oviraptor* may have died shielding its eggs from a predator, 75 million years ago.

523 **Some amazing fossils of the 1990s–2000s are from Liaoning Province in northeast China.** Dated to 130 million years ago, they show details of creatures and plants, including dinosaurs with feathers and a cat-sized mammal that preyed on baby dinosaurs.

▲ Fossils of the tiny feathered dinosaur *Microraptor* have been found in China.

524 **New fossils provide more evidence for evolution, such as how fish changed gradually into land animals.** *Panderichthys* was a fish-like creature from 380 million years ago. It had features such as finger-like bones developing in its fins.

525 **Important fossil discoveries cause news and excitement around the world.** They affect our ideas about prehistoric life, how Earth has changed through time, evolution and extinction. They can also help to fill in the details of where we came from.

NAME GAME

Match these nicknames of fossils with their scientific names.
A. 'Lucy' B. 'Stan' C. 'Jaws' D. 'Spike'

1. Triceratops (dinosaur)
2. Megalodon (giant shark)
3. Australopithecus afarensis (early human)
4. Tyrannosaurus (dinosaur)

Answers:
A3 B4 C2 D1

▲ *Panderichthys* was about one metre long. Its fossils come from Latvia in northeastern Europe.

POLAR LANDS

526 The polar regions are found at the top and bottom of the Earth and they are the coldest, windiest places in the world. Here, the land and sea stay frozen for most of the year, and snow and ice stretch as far as the eye can see. Only a few creatures are tough enough to survive these frozen conditions.

▼ Ice-breakers like the *Apu* have enough power to smash through metre-thick ice in polar seas. They clear the way for following ships, which must keep up because the ice re-freezes in a few hours.

The ends of the Earth

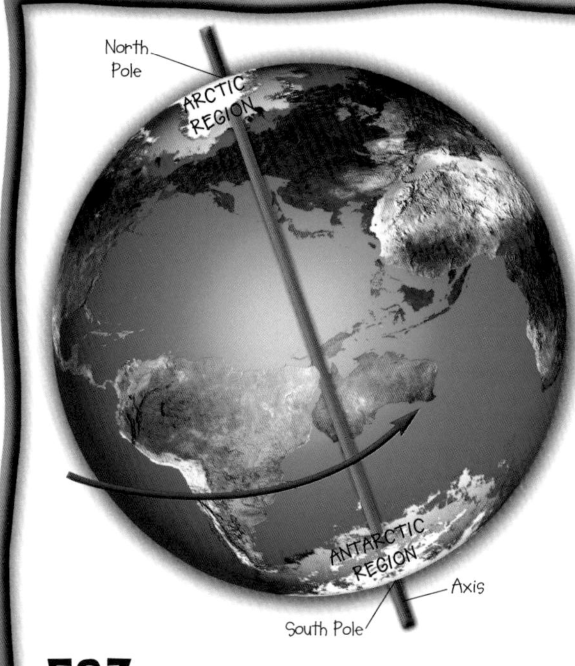

◀ The Earth spins around an imaginary line called the axis, which passes through the Geographic North and South Poles.

527 The North and South Poles are at the top and bottom of the Earth. Every 24 hours, Earth turns once around its axis. The axis is an invisible line that runs through the middle (core) of the Earth, from Pole to Pole.

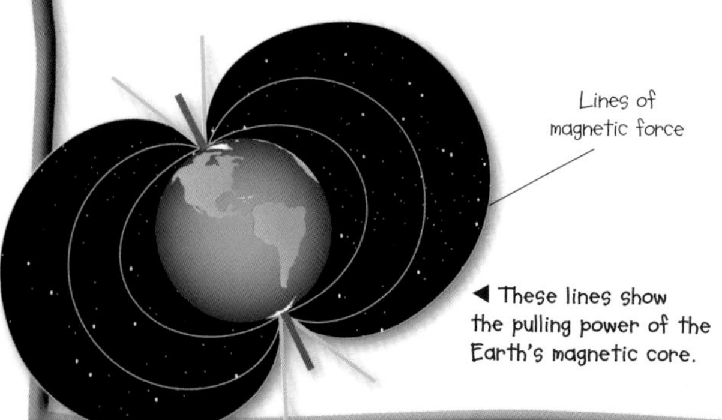

◀ These lines show the pulling power of the Earth's magnetic core.

528 The Earth really has four poles! There are the Geographic North and South Poles, which are defined by the position of the Earth's axis, but there are also the Magnetic North and South Poles. The Magnetic Poles are some distance from the Geographic Poles.

529 The Earth is like a giant magnet. Deep inside the Earth are layers of hot, liquid metals, especially iron. As the Earth turns, the iron moves, creating a magnetic force. The Magnetic Poles are the two places where this force is strongest.

Antarctic Peninsula

530 Because of the moving liquid metals inside the Earth, the magnetic poles wander, and may move a few metres every year. Throughout history, the poles have flipped. This is known as magnetic reversal – the Magnetic North Pole becomes the Magnetic South Pole, and the Magnetic South Pole becomes the Magnetic North Pole. The last flip was about 780,000 years ago.

▶ The North Pole is in the middle of the Arctic Ocean, which is covered by a floating ice sheet.

ARCTIC OCEAN
(ice sheet)

Geographic North Pole

GREENLAND

531 The northern polar region is called the Arctic. The word Arctic comes from the ancient Greek word *arktos*, meaning 'bear'. This refers to the star pattern (constellation) called the Little Bear, or *Ursa Minor*. It contains a star near the North Pole, known as the Pole Star.

Antarctica is the coldest place on Earth. At Vostok Base, the coldest-ever temperature was –89°C in 1983. That's more than four times colder than inside a freezer!

◀ ▼ The South Pole is towards one side of the vast, ice-covered land mass of Antarctica. In early April penguins gather at traditonal breeding sites on the sea ice.

Geographic South Pole

ANTARCTICA

SOUTHERN OCEAN

532 The southern polar region is called the Antarctic. Ant or anti means 'against' or 'opposite to'. So the Antarctic is simply the region opposite the Arctic, on the other side of the Earth.

Extreme seasons

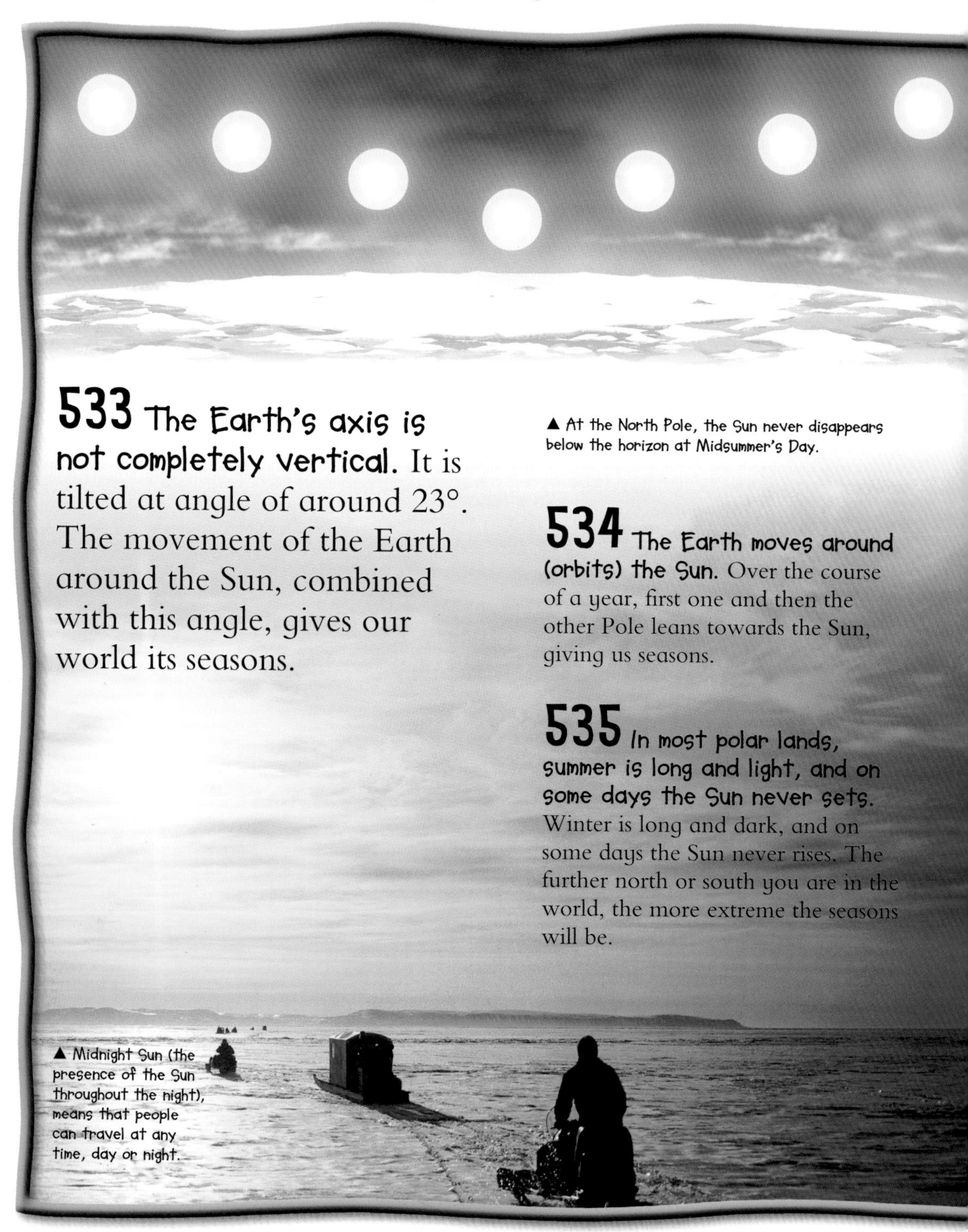

▲ At the North Pole, the Sun never disappears below the horizon at Midsummer's Day.

533 The Earth's axis is not completely vertical. It is tilted at angle of around 23°. The movement of the Earth around the Sun, combined with this angle, gives our world its seasons.

534 The Earth moves around (orbits) the Sun. Over the course of a year, first one and then the other Pole leans towards the Sun, giving us seasons.

535 In most polar lands, summer is long and light, and on some days the Sun never sets. Winter is long and dark, and on some days the Sun never rises. The further north or south you are in the world, the more extreme the seasons will be.

▲ Midnight Sun (the presence of the Sun throughout the night), means that people can travel at any time, day or night.

536 When the North Pole is facing away from the Sun, the area around it is in perpetual darkness. The Sun does not rise for at least one night in midwinter. This area is known as the Arctic Circle. The Antarctic Circle is a similar area around the South Pole. When it is midwinter in the Arctic it is midsummer in Antarctica, so at the Antarctic Circle, the Sun does not set for at least one day.

NO SUNSET

You will need:
an apple a desk lamp

Imagine your apple is the Earth, and the lamp is the Sun. The stem of the apple represents the North Pole. Hold the apple in front of the lamp and angle the stem towards the light. Spin the apple around its core. Despite the spinning, the area around the North Pole has light all the time, while the other side stays in darkness. This illustrates midsummer at the Arctic Circle.

537 Sometimes at night, the polar skies are lit by shimmering, waving curtains of multi-coloured lights. These are called the *Aurora Borealis* or Northern Lights in the Arctic. Around Antarctica they are called the *Aurora Australis* or Southern Lights.

538 The lights are made by tiny particles given off by the Sun, known as the solar wind. These get trapped by the Earth's magnetism and start to glow. This happens very high in the sky, above 100 kilometres, which is three times higher than a passenger jet plane can travel.

▼ Campers in the forests of the far north see the Northern Lights as a wavy glow. Tonight it is yellow-green. Tomorrow it may be blue or red!

Land around a frozen sea

539 The Arctic is a mostly frozen area of the Arctic Ocean that is surrounded by land. The Arctic Ocean is the smallest, shallowest ocean, with an area of about 14 million square kilometres, and an average depth of 1000 metres. During winter, the ice over the ocean becomes up to 3 metres thick. In summer it shrinks, but it never disappears.

540 The floating ice layer over the Arctic Ocean cracks and melts around the edges to form dangerous pack ice (icebergs) and icefields. Around the shores of the Arctic Ocean, massive lumps of ice break from ice sheets and form glaciers (frozen rivers), which float out into the ocean as icebergs.

541 Around the Arctic Ocean it is too cold and windy for any trees to grow. The main plants are tussock grass, small bushes, low-growing mosses and lichens. These treeless zones are known as tundra. The Arctic hares that live here have very short ears, to stop them losing body heat.

▼ In spring, enormous herds of caribou (reindeer) migrate north to feed on the plants of the tundra.

542 Around the tundra, millions of conifers form huge areas known as boreal forests, or taiga. These are some of Earth's last unexplored wildernesses. Conifer trees' needle-like leaves and downward-sloping branches mean that snow slides off easily. If too much snow gathered, the branches would become heavy and break.

543 The deer known as caribou in North America are called reindeer in northern Europe and Asia. They wander through the forests in winter, then trek out to tundra areas for the summer, in long journeys known as migrations. Packs of wolves follow them and pick off the old, young, sick and dying.

544 In some Arctic regions, the soil just below the surface never thaws, even in summer. These areas are called permafrost. The layer of ice does not let surface water drain through down into the soil below. So permafrost areas are usually boggy and swampy.

FLOATING ICEBERG

Icebergs are much bigger than they look. Make a big lump of ice by putting a plastic bowl of water into a freezer. Float this lump in a sink filled with water. How much is above the surface? In an iceberg it is usually about one-eighth of the total volume above, leaving seven-eighths below.

▶ When there is less ice in summer, brown bears wander from the forests towards the Arctic Ocean shores.

Sea around a frozen land

545 Antarctica is different to the Arctic in many ways. The Arctic is a sea surrounded by land, while the Antarctic is land surrounded by sea. Antarctica is a huge landmass about 14 million square kilometres in area, mostly covered by ice. It has mountains, valleys, and old volcanoes, but nearly all of these are hidden under the ice.

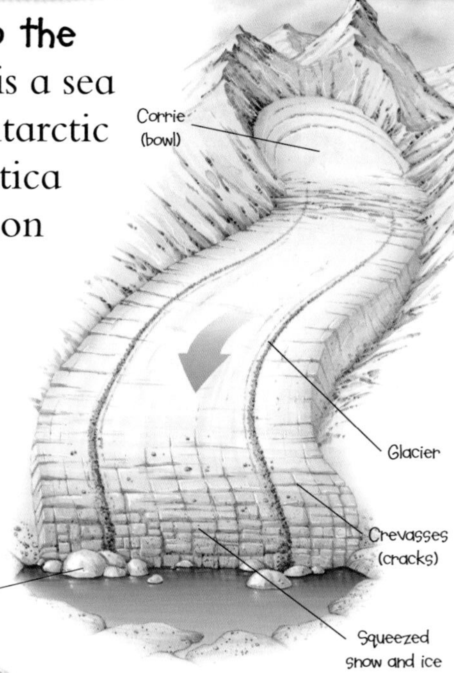

▶ Snow and ice slide slowly from the polar ice caps as long glaciers, down to the sea.

546 Around Antarctica is the Southern Ocean, also called the Antarctic or Southern Polar Ocean. It is larger and deeper than the Arctic Ocean, with an area of around 20 million square kilometres and an average depth of 4500 metres. It merges into southern parts of the Atlantic, Indian and Pacific Oceans.

◀ Massive chunks split off the ice cap into the sea, and float away as they melt.

547 During the long, dark winter, the Antarctic ice sheet spreads into the surrounding ocean. It forms layers known as ice shelves, which float on the surface. As summer arrives, the shelves shrink back again.

548 Huge ice blocks break off the ice shelves to form massive icebergs. This ice was originally snow, so it is made of fresh water. It differs from the sea ice that forms in the middle of the Arctic Ocean.

549 Each summer, a small area of Antarctica becomes ice-free. This is mainly along the Antarctic Peninsula towards South America. The land is mostly rock and thin soil, where only a few small plants and animals can survive.

I DON'T BELIEVE IT!

Antarctica's ice cap is an average of 1600 metres deep. In places the ice goes down 3350 metres before reaching the rocky surface of the continent. Here there are streams, rivers and lakes, all far below the ice surface.

▶ Most of an iceberg is hidden below the sea's surface, and sometimes scrapes along the sea bed.

Animals of Arctic lands

550 Many kinds of animals live on the lands of the far north. Most of them have thick fur or feathers to keep out the cold and wind in winter. In spring, they shed (moult) their winter fur or feathers, and grow a thinner summer coat.

◀ Ptarmigan change their feathers for camouflage, from white in winter to brownish in summer.

551 Snowy owls make nests on the tundra. They lay their eggs in shallow hollows in the ground. The female looks after her chicks while the male finds food.

▶ Snowy owl chicks feed on small animals such as mice, voles, lemmings and young birds.

552 The ptarmigan gets new feathers for winter. In preparation for the colder months, the ptarmigan grows thick, white feathers. These help it to merge into the natural background, which is known as camouflage. Its winter feathers are also warmer than its brown summer feathers.

WHITE ON WHITE

How do snowy owls 'hide' out in the open? Make a snowy owl by cutting out an owl face shape and feathers from white paper. Draw the eyes and beak. Hold the owl in front of surfaces of different colours. See how it stands out more against dark colours and less against pale colours.

◀ The Arctic ground squirrel hibernates for up to seven months every year. When it emerges from its burrow it feeds mostly on a variety of plants, seeds and berries.

553 **Smaller animals of the far north include the Arctic hare, snowshoe hare, various kinds of voles, Siberian and Norway lemmings, and Arctic ground squirrels.** Some of them live under the snow in winter, which is warmer than out in the freezing winds above.

554 **The moose of North America is known as the elk in Europe.** It eats all kinds of plant foods, from soft waterweeds in summer to twigs and bark in winter. Some move south in autumn to the shelter of the forests for the cold winter. Only the males have antlers.

555 **In North America, musk oxen live out on the tundra.** They have very long, thick fur, with some hairs reaching almost one metre in length. Herds of musk oxen are hunted by arctic wolves. If the adult musk oxen sense danger, they form a defensive circle around their young to protect them.

▶ The moose, or elk, is the biggest deer. A large male can be 2 metres in height.

Realm of bears and wolves

▲ Arctic foxes often follow polar bears, to feed on the leftover bits of their kill.

556 The biggest land hunter in the Arctic, and in the world, is the polar bear. However, it often hunts in water and on ice, too! A big male polar bear can measure 3 metres in length and weigh over half a tonne.

557 The polar bear's favourite food is seals. Camouflaged against the snow, polar bears hunt by creeping up on their prey, then pouncing. They also wait by seals' breathing holes for one to appear above the water. Then the bear bites the seal or hooks it out of the water with its huge claws.

What is a rainforest?

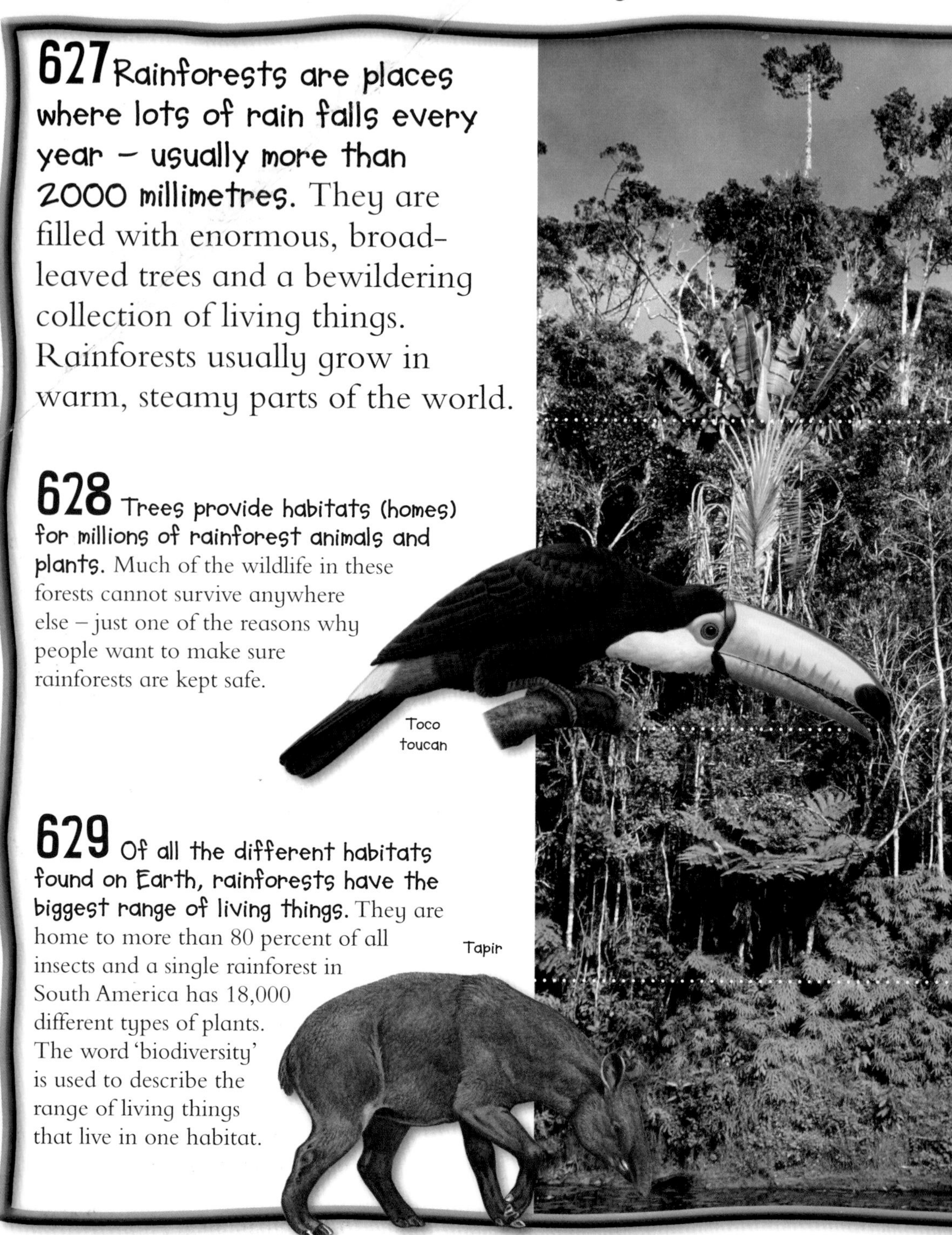

627 Rainforests are places where lots of rain falls every year – usually more than 2000 millimetres. They are filled with enormous, broad-leaved trees and a bewildering collection of living things. Rainforests usually grow in warm, steamy parts of the world.

628 Trees provide habitats (homes) for millions of rainforest animals and plants. Much of the wildlife in these forests cannot survive anywhere else – just one of the reasons why people want to make sure rainforests are kept safe.

629 Of all the different habitats found on Earth, rainforests have the biggest range of living things. They are home to more than 80 percent of all insects and a single rainforest in South America has 18,000 different types of plants. The word 'biodiversity' is used to describe the range of living things that live in one habitat.

Whales of the far north

567 **The beluga is also called the white whale.** It makes a variety of sounds such as whistles, squeals, twitters and chirps. These can be heard even above the surface. Old-time sailors nicknamed it the 'sea canary'. Both the beluga and narwhal are 4 to 6 metres in length and weigh about one tonne. They eat prey such as fish, squid and shellfish.

▲ The beluga whale has very bendy lips, and purses them as though kissing, to suck in its food.

568 **The beluga and narwhal migrate within the Arctic, from the southern areas of the Arctic Ocean to the even icier waters further north.** They follow the edge of the ice sheet as it shrinks each spring, then grows back again each autumn.

566 **The cold seas of the Arctic are visited in summer by many kinds of whales, including the biggest of all, the blue whale.** However, there are some whales that stay in the Arctic all year round, such as the beluga and narwhal.

I DON'T BELIEVE IT!

The massive bowhead whale has the largest head and mouth of any animal. Its head is almost one-third of its 18 metre-long-body. The brush-like baleen strips in its huge curved mouth can be more than 4 metres in length!

▼ Walruses often use their flippers and tusks to haul themselves out of the water onto rocky shores, to sunbathe during the brief summer.

564 **Mother seals have to return to the water to feed, leaving their pups alone on the ice.** At this time pups are in danger from polar bears, wolves and other predators. Within a couple of weeks the young seal is big enough to look after itself.

565 **The walrus is a huge seal with two long upper teeth, called tusks.** It shows these off at breeding time to impress its partner. Tusks are also used in feeding, to lever shellfish off the seabed. A big walrus can grow to 3 metres in length and weigh 1.5 tonnes!

Arctic seals

561 Many kinds of seals live in the Arctic region. These include ringed seals, bearded seals, harp seals, spotted seals, ribbon seals and hooded seals. Most feed on fish, squid and small shrimp-like creatures called krill, which are also eaten by whales.

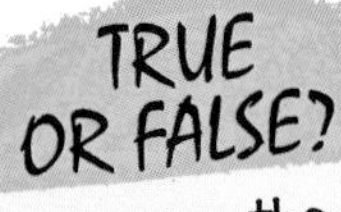

1. Seals are the only animals that eat krill.
2. Seals have a layer of blubber.
3. Walruses sunbathe in summer.
4. Seals usually give birth to three pups.
5. Polar bears prey on seals.

Answers:
1. False 2. True 3. True
4. False 5. True

◀ Seals make breathing holes by bashing their noses, teeth and flippers against the thin ice.

562 Seals have very thick fur to keep out the cold water. Like their main enemy, the polar bear, they also have a layer of fatty blubber under the skin to keep them warm. They swim well but have to come up to breathe every few minutes. Sometimes they use breathing holes they make in the ice.

563 In spring, mother seals come onto the ice to give birth. Their babies, or pups, have very thick, fluffy fur to keep them warm. Each mother seal usually has only one pup. She feeds it on very rich milk, and it grows very quickly.

I DON'T BELIEVE IT!

Mother polar bears are enormous, weighing as much as four adult humans, but cubs are tiny, weighing around half a kilogram – that's only one-eighth of the weight of a human baby.

559 **Wolves of the far north tend to follow their prey, such as caribou and musk oxen, until it tires.** Wolves work in packs to kill a large victim, or they can hunt alone for smaller prey such as Arctic hares, voles and lemmings.

▶ In midwinter, the mother polar bear gives birth to two or three tiny babies, called cubs, in a snow cave she digs.

558 **Polar bears can swim for hours in icy water, and walk across land, ice or frozen snow.** Their fur is very thick, and their paws are wide so they sink less in soft snow. They also have a layer of fat under their skin, called blubber, which keeps in body heat.

560 **Only the chief male and female of the wolf pack (the alpha pair), mate and have cubs.** Other pack members help look after the cubs, and bring them food. They also help to defend the pack from polar bears and brown bears.

▼ Wolves try to break up and scatter a herd of musk oxen so they can attack the young.

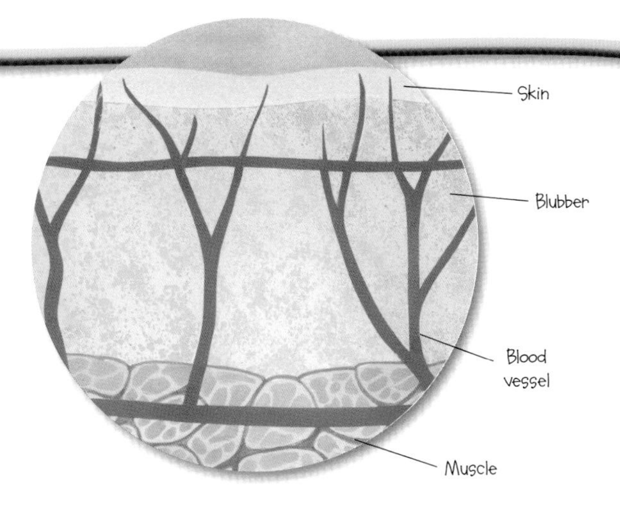

▲ Whales, seals and other polar mammals have a thick layer of blubber under their skin. In whales it is about five times thicker than the fat beneath human skin.

569 **The male narwhal has a tooth in its upper jaw that grows very long and pointed, to form a spear-like tusk.** This can reach 3 metres in length. It is sometimes used to pierce a hole in the ice so the whale can come up to breathe.

570 **The northern right and the bowhead whale are baleen whales.** They have long brush-like fringes of baleen in their mouths to filter tiny animals, called plankton, from the sea. These whales can weigh up to 80 tonnes! They are among the world's rarest whales, with just a few hundred right whales left.

571 **One of the most powerful Arctic hunters is the killer whale, or orca.** It is not a true whale, but the largest kind of dolphin. It lives in large family groups called pods and hunts fish, seals and even great whales.

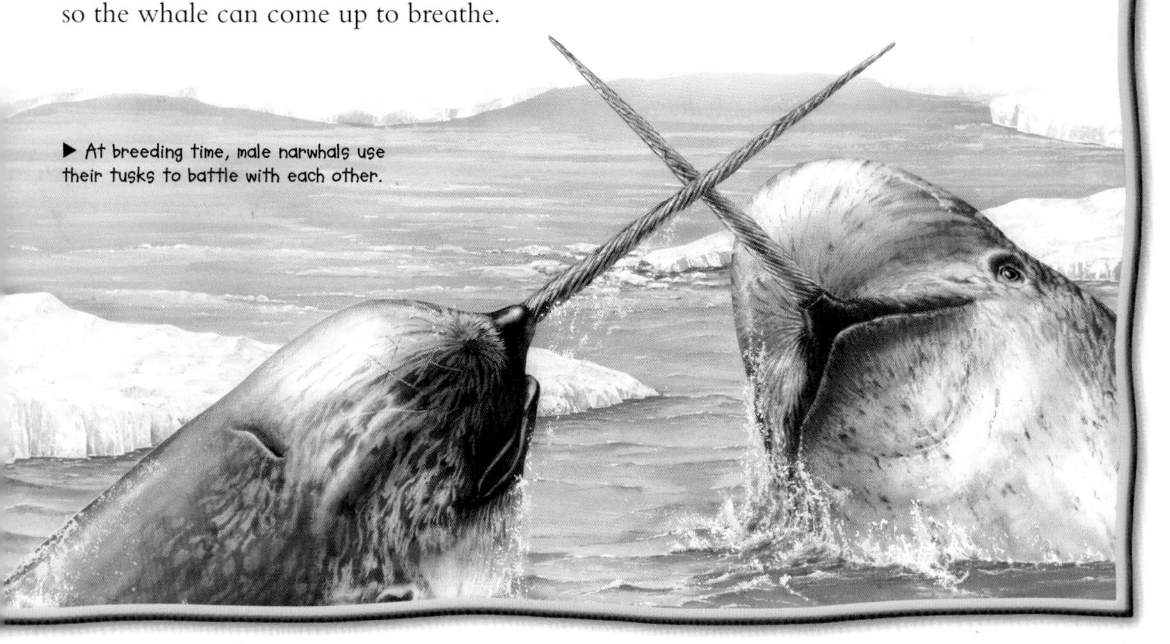

▶ At breeding time, male narwhals use their tusks to battle with each other.

Summer visitors

572 Some animals migrate north to the Arctic for its short summer. At this time, Arctic days are long and food is plentiful. In autumn, as the long winter approaches, animals return south to warmer regions.

573 The Arctic tern has the longest migration of all animals. It breeds in summer at the Arctic, then follows the warm weather south to the Antarctic, to have another summer. It covers an amazing 35,000 kilometres every year.

▼ The Arctic tern swoops down to the sea's surface to eat small creatures such as baby fish and krill.

▼ Snow geese flock to the tundra of North America in huge family groups, where each pair raises three to five chicks.

574 **The mighty sperm whale is also a summer visitor to the Arctic.** The huge males swim from the tropics to the edge of the pack ice. They dive to great depths to catch fish and giant squid.

▲ Grey whale babies (calves) join their mothers on the long journey north each spring, but many are attacked by sharks and killer whales.

575 **Many kinds of geese and other birds migrate to the Arctic in summer, such as snow geese, Brent geese and barnacle geese.** These birds make nests and rear their chicks quickly. They feed on grasses, rushes, sedges and other plants of the boggy tundra, as well as eating flies, grubs and other small creatures from pools along the seashore.

576 **Grey whales swim along the coasts of the North Atlantic in spring, to feed in the waters off Alaska and in the Bering Sea throughout the summer.** Then they return to subtropical waters off Baja California, Mexico, and spend the winter resting and giving birth. Their yearly journeys total 20,000 kilometres, and are the longest migration of any mammal.

QUIZ

Do some research and see if you can put these animals in order of the distance they cover on their yearly migration:

A Bowhead whale
B Barnacle goose
C Sperm whale
D Arctic tern
E Caribou

Answers:
D C B E A

In the Southern Ocean

577 During summer, the Southern Ocean around Antarctica is rich with life. The water is not very warm, but it contains many nutrients and there is lots of daylight. This means billions of tiny plants and animals, called plankton, grow. They become food for bigger creatures such as fish and squid.

578 The great supply of krill and plankton attracts some huge visitors to the Antarctic region. These include the world's largest animals, such as the blue whale, fin whale and humpback whale, which migrate here for summer.

579 Southern Ocean seals include the leopard, crabeater and Southern elephant seal. Despite its name, the crabeater seal does not actually eat crabs – it is mainly a krill-feeder. The leopard seal is about 3 metres in length and very fierce. It catches fish, seabirds, penguins, and even other seals.

580 A Southern elephant seal is almost as big as a real elephant! These seals spend weeks at sea feeding, then come to remote beaches to breed. The huge males, called beachmasters, rear up, roaring and biting each other, before mating with the females.

581 Elephant seals are the deepest-diving of all seals. They can dive down more than 1000 metres and stay under the water for over an hour before they need to surface for breath. They eat mainly fish and squid, as well as crabs and shrimps from the ocean floor.

▼ Male elephant seals battle each other to win an area of the beach, otherwise they do not breed. Sometimes they become badly injured in the fight, and die.

I DON'T BELIEVE IT!

A male southern elephant seal can be more than 5 metres in length. When it is well fed, it weighs almost two tonnes! It gets its name from its huge size, and from its long, floppy nose.

Antarctic waters

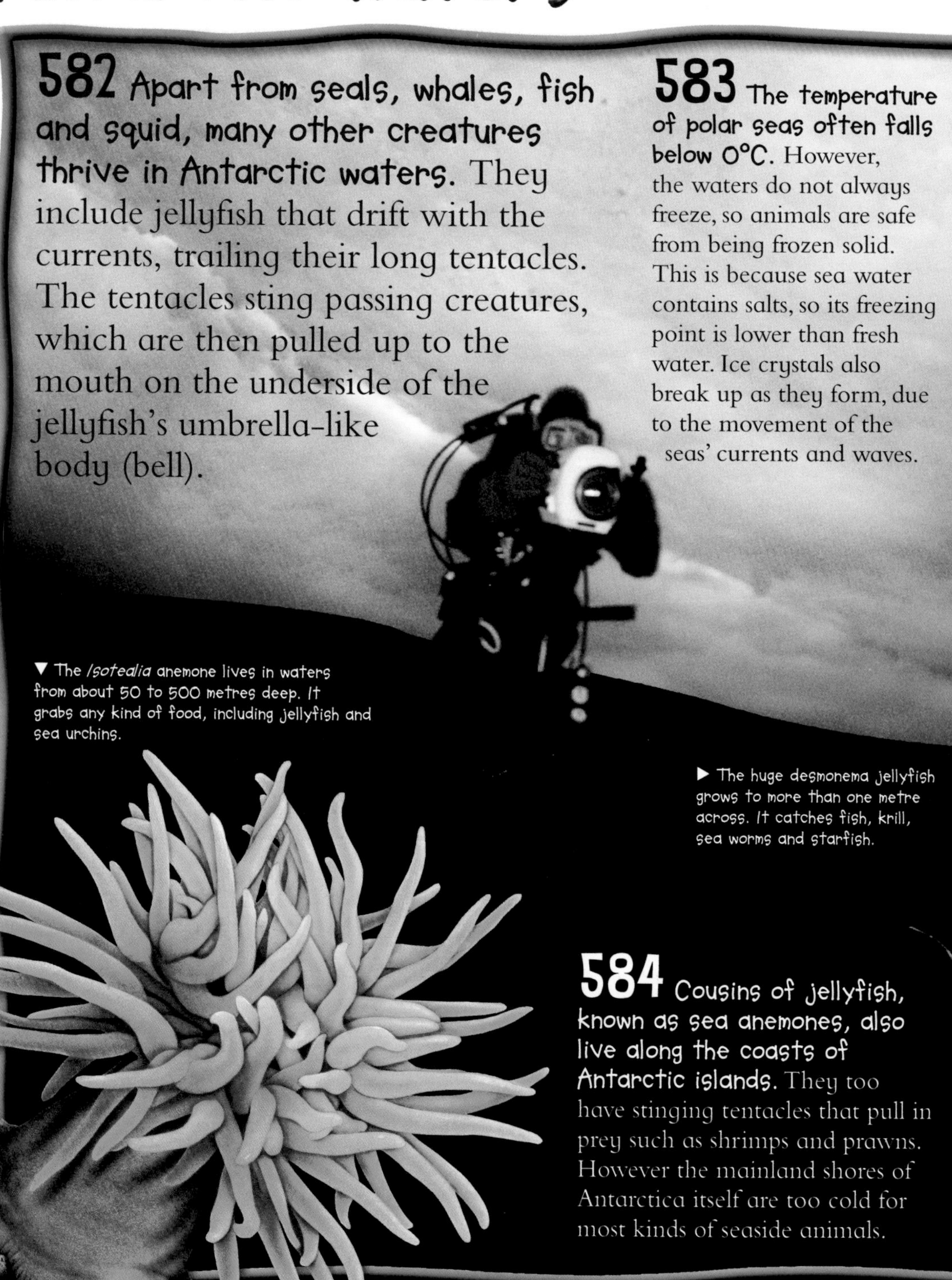

582 Apart from seals, whales, fish and squid, many other creatures thrive in Antarctic waters. They include jellyfish that drift with the currents, trailing their long tentacles. The tentacles sting passing creatures, which are then pulled up to the mouth on the underside of the jellyfish's umbrella-like body (bell).

583 The temperature of polar seas often falls below 0°C. However, the waters do not always freeze, so animals are safe from being frozen solid. This is because sea water contains salts, so its freezing point is lower than fresh water. Ice crystals also break up as they form, due to the movement of the seas' currents and waves.

▼ The *Isotealia* anemone lives in waters from about 50 to 500 metres deep. It grabs any kind of food, including jellyfish and sea urchins.

▶ The huge desmonema jellyfish grows to more than one metre across. It catches fish, krill, sea worms and starfish.

584 Cousins of jellyfish, known as sea anemones, also live along the coasts of Antarctic islands. They too have stinging tentacles that pull in prey such as shrimps and prawns. However the mainland shores of Antarctica itself are too cold for most kinds of seaside animals.

QUIZ

Do some research to find out which fish is most closely related to the Antarctic ice-fish.

A Flatfish
B Sharks
C Trout
D Perch

Answer: D

585 Several polar fish have special substances in their blood and body fluids that work like natural anti-freeze. Even if trapped in solid ice, these animals can survive for a while by going into suspended animation – staying still and using almost no energy.

▶ There are several kinds of Antarctic ice-fish, which have blood that is thickened by certain natural chemicals to stop it freezing.

Antarctic birds

586 Antarctica is visited by hundreds of kinds of birds each year. Most of them fly over the open ocean, since there is very little unfrozen land on which to nest. In contrast, the islands close to Antarctica are home to some breeding birds, such as albatrosses and petrels.

I DON'T BELIEVE IT!

After a young albatross first takes off, it may stay in the air for more than five years, swooping to grab food at the sea's surface, before touching down again.

587 The wandering albatross has longer wings than any other bird, at more than 3 metres from tip to tip. Albatrosses form long-lasting breeding pairs that come together on remote islands to raise their single chick. The young albatross may not fly until it is almost one year old.

▼ Research scientists measure the wingspan of an albatross.

▶ Tussock birds are always on the lookout for any morsels of food. This bird is pecking bits of flaking skin from an elephant seal.

588 The blackish cinclodes, also called the tussock bird, eats almost anything it can find. It snaps up shellfish and shrimps along the coast and eats dead crabs and starfish washed up on the shore. Tussock birds also wander around seabird colonies to feed on the rotting fish that the parent birds cough up, or regurgitate, for their chicks.

589 Skuas are powerful seabirds with large, sharp beaks. They chase terns, gulls and similar birds and attack them in mid air, forcing them to drop their food, which the skua then gulps down.

▶ The skua's strong beak can easily stab into a penguin's egg. Then the bird laps up the soft inner parts or hacks apart the chick inside.

Sliding and diving

590 Penguins live only in the south, around Antarctica – there are none in the Arctic. They cannot fly, but they use their flipper-like wings to swim with great speed and skill. Most of the 17 kinds of penguins live on the islands and shores of the Southern Ocean, on the icebergs and ice floes there, and on the continent of Antarctica itself.

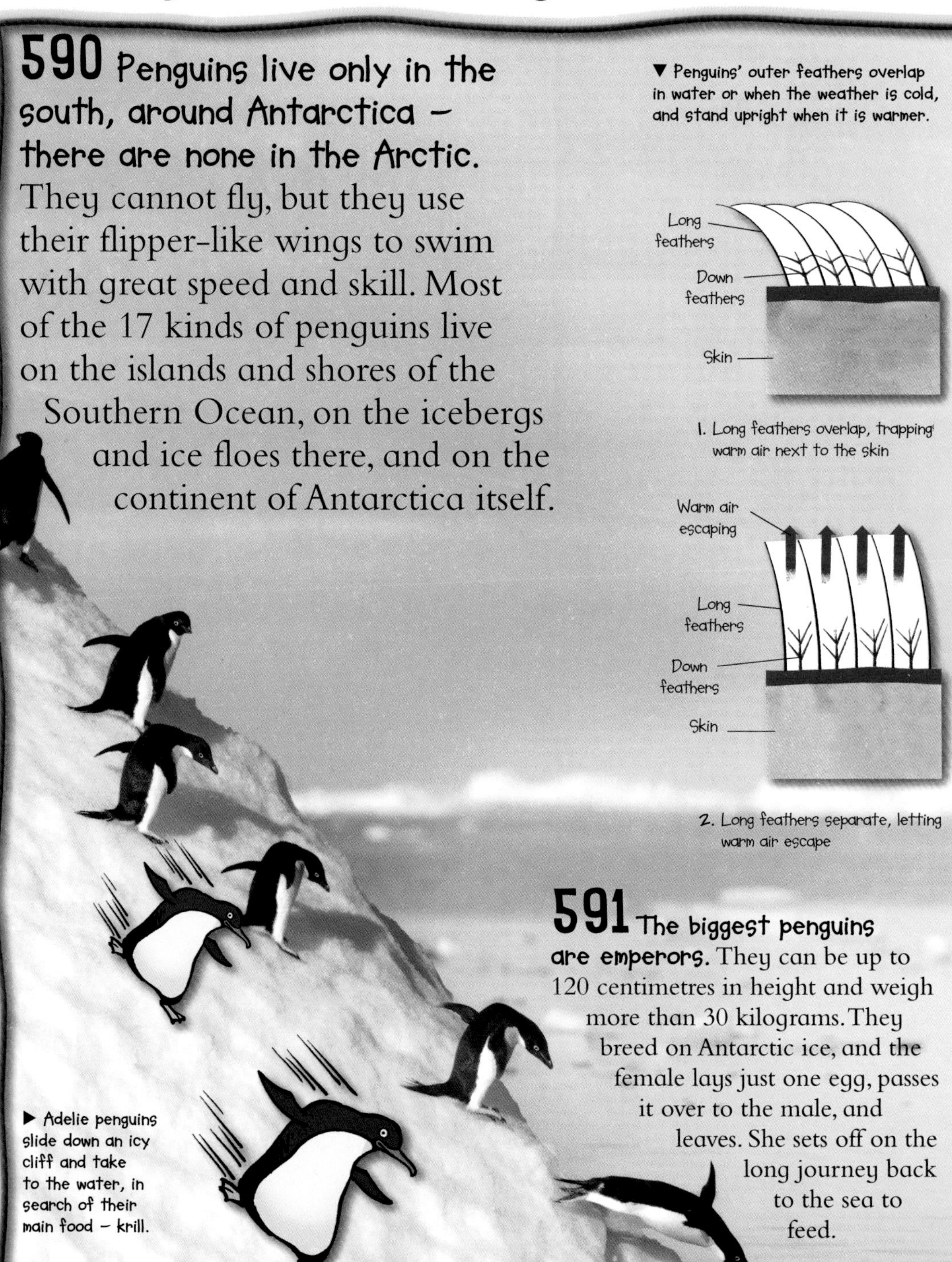

▼ Penguins' outer feathers overlap in water or when the weather is cold, and stand upright when it is warmer.

1. Long feathers overlap, trapping warm air next to the skin

2. Long feathers separate, letting warm air escape

▶ Adelie penguins slide down an icy cliff and take to the water, in search of their main food – krill.

591 The biggest penguins are emperors. They can be up to 120 centimetres in height and weigh more than 30 kilograms. They breed on Antarctic ice, and the female lays just one egg, passes it over to the male, and leaves. She sets off on the long journey back to the sea to feed.

STAND UP!

You will need:
card felt-tip pens tape

Make a penguin about 30 centimetres tall from card. Carefully cut out the head and body, two flippers, and two feet, and colour them with felt-tip pens. Tape the parts together and try to make the penguin stand upright. It's quite tricky! Luckily a penguin has a short, stiff tail. Cut this out and tape it on to make standing easier.

▲ Emperor penguins travel to traditional breeding sites to find a partner and mate. When an egg hatches, the parent bird brings up (regurgitates) food from its stomach to feed its chick.

592 The male emperor penguin spends almost two months of the worst midwinter weather with the egg on his feet, keeping it warm until it hatches. Then the female returns, walking and sliding across the ice, to take over caring for the chick. At last the hungry male can head to the sea to feed.

593 The king penguin is the second-largest penguin. It stands about 90 centimetres in height and weighs up to 15 kilograms. Its main foods are fish, squid and plankton. King penguins can dive down to 200 metres.

Polar peoples

594 People have lived in Arctic regions for over 10,000 years. Today, groups exist around northern North America, Scandinavia (northern Europe) and Siberia (north Asia). They include Inuit, Aleuts, Koryak, and Chukchi people. They live in some of the world's most difficult conditions.

Wind chill makes cold temperatures much worse! Cold wind blowing past a warmer object, such as a human body, draws away heat in seconds. If the temperature is –20°C, strong winds can double this to –40°C. It freezes body parts in seconds.

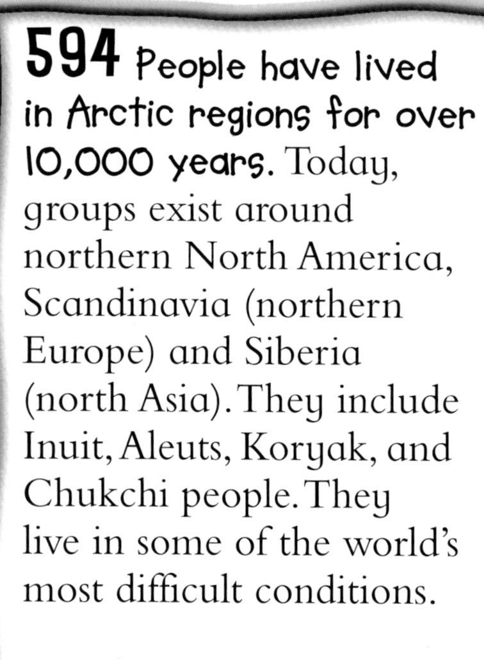

595 In recent times, the traditional way of life in polar regions has changed greatly. New ways of travel are available, from skidoos and other snowmobiles to helicopters, snowplanes and icebreaker ships. Many polar people are no longer cut off from the lands farther south. They can trade more easily for consumer goods such as clothes, tools, TVs and prepared foods.

▼ Snowmobiles have skis at the front for steering, and tracks at the rear to push the vehicle along. Here, a Saami person crosses a snow-covered lake in Finland.

596 Commercial fishing is big business in some Arctic areas. Ships catch large numbers of fish or krill, especially in summer. Whaling and sealing are banned, but ships continue to catch food that these animals eat, so the populations can still be harmed.

▶ Traditional fishing skills are still vital. This man is fishing for halibut through a hole in the ice in Greenland.

597 One of the most helpful modern items for northern people has been the gun. In the past, spears or hooks and lines were used to catch seals and other food. Even when using guns, hunters still need patience. Arctic animals are very wary and it is difficult to creep up on them unseen in the white, icy wilderness.

598 The discovery of oil, coal, minerals and other resources have brought many newcomers to the Arctic. Settlements have grown up along the coasts. The houses are heated by oil, from wells in the area, or coal mined locally, since there are no trees to burn as fuel.

▼ Tourism is a growing business in Ilulissat, Greenland, a World Heritage Site. Visitors come to see icebergs breaking off the Sermeq Kujalleq glacier.

Living in the cold

599 Over time, Arctic people have developed skills and knowledge to survive in this harsh environment. Plants are scarce, so food is mainly animals such as seals, shellfish, fish and whales. A stranded whale can provide enough food for a week.

600 Arctic animals provide not just food, but many other resources for polar people. The fatty blubber is burned in lamps for heat and warmth. Weatherproof clothes and boots are made from the furry skins of seals, caribou and other creatures.

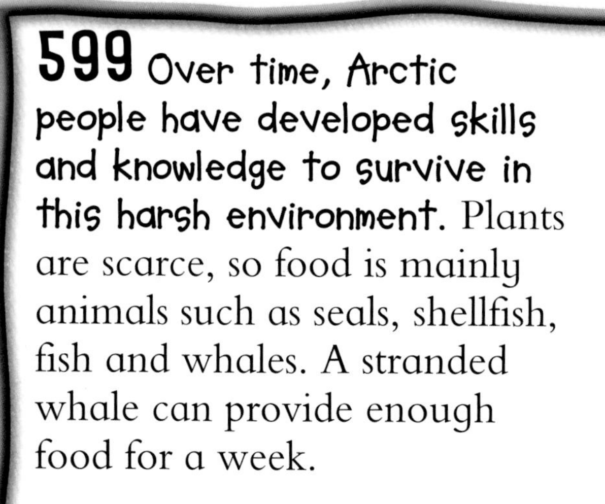

1. Large blocks of squashed snow or loose ice are cut with a large-bladed snow-knife.

601 Tools and utensils such as knives, bowls and spoons are also made from local animals. They are carved from the bones and teeth of smaller toothed whales, from the horns of caribou and musk oxen, from the tusks of walrus and narwhals, and from the bendy, springy baleen or whalebone of great whales.

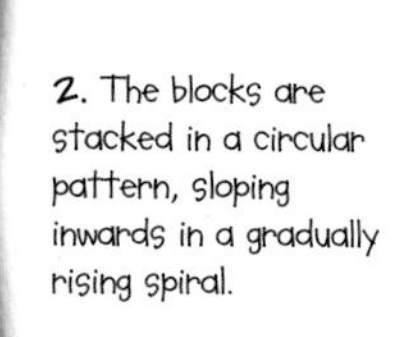

2. The blocks are stacked in a circular pattern, sloping inwards in a gradually rising spiral.

◀ Snow houses called igloos are usually a temporary shelter, made for just a night or two while out on a winter hunting expedition.

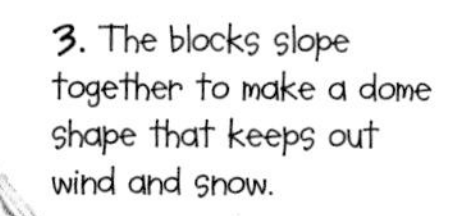

3. The blocks slope together to make a dome shape that keeps out wind and snow.

▶ Kayaks are usually paddled by hand with paddles made from driftwood. Some modern ones have outboard motors. Here, a kayak is launched by hunters in Alaska.

602 **Since so much food is obtained from the sea, boats are very useful.** The canoe-like kayak is made by stretching waterproof animal skin such as whale hide over a frame of carved driftwood, or perhaps bone. The parts are tied together with animal sinews.

603 **Kayaks are light and easily carried, and slide well across snow and ice.** Larger kayaks are used for carrying a family's possessions to a new hunting area.

◀ The joints between the blocks in an igloo are sealed with snow to keep out the wind. The entrance is low down to prevent the warm air inside from escaping.

QUIZ

Try and find out which materials Antarctic people use to make the following items:

A. Boots
B. An overcoat
C. A head-dress

Answers:
A. Waterproof sealskin
B. Reindeer hide
C. Seabird feathers

Life of a herder

604 Some people of the far north live inland. People in northern Europe such as the Saami (Lapps), and the Nenet of Siberia, depend on reindeer herds that provide them with almost everything they need.

605 The reindeer herds follow their natural migrations. They move north to tundra areas for summer and head south to the forests for winter. Herders travel with them, to keep the herds together and protect them from wolves and bears.

606 As the people and deer move, the reindeer pull sleds loaded with the herder's tents, utensils and other belongings. The animals are counted regularly and spare reindeer are herded to the local towns, where they are traded for items such as sharp metal knives.

▼ Nenet people gather reindeer in a herd to be checked and counted.

I DON'T BELIEVE IT!

In the last 50 years the Nenet people have lost more than 7 million hectares of reindeer grazing lands due to pollution, the creation of coal mines, new vehicle tracks, oil pipelines, and introduced animals eating the plant food.

607 Reindeer can provide a huge variety of resources. Their fur and skins make clothes, boots, floor rugs, sleeping blankets and tents. They provide fresh milk and blood to drink, and their meat is very nutritious. The antlers and bones are carved into utensils and tools. They are also used, along with teeth, to make beautiful works of art, showing scenes of fishing, hunting, herding and the natural world.

▲ Saami hunters live in tents of reindeer hide stretched over log poles, which can be easily packed and transported by sled.

On top of the world!

608 Many adventurers have tried to reach the North Pole, which is located near the middle of a floating layer of ice in the Arctic Ocean. Before today's satellite navigation, it was hard to know if you were in the right place. Then, explorers had to prove that they really did reach their destination. They couldn't leave a flag in the floating, breaking ice.

▶ Nansen's ship *Fram* was stuck in ice for almost three years, but its design meant that it survived.

609 English admiral William Parry tried to reach the North Pole in 1825. So did Norwegian explorer Fridtjof Nansen in 1893–96 in his ship *Fram*. Yet neither of them made it. In 1909, American Robert Peary and his team claimed to have reached the North Pole, but experts do not agree if they really did.

610 The first people to fly over the North Pole in a plane may have been Richard Byrd and Floyd Bennet in 1926. However, as with Peary, it's not certain if they really did. A few days later, Roald Amundsen – the first person to reach the South Pole – flew over the North Pole in an airship, the *Norge*.

◀ Some experts disagree with Robert Peary's claim that he marched across the floating ice to the North Pole.

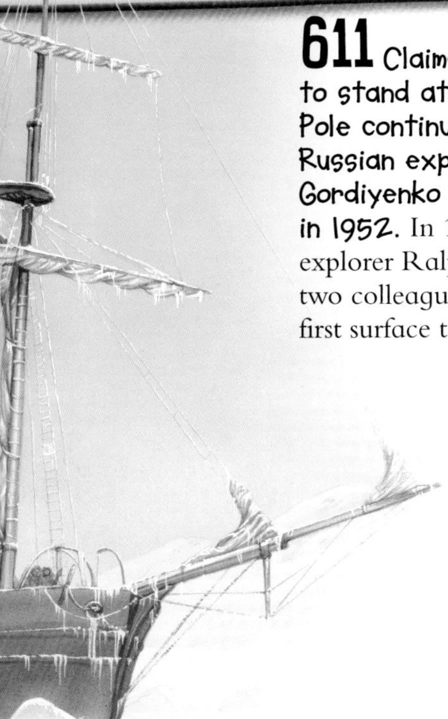

611 Claims to be first to stand at the North Pole continued, such as Russian explorer Pavel Gordiyenko and his team in 1952. In 1968, American explorer Ralph Plaisted and two colleagues made the first surface trip there.

QUIZ

You're off to the North Pole. What do you pack?

A. Swimming costume
B. GPS satellite-navigation recorder
C. Skis or snow boots

Answers:
A. No – too cold!
B. Yes – shows where you are.
C. Yes – allows you to move over the ice, to and from your waiting ship.

612 In modern times, more and more expeditions have reached the North Pole across the ice. In 2007, Dutch performer Guido van der Werve spent a day there, turning in the opposite direction to the Earth's spinning, so in fact he stayed completely still. It is even possible for rich tourists to fly to the exact North Pole for a few hours' visit.

▶ In 2007, Lewis Gordon Pugh swam one kilometre through water in cracks between the North Pole ice, to highlight the problem of global warming.

Race to the South Pole

614 Once ships arrived at Antarctica, there was still a dangerous journey across the ice to the South Pole. Irish explorer Ernest Shackleton made several trips there. In 1901–02 in the ship *Discovery*, and in 1914–16 in *Endurance*. These trips did not reach the South Pole, but helped to establish bases for further exploring across the ice cap.

▶ In Ernest Shackleton's 1914–15 expedition, his ship *Endurance* was frozen into the ice for ten months and finally crushed. Yet all the crew were eventually rescued.

613 It was difficult to even get close to the South Pole. In 1820, Russian naval officer Fabian Gottlieb von Bellingshausen was perhaps the first person to see the Antarctic mainland. American seal-hunter John Davis may have been first to set foot on the continent, in 1821. In 1839, English naval commander James Clark Ross set sail on a voyage to map Antarctica's outline. Many of these people have areas of Antarctica named after them.

SLIPPERY SLOPE

You will need:
length of wood ice cubes stones wood plastic

Hold up one end of the wood, like a ramp. Put an ice cube at the top and let it slide down. The ice melts into water, which works like slippery oil. Try sliding the other substances such as plastic, wood and stone. The ramp has to be much steeper!

▲ Amundsen's expedition saved the weight of carrying food by killing and eating the sled dogs one by one.

615 In 1911 two expeditions set off to reach the South Pole, led by Norwegian Roald Amundsen, and English naval officer Robert Scott. The world was gripped by news of their 'race to the Pole'. Amundsen, his team and his dog sleds got there first on 14 December 1911, and returned safely. Scott and his team, pulling their own sledges, arrived a month later. Tragically, on the way back they ran out of supplies and were stranded by blizzards. They did not survive.

616 The South Pole can now be visited by rich tourists. Several overland expeditions make the trek each year. There is a permanent scientific base called the Amundsen-Scott South Pole Station, where people live and work, usually for a period of six months.

▶ In 1997, mother-of-two Laurence de la Ferriere walked across Antarctica to the South Pole unaided.

Polar lands in peril

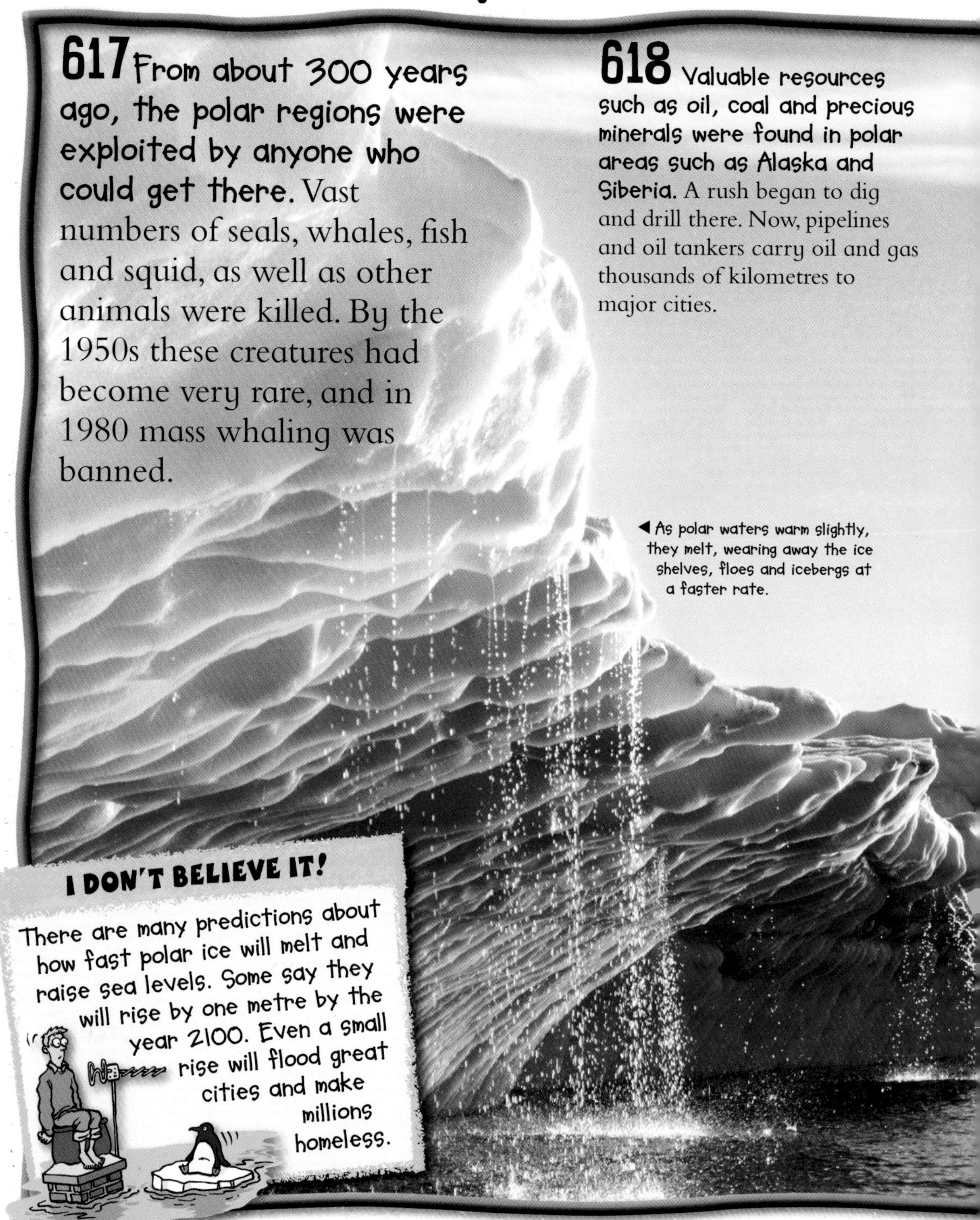

617 From about 300 years ago, the polar regions were exploited by anyone who could get there. Vast numbers of seals, whales, fish and squid, as well as other animals were killed. By the 1950s these creatures had become very rare, and in 1980 mass whaling was banned.

618 Valuable resources such as oil, coal and precious minerals were found in polar areas such as Alaska and Siberia. A rush began to dig and drill there. Now, pipelines and oil tankers carry oil and gas thousands of kilometres to major cities.

◀ As polar waters warm slightly, they melt, wearing away the ice shelves, floes and icebergs at a faster rate.

I DON'T BELIEVE IT!

There are many predictions about how fast polar ice will melt and raise sea levels. Some say they will rise by one metre by the year 2100. Even a small rise will flood great cities and make millions homeless.

619 Pollution has begun to affect the polar lands. Dangerous chemicals such as pesticides from farming, and toxins from industry, flow into Arctic waters. The protective ozone layer above Antarctica has been made thinner by chemicals from aerosol spray cans. Oil spills from tankers have devastated parts of the Arctic.

▶ Cleaning penguins' coats of pollution strips their feathers of natural oils, without which the birds could freeze to death. Rescued birds are fitted with woolly jumpers to keep them warm.

620 Climate change will have terrifying results around the world. The habitats of polar bears, seals, penguins and many other animals are disappearing. Floods will affect low-lying areas far from polar lands, where billions of people live in cities. Polar scientific bases have been set up to study these problems.

621 The greatest threat to polar regions may still be to come. Global warming due to the greenhouse effect is causing climate change, as world temperatures rise. This is making the ice caps melt, causing sea levels to rise.

▼ The striped pole marks the exact spot of the South Pole. It is repositioned every New Year's Day, as the ice moves around 10 metres yearly.

Protecting the Poles

622 Countries have signed agreements to protect polar lands and oceans from damage. Even tourism can be a problem. Cruise ships bring visitors that disturb whales and other wildlife, and leave waste.

▼ Scientists monitor emperor penguin breeding colonies near the Weddell Sea, Antarctica, to see the effect of climate change on their breeding.

623 In 1994 the Southern Ocean was declared a vast sanctuary, or safe area, for whales. This meant it was also safe for many other kinds of wildlife. However some countries still hunt whales, and ships also go there to catch krill, fish and squid. As we catch more, whales and other large animals have less to eat.

624 Some parts of the Arctic are also being protected. Some countries want to drill for oil and gas, and mine for coal, precious minerals and metals. Big companies sometimes try to change the minds of governments or break the rules. These activities create jobs for people, but create risks of pollution.

QUIZ

Arrange these ways of travelling across polar lands from fastest to slowest:

A. Walk
B. Skidoo
C. Ski
D. Dog-pulled sled

Answer:
Fastest to slowest – D C B A

625 The polar lands and oceans are far away from most of us. Yet they are the last great wildernesses on Earth. They have the harshest habitats in the world, where animals have had to adapt or perish. These places need our help to survive.

RAINFORESTS

626 In the world's rainforests animals and plants are closely linked in a daily struggle for survival. It's a battle for life that has been going on for millions of years, and has led to these unique environments becoming home to a huge variety of living things, from the deadliest frogs to the foulest-smelling flowers.

▼ In a rainforest, plants of all types fight for light and space. They create an emerald-green landscape of leafy undergrowth and towering trees.

Queen Alexandra's birdwing butterfly

630 Rainforests have four main layers. The bottom layers are the dark, dank forest floor and understorey, where the shortest plants live. Here, bugs, frogs, fungi and many other living things thrive. The middle layer is the forest canopy and the top layer is the emergent layer. This is where the tallest trees poke up above a blanket of green leaves. The trees are home to vines, mosses, monkeys, lizards, snakes, insects and thousands of species (types) of bird.

◀ Most animals and plants live in the rainforest canopy layer. The understorey is very gloomy because not much sunlight reaches it.

I DON'T BELIEVE IT!

People who live in rainforests can build their entire homes from plant materials. Walls are made from palm stems or bamboo and leaves can be woven to make roofs and floors.

Red-eyed tree frog

631 Rainforests are home to people as well as animals and plants. Many tribes (groups of people) live in these dense, green forests around the world, finding food, medicines and shelter amongst the trees. Some of them still follow a traditional lifestyle, hunting animals and gathering plants for food.

Not just jungles

632 Hot, steamy rainforests are sometimes called jungles. They are found in Earth's tropical regions. These are areas near the Equator, an imaginary line that encircles the Earth, where daily temperatures are around 25°C and it rains most days.

▼ A boy rows a canoe made from a hollow tree trunk on the Amazon River in Brazil.

633 Around 60–100 million years ago, most of the world's land was covered with tropical rainforest. Now only a tiny area – six percent – is covered. This is partly due to deforestation (people cutting down trees) and partly because the Earth's climate has changed, becoming cooler and drier.

634 Temperate rainforests grow in cool, wet places. 'Temperate' means having a moderate climate. Trees here are usually conifers such as pine trees. Temperate rainforests are home to the world's largest trees – Californian redwoods. These can live for 2000 years, and the tallest reach 115 metres in height.

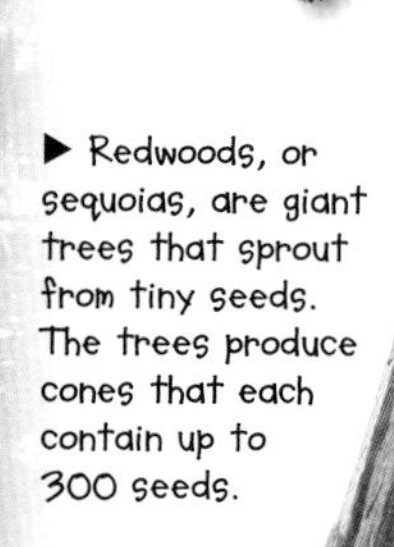

▶ Redwoods, or sequoias, are giant trees that sprout from tiny seeds. The trees produce cones that each contain up to 300 seeds.

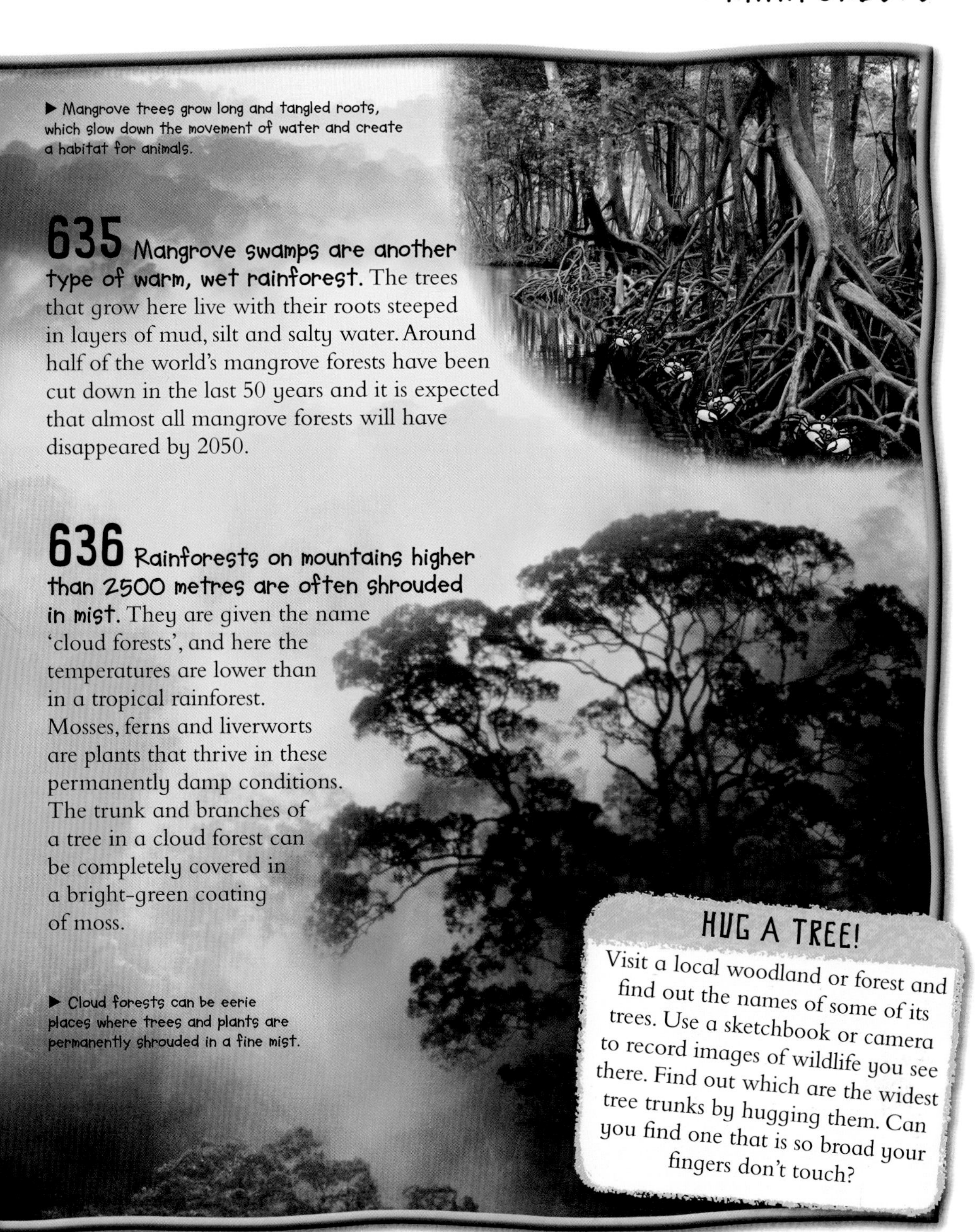

▶ Mangrove trees grow long and tangled roots, which slow down the movement of water and create a habitat for animals.

635 Mangrove swamps are another type of warm, wet rainforest. The trees that grow here live with their roots steeped in layers of mud, silt and salty water. Around half of the world's mangrove forests have been cut down in the last 50 years and it is expected that almost all mangrove forests will have disappeared by 2050.

636 Rainforests on mountains higher than 2500 metres are often shrouded in mist. They are given the name 'cloud forests', and here the temperatures are lower than in a tropical rainforest. Mosses, ferns and liverworts are plants that thrive in these permanently damp conditions. The trunk and branches of a tree in a cloud forest can be completely covered in a bright-green coating of moss.

▶ Cloud forests can be eerie places where trees and plants are permanently shrouded in a fine mist.

HUG A TREE!

Visit a local woodland or forest and find out the names of some of its trees. Use a sketchbook or camera to record images of wildlife you see there. Find out which are the widest tree trunks by hugging them. Can you find one that is so broad your fingers don't touch?

Where in the world?

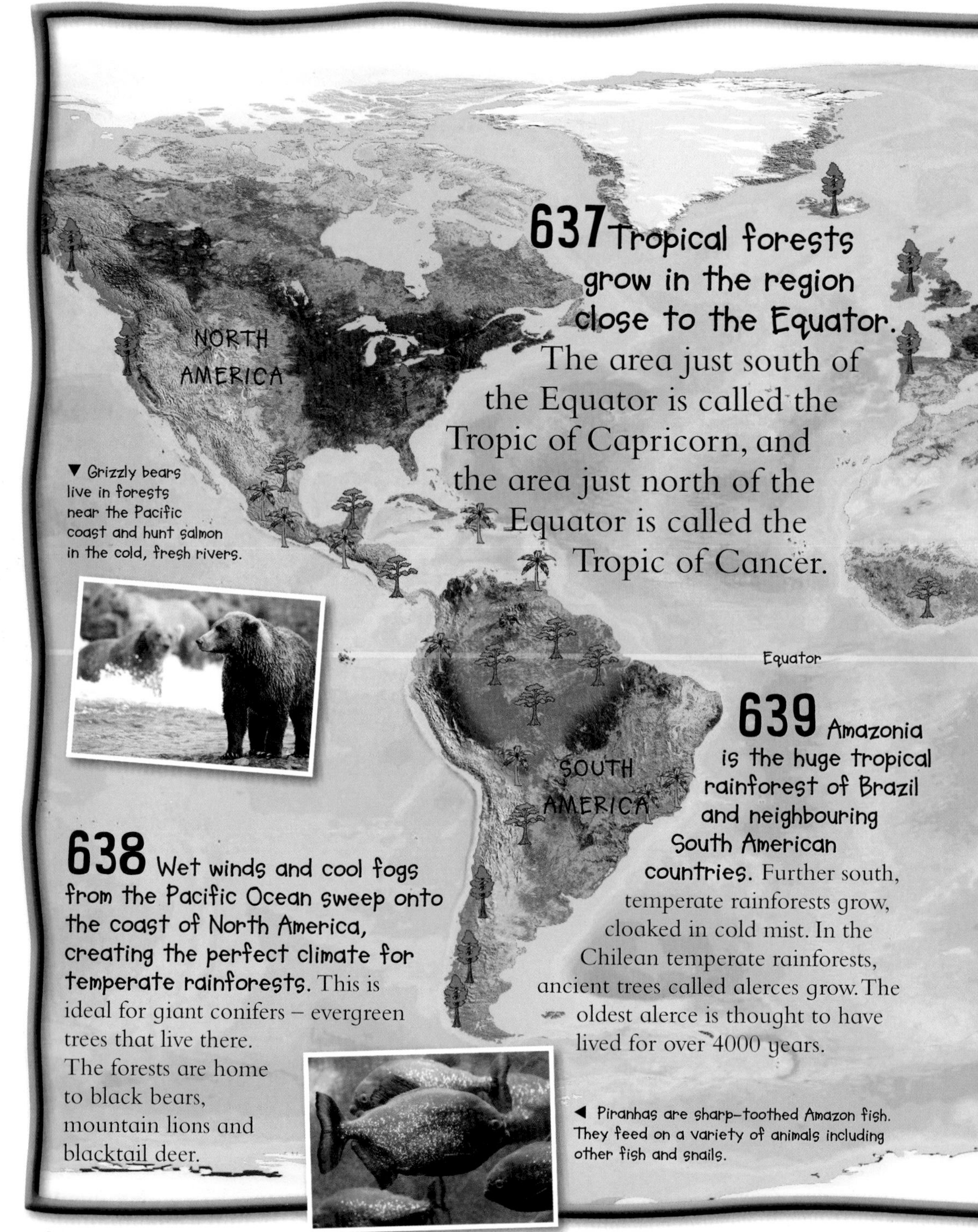

637 Tropical forests grow in the region close to the Equator. The area just south of the Equator is called the Tropic of Capricorn, and the area just north of the Equator is called the Tropic of Cancer.

▼ Grizzly bears live in forests near the Pacific coast and hunt salmon in the cold, fresh rivers.

639 Amazonia is the huge tropical rainforest of Brazil and neighbouring South American countries. Further south, temperate rainforests grow, cloaked in cold mist. In the Chilean temperate rainforests, ancient trees called alerces grow. The oldest alerce is thought to have lived for over 4000 years.

638 Wet winds and cool fogs from the Pacific Ocean sweep onto the coast of North America, creating the perfect climate for temperate rainforests. This is ideal for giant conifers – evergreen trees that live there. The forests are home to black bears, mountain lions and blacktail deer.

◀ Piranhas are sharp-toothed Amazon fish. They feed on a variety of animals including other fish and snails.

◀ Atlas moths are the world's largest moths. They flutter through the canopies of Asian cloud forests.

▼ Cassowaries are large birds that cannot fly. They live in the forests of Australia and New Guinea.

◀ African bush vipers live in the forest canopy, slithering down to hunt frogs and lizards.

640 Cloud forests usually grow on, or near, mountain ranges, where there is plenty of rain and mist. In China, the Yunnan cloud forest grows over tall mountains and deep gorges. The name *Yunnan* means 'south of the clouds' – it's a mysterious place that few people have visited.

QUIZ

1. What is the Equator?
2. Where does the cassowary live?
3. How old is the oldest-known alerce?

Answers:
1. An imaginary line that encircles the Earth 2. New Guinea and Australia 3. More than 4000 years old

Tree of life

641 The brazil-nut tree produces balls of seeds. Each ball is the size of a melon and as hard as stone. This amazing tree grows in tropical rainforests and provides a home and food for many living things.

642 When the seed balls are ripe they crash to the ground. Only the agouti, a dog-sized rodent, has teeth tough enough to break through the case to reach the tasty brazil nuts inside. Agoutis bury some of the nuts, which may then grow into trees. Without agoutis new brazil-nut trees could not grow.

▲ Between 12 and 24 nuts grow inside each brazil-nut tree seed case. Inside each nut is a seed.

Strangler fig

643 Strangler figs grow up and around the trunks of rainforest trees. Over years, the fig continues to grow until it eventually strangles its host tree to death. Once the tree has rotted, only the tangled web of fig roots and stems remain, like a spooky tree skeleton.

◀ Agoutis' teeth continue to grow throughout their lives, allowing them to bite through nutshells.

▼ Brazil-nut tree flowers open before sunrise. By the end of the day, all the petals will have fallen off.

644 Brazil-nut trees also depend on a single type of insect to survive – orchid bees. These are the only insects strong enough to get inside the tree's heavy, hooded flowers to pollinate them, so the nuts – which contain seeds – can grow into new plants.

▶ Female orchid bees visit brazil-nut flowers to feed on nectar, while male orchid bees visit orchids to collect perfume.

Male orchid bee

645 Fallen leaves at the base of tropical trees quickly disappear. Dead matter, called leaf litter, is broken down by fungi, or eaten by bugs. This process is known as decomposition, and it helps the goodness from the leaves return to the forest soil in a natural method of recycling.

646 When a number of different living things all depend on one another for survival they are described as an ecosystem. Rainforest habitats are large ecosystems, and a brazil-nut tree is a small ecosystem. When brazil-nut trees are cut down, many other living things that depend on them die, too.

◀ A brazil-nut tree can grow to 60 metres in height and produce more than 100 kilograms of nuts every year.

Amazing Amazon

647 The Amazon rainforest is the largest tropical rainforest in the world. It covers 6 million square kilometres, which means it is nearly the same size as Australia. Around half of all animal and plant species live in Amazonia, as this forest is known.

◀ An Amazonian Hercules beetle can grow to 18 centimetres in length. It is one of the world's largest insects.

648 The giant Amazon River wends its way through the forest, bringing life and death to many of its inhabitants. This is the world's biggest river, stretching for about 6400 kilometres and pouring 770 billion litres of water into the Atlantic Ocean every day. People and animals of the forest use the river for transport, food and water.

649 Insect experts who travelled to Amazonia in the 1840s discovered more than 8000 new species (types) of beetle. Alfred Wallace and Henry Bates were amongst the first of many scientists who realized that this rainforest has a fantastic range of animal and plant life, many of which do not exist anywhere else. Charles Darwin, a 19th century scientist, described it as 'a great wild, untidy, luxuriant hothouse'.

▼ The Amazon River basin holds 20 percent of the world's fresh water.

650 The waters of the Amazon are home to many types of animal and plant. Giant waterlilies with 2-metre-wide leaves grow in slow-moving stretches of the river, but just beneath them lurk hungry alligators, sharp-toothed piranha fish and blood-sucking leeches.

651 There are more than 400 species of reptile, such as snakes and lizards, in the Amazon rainforest. More freshwater fish live in the Amazon River than anywhere else on Earth, and more than 225 types of amphibian, such as frogs and toads, live in and around the water.

▶ Large green iguanas like to lie on branches that hang over the Amazon River and soak up the sun's warming rays.

I DON'T BELIEVE IT!

Giant Amazonian leeches are blood-sucking worms that can grow up to 30 centimetres in length! They have sharp teeth and pain-numbing spit that stops blood from clotting so they can enjoy a long feast.

People of the Amazon

652 The Amazon was given its name by a Spanish explorer who ventured down the river in the 1540s. Francisco de Orellana was attacked by the local long-haired people who reminded him of the mythical female warriors described by the ancient Greeks, so he named the Amazon after them.

▶ Inside the *shabono*, Yanomani people build circular huts called *malocas*. At night, the young people sleep in hammocks, outside the *malacos*.

653 When Europeans first went to the Amazon rainforest in search of treasure, there were around seven million people living there. Today, 500 years later, there are fewer than a million. The Amazonian people live as groups, or tribes, and have different cultures and languages from one another.

654 The Yanomani people still follow many of their ancient traditions today. Villagers share one large home, known as the *shabono*, and women grow crops such as sweet potatoes. Men hunt using blowpipes and bows and arrows. The rainforest is the children's school, where they learn how to survive in, and protect, their jungle home.

◀ Several families make up one Yanomani village. They live, work and play together, passing on traditions and skills.

655 The Embera people use the poison produced by rainforest frogs to hunt animals to eat. Men wipe the tips of their blowpipe darts on the frogs' backs before firing them. One golden poison dart frog has enough poison to kill ten men. In recent years several rainforest frogs have become extinct (died out), but no one knows why this is.

▲ The golden poison frog produces poison on its skin, which the people of the Embera tribe carefully wipe on their darts.

656 Although many Amazonian people live in protected areas of rainforest, many more face an uncertain future. Large parts of Amazonia are being taken over by mining and logging companies. They cut down large parts of the forest, forcing local people to move elsewhere.

► Embera women clean and prepare food in rivers and lakes, but many have become polluted.

Forests of Oceania

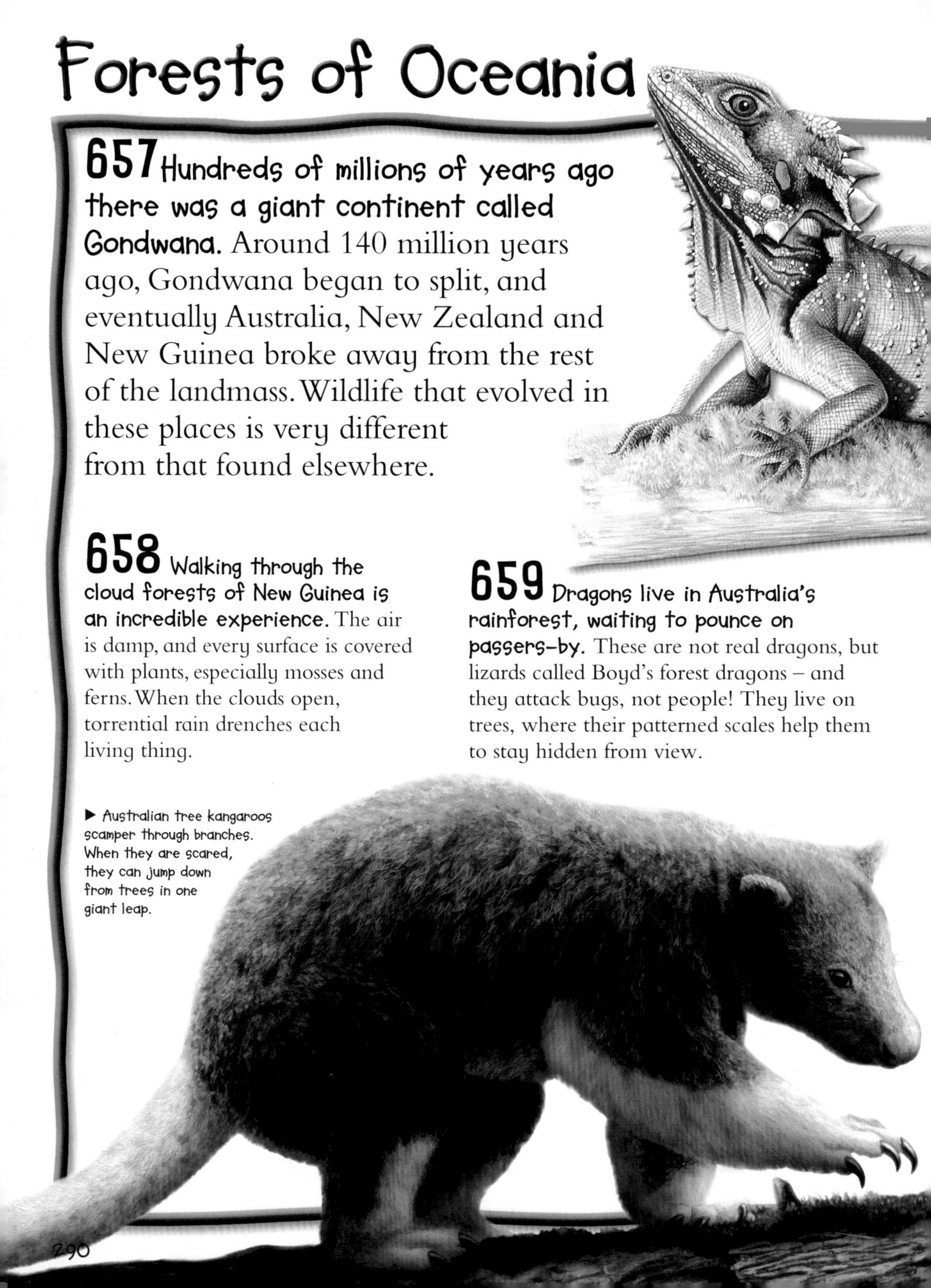

657 Hundreds of millions of years ago there was a giant continent called Gondwana. Around 140 million years ago, Gondwana began to split, and eventually Australia, New Zealand and New Guinea broke away from the rest of the landmass. Wildlife that evolved in these places is very different from that found elsewhere.

658 Walking through the cloud forests of New Guinea is an incredible experience. The air is damp, and every surface is covered with plants, especially mosses and ferns. When the clouds open, torrential rain drenches each living thing.

659 Dragons live in Australia's rainforest, waiting to pounce on passers-by. These are not real dragons, but lizards called Boyd's forest dragons – and they attack bugs, not people! They live on trees, where their patterned scales help them to stay hidden from view.

▶ Australian tree kangaroos scamper through branches. When they are scared, they can jump down from trees in one giant leap.

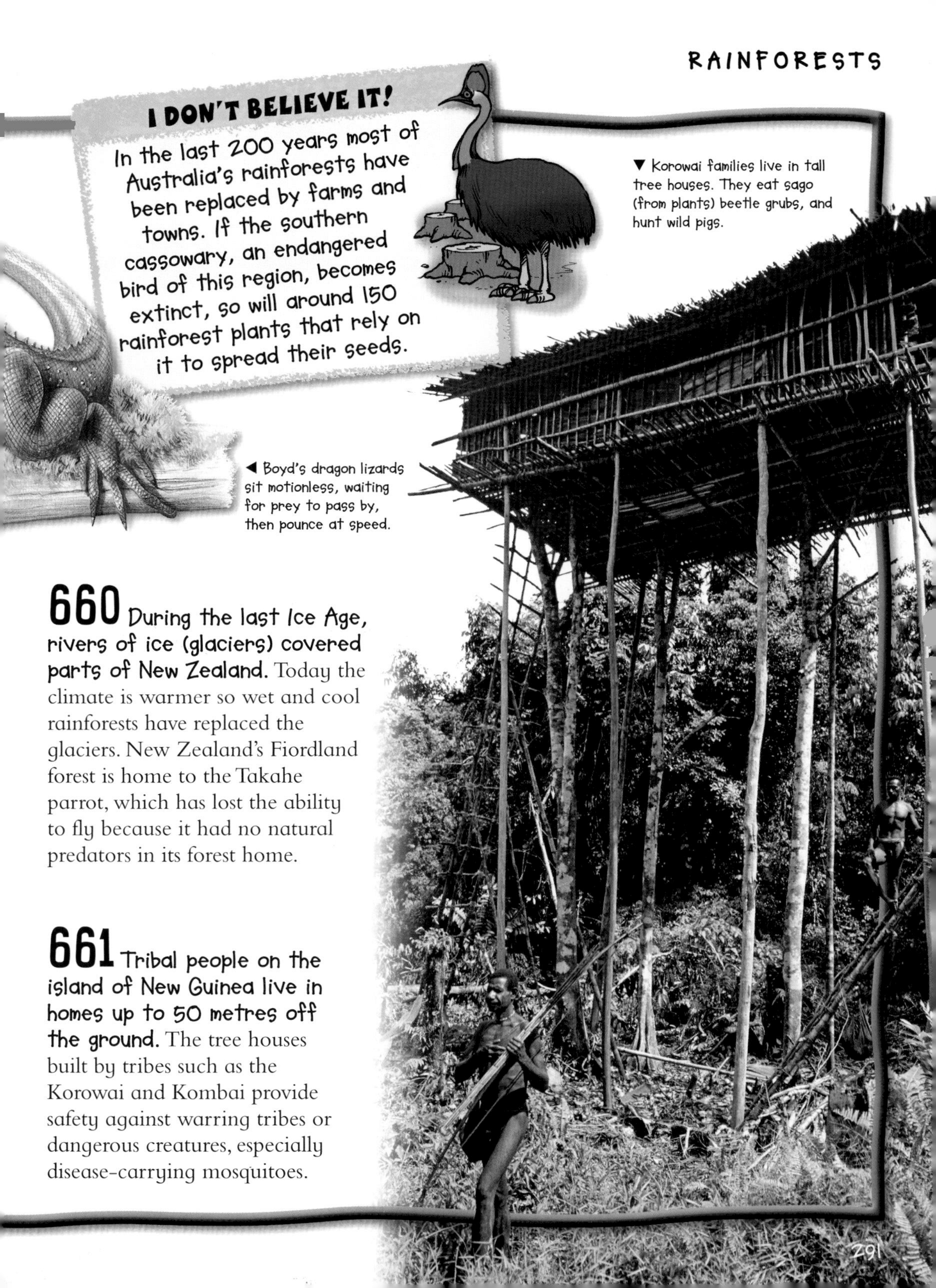

I DON'T BELIEVE IT!

In the last 200 years most of Australia's rainforests have been replaced by farms and towns. If the southern cassowary, an endangered bird of this region, becomes extinct, so will around 150 rainforest plants that rely on it to spread their seeds.

▼ Korowai families live in tall tree houses. They eat sago (from plants) beetle grubs, and hunt wild pigs.

◀ Boyd's dragon lizards sit motionless, waiting for prey to pass by, then pounce at speed.

660 During the last Ice Age, rivers of ice (glaciers) covered parts of New Zealand. Today the climate is warmer so wet and cool rainforests have replaced the glaciers. New Zealand's Fiordland forest is home to the Takahe parrot, which has lost the ability to fly because it had no natural predators in its forest home.

661 Tribal people on the island of New Guinea live in homes up to 50 metres off the ground. The tree houses built by tribes such as the Korowai and Kombai provide safety against warring tribes or dangerous creatures, especially disease-carrying mosquitoes.

Magical Madagascar

662 Madagascar is the world's fourth largest island. It lies to the east of Africa, in the warm waters of the Indian Ocean. The rainforests here cover 10,000 square kilometres, and are mostly found on the island's eastern coast.

663 When Madagascar split away from the rest of Africa about 165 million years ago, its animals and plants began moving on a unique path of change. Now this tropical place is a haven for some amazing animals such as lemurs and coloured lizards called chameleons. Between 80 and 90 percent of the 250,000 species found here live nowhere else, and new species are discovered all the time.

▼ Ring-tailed lemurs live together in groups that are ruled by females. They feed on plants and, unlike most lemurs, spend much of their time on the ground.

664 Lemurs are animals with long legs and bushy tails that leap through trees. They are related to monkeys and apes and, like their cousins, are intelligent and inquisitive creatures. The ring-tailed lemur lives in groups of up to 25 family members. They like to sit in the sun, but scatter if a member of the group sounds an alarm call to warn of danger nearby.

◀ The wings of the African sunset moth are ablaze with beautiful colours. Like most colourful moths, it is active during the day.

665 **People have been living on Madagascar for around 2000 years.** Travellers from Arabia, Asia, Africa and Indonesia have all settled here, along with Europeans. Four out of every five adults earns a living from agriculture. More than 90 percent of Madagascar's rainforests have been destroyed to provide farmland for the growing population.

◀ The rosy periwinkle is used to make drugs that fight deadly diseases.

666 **The pretty rosy periwinkle plant is found in Madagascar's rainforests and is used to fight cancer.** It contains chemicals that are used to make drugs that combat this deadly disease. The rosy periwinkle is endangered in the wild because its forest home has been largely destroyed.

I DON'T BELIEVE IT!

Lemurs in Madagascar have been seen rolling giant millipedes over their fur. No one knew why, until scientists discovered that the many-legged bugs release chemicals that keep flies and fleas off the lemurs – like a natural fly spray!

▶ A Madagascan aye-aye taps a tree with its long middle finger. It listens for sounds of moving grubs beneath, and hooks them out.

African adventures

▲ The Central African rainforest is home to more than 11,000 types of plant and 400 types of mammal, such as African forest elephants.

667 The Congo rainforest (or Central African rainforest) lies in the centre of Africa, in the basin of the Congo River. It is the second largest rainforest, with an area around twice the size of France. More than 50 million people depend on it for survival.

668 Before European explorers ventured into Africa's jungles the native people lived in harmony with their environment. They survived as hunter-gatherers – they only killed what they needed to eat, and collected fruits by hand. Europeans wanted to use the rainforests to make money – a practice that continues today.

669 Walking through the African rainforest is a challenging, frightening, noisy activity! Plants block every step and strange noises come from all corners, including squeaks, trilling, singing, cheeps, growls and roars. Deadly snakes and spiders lurk in dark corners, and biting or stinging insects will sniff out human flesh in seconds.

◀ Grey parrots are common in Arican rainforests, where they feed on fruits and seeds.

670 The Batwa people of Central Africa are pygmies, which means they are unusually short. They have lived in African rainforests for thousands of years, collecting honey and hunting. When farmers destroyed the Batwas' forests, they were left without homes and with no way to get food. Most now live in great poverty.

▶ Some Batwa men still climb trees to collect honey, but most members of the tribe have been forced to leave their forest homes.

671 African hardwoods are prized for their great beauty and durability. These woods come from tropical trees and have been used for centuries to make fine furniture and decorative objects. Mahogany, ebony and teak are all exotic woods from African rainforests.

▼ Around 90 percent of the rainforests in West Africa have been wiped out by farming.

QUIZ

Three of these countries are in Africa, and three are in South America. Can you put them in the right continents?

Colombia Gabon Congo
Guyana Brazil Ghana

Answers:
Africa: Congo Gabon Ghana
South America: Brazil Colombia Guyana

Forests of the Far East

672 The word 'jungle' comes from a Hindi word meaning 'thick forest'. Most Asian rainforests lie on the mainland, from India to Bhutan and Malaysia, or on tropical islands such as Sumatra.

▼Orang-utans live in trees, but they do spend some time on land. They can walk through water, but do not swim.

673 Borneo cloud forests provide shelter and food for one of the world's most endangered apes. Orang-utans live in trees and feed on the fruit of more than 400 different types of tree, especially durians and figs. If they can't find fruit, they eat leaves and bark.

674 Palm trees provide an important source of food – sago. Women make it from palm pith (the spongy substance inside a trunk or branch). They chop and soak it, before treading on it to turn it into a pulp. The pulp dries to a flour that can be cooked. Tribal people also enjoy delicious sago grubs – the large maggots that live inside rotting palm trees.

RAIN RECORD

It rains almost every day in a rainforest. To measure your rainfall you need a clear plastic container, a ruler and a notebook.

1. Place the empty container outside, away from trees.
2. At the same time every day measure the water in the container.
3. Empty your container after each measurement.
4. Record your results in a notebook.

Powerful, curved beak

◀ The Philippine eagle has a wingspan of more than 2 metres and is a formidable predator, catching prey such as flying lemurs in mid-flight. It is in danger of extinction because more than 90 percent of its Philippine forest home has been cut down.

Sharp talons

675 The people of the Indonesian rainforests are called Orang Asli and they have had a hard battle for survival in recent times. In Malaysia, they were often captured and sold as slaves to local chiefs. Many Orang Asli still live in the rainforests, hunting monkeys with blowpipes made from bamboo.

676 Known as the lord of the jungle, the Philippine eagle soars over Asian rainforests, hunting monkeys and squirrels. It is one of the world's biggest raptors (birds of prey), but also one of the most endangered. There are now probably no more than 500 alive.

Cloud forests

677 Trekking through the Monteverde cloud forest of Costa Rica can be done on foot – or by air! Visitors can fly between the trees on zip wires, passing through low-lying clouds to get a bird's-eye view of the treetops. On the ground, every surface is wet, as it is either drizzling or pouring with rain for much of the day.

▲ Three-toed sloths are slow-moving mammals. Their camouflage is their only defence against jaguars – the big cats of South America that hunt them.

▼ Mountain gorillas live in the cloud forests of Africa's Virunga National Park. They are highly endangered animals, despite being our close cousins.

678 At night, cloud forests buzz with life, but the sleepy sloth rarely stirs. These animals from Central and South America are such slow movers that plants grow in their fur, giving perfect camouflage! Three-toed sloths hang from branches and sleep upside-down for up to 18 hours every day, only coming down to the ground once a week. It takes them one minute to travel just 3 metres.

679 Epiphytes are rainforest plants that grow very well in cloud forests. They emerge from the nooks and crannies of tree trunks and branches, to reach more sunlight than they would on the forest floor. Dirt collects in these places and turns to soil. The epiphytes' roots grow into this soil, where they collect nutrients and water.

▲ Trees in cloud forests are covered in epiphytes and they grow roots from their trunks and branches. These hanging roots can be tens of metres in length and absorb water from the damp atmosphere.

◀ In the mating season a male quetzal grows two tail feathers that may reach one metre in length.

GO SLOW

Measure out 3 metres on the floor. How quickly can you cover this distance when you run? Probably very quickly! Now try to cover the same distance as slowly as you can, so it takes a whole minute – just like a three-toed sloth. Now do it again, upside down (only joking!)

680 As a resplendent quetzal flies through Mexico's cloud forest its tail feathers shimmer in the sunlight. Male quetzals, known as birds of the gods, have the longest tail feathers of any bird in the region, and they are often regarded as one of the world's most beautiful birds. Quetzals eat wild avocados, swallowing the fruit whole. The seeds pass through their bodies, helping new avocado trees to grow.

Peculiar plants

681 It is thought that more than 60 percent of plant species live in rainforests. Plants do an important job in making the soil stable so rain doesn't wash it away. They also take carbon dioxide out of the air, and put oxygen – the gas we breathe – back into it.

682 One of the stinkiest plants is the giant titan arum. This freaky flower can grow to 3 metres in height and produces a pongy perfume to attract insects. The insects pollinate the plants so that it can produce seeds. The titan arum only flowers once every seven years.

◀ Titan arums only grow wild in the Indonesian island of Sumatra. They smell of rotting meat.

▶ Durians are called 'kings of fruits' and are eaten in Indonesia and Malaysia.

683 The smell of a ripe durian fruit can be detected nearly one kilometre away. Visitors to the rainforests of Southeast Asia say durians stink like rotting fish, but the local people and the animals don't mind – they know the soft flesh tastes sweet. Tigers, sun bears and mouse deer all eat durians that have fallen to the forest floor.

▶ Look inside a pitcher plant and you can see how it traps bugs.

Slippery surface

Insects caught in thick liquid

684 Pitcher plants are killers. These pretty green plants lure bugs using a tempting scent. As insects land on the rim of the pitcher, their feet lose their grip on the waxy surface, sending them tumbling into the trap. The plant produces acid, which digests the insect's body, dissolving it within hours. The enormous rajah pitcher plant can even digest mice and birds!

I DON'T BELIEVE IT!

Scientists recently discovered that the water in a pitcher plant is thickened with slime, which sucks the insect down like quicksand. It may be possible to use this slime to develop chemicals that kill insect pests.

685 The biggest flower on Earth – the rafflesia – grows in the rainforests of Borneo. This monster bloom can reach one metre across and smells of rotting flesh. The rafflesia lives on other plants and steals its food and water from its 'host'.

▶ Rafflesia plants are parasites so they do not need roots, stems or leaves. Their foul smell attracts flies that pollinate the flowers.

On the move

◀ Green vine snakes live in Southeast Asia and mostly prey upon frogs and lizards.

686 Moving through a rainforest is difficult. Trees, roots and shrubs fill every space, and there are few natural paths, so animals have to fly, swing, crawl or leap to find food, shelter and mates.

687 Walking in a jungle at night is especially challenging, as an inky darkness descends when the sun sets. Animals that hunt at night are called nocturnal. Some bats use echolocation – a type of sixth sense – to hunt and find their way through the web of branches, while others, such as flying foxes, use their exceptional eyesight.

688 Green vine snakes have pencil-thin bodies and can move between branches soundlessly, reaching up to one metre between trees. With their tails firmly wrapped around a branch these snakes dangle down, looking for prey they can catch with a single venomous bite.

▲ Gibbons can swing from tree to tree using their long, strong arms. This movement is called brachiation.

689 Geckos can run along branches upside down, thanks to millions of tiny hairs on the soles of their feet. Each hair may be too small to see with the naked eye, but together they create a sticky force that holds the lizard to the tree. Scientists have been able to copy geckos' feet to make a super-sticky tape for use by humans.

690 Monkeys have prehensile (gripping) tails to help them keep their balance on branches. White-faced capuchins are small monkeys that live in groups, scampering through forests looking for bugs and fruit to eat. They can leap from tree to tree, but will sometimes run along the ground while keeping a watchful eye for jaguars.

◀ Like other big cats, jaguars move with stealth and in silence. Fur on their large padded paws helps to dampen the sound of their footsteps.

QUIZ

A monkey leaps through the treetops at a speed of 4 kilometres an hour. How far would it travel in 15 minutes?

a) 15 metres
b) 5 kilometres
c) 1 kilometre

Answer:
1 kilometre

Fantastic feathers

691 Birds of paradise are the jewels in a rainforest crown. These animals are dressed in feathers of fine colours and are adorned with crests, ruffs and streamers. Males use their bright, bold plumage to catch the attention of females, but they also do splendid dances and displays to make sure they can't be ignored!

692 The mating dance of the male cock-of-the-rock is one of nature's most extraordinary sights. Groups of males, with their bright-orange heads, collect on a branch near the forest floor, and put on a performance for a watching female. They flutter their wings, bob their heads and scuttle along the branch. The female mates with the male whose show has most impressed her.

▼ Male cocks-of-the-rock never hide themselves behind dull colours. Their startling plumage catches the attention of females – and predators.

693 Wilson's bird of paradise has bare blue skin on its head, which is so bright it can be seen at night. Males prepare a patch of ground to use as a stage, clearing it of all leaves and twigs. Their tails contain two skinny, curly silver feathers and their backs are metallic green. Like all birds of paradise, the females are not as brightly coloured as their mates.

I DON'T BELIEVE IT!

Hummingbirds are tiny, colourful birds of the rainforest that feed on sugary nectar from flowers. The bee hummingbird is the world's smallest bird, with a body length of just 57 millimetres and a wingspan of only 65 millimetres.

▼ When a male Raggiana bird of paradise is resting, its fan of orange-red feathers is hidden from view, but if a female nears, it will show itself in all its glory.

694 **Birds of paradise live in Australia, New Guinea and some Asian islands.** When dead samples of these birds were sent to Europe hundreds of years ago, their legs had been removed. This led scientists to believe that these creatures had come straight from paradise, and could not touch the ground until death, which is how they got their name.

Kaleidoscope of colour

695 Rainforests are full of shades of green, but the animals that live in them are often bold and bright in colour. Strong colours help animals send signals to one another in a habitat where it is easy to be hidden from view.

Postman butterfly

Birdwing butterfly

Blue morpho butterfly

▲ The wings of many butterflies are covered in tiny scales that reflect light rays to create a range of shimmering colours.

▶ A strawberry poison-dart frog from Costa Rica has bright colours to warn of the poison it has on its skin.

696 While some animals use colour to draw attention to themselves, others use it to hide. Giant stick insects, like many other bugs in the forest, are patterned in mottled shades of green, grey or brown so they blend in with their surroundings. Camouflage is one way to avoid being eaten in the jungle, but there are many other ways to stay alive.

697 The forest floor is littered with brightly coloured 'umbrellas'. These little growths, called toadstools or mushrooms, are fungi – living things that are similar to plants but do not need sunlight. Orange, gold, red, blue and yellow are common fungi colours, which may alert grazing animals to the poisons they contain.

◀ The giant stick insect can reach 45 centimetres in length.

Parasol fungi

Cup fungi

▲ Chameleons can change their skin colour, often to make themselves attractive to possible mates.

HIDE AND SEEK

With an adult's help, use the Internet to find out how these insects use camouflage to survive:

Mantis Glasswing butterfly Agrippa moth Leaf moth Leaf insect

698 Chameleons are masters of disguise. These lizards are able to change the colour of their skin according to heat, light and their mood. When chameleons are feeling relaxed and calm they are most likely to appear green, but they can turn yellow in a flash if they are angry.

▼ Fungi grow on old trees and rotting leaves on the forest floor.

Stinkhorn

699 Scarlet macaws, with their feathers of red, blue and green, brighten up cliff faces where they settle. They visit cliffs to eat clay, which helps them deal with poisons found in some of the seeds they eat. A flock of macaws is an explosion of colour and sound. They squawk and squabble as they feed, but fall silent if a predator nears.

▶ The rainbow colours of a scarlet macaw's plumage have led to this beautiful bird being trapped for the pet trade.

The key to survival

700 Surviving in a rainforest is a battle for most animals. Food and shelter are plentiful, but habitats are so crowded it is easy for predators to hide. As a result, many creatures have developed amazing ways to stay alive.

▲ Leaflitter toads are named for their clever camouflage. They resemble the decaying leaves of their forest floor habitat.

701 Some rainforest animals pretend to be poisonous. When explorer Henry Bates (1825–1892) examined butterflies in the Amazon he found one type of patterned butterfly that tasted foul to birds, and another type that looked very similar, which didn't. He concluded that some animals copy (mimic), the appearance of others that are poisonous to avoid being eaten.

▼ Goliath tarantulas don't build webs to catch their prey – they hunt just like bigger predators, stalking animals such as frogs.

702 Poisons are common in many rainforest creatures. However, the Goliath tarantula spider uses flying hairs, as well as poisons, to keep safe! Probably the world's largest spider, it reaches 30 centimetres across, with 2.5-centimetre-long fangs. If threatened, Goliath tarantula spiders shoot hairs at attackers, which cause irritation and pain.

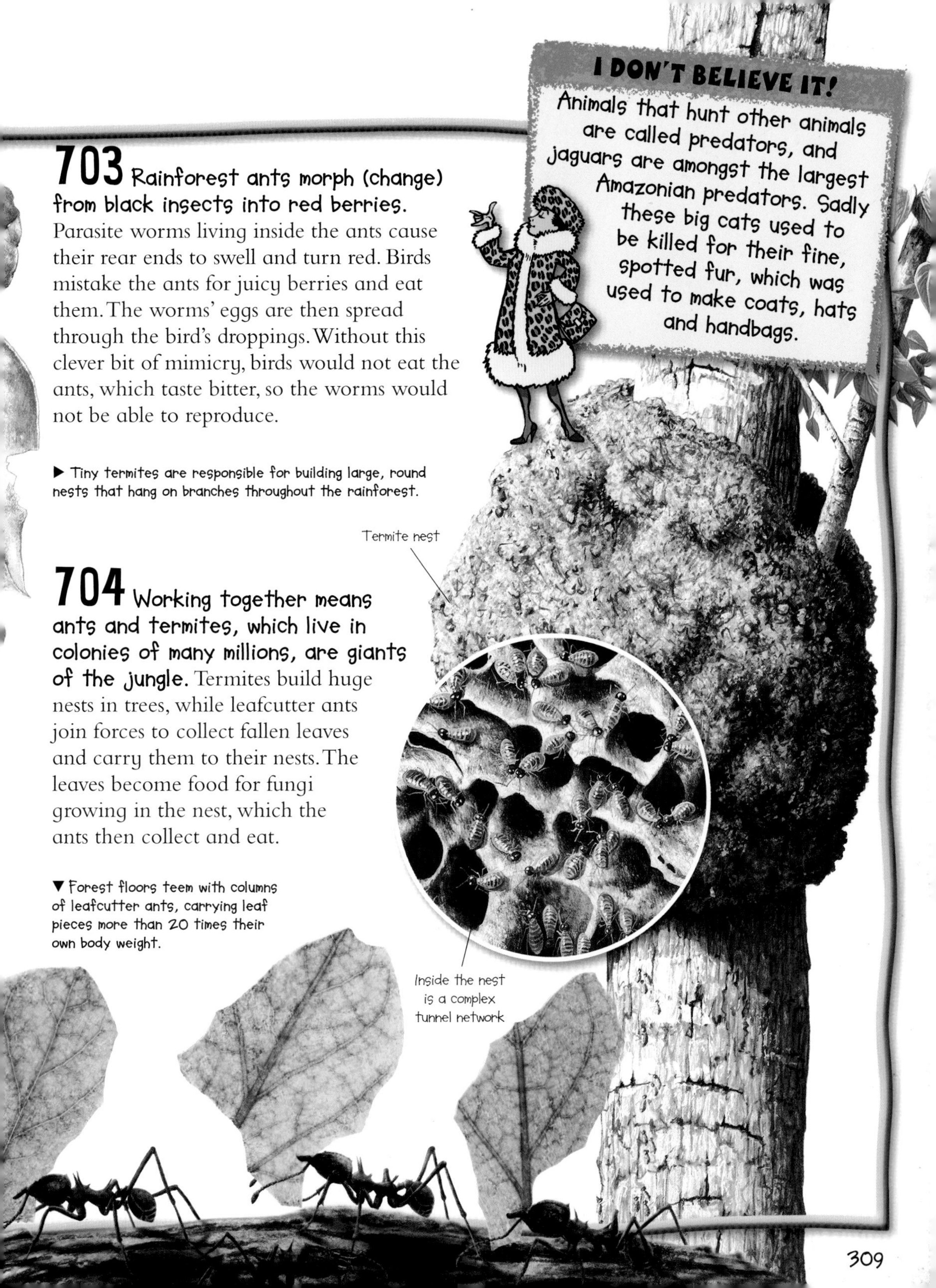

703 **Rainforest ants morph (change) from black insects into red berries.** Parasite worms living inside the ants cause their rear ends to swell and turn red. Birds mistake the ants for juicy berries and eat them. The worms' eggs are then spread through the bird's droppings. Without this clever bit of mimicry, birds would not eat the ants, which taste bitter, so the worms would not be able to reproduce.

▶ Tiny termites are responsible for building large, round nests that hang on branches throughout the rainforest.

704 **Working together means ants and termites, which live in colonies of many millions, are giants of the jungle.** Termites build huge nests in trees, while leafcutter ants join forces to collect fallen leaves and carry them to their nests. The leaves become food for fungi growing in the nest, which the ants then collect and eat.

▼ Forest floors teem with columns of leafcutter ants, carrying leaf pieces more than 20 times their own body weight.

The jungle's bounty

705 When Christopher Columbus (1451–1506) trekked through the rainforests of Central America he searched in vain for treasure. Eventually, other explorers and invaders came to realize that the rainforests of the world are home to plenty of other valuables. Sadly, it is this discovery that has led to the destruction of so much of the rainforest habitat.

706 For many people who rely on rainforests for survival, the jungle's most precious bounty is wood. Trees provide fuel for cooking, keeping warm and heating water. People also cut down large numbers of trees to sell the wood – this is called logging.

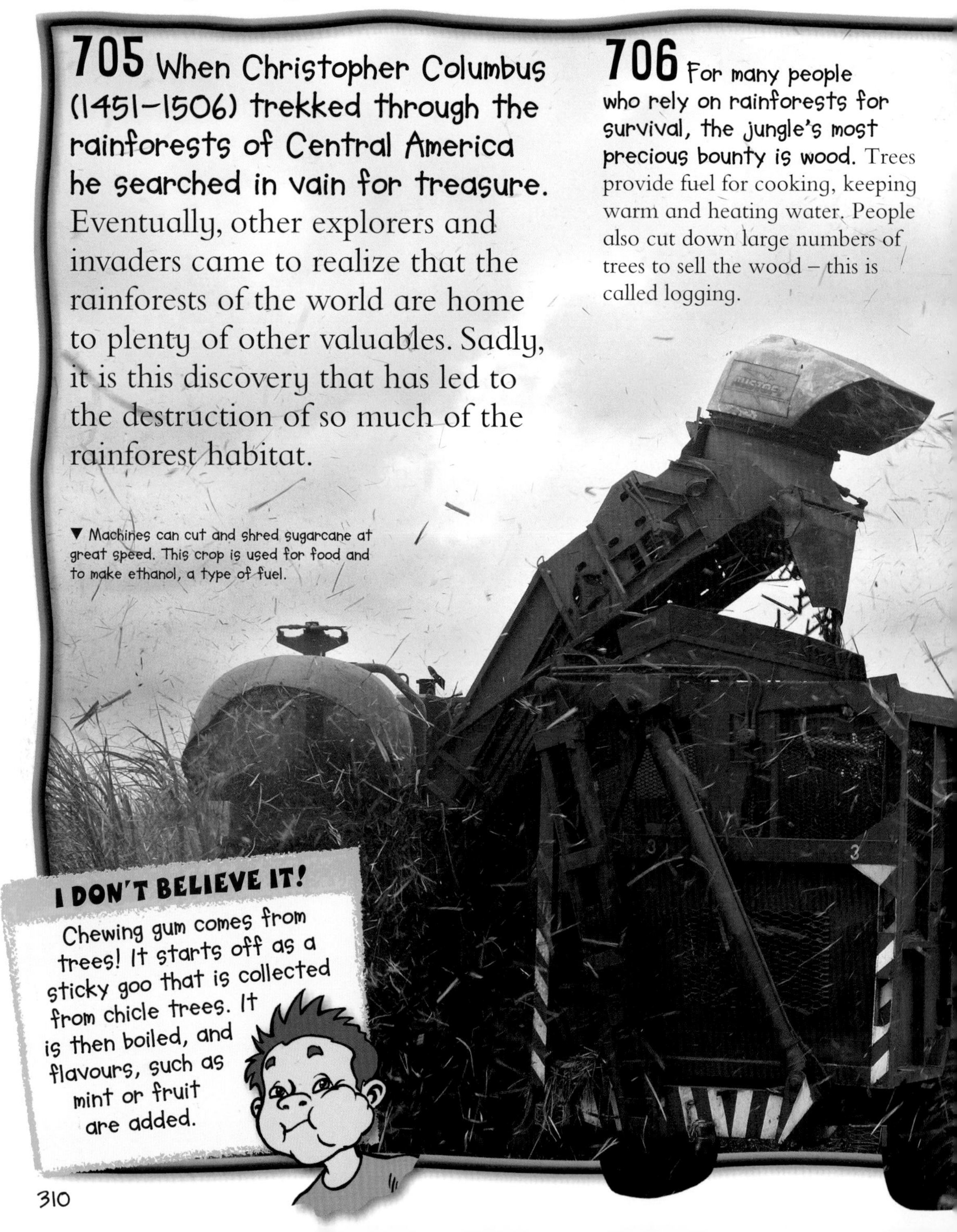

▼ Machines can cut and shred sugarcane at great speed. This crop is used for food and to make ethanol, a type of fuel.

I DON'T BELIEVE IT!

Chewing gum comes from trees! It starts off as a sticky goo that is collected from chicle trees. It is then boiled, and flavours, such as mint or fruit are added.

▲ Cocoa beans grow inside pods.

▲ Latex drips into a collecting cup.

▲ Star fruits, or carambolas, can be sweet or sour.

707 Chocolate, sugar and rubber come from rainforest plants. Cocoa pods are cut open to reveal seeds (cocoa beans) which are dried, cleaned and made into chocolate. Sugar comes from a grass called sugarcane that grows in tropical areas. Rubber is harvested from trees as a white sticky gum called latex, which is made into many useful products such as tyres and hoses.

708 Scientists are discovering that rainforest plants can be used to treat diseases. The people of the rainforests have known this for thousands of years. Quinine is a chemical that comes from the bark of the cinchona tree. It has been used by Amazonian Indians to prevent malaria – a deadly disease spread by mosquitoes. It is thought many rainforest plants could be used to treat cancer in the future.

709 Many delicious fruits, vegetables, nuts, spices and herbs come from rainforests, although they may be cultivated (grown) in other places. Shops around the world sell ginger, cloves, pepper, nutmeg, pineapples, bananas, starfruits and sweet potatoes, all of which originally came from rainforests.

▶ The outer bark of a cinchona tree is peeled back to reveal yellow inner bark, which contains quinine.

Paradise lost

710 Mangrove forests are one of the world's fastest disappearing habitats. Half of them have been destroyed in just 50 years. The trees are cut down so the swampy ground can be used to cultivate shrimps to be sold as food. Coastal areas that have lost their mangrove forests are more likely to suffer from tsunamis, storms and flooding.

711 The red-vented cockatoo is one of the world's rarest birds. Chicks are taken from nests and sold as pets – there may now be as few as 1000 left. The giant elephant birds of Madagascar died out centuries ago when their eggs were taken for food.

712 Gold mines, which use the poisonous metal mercury, have been established in some rainforests. Water that contains mercury can kill anything that comes into contact with it, and may have caused the disappearance of many types of frog and toad.

QUIZ

Which of these words means a type of animal has completely disappeared?
a) Existing
b) Extinct
c) Extinguished

Answer:
b

▲ This mangrove swamp in Indonesia has been devastated by shrimp farming. Mangroves protect land from water damage and are home to many animals, which, once destroyed, may take centuries to recover.

713 Humans' closest relatives are being eaten to extinction. Primates such as gorillas, chimps and bonobos are sold as meat in Africa, while monkeys and langurs are served as luxury dishes in Asia. Primates also suffer when their habitats are affected by human conflicts.

▲ WWF international staff patrols search for evidence of poaching activities in central Africa.

714 When the forest dies, so does a way of life. Now the future looks uncertain for millions of tribal people whose families have depended on rainforests for centuries. When they lose their forest homes, it is hard for people to retain the knowledge and skills that help them to survive.

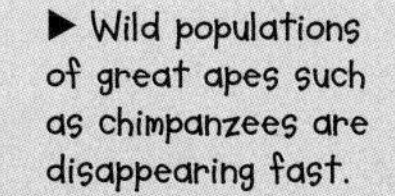

► Wild populations of great apes such as chimpanzees are disappearing fast.

Burning issues

715 Cutting down forests is called deforestation. Many forests are lost when they are turned into plantations – large fields that are used to grow single crops, such as bananas or rubber. Scientists believe that at least 19 million precious rainforest trees are cut down every day for wood or to make way for crops.

716 Around one-sixth of the Amazon rainforest has been destroyed, yet deforestation continues around the world. New roads are being built in the South American and African rainforests, which make it easier to fell trees. As many countries with rainforests are poor, selling wood can seem a good way for people to pay for food.

▼ It only takes a few hours for modern machines to fell trees and remove vegetation so the land can be used for farming.

I DON'T BELIEVE IT!

Orang-utans are close to extinction because their forests are becoming palm plantations. Palm oil is used in food and as a fuel. It is expected that orang-utans will be gone from the wild in less than ten years.

▲ Aerial photos show how huge areas of rainforest are being destroyed so the land can be used for cattle and crops.

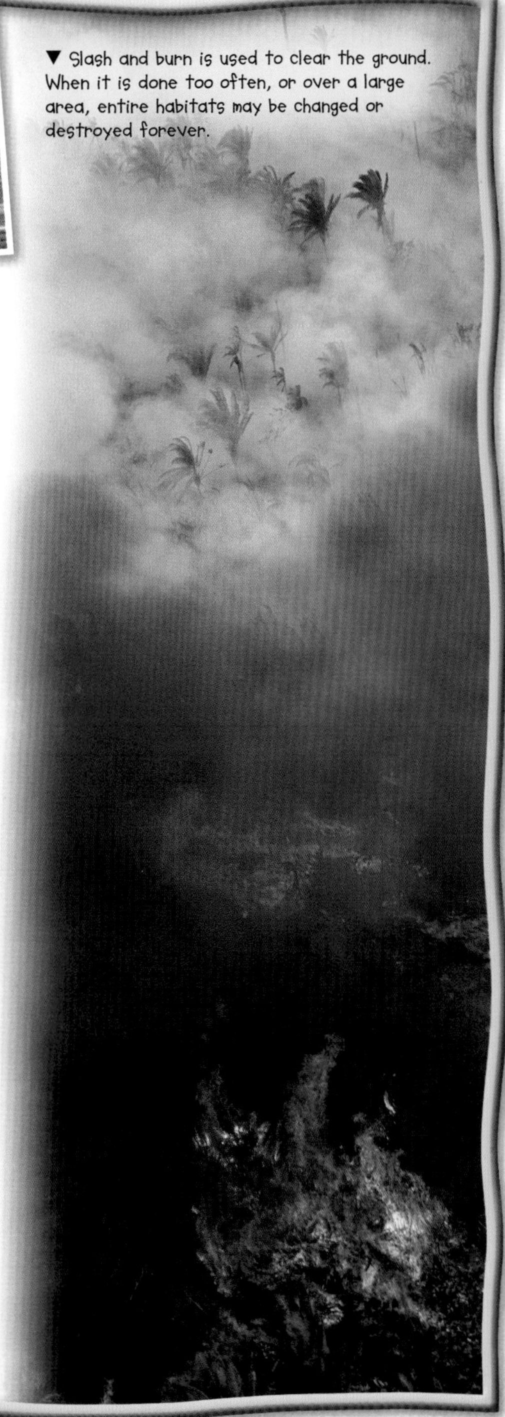

▼ Slash and burn is used to clear the ground. When it is done too often, or over a large area, entire habitats may be changed or destroyed forever.

717 **The Amazon rainforest is being cut down to provide land for cattle.** These animals are used for beef, which is sent to developed nations for use in hamburgers and similar foods. There are more than 200 million herds of cattle in the region, and that number is likely to grow.

718 **Large areas of rainforest are destroyed using 'slash and burn'.** Trees and plants are cut down, and the remains are burned. The cleared ground is used for growing crops, or as land for cattle. This method of deforestation ruins the soil, so the farmers then have to move on to a new patch of forest.

719 **Deforestation has been found to affect our atmosphere and climate.** Removing these massive ecosystems could cause droughts and flooding. Once forests are gone, the soil is not held together so well, causing soil erosion, so landslides become more common and plants can no longer grow.

Forests for the future

720 We must preserve the world's rainforests if we value the people and wildlife that live in them. Less than eight percent of these ecosystems are currently strictly protected from deforestation, but governments could turn rainforests into national parks so they cannot be used for farming or logging.

▲ Tourists pay to go on canopy walks and admire the rainforests from above. Money from tourism can be used to protect these habitats and give local people jobs.

▼ Solar panels collect the Sun's energy, which can be turned into electrical energy to provide light and heat.

721 Rainforest people can be shown how to use solar power to produce energy for light and cooking. Solar power is sustainable, which means it will never run out – unlike rainforest trees. Wood fires produce dirty smoke, but solar energy, which comes from the sun, is pollution-free.

722 Technology may help save the Congo rainforest in Africa. Local people who find better ways to earn money than cutting down trees will be helped with money from a special fund. Their progress will be checked using satellite images of the forest.

724 Everyone can make a difference to the future of the rainforests. Shoppers can check they are not buying products that come from rainforest regions, and governments can develop tourism so that local people can earn a living protecting forests, rather than destroying them.

Products that may come from rainforest regions:

* Wood
* Soya
* Beef
* Palm oil

Check labels before buying

723 It was once thought that when a rainforest had gone, it would be gone forever. However, scientists have grown a fresh forest in Borneo to replace one that has been destroyed. Seeds from more than 1300 trees were planted, and the soil was treated with a special fertilizer. Now 30 types of mammal and 116 types of bird have moved in. Local people have been involved with the project, and helped it to succeed.

725 Rainforests will only be preserved if people respect all of Earth's delicate ecosystems. Everyone who cares about nature hopes that there is still time to halt the damage, and that rainforests will still be around in the centuries to come.

▶ Workers at an orang-utan orphanage in Borneo care for baby orangs that have lost their parents to hunting or the illegal pet trade.

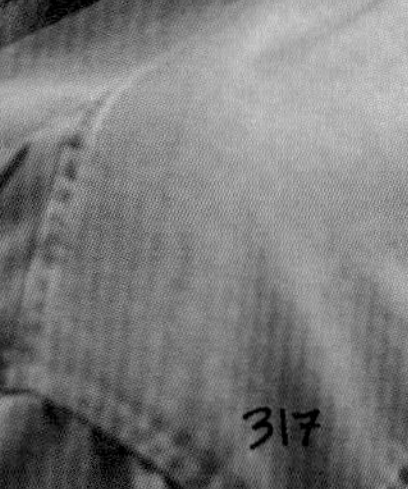

OCEANS

726 Oceans cover more than two-thirds of the Earth's rocky surface. Their total area is about 362 million square kilometres, which means there is more than twice as much ocean as land! Although all the oceans flow into each other, we know them as four different oceans – the Pacific, Atlantic, Indian and Arctic. Our landmasses, the continents, rise out of the oceans.

ARCTIC OCEAN
ATLANTIC OCEAN
PACIFIC OCEAN
ATLANTIC OCEAN
SOUTHE

727 The largest, deepest ocean is the Pacific. It covers nearly half of our planet and is almost as big as the other three oceans put together! In places, the Pacific is so deep that the Earth's tallest mountain, Everest, would sink without a trace.

▶ Mount Everest is the highest point on Earth, rising to 8848 metres. Parts of the Pacific Ocean are deeper than 10,000 metres.

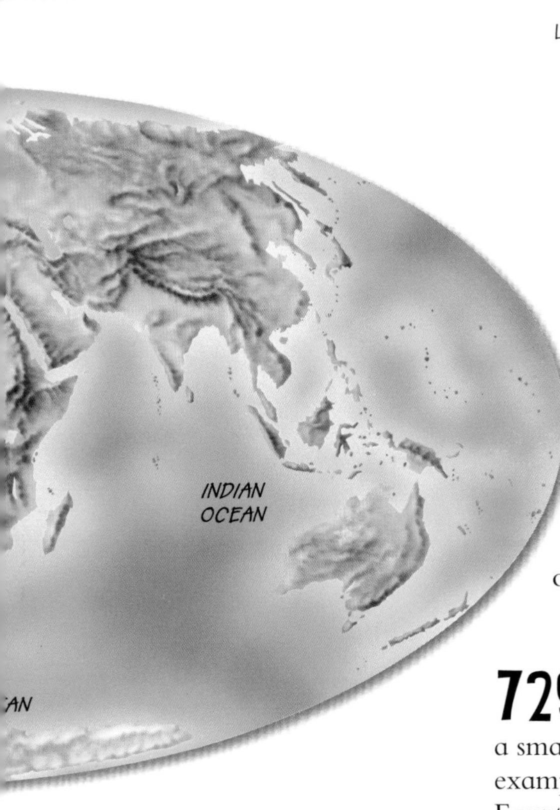

▲ The world's oceans cover most of our planet. Each ocean is made up of smaller bodies of water called seas.

Light hits the surface of the water

Scattered blue and green

▶ A cup of sea water appears see-through. It is only when you look at a large area of sea that it has colour.

728 Oceans can look blue, green or grey. This is because of the way light hits the surface. Water soaks up the red parts of light but scatters the blue-green parts, making the sea look different shades of blue or green.

729 Seas can be red or dead. A sea is a small part of an ocean. The Red Sea, for example, is the part of the Indian Ocean between Egypt and Saudi Arabia. Asia's Dead Sea isn't a true sea, but a landlocked lake. We call it a sea because it is a large body of water.

Oceans hold 97 percent of the world's water. Just a fraction is in freshwater lakes and rivers.

730 There are streams in the oceans. All the water in the oceans is constantly moving, but in some places it flows as currents, which take particular paths. One of these is the warm Gulf Stream, that travels around the edge of the Atlantic Ocean.

Ocean features

731 There are plains, mountains and valleys under the oceans, in areas called basins. Each basin has a rim (the flat continental shelf that meets the shore) and sides (the continental slope that drops away from the shelf). In the ocean basin there are flat abyssal plains, steep hills, huge underwater volcanoes called seamounts, and deep valleys called trenches.

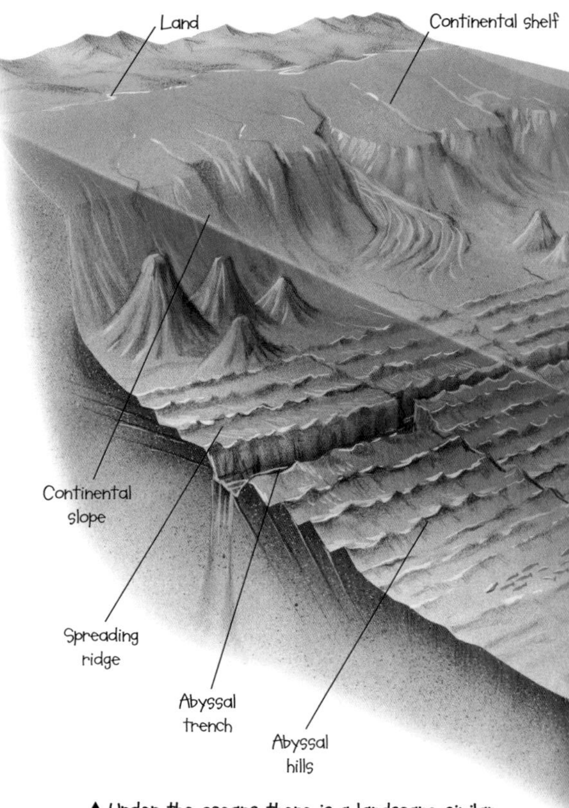

▲ Under the oceans there is a landscape similar to that found on land.

▼ Magma (molten rock) escapes from the seabed to form a ridge. This ridge has collapsed to form a rift valley.

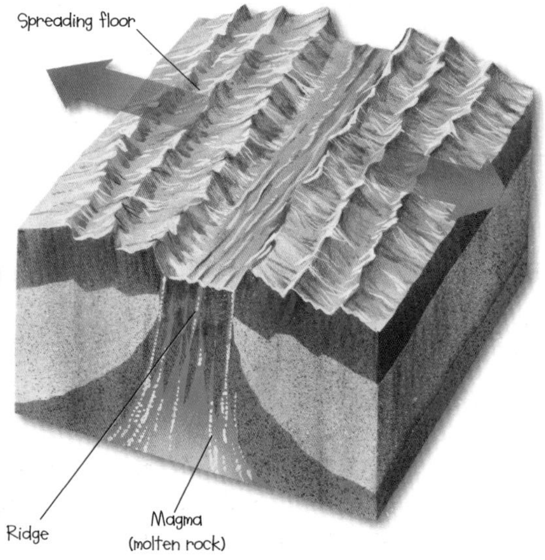

732 The ocean floor is spreading. Molten (liquid) rock inside the Earth seeps from holes on the seabed. As the rock cools, it forms new sections of floor that creep slowly out. Scientists have proved this fact by looking at layers of rock on the ocean floor. There are matching stripes of rock either side of a ridge. Each pair came from the same hot rock eruption, then slowly spread out.

▼ An atoll is a ring-shaped coral reef that encloses a deep lagoon. It can form when a volcanic island sinks underwater.

733 Some islands are swallowed by the ocean.

Sometimes, a ring-shaped coral reef called an atoll marks where an island once was. The coral reef built up around the island. After the volcano blew its top, the reef remained.

▶ There are more Hawaiian islands still to come – Loihi is just visible beneath the water's surface.

I DON'T BELIEVE IT!

The world's longest mountain chain is under the ocean. It is the Mid-Ocean range and stretches around the middle of the Earth.

734 New islands are born all the time.

When an underwater volcano erupts, its lava cools in the water. Layers of lava build up, and the volcano grows in size. Eventually, it is tall enough to peep above the waves. The Hawaiian islands rose from the sea like this.

Swimming machines

735 There are over 21,000 different types of fish in the sea. They range from huge whale sharks to tiny gobies. Almost all are covered in scales and use fins and a muscular tail to power through the water. Like their freshwater cousins, sea fish have slits called gills that take oxygen from the water so they can breathe.

736 The oarfish is bigger than an oar – it is as long as four canoes! It is the longest bony fish and is found in all the world's oceans. Oarfish are handsome creatures – they have a striking red fin along the length of their back.

737 Sunfish like sunbathing! Ocean sunfish are very large, broad fish that can weigh as much as a tonne. They are named after their habit of sunbathing on the surface of the open ocean.

◀ People once thought oarfish swam horizontally through the water. Now they know they swim upright.

▶ At over 3 metres long, sunfish are the biggest bony fish in the oceans. They feed on plankton.

▲ In a large group called a school, fish like these yellow snappers have less chance of being picked off by a predator.

▶ Flying fish feed near the surface so they are easy to find. Their gliding flight helps them escape most hunters.

738 Flying fish cannot really fly. Fish can't survive out of water, but flying fish sometimes leap above the waves when they are travelling at high speeds. They use their wing-like fins to keep them in the air for as long as 30 seconds.

QUIZ

1. Which fish like to sunbathe?
2. How many types of fish live in the sea?
3. How does a fish breathe?
4. Can flying fish really fly?

Answers:
1. Sunfish 2. 21,000
3. With its gills 4. No

739 Not all fish are the same shape. Cod or mackerel are what we think of as a normal fish shape, but fish come in all shapes and sizes. Flounder and other flatfish have squashed-flat bodies. Eels are so long and thin that the biggest types look like snakes, while tiny garden eels resemble worms! And of course, seahorses and seadragons look nothing like other fish at all!

▶ The flounder's flattened shape and dull colouring help to camouflage (hide) it on the seabed.

Shark!

740 Great whites are the scariest sharks in the oceans. These powerful predators have been known to kill people and can speed through the water at 30 kilometres per hour. Unlike most fish, the great white is warm-blooded. This allows its muscles to work well, but also means the shark has to feed on plenty of meat.

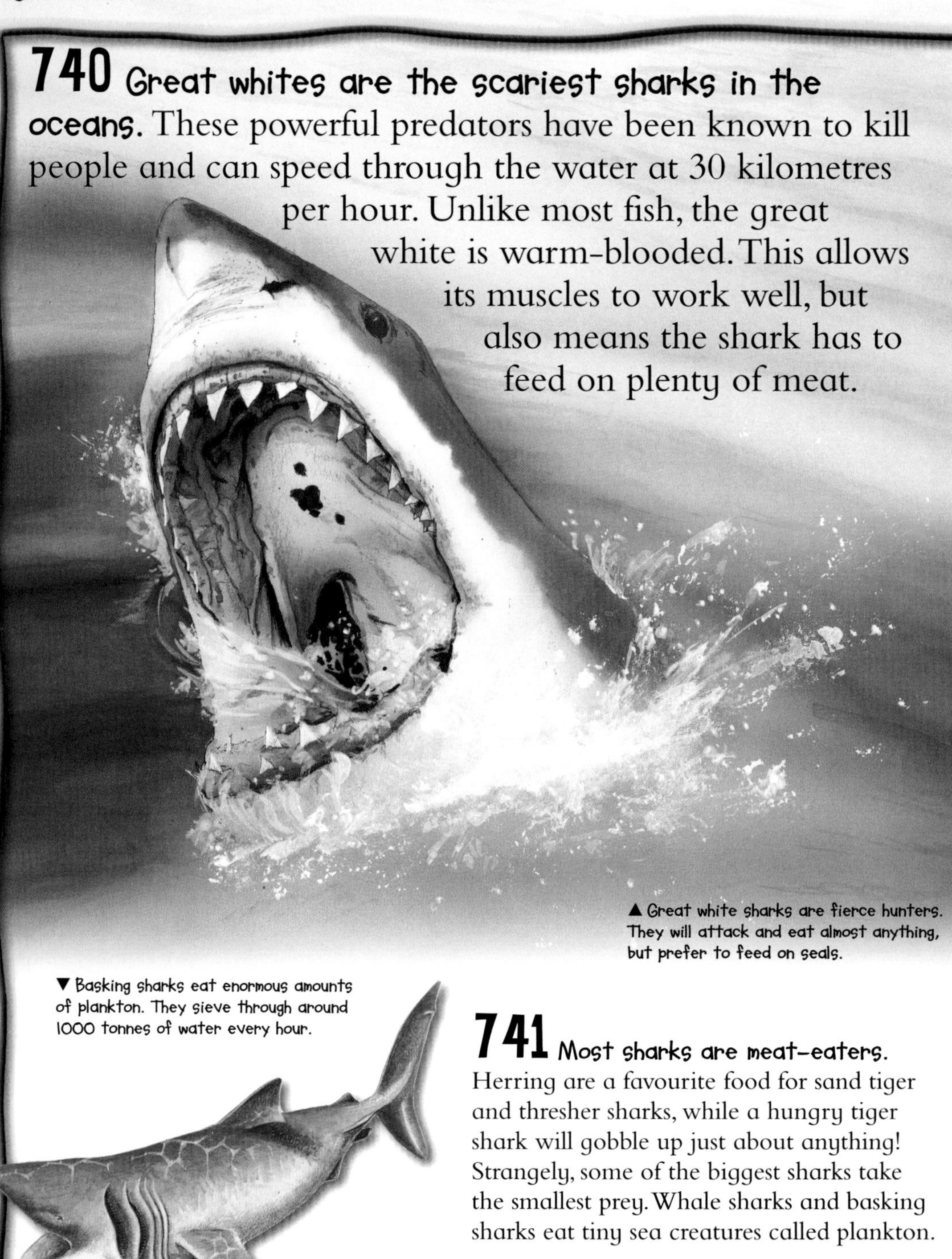

▲ Great white sharks are fierce hunters. They will attack and eat almost anything, but prefer to feed on seals.

▼ Basking sharks eat enormous amounts of plankton. They sieve through around 1000 tonnes of water every hour.

741 Most sharks are meat-eaters. Herring are a favourite food for sand tiger and thresher sharks, while a hungry tiger shark will gobble up just about anything! Strangely, some of the biggest sharks take the smallest prey. Whale sharks and basking sharks eat tiny sea creatures called plankton.

SHARK PARTS

Study the labels to learn the shark's special features. Trace the shark without the labels, then see how many parts you can name.

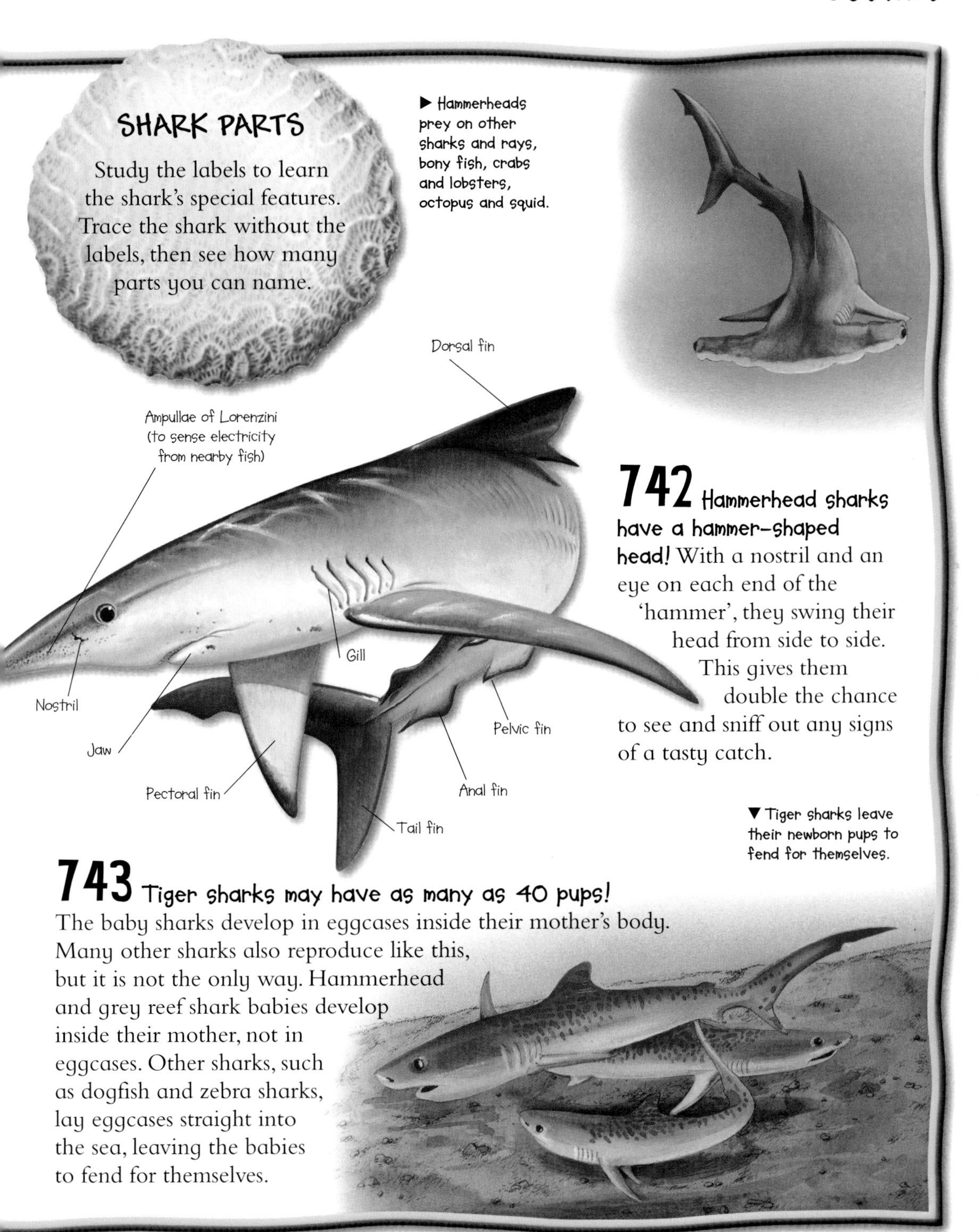

▶ Hammerheads prey on other sharks and rays, bony fish, crabs and lobsters, octopus and squid.

742 **Hammerhead sharks have a hammer-shaped head!** With a nostril and an eye on each end of the 'hammer', they swing their head from side to side. This gives them double the chance to see and sniff out any signs of a tasty catch.

▼ Tiger sharks leave their newborn pups to fend for themselves.

743 **Tiger sharks may have as many as 40 pups!** The baby sharks develop in eggcases inside their mother's body. Many other sharks also reproduce like this, but it is not the only way. Hammerhead and grey reef shark babies develop inside their mother, not in eggcases. Other sharks, such as dogfish and zebra sharks, lay eggcases straight into the sea, leaving the babies to fend for themselves.

Whales and dolphins

744 The biggest animal on the planet lives in the oceans. It is the blue whale, measuring about 28 metres in length and weighing up to 190 tonnes. It feeds by filtering tiny, shrimp-like creatures called krill from the water – about four tonnes of krill a day! Like other great whales, it has special, sieve-like parts in its mouth called baleen plates.

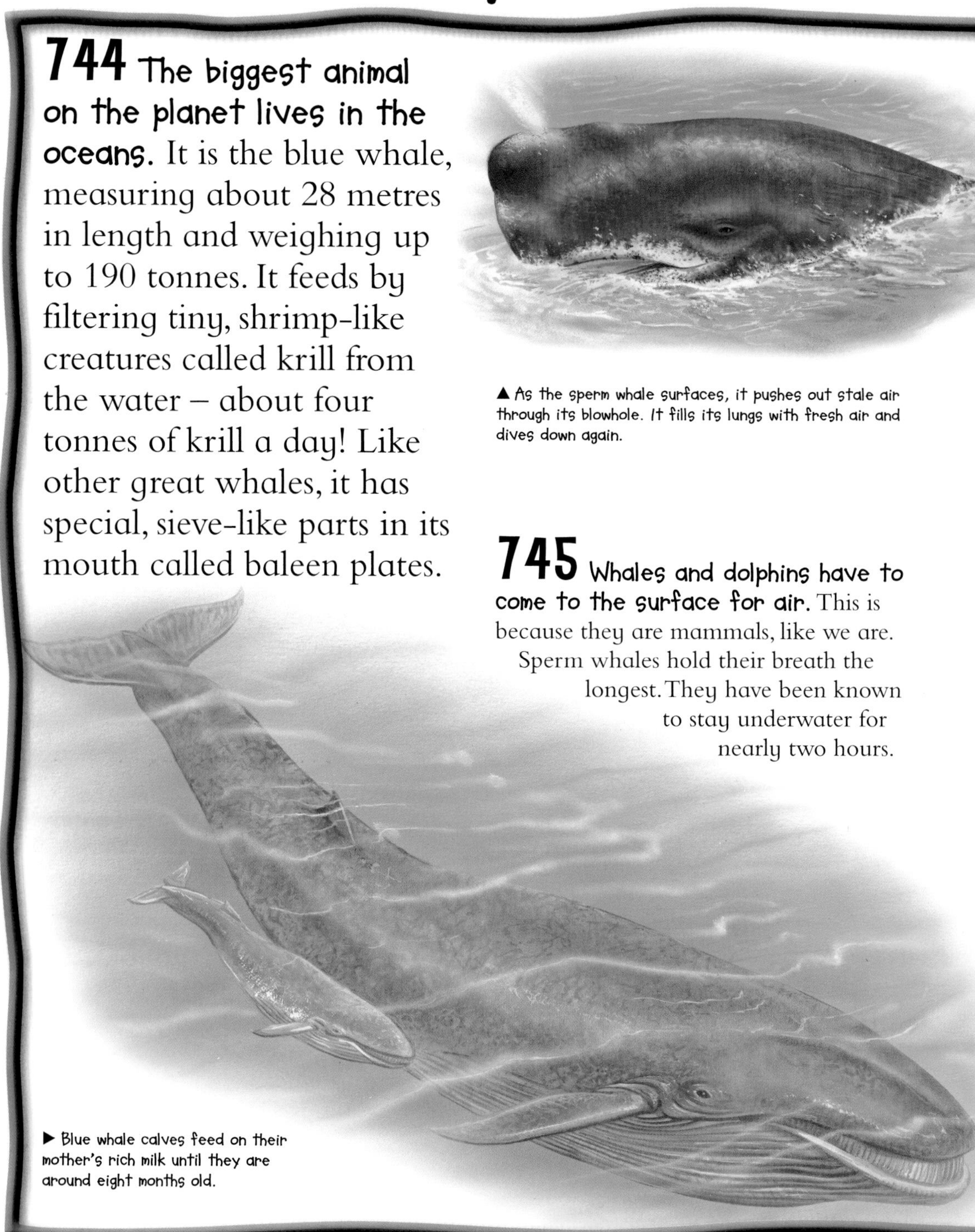

▲ As the sperm whale surfaces, it pushes out stale air through its blowhole. It fills its lungs with fresh air and dives down again.

745 Whales and dolphins have to come to the surface for air. This is because they are mammals, like we are. Sperm whales hold their breath the longest. They have been known to stay underwater for nearly two hours.

▶ Blue whale calves feed on their mother's rich milk until they are around eight months old.

▲ Killer whales carry the baby seals out to sea before eating them.

▶ The beluga is a type of white whale. It makes a range of noises – whistles, clangs, chirps and moos!

746 Dolphins and whales sing songs to communicate. The noisiest is the humpback whale, whose wailing noises can be heard for hundreds of kilometres. The sweetest is the beluga – nicknamed the 'sea canary'. Songs are used to attract a mate, or just to keep track of each other.

747 The narwhal has a horn like a unicorn's. This Arctic whale has a long, twirly tooth that spirals out of its head. The males use their tusks as a weapon when they are fighting over females.

▲ The narwhal's 3 metre tusk seems too long for its body.

748 Killer whales play with their food. They especially like to catch baby seals, which they toss into the air before eating. Killer whales are not true whales, but the largest dolphins. They have teeth for chewing, instead of baleen plates.

749 Moby Dick was a famous white whale. It starred in a book by Herman Melville about a white sperm whale and a whaler called Captain Ahab.

I DON'T BELIEVE IT!

Barnacles are shellfish. They attach themselves to ships' hulls, or the bodies of grey whales and other large sea animals.

Ocean reptiles

750 Marine iguanas are the most seaworthy lizards. Most lizards prefer life on land, where it is easier to warm up their cold-blooded bodies, but marine iguanas depend on the sea for their food. They dive underwater to graze on the algae and seaweed growing on rocks.

▲ Marine iguanas are found around the Galapagos Islands in the Pacific. When they are not diving for food, they bask on the rocks that dot the island coastlines. The lizards' dark skin helps to absorb the Sun's heat.

751 Turtles come ashore only to lay their eggs. Although they are born on land, turtles head for the sea the minute they hatch. Females return to the beach where they were born to dig their nest. After they have laid their eggs, they go straight back to the water. Hawksbill turtles may lay up to 140 eggs in a clutch, while some green turtle females clock up 800 eggs in a year!

▲ *In a single breeding season, a female green turtle may lay as many as ten clutches, each containing up to 80 eggs!*

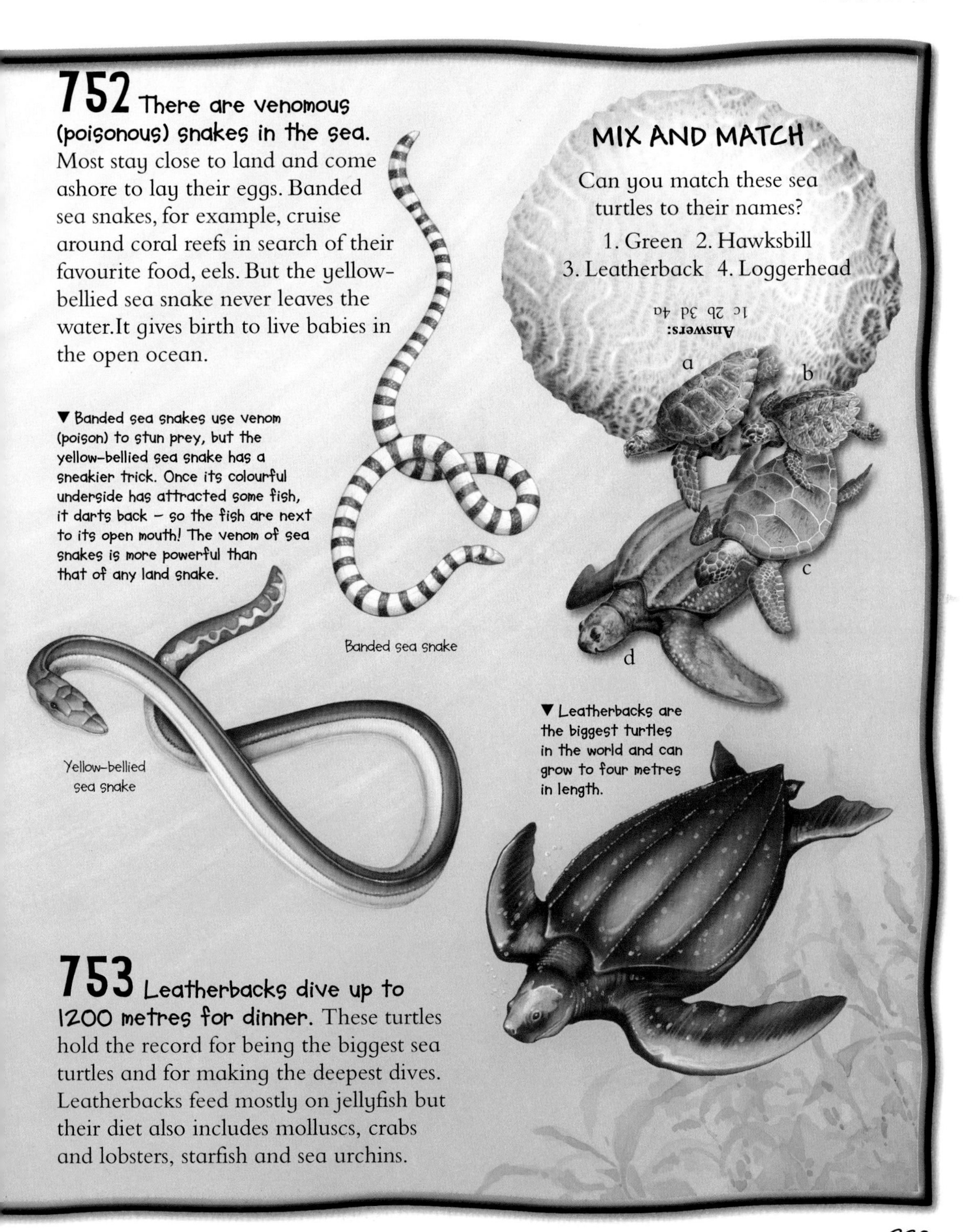

752 There are venomous (poisonous) snakes in the sea. Most stay close to land and come ashore to lay their eggs. Banded sea snakes, for example, cruise around coral reefs in search of their favourite food, eels. But the yellow-bellied sea snake never leaves the water.It gives birth to live babies in the open ocean.

▼ Banded sea snakes use venom (poison) to stun prey, but the yellow-bellied sea snake has a sneakier trick. Once its colourful underside has attracted some fish, it darts back – so the fish are next to its open mouth! The venom of sea snakes is more powerful than that of any land snake.

MIX AND MATCH

Can you match these sea turtles to their names?

1. Green 2. Hawksbill 3. Leatherback 4. Loggerhead

Answers:
1c 2b 3d 4a

▼ Leatherbacks are the biggest turtles in the world and can grow to four metres in length.

753 Leatherbacks dive up to 1200 metres for dinner. These turtles hold the record for being the biggest sea turtles and for making the deepest dives. Leatherbacks feed mostly on jellyfish but their diet also includes molluscs, crabs and lobsters, starfish and sea urchins.

Harvests from the sea

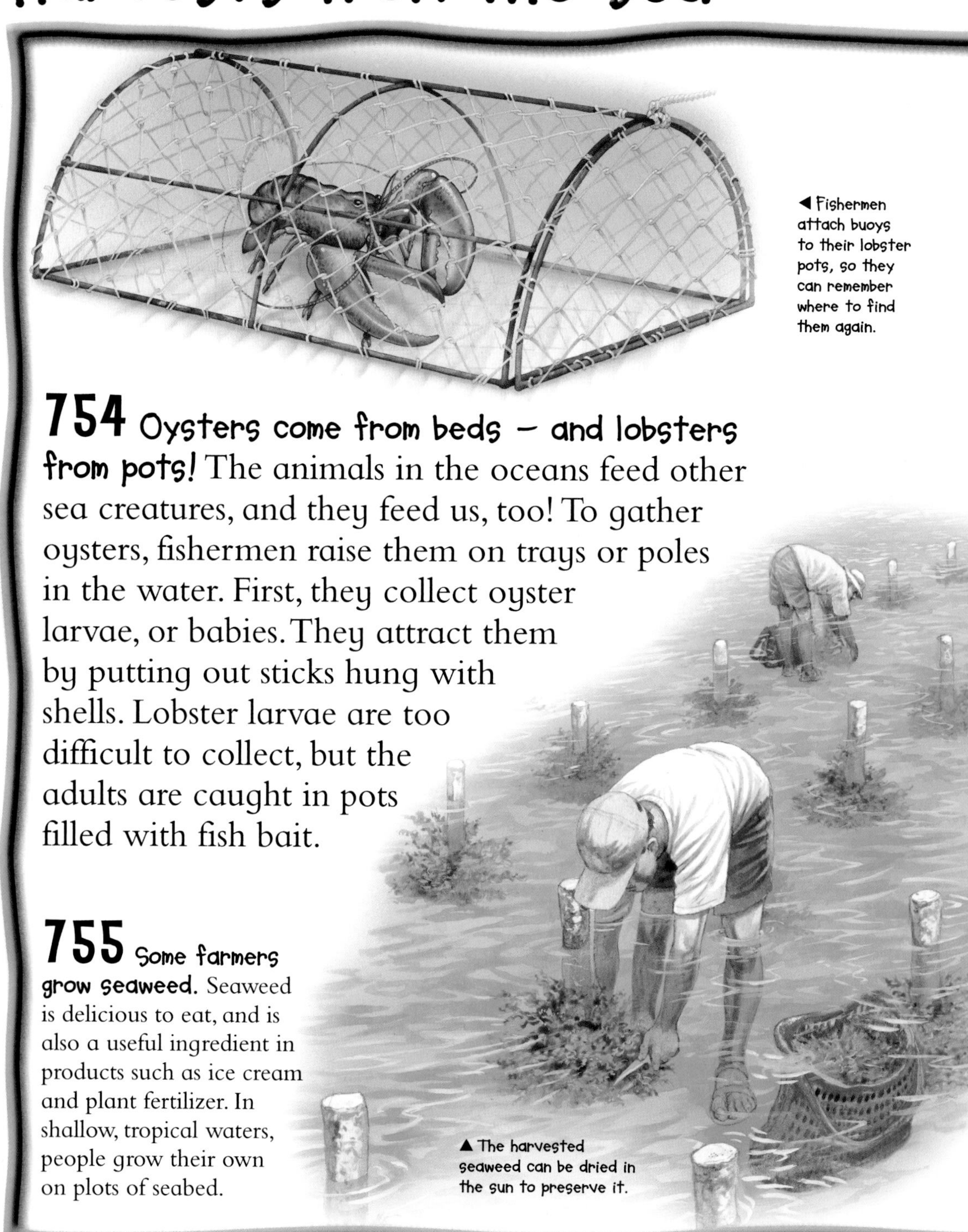

◀ Fishermen attach buoys to their lobster pots, so they can remember where to find them again.

754 Oysters come from beds – and lobsters from pots! The animals in the oceans feed other sea creatures, and they feed us, too! To gather oysters, fishermen raise them on trays or poles in the water. First, they collect oyster larvae, or babies. They attract them by putting out sticks hung with shells. Lobster larvae are too difficult to collect, but the adults are caught in pots filled with fish bait.

755 Some farmers grow seaweed. Seaweed is delicious to eat, and is also a useful ingredient in products such as ice cream and plant fertilizer. In shallow, tropical waters, people grow their own on plots of seabed.

▲ The harvested seaweed can be dried in the sun to preserve it.

▶ The oil platform's welded-steel legs rest on the seabed. They support the platform around 15 metres above the surface of the water.

756 Sea minerals are big business. Minerals are useful substances that we mine from the ground – and oceans are full of them! The most valuable are oil and gas, which are pumped from the seabed and piped ashore or transported in huge supertankers. Salt is another important mineral. In hot, low-lying areas, people build walls to hold shallow pools of sea water. The water dries up in the sun, leaving behind crystals of salt.

757 There are gemstones under the sea. Pearls are made by oysters. If a grain of sand is lodged inside an oyster's shell, it irritates its soft body. The oyster coats the sand with a substance called nacre, which is also used to line the inside of the shell. Over the years, more nacre builds up and the pearl gets bigger.

QUIZ

1. What are the young of lobster called?
2. What substances are pumped from the seabed?
3. Is seaweed edible?
4. Which gemstone is made by oysters?

Answers:
1. Larvae 2. Oil and gas
3. Yes 4. Pearl

▶ Pearl divers carry an oyster knife for prising open the oyster's shell.

DEEP OCEAN

758 Far down in the dark waters of the deep oceans lies a mysterious wilderness. The deep ocean is a place without light, where the water pressure can crush human bones. Until modern times, people did not believe that anything could live here. Now scientists are discovering new creatures all the time, from colossal squid with huge eyes to giant worms that are 2 metres in length.

▶ Almost 2.5 kilometres below the surface of the ocean, an eelpout fish hides among giant tube worms and crabs at a hydrothermal vent. Only two people have been to the deepest part of the oceans, which is about 11 kilometres below the waves. In contrast, 12 human explorers have walked on the surface of the Moon, which is 384,400 kilometres from Earth.

The ocean zones

759 Oceans are enormous areas of water. They cover more than two-thirds of the Earth's surface. There are five oceans and they make up a giant ecosystem of creatures that depend on seawater to survive.

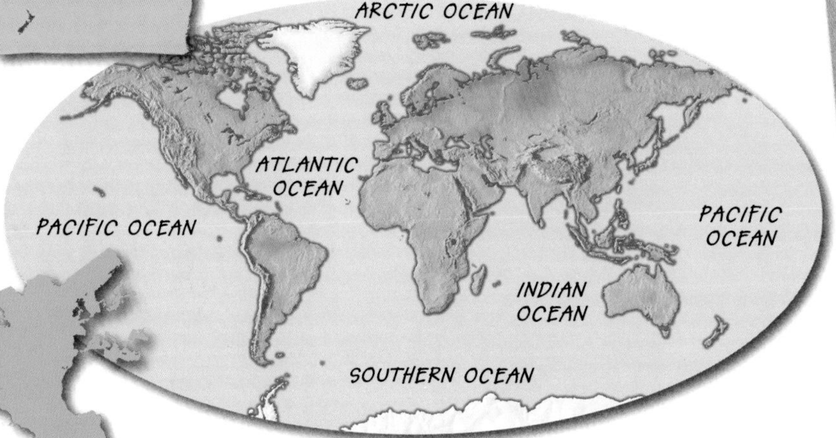

ARCTIC OCEAN

PACIFIC OCEAN

ARCTIC OCEAN

ATLANTIC OCEAN

PACIFIC OCEAN

PACIFIC OCEAN

INDIAN OCEAN

SOUTHERN OCEAN

ATLANTIC OCEAN

SOUTHERN OCEAN

INDIAN OCEAN

LIGHT ZONE 0–200 metres

Jellyfish

TWILIGHT ZONE 200–1000 metres

DARK ZONE 1000–4000 metres

Sea lily

ABYSSAL ZONE 4000–6000 metres

Tube worms

HADAL ZONE 6000–10,000 metres

760 At their edges, oceans are shallow and teem with life. These places are called continental shelves. However continental shelves only take up 5 percent of the total area of the oceans. The shelves fall away into deep slopes and from there, the seabed stretches out as dark, enormous plains.

◀▲ There are five oceans. They are all connected and make up one giant mass of water.

▶ Scientists divide the ocean into five layers, or zones. Different types of animals live in the different zones.

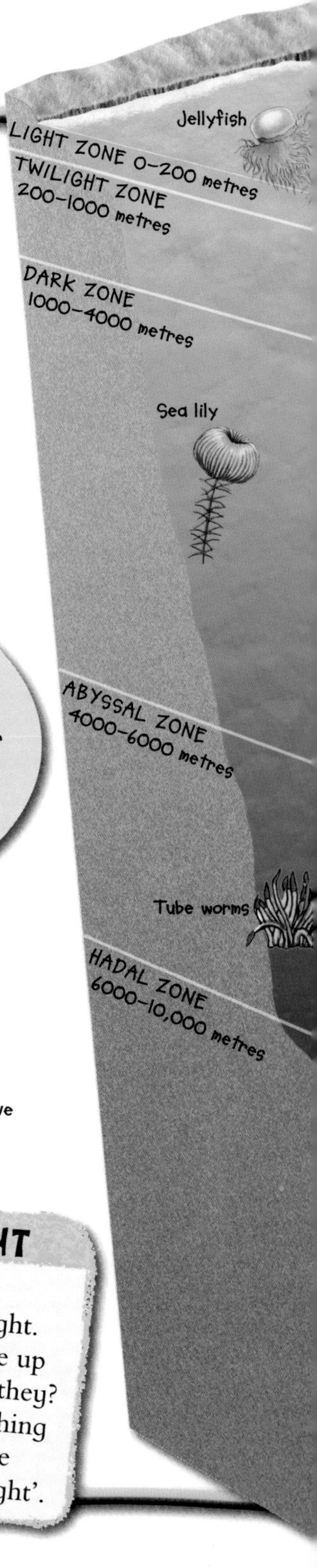

DELIGHT IN LIGHT

Find out about the wavelengths of white light. How many colours make up white light, and what are they? Find the answers by searching on the Internet with the keywords 'rainbow' and 'light'.

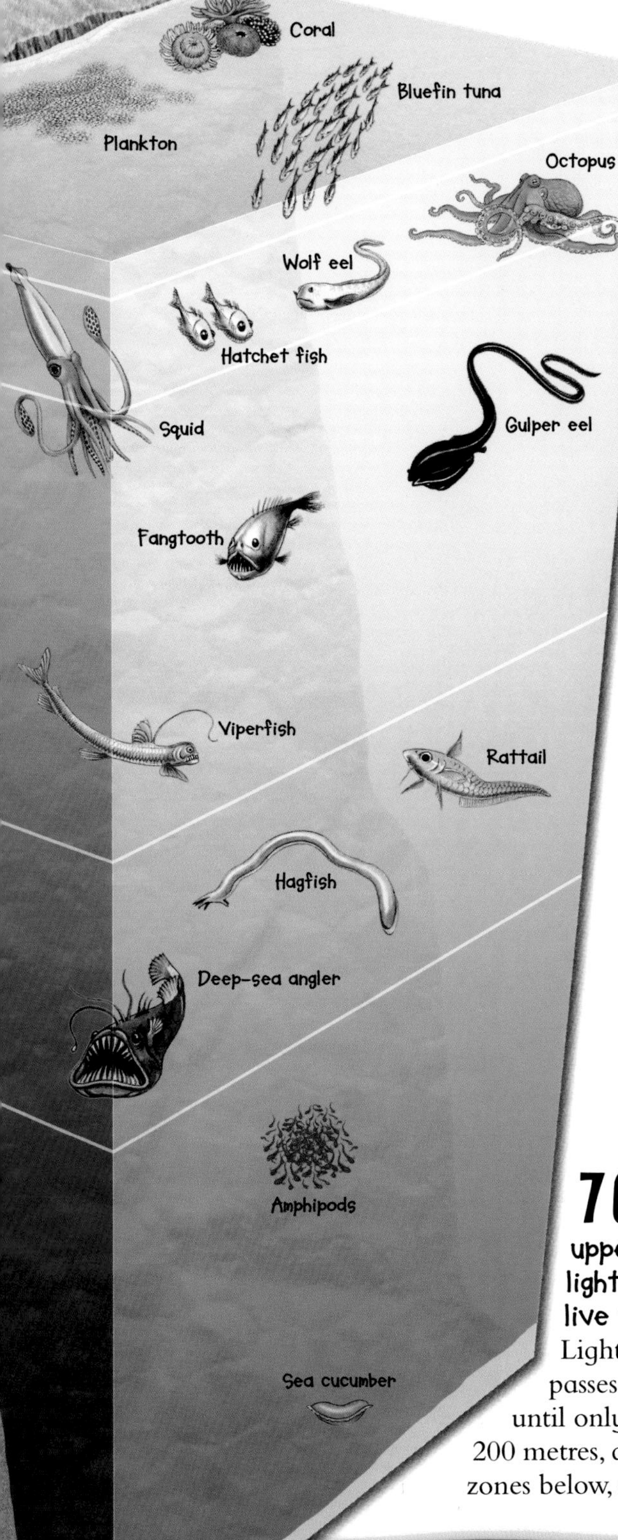

761 Oceans are deep places. The average depth is 3800 metres, but in some places the seabed lies as deep as 11,000 metres. If all the water in the oceans was removed, a dramatic landscape would be revealed – giant mountains, volcanoes, smooth flat plains and deep trenches.

▲ Sunlight can only pass through the ocean's uppermost layer. Everything below is in perpetual darkness.

762 Sunlight streams through the upper zone of the ocean, giving warmth, light and energy to the creatures that live there. This is called the Light Zone. Light is made up of many colours, and as it passes through water, the colours get absorbed, until only blue light is left. At a depth of around 200 metres, all blue light has disappeared and in the zones below, darkness takes over.

In deep water

763 Living in water is nothing like living in air. The ocean is one of Earth's most remarkable habitats. Ocean water is constantly moving and changing. The creatures that live here have to cope without light, and the weight of many tonnes of water above them.

765 As you travel deeper into the ocean you will feel a great weight on your body. Water is 830 times denser than air, and it is very heavy. It is water's density that helps things to float, or stay buoyant. However, the further down you go, the more pressure the water forces on you.

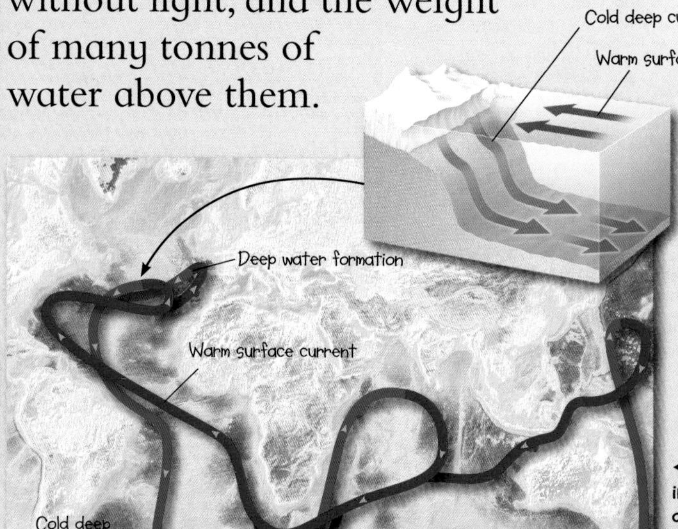

◄ Cold water is denser than warm water, and it sinks to the ocean depths near the polar regions.

◄ Water travels in currents around the world. The largest and deepest of these form a system called the global conveyor.

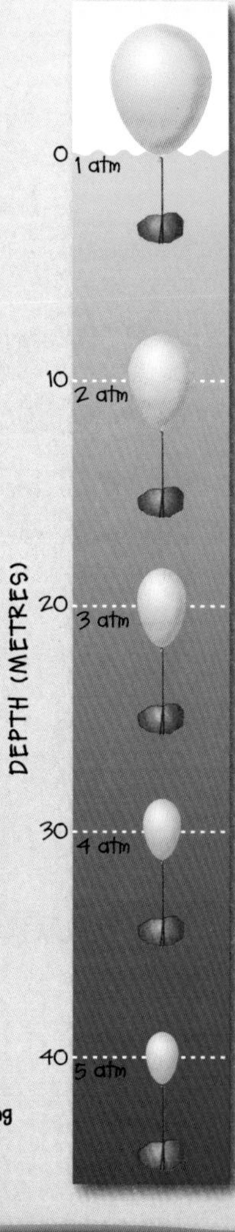

764 At the surface, wind creates waves and the Moon's gravitational pull causes tides. Further down, other forces are in action. Ocean water is continually moving, passing around the globe in giant streams called currents. If you were to get caught in one of these strong, deep currents, after 1000 years you would have journeyed all around the world!

► Water pressure is measured in atmospheres (atm). Pressure increases with depth, squashing the molecules of air in this balloon.

766 **Although you will soon be cold, you may notice that the temperature of the water around you doesn't change much.** Ocean water has great heat capacity, which means that it warms up slowly and cools down slowly too. It can hold on to its temperature about 4000 times better than air can.

▼ Many enormous animals, such as this basking shark, live in the ocean. The dense, salty seawater supports their great weight.

767 **The good news is that you won't have to work hard to get food.** If you stay still, it will float right past your nose. Because water is dense, tiny creatures and particles of food are suspended in it. Some sea creatures can wave tentacles to catch food, or just open their mouths as they swim!

◀ A magnified view of plankton, tiny animals and plants that float or swim in seawater. They often become food for bigger animals.

768 **You should never drink seawater.** It has lots of minerals, called salts, dissolved in it. A single bath of seawater contains 2.8 kilograms of salts. Most of that is sodium chloride (common salt). Gases, such as oxygen and nitrogen are also dissolved in seawater.

MAKING WATER HEAVY

You will need:

two identical cups containing the same amount of water salt

Add salt to one of the cups and stir. Continue until no more salt will dissolve. Weigh both cups – the salty one should be heavier. Salty water is denser and heavier than fresh water.

Water 96.5%
Other elements 0.6%
Sodium 1%
Salt 3.5%
Chloride 1.9%

▶ A beaker of ocean water may look dirty, but it is full of substances that are food for tiny organisms called phytoplankton.

The Light Zone

769 The top 200 metres of the ocean is called the Light Zone. At the continental shelf, sunlight can reach all the way to the seabed. However, within 10 metres of the water's surface, nearly all of the red parts of light have been absorbed, which means that many creatures appear dull in colour.

▲ The shiny scales on tuna fish reflect sunlight as they dart from side to side, to confuse their predators.

▶ Green turtles have to visit the surface to breathe air, then they dive to feed on marine plants.

770 Sunlight provides the energy for plants to grow. Marine plants such as seaweed need light in order to make food from carbon dioxide and water, in a process called photosynthesis. Plants also produce oxygen, the gas we breathe, and without it there would be no life in the oceans.

◀ Marine plants, including seaweed (shown here) and phytoplankton, are called algae.

◀ Emperor penguins can stay underwater for up to 20 minutes at a time, hunting for fish.

I DON'T BELIEVE IT!

Six billion tonnes of phytoplankton grow in the Light Zone every year and they produce half of the oxygen in our atmosphere. Without them there would be almost no animal life in the oceans, and few animals on land either.

771 Many marine plants are almost invisible. They are called phytoplankton and are so tiny that they have to be viewed with a microscope. Phytoplankton begin a food web that supports nearly all ocean life. They are eaten by microscopic animals, called zooplankton, and bigger animals too.

772 The Light Zone is bright and full of food, making it a busy habitat. Fish such as anchovies and sardines come to feed on swarms of plankton. In turn larger animals, such as sharks, come to prey upon the fish. Even birds, such as pelicans and penguins, enter this habitat to grab what food they can.

773 Most swimming animals of the Light Zone can move into deeper water to escape from predators. At around a depth of 200 metres almost all sunlight has been absorbed and darkness takes over in the Twilight Zone.

▼ Warm-water corals need sunlight to grow, and they build reefs in the Light Zone.

The Twilight Zone

774 From a depth of 200 to 1000 metres lies the Twilight Zone. Just enough light reaches this zone for animals to see, and be seen by. Predators and prey battle it out in a constant fight for survival.

Siphuncle
Jaws
Digestive gland
Stomach
Brain
Gonad
Tentacles
Funnel
Gills
Heart

▲ A nautilus fills the chambers in its shell with water or gas by a tube called a siphuncle. Like octopuses and squid, a nautilus propels itself by pushing water out of its funnel.

775 The nautilus can swim, float and move up and down in the Twilight Zone. It lives in the outermost chamber of its shell, and its inner chambers are filled with gas or liquid. By pushing gas into the chambers, liquid is forced out and the nautilus becomes lighter – and floats up. When the gas is replaced with liquid, the nautilus sinks.

776 Mighty sperm whales plunge into the Twilight Zone when they are hunting squid. They can dive to depths of 1000 metres and hold their breath for up to 90 minutes at a time. The deepest known dive of any sperm whale was 3000 metres, and the whale swam at a speed of 4 metres a second to get there!

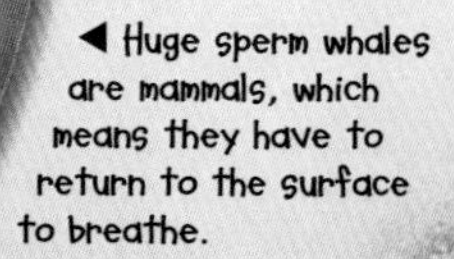

◀ Huge sperm whales are mammals, which means they have to return to the surface to breathe.

777 It is hard to see if your eyes are deep inside your head. Barreleye fish don't mind because they have see-through heads. They swim with their big, green eyes peering upwards. When the fish sees its prey, it flips its body upright and rotates its eyes in its head. This allows the fish to keep its prey in view while swimming up to grab it.

◀ A barreleye fish's eyes are very sensitive, which help it to spot its prey in low light.

778 There are few hard surfaces to attach to, so animals in the Twilight Zone are mostly floaters and swimmers. Many have unusual shapes and their bodies are often soft and watery. Comb jellies are soft-bodied animals, but they can turn hard by contracting muscles. Some have long, sticky tentacles to grab prey.

▼ Comb jellies swim by beating rows of comb-like plates, which bend light rays to make colourful shimmers.

▼ Sea pens anchor themselves to the seafloor in the Twilight Zone. They feed on plankton by catching it in their feathery branches.

TRUE OR FALSE?

1. Barreleye fish have see-through heads.
2. Sperm whales can breathe underwater.
3. Nautiluses swim using fins.
4. The Twilight Zone is pitch black.

Answers:
1. True 2. False 3. False
4. False

Monster of the deep

779 Giant squid are monsters of the deep. They can grow to 15 metres in length, including tentacles, which alone can grow to 12 metres. Their eyes are thought to be the largest of any animal. Each one is up to 40 centimetres in diameter!

780 Little is known about these mysterious animals because they live in the Twilight Zone. Giant squid can swim well, and with their good eyesight they can spot fishing nets and move swiftly away. Very few have ever been caught, and what is known about them has been revealed from dead specimens, or remains that have been found in the stomachs of sperm whales.

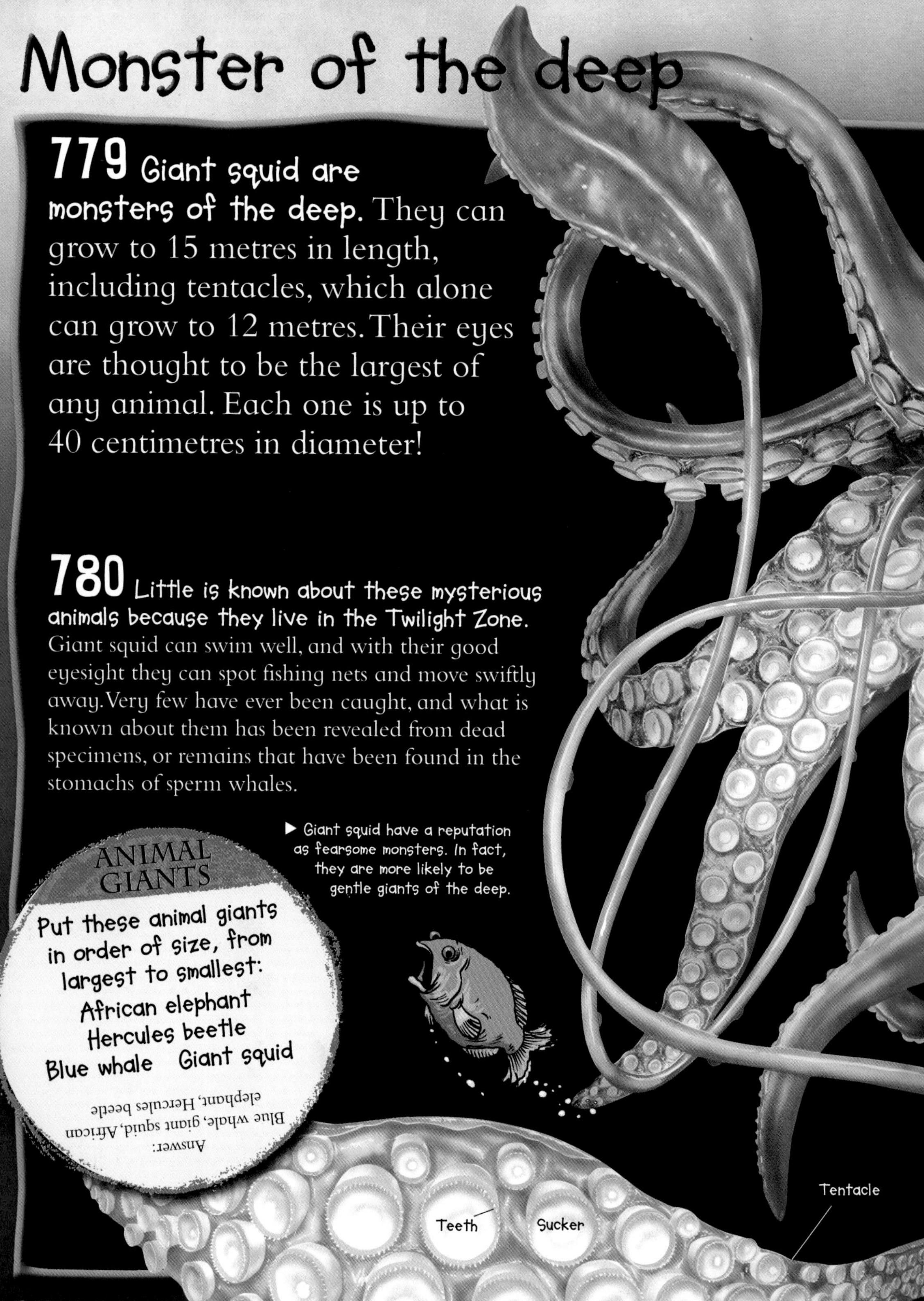

▶ Giant squid have a reputation as fearsome monsters. In fact, they are more likely to be gentle giants of the deep.

ANIMAL GIANTS

Put these animal giants in order of size, from largest to smallest:

African elephant
Hercules beetle
Blue whale   Giant squid

Answer:
Blue whale, giant squid, African elephant, Hercules beetle

The Abyssal Zone

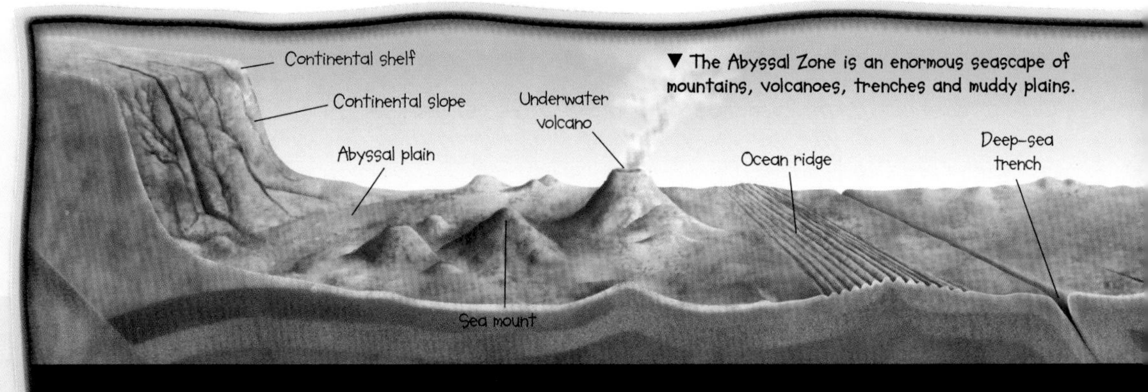

▼ The Abyssal Zone is an enormous seascape of mountains, volcanoes, trenches and muddy plains.

788 Below the Dark Zone is the Abyssal Zone, or abyss, which reaches from 4000 to 6000 metres. Where the continental slope ends, the sea floor stretches out in a giant plain. Around one-third of the seabed is in the Abyssal Zone.

789 The abyssal plains have mountains (called sea mounts), trenches and valleys. Many sea mounts are drowned volcanoes, and there may be 30,000 of them in the world's oceans. The sides of the mounts are sheer, which causes water to flow upwards in a process called upwelling. This flow of water brings nutrients to the area, and many animals live in these habitats.

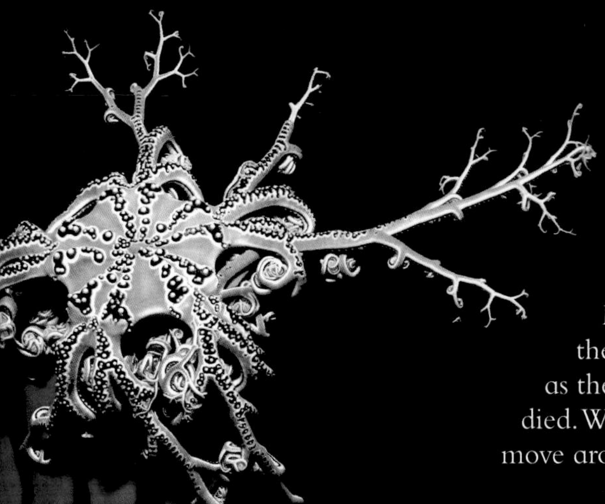

790 Most waters of the Abyssal Zone contain little food. Animals rely on finding marine snow, which may take several months to fall from the surface, or hunting other deep-sea creatures. Many are scavengers, which means they only feed when they find food, such as the remains of other animals that have died. With a shortage of food, creatures here move around very little to save energy.

◀ Basket stars can survive in the abyss. Each arm is branched into many smaller parts to catch particles of marine snow

786 Greenland sharks live under the Arctic ice at depths of up to 2000 metres. Not much is known about how these giant fish live because of their unusual habitat. Nearly all Greenland sharks are blind because of parasites, tiny creatures that damage their eyes. However, they have a good sense of smell, which they use to sniff out the rotting flesh of other dead animals to eat. They also prey on seals and other sharks.

▲ Greenland sharks can grow to 6 metres long. They live in the Arctic and often swim close to shore, but pose little threat to humans.

▼ Giant isopods are crustaceans that live in the Dark Zone. They are related to crabs, shrimps, lobsters and woodlice, and can reach a length of 35 centimetres. Isopods have long antennae that help them feel their way in the dark.

787 Giant isopods are peculiar crawling creatures that look like huge woodlice. Their bodies are protected by tough plates, and they can roll themselves up into a ball when they come under attack. Isopods live on the seabed, searching for soft-bodied animals to eat.

The Dark Zone

783 Below 1000 metres absolutely no light can penetrate. So far from the Sun's rays, this habitat is intensely cold, and there is bone-crushing pressure from the enormous weight of water above. It is called the Dark Zone, and it extends to 4000 metres below the ocean's surface.

784 It snows in the Dark Zone! Billions of particles fall down towards the seabed, and this is called marine snow. This 'snow' is made up of droppings from animals above, and animals and plants that have died. Small flakes often collect together to become larger and heavier, drifting down up to 200 metres a day. Marine snow is an important source of food for billions of deep-sea creatures.

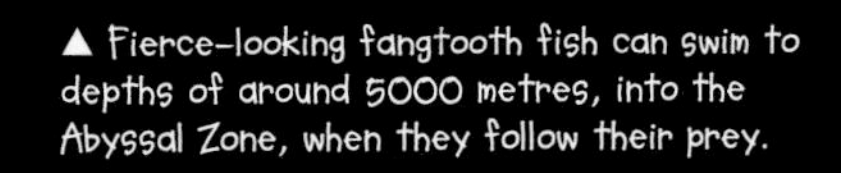

▲ Fierce-looking fangtooth fish can swim to depths of around 5000 metres, into the Abyssal Zone, when they follow their prey.

I DON'T BELIEVE IT!

The orange roughy lives in deep water where its colour appears black if any light reaches it. This is believed to be one of the longest living fish – one individual allegedly reached 149 years of age.

785 A fangtooth fish may have enormous teeth, but at only 15 centimetres in length, these fish are not as scary as they sound. Fangtooths have poor eyesight, and in the Dark Zone other senses are just as valuable. These fish can detect tiny movements in the surrounding water, which they follow to find their prey.

781 People have known about giant squid for hundreds of years. The first one to be recorded was found in Iceland in 1639, and the stories and myths began. People feared that these creatures could sink ships or grab people on deck. When sperm whales were discovered with scars caused by giant squid suckers, people realized that these predators battle with large whales.

782 Giant squid are predators. No one knows for sure how they live, but like other squid they probably hunt fish, octopuses and smaller squid. Their muscular tentacles are equipped with giant, toothed suckers that can grab hold of wriggly prey.

▶ The eye of a giant squid has a diameter bigger than a person's head.

▼ There are around 60 types of hagfish. They have eel-like bodies with four hearts, but no bones.

I DON'T BELIEVE IT!

Sea cucumbers, also known as sea pigs, are sausage-like animals of the abyss. They are enjoyed as a tasty delicacy in some parts of the world.

791 An Atlantic hagfish is a slimy, fish-like animal of the abyss with disgusting eating habits. It is nearly blind but has a good sense of smell, which helps it to find prey. A hagfish has tentacles and hooks around its mouth to grab hold of its victim's flesh. Then it burrows into the prey's body, eating its insides. A hagfish can survive for many months without feeding again.

792 The most common fish in the Abyssal Zone are called rattails, or grenadiers. There are around 300 different types of rattails in the world and scientists estimate that there are at least 20 billion of just one type – that's more than three times the number of humans!

▼ Rattails are slow movers so they probably creep up on their prey to catch them. They are also scavengers, eating anything they can find on the seabed. Here, they swarm around a bait cage and the submersible *Mir I*.

793 **One of the world's strongest types of glass is made by a creature of the abyss.** The Venus' flower basket is a type of glass sponge that has a strong skeleton. Glass sponges build their structures from strands of silica, the material used to make glass.

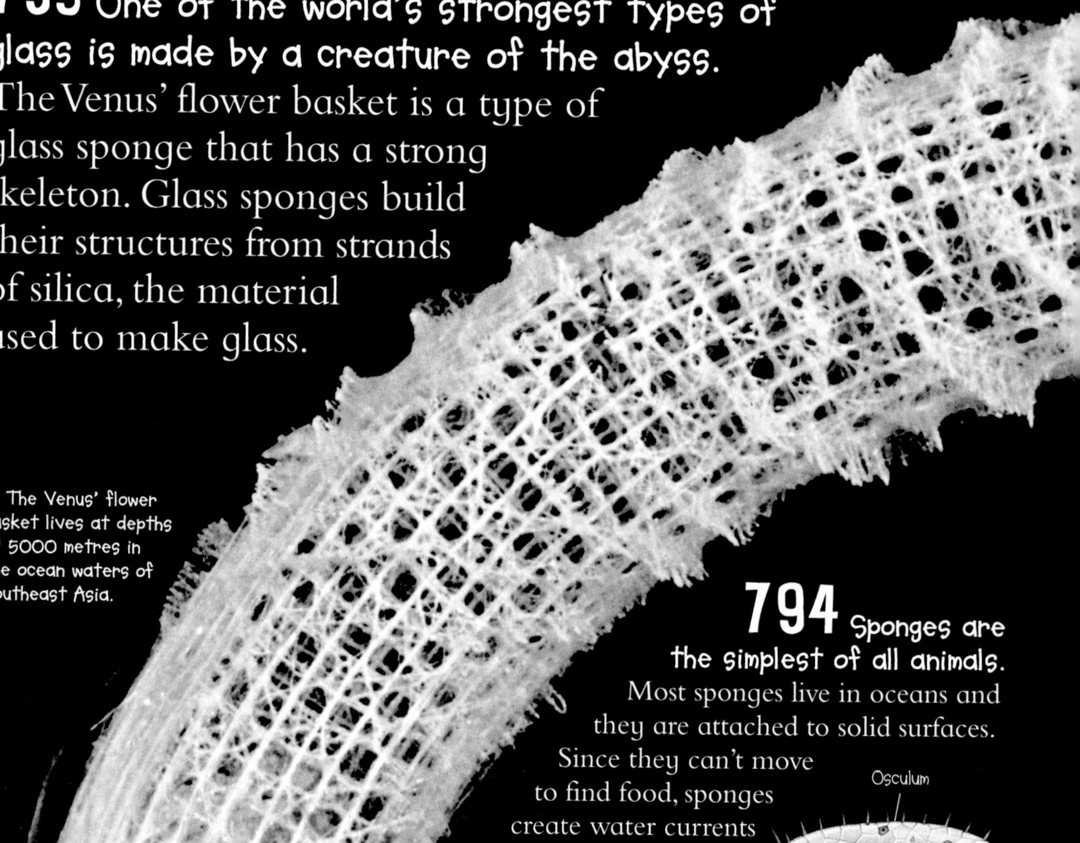

▶ The Venus' flower basket lives at depths of 5000 metres in the ocean waters of Southeast Asia.

794 **Sponges are the simplest of all animals.** Most sponges live in oceans and they are attached to solid surfaces. Since they can't move to find food, sponges create water currents that move through their bodies so they can filter out any particles of food.

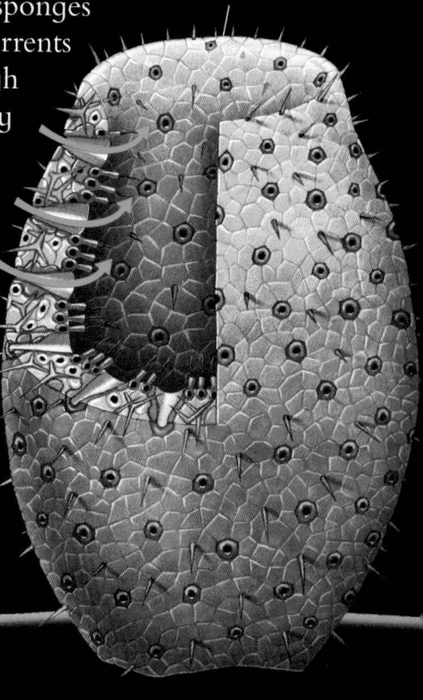

▶ Special cells near the pores have tail-like parts, that move in a beating motion. This sucks water into the sponge, and out through the osculum.

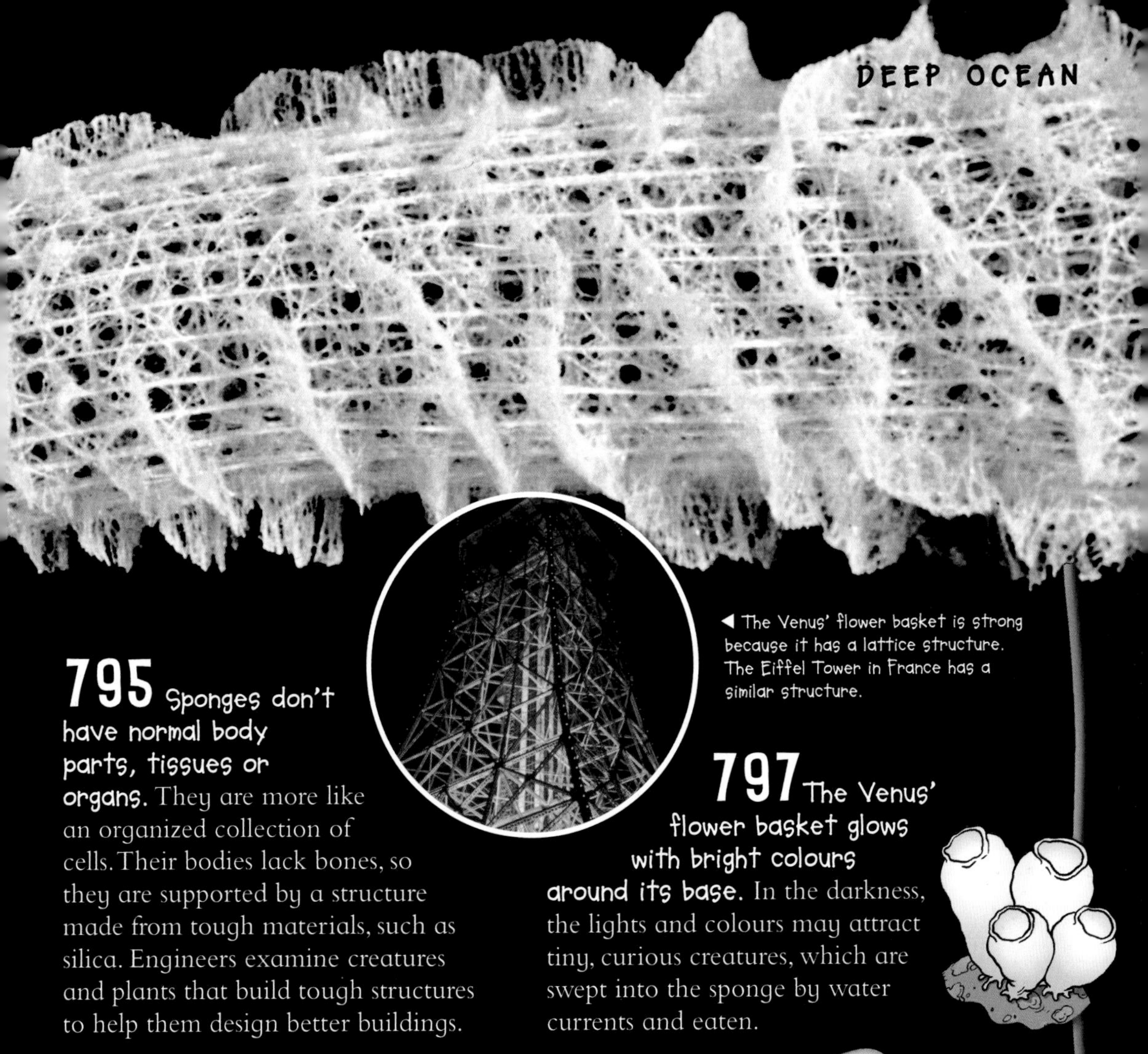

◀ The Venus' flower basket is strong because it has a lattice structure. The Eiffel Tower in France has a similar structure.

795 Sponges don't have normal body parts, tissues or organs. They are more like an organized collection of cells. Their bodies lack bones, so they are supported by a structure made from tough materials, such as silica. Engineers examine creatures and plants that build tough structures to help them design better buildings.

797 The Venus' flower basket glows with bright colours around its base. In the darkness, the lights and colours may attract tiny, curious creatures, which are swept into the sponge by water currents and eaten.

796 The Venus' flower basket builds its structure by 'gluing' together needles of silica, each no thicker than a human hair. The construction follows a beautiful pattern, which gives the sponge great strength to withstand the water pressure at depths of 5000 metres or more.

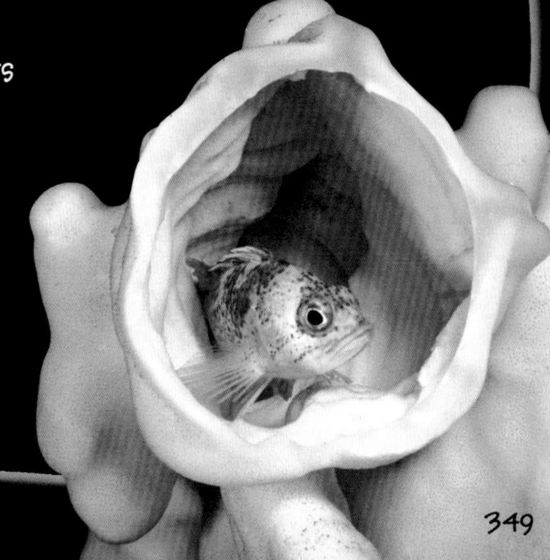

▶ Cloud sponges are another type of deep-living glass sponge. They can provide a safe living area for other small animals.

The Hadal Zone

798 The oceans plunge to depths greater than 6000 metres in only a few places, called trenches. This is called the Hadal Zone, named after the Greek word 'hades', which means 'unseen'. It's the perfect name for the most mysterious habitat on Earth.

▲ Earth's largest mountain, Everest, could fit into eight of the world's deepest trenches.

799 The deepest of all trenches is the Mariana Trench in the Pacific Ocean, which plunges to 11,034 metres. It is 2550 kilometres long and about 70 kilometres wide. This trench was created when two massive plates in the Earth's crust collided millions of years ago.

800 Scientists know very little about animals that live in the Hadal Zone. Collecting live animals from this depth causes great problems because their bodies are suited to high water pressure. When they are brought to the surface the pressure drops, and they die.

▶ Snailfish thrive in the ocean's deepest waters and have been found at depths of more than 7000 metres. They have large heads and bodies that taper to slender tails.

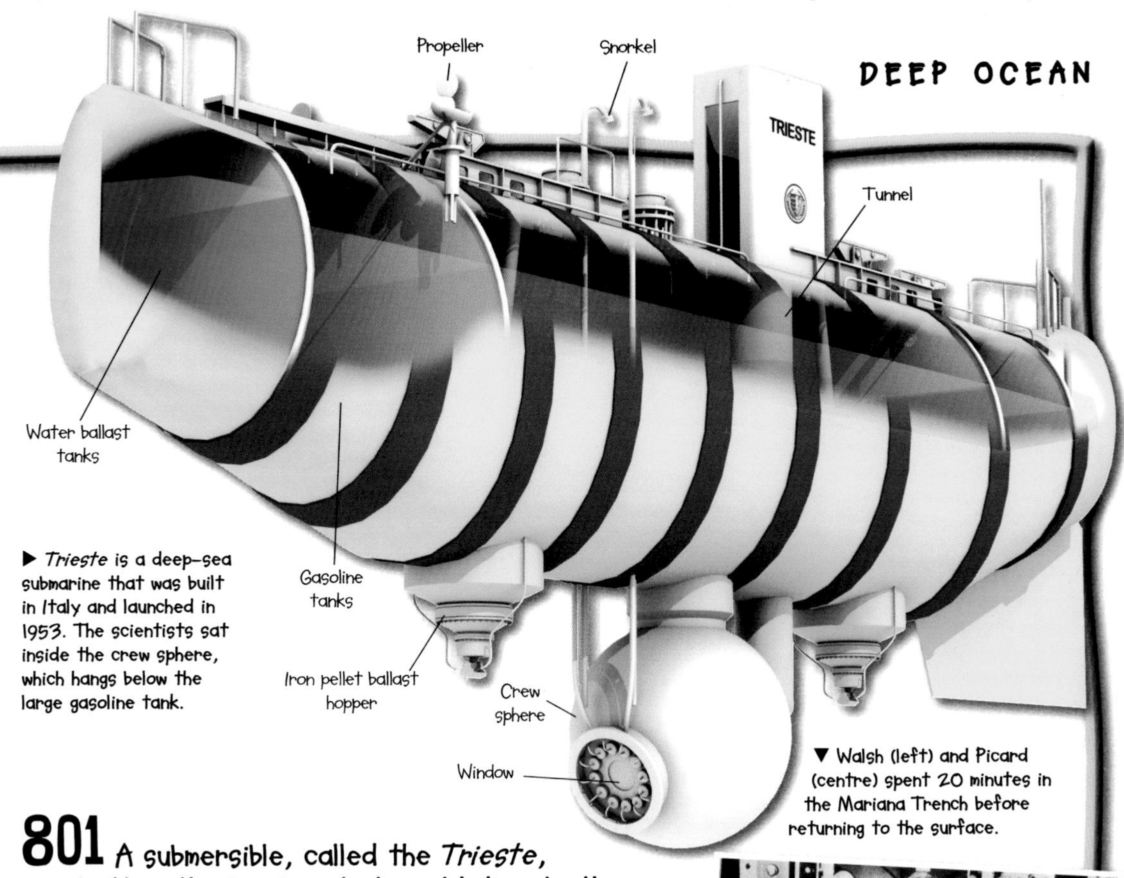

▶ *Trieste* is a deep-sea submarine that was built in Italy and launched in 1953. The scientists sat inside the crew sphere, which hangs below the large gasoline tank.

▼ Walsh (left) and Picard (centre) spent 20 minutes in the Mariana Trench before returning to the surface.

801 A submersible, called the *Trieste*, was built in the 1950s, which could dive to the Hadal Zone. In 1960, explorers Don Walsh and Jacques Piccard climbed aboard and began one of the most dangerous journeys ever undertaken. It took five hours to descend to 10,911 metres in the Mariana Trench and here they saw the deepest-known crustacean – a red shrimp. Other similar creatures called amphipods have been collected at depths of 10,500 metres.

CURIOUS CREATURES

Draw a picture of your own Hadal Zone creature. It should probably be dark-coloured, with tiny eyes, or none at all, and very ugly. Body parts that help it feel its way around a dark habitat would be helpful.

802 The deepest-living fish are believed to belong to a family called *Abyssobrotula*. One fish, *Abyssobrotula galatheae*, was captured in 1970 at a depth of 8370 metres. It was found by explorers in the Puerto Rico Trench. Scientists tried to bring the fish to the surface, but it did not survive the journey.

Muds and oozes

803 The remains of all marine creatures eventually get eaten or drift down to the seabed. These remains, which are mostly marine snow, become deep-sea sediments. They form layers of muddy ooze that can be up to 450 metres thick.

804 Most creatures that live on the seafloor are scavengers. A dead whale can provide food for millions of other animals, including shrimp-like amphipods and copepods, worms, rattails and hagfish.

KEY

1. Crabs, hagfish, amphipods, rattails and sharks strip the flesh from the fresh body.
2. Next, worms are the main colonizers, living off the enriched sediments.
3. Finally, the whale's bones produce sulphides – chemicals that bacteria, mussels and clams feast on.

805 The muddy layer of the abyssal plain may look smooth, but close up there are tiny trails and holes. Every handful of mud contains millions of microscopic animals. Foraminifera and radiolarians are tiny shelled single-celled organisms that live in the sediments. When they die, their shells dissolve into the muddy ooze.

806 The abyssal plains are home to many types of sea cucumbers. These sausage-shaped animals are common in this habitat. Some burrow in the mud, while others can swim. Most move over the seafloor, picking up any bits of food they can find.

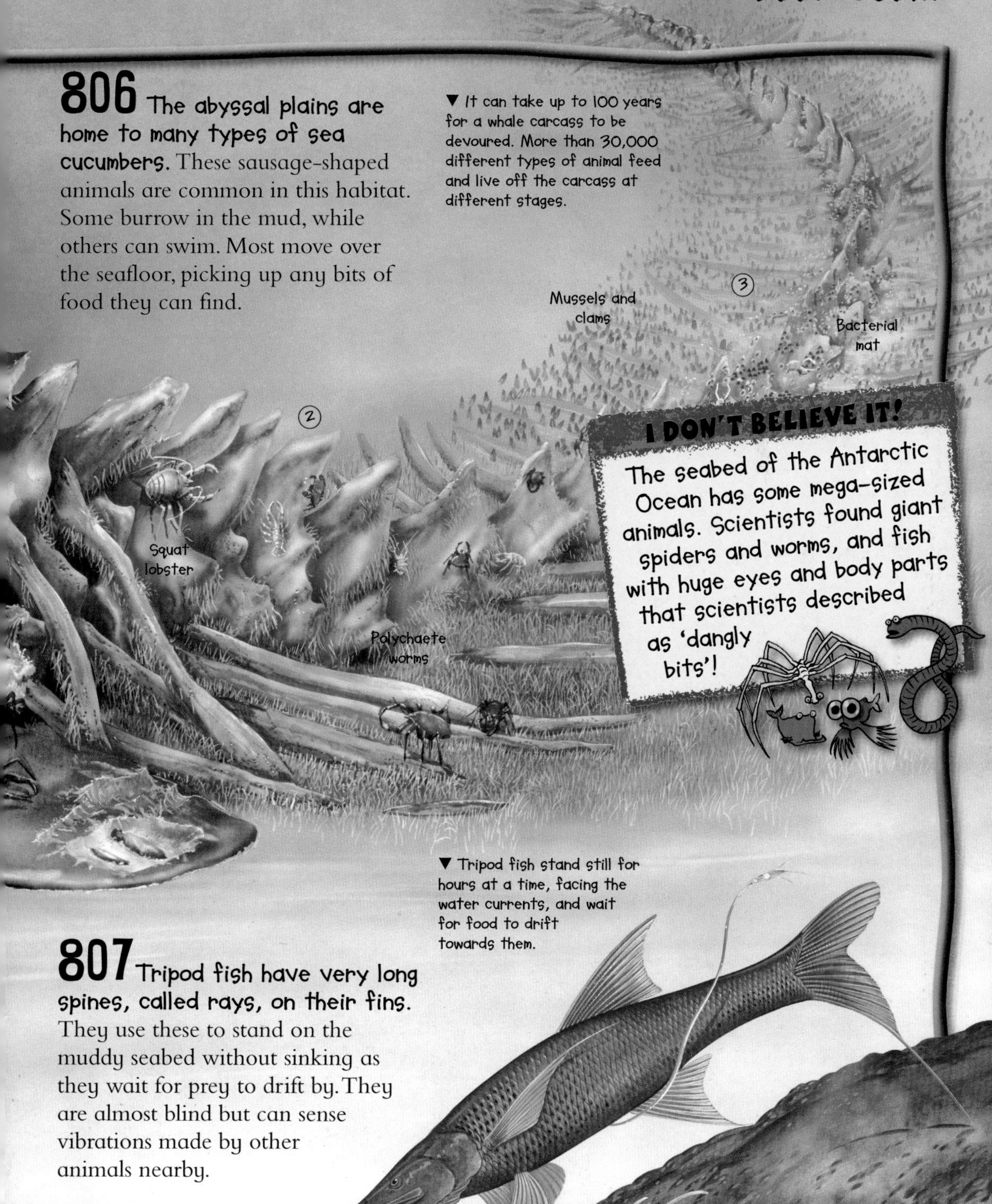

▼ It can take up to 100 years for a whale carcass to be devoured. More than 30,000 different types of animal feed and live off the carcass at different stages.

▼ Tripod fish stand still for hours at a time, facing the water currents, and wait for food to drift towards them.

807 Tripod fish have very long spines, called rays, on their fins. They use these to stand on the muddy seabed without sinking as they wait for prey to drift by. They are almost blind but can sense vibrations made by other animals nearby.

Deep heat

808 The deep ocean floor is mainly a cold place, where animals struggle to survive. However, there are some extraordinary areas where the water is heated to temperatures of 400°C and living things thrive.

809 Below the Earth's surface is a layer of hot, semi-liquid rock, called magma. In places, magma is close to the ocean floor. Water seeps into cracks in rocks, called hydrothermal vents, and is heated. The water dissolves minerals from the rocks as it travels up towards the ocean floor, and bursts through a vent like a fountain.

810 The first hydrothermal vents were discovered in the Pacific Ocean in the 1970s. Since then, others have been found in the Atlantic, Indian and Arctic Oceans. The largest known region of hydrothermal vents lies near the Mid-Atlantic Ridge and is the size of a football pitch.

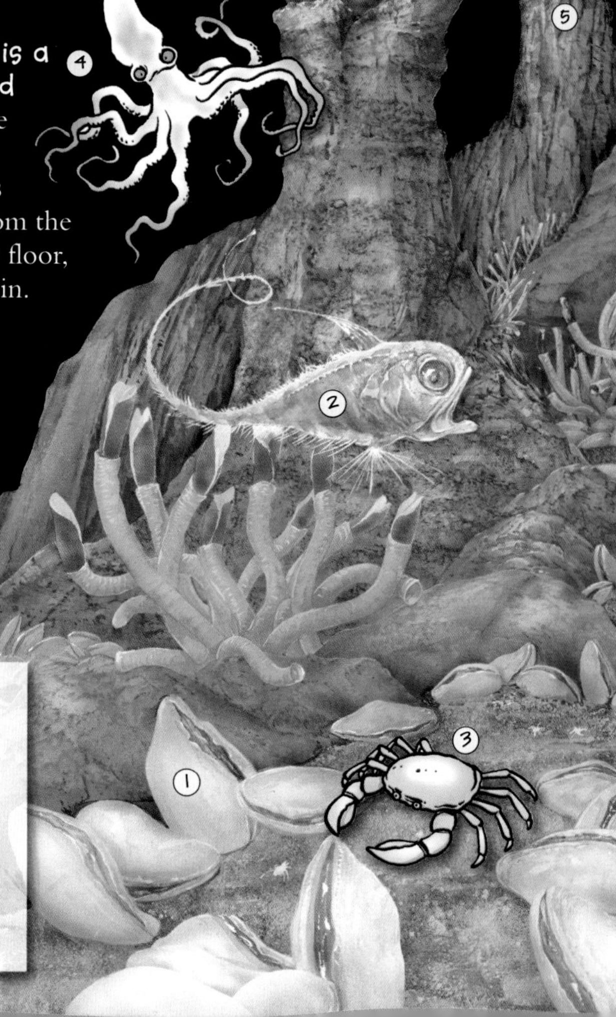

▼ The minerals in the water produce dark clouds that look like smoke, and these vents are called 'black smokers'. Over time, they build up rocky structures called chimneys, which can grow to the height of a 15-storey building.

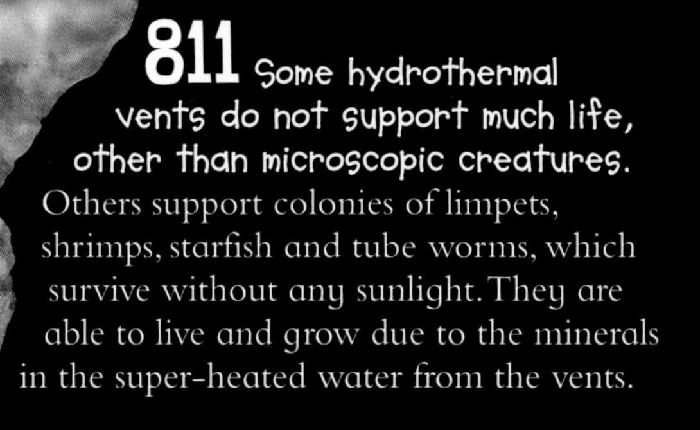

811 Some hydrothermal vents do not support much life, other than microscopic creatures. Others support colonies of limpets, shrimps, starfish and tube worms, which survive without any sunlight. They are able to live and grow due to the minerals in the super-heated water from the vents.

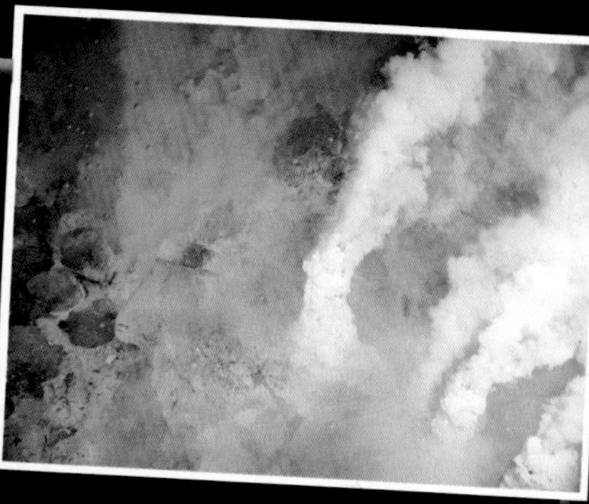

▲ Hydrothermal vents known as 'white smokers' release cooler water and plumes of different minerals to black smokers.

812 Vent tube worms can grow to 2 metres long and they live without eating anything. Each worm is attached to the seabed and is protected by the tube it lives in. A red plume at the top collects seawater, which is rich in minerals. These minerals are passed to bacteria in the worm's body, and are then turned into nutrients.

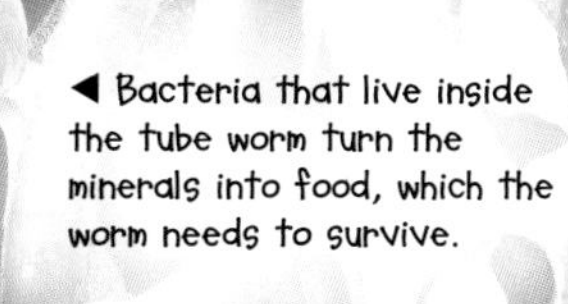

◀ Bacteria that live inside the tube worm turn the minerals into food, which the worm needs to survive.

UNDER PRESSURE

You will need:
milk carton   sticky tape

With an adult's help, make four holes on one side of an old milk carton, one above the other. Put sticky tape over the holes and fill the carton with water. Hold it over a bowl while you pull the tape off. Water will pour out fastest from the bottom hole because it has the most pressure on it.

Deep-sea coral

813 Tiny creatures called coral polyps build large reefs in the cold, deep ocean. Coral reefs are often found in warm, shallow waters, and they attract a wide variety of life. Cold-water reefs are not such varied habitats, but there may be more cold-water reefs than warm-water ones.

814 Coral polyps have tube-shaped bodies and tentacles around their mouths. All polyps feed by filtering food particles from the water, and they have thousands of tiny stingers to stun bigger prey.

815 Coral polyps produce a hard substance called calcium carbonate, which forms a protective cup around them. Over time, the stony cups collect and grow into a reef, held together by a cement of sand, mud and other particles.

I DON'T BELIEVE IT!

Air pollution from carbon dioxide causes the oceans to become more acidic. This stops polyps, especially cold-water ones, from being able to grow their stony skeletons.

Bubble gum coral

Flytrap anemone

Lophelia pertusa

Squat lobster

▲ A specimen of bamboo coral is carefully lifted from the deep sea in a collection box that is attached to a submersible.

▼ Cold-water coral creates a special habitat where other animals can live, find food and shelter. A group of living things that depend on one habitat like this is called an ecosystem.

816 **A type of cold-water coral polyp called *Lophelia* is the most common reef builder in the Atlantic Ocean.** One reef can cover 2000 square kilometres and is home to animals such as squat lobsters, long-legged crabs, and fish – especially babies called larvae.

817 **Other cold-water communities have been found in the deep oceans.** Engineers drilling for oil in the Gulf of Mexico found cold seeps (places where gases leak out of cracks in the rocks) and animal life thrived nearby. The gases are an energy source for bacteria that feed there. Animals that feed on the bacteria are in turn eaten by crabs, corals, worms and fish.

On the move

818 Travelling in the ocean is different from travelling in air. Animals can simply float or drift along because they weigh 50 times less in water than they do in air. Currents help too. They can bring food to animals that are attached to the seabed, or they can carry animals towards food.

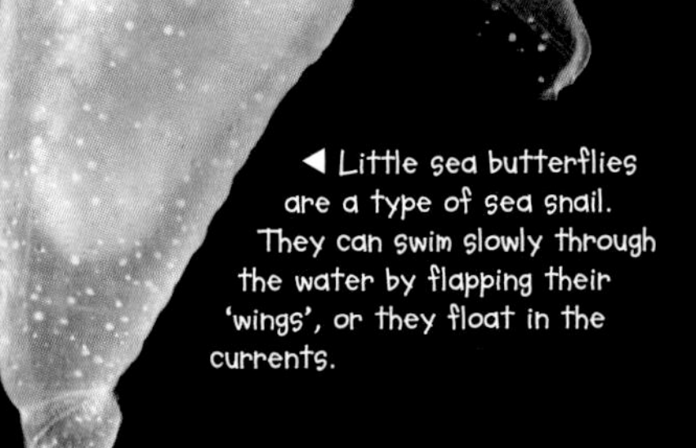

◀ Little sea butterflies are a type of sea snail. They can swim slowly through the water by flapping their 'wings', or they float in the currents.

▼ For this tube anemone, being attached to the seabed means it is impossible to make a quick getaway from the giant nudibranch that is attacking it (bottom).

819 Animals caught in deep-sea currents have to go with the flow, unless they are strong swimmers. Swimming takes 830 times as much energy as staying still because water is dense and heavy. Tiny zooplankton are weak swimmers, so when they get caught in currents, they drift along until they become free.

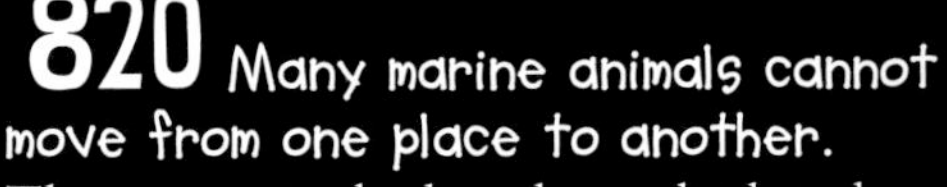

820 Many marine animals cannot move from one place to another. They are attached to the seabed and stay there, waiting for food to come to them. These animals, such as sea lilies and tube anemones, have feathery tentacles that they use to filter the seawater and collect particles of food.

821 Billions of animals undertake a journey every night. They travel up from the Twilight and Dark Zones into the Light Zone to feed, and return to deeper water in the morning. This mass movement is called a vertical migration and it represents the largest migration, or animal journey, on Earth.

822 Lantern fish are mighty movers of the ocean. The champion is called *Ceratoscopelus warmingii* and it lives at a depth of 1800 metres in the day. At night it swims upwards to depths of 100 metres to feed and avoid predators, and then it swims back. This feat is like a person running three marathons in a day!

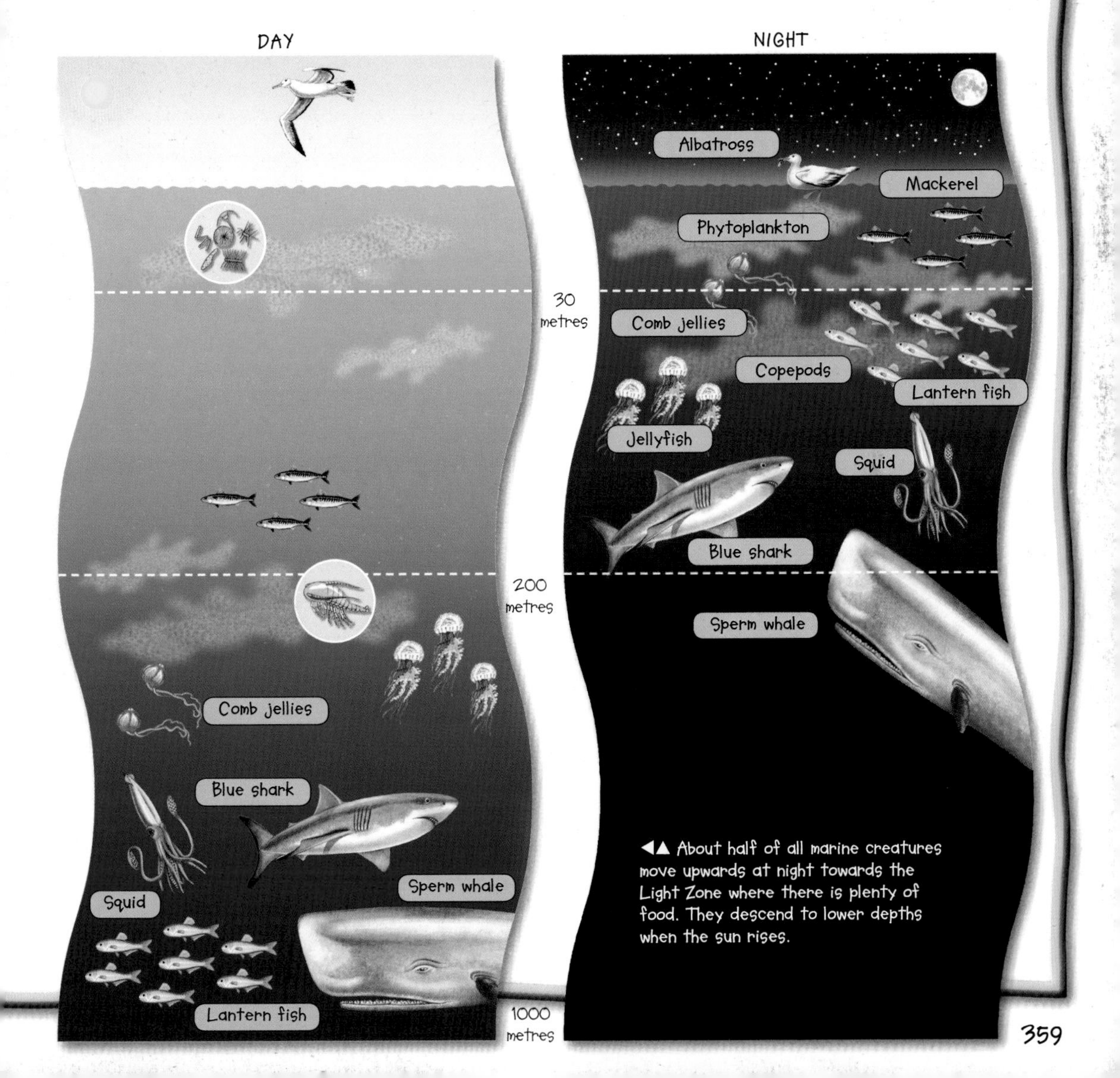

◄▲ About half of all marine creatures move upwards at night towards the Light Zone where there is plenty of food. They descend to lower depths when the sun rises.

Breathing and diving

Gill slits

823 Animals need to take a gas called oxygen into their bodies to release energy from food. Taking in oxygen is called breathing, and the process of using it to release energy is called respiration. Most marine animals are specially adapted to take in dissolved oxygen from seawater.

▲ As a shark swims, water enters its mouth, passes over its gills where oxygen is absorbed, and then leaves through the gill slits.

MAKE A SWIM BLADDER

Blow up a balloon. It is now filled with gas, like a swim bladder. Put the balloon in a bowl or bath of water and try to make it sink. Now fill the balloon with water, and see if it will float.

824 Fish breathe using gills. Like our lungs take oxygen from air, gills take in oxygen from water. Most fish also have a swim bladder, which helps them to cope with the changing pressure as they swim deeper. A swim bladder is a gas-filled sac that expands as a fish moves upwards, and shrinks as it descends. All deep-sea fish have gills, but they do not have swim bladders because the immense pressure would crush them.

Blowhole

◀ Whales, such as this killer whale, come to the surface to breathe. They have one or two blowholes on the top of their heads. These are like nostrils, and this is where air enters the body. When air is breathed out of a blowhole it creates a water spout.

As a sperm whale dives, its ribs and lungs contract (shrink). They expand again when the whale surfaces.

The whale's heartbeat slows by half so less oxygen is needed.

The spermaceti organ is a huge mass of oil. It probably helps the whale to dive deep by changing its ability to float.

The nasal passages fill with cool water to help the whale sink.

▲ The sperm whale is adapted for diving in very deep water. It can stay underwater for up to 90 minutes while hunting for giant squid.

825 **Seals, dolphins and whales are air-breathing mammals, but their bodies are adapted to life in water.** The sperm whale can store oxygen in its blood and muscles, which allows it to descend to over 1000 metres to hunt. Its flexible ribcage allows the whale's lungs to shrink during a dive.

826 **Super-speedy pilot whales are called 'cheetahs of the deep'.** During the day, these predators swim at depths of around 300 metres, but at night they plunge to 1000 metres in search of prey. Pilot whales can plummet 9 metres a second at top swimming speed. They need to be fast to catch their prey of large squid, but also because they need to get back to the surface to breathe.

▼ Most marine worms have feathery gills that absorb oxygen from the water. However, some do not have gills and absorb oxygen through their skin.

827 **Simple creatures do not have special body parts for breathing.** They can absorb oxygen from the water directly through their skins. The amount of oxygen in the water falls from the surface to a depth of around 1000 metres, but it increases again at greater depths.

Glow in the dark

828 Animals of the deep create their own light to attract prey, a mate or to confuse predators. This is called bioluminescence and it takes place in organs called photophores. These usually produce blue light, but some animals can glow with green, red or yellow light.

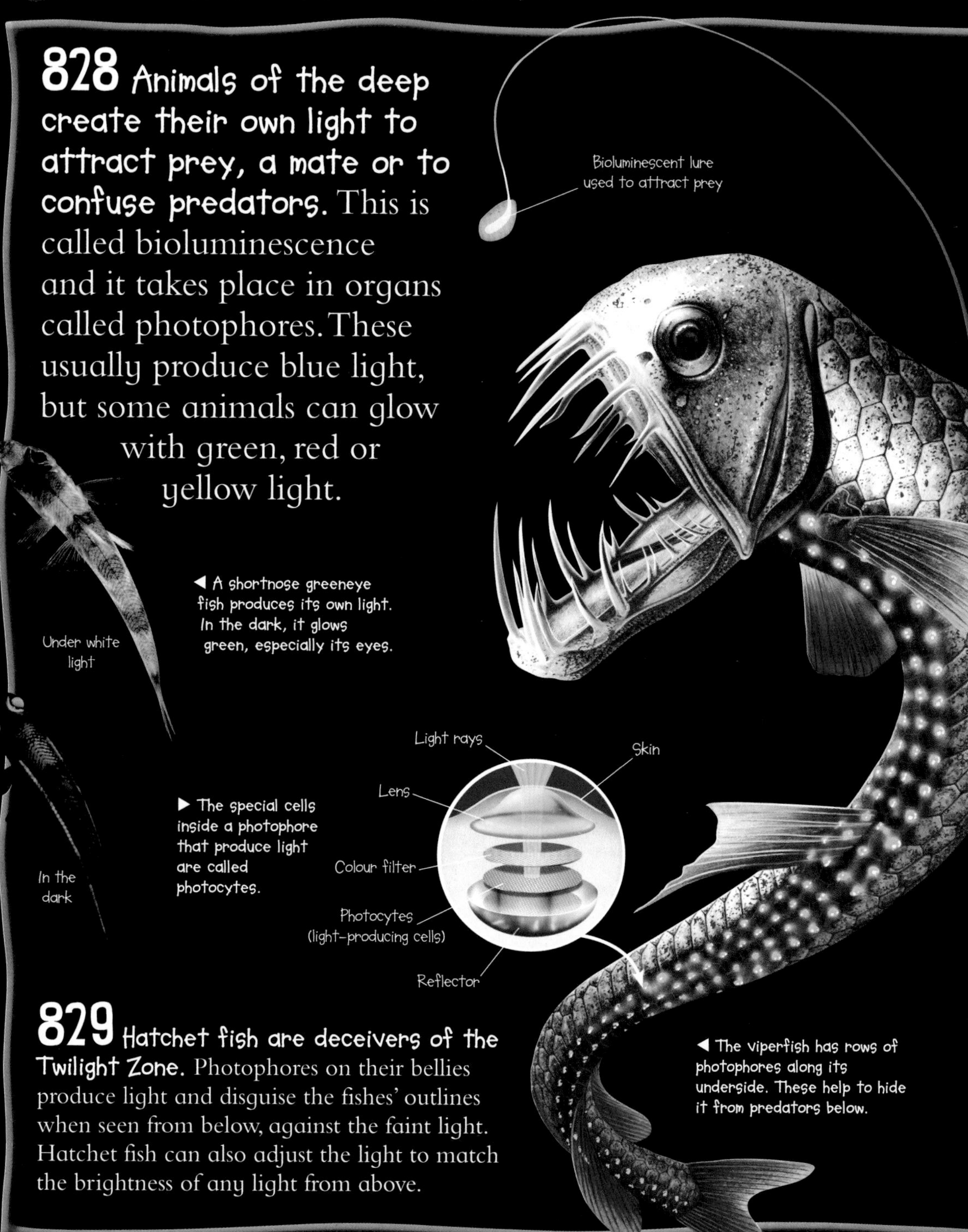

◀ A shortnose greeneye fish produces its own light. In the dark, it glows green, especially its eyes.

▶ The special cells inside a photophore that produce light are called photocytes.

◀ The viperfish has rows of photophores along its underside. These help to hide it from predators below.

829 Hatchet fish are deceivers of the Twilight Zone. Photophores on their bellies produce light and disguise the fishes' outlines when seen from below, against the faint light. Hatchet fish can also adjust the light to match the brightness of any light from above.

830 Spotted lantern fish use their photophores to attract mates. They are one of the brightest deep-sea fish, with brilliant displays of bioluminescence along their sides and bellies. The photophores are arranged in different patterns depending on whether the fish is male or female, and what type of lantern fish it is. This helps the fish to find the right mate.

831 It is not just fish that can glow in the dark. Mauve stinger jellyfish emit a beautiful violet-blue colour when they are disturbed. Firefly squid not only cover their bodies with lights, they can also produce a cloud of glowing particles that distracts predators while they make a quick getaway.

▶ Mauve stinger jellyfish produce quick flashes of light when they sense movement in the water. They even flash when waves pass over them at the ocean's surface.

832 Tiny vampire squid have enormous eyes and can produce light all over their bodies whenever they want to. These squid are able to control their bioluminescence, producing dazzling displays of patterned light that can be dimmed or brightened, probably to scare off predators. When a vampire squid is hunting it does not light up. This means it can surprise its prey.

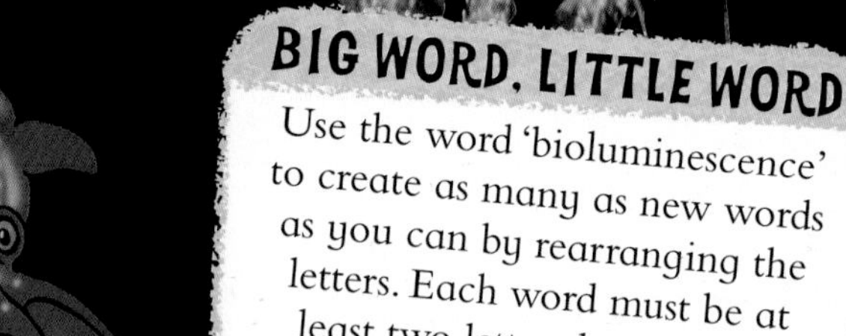

BIG WORD, LITTLE WORD

Use the word 'bioluminescence' to create as many as new words as you can by rearranging the letters. Each word must be at least two letters long. Use a dictionary to check the spelling of your words.

Deep-sea food

833 The ocean food chain begins in the Light Zone. Phytoplankton use the Sun's energy to grow. In turn, they are eaten by other creatures, passing on energy and nutrients. It takes a long time for energy and nutrients to filter down to the sea floor, so many deep-sea animals scavenge food, eating whatever they find, while others hunt.

▼ Nearly all energy used by marine life comes from the Light Zone. Phytoplankton begin the nutrient cycle, and upward-flowing water currents complete it by bringing nutrients back to the surface.

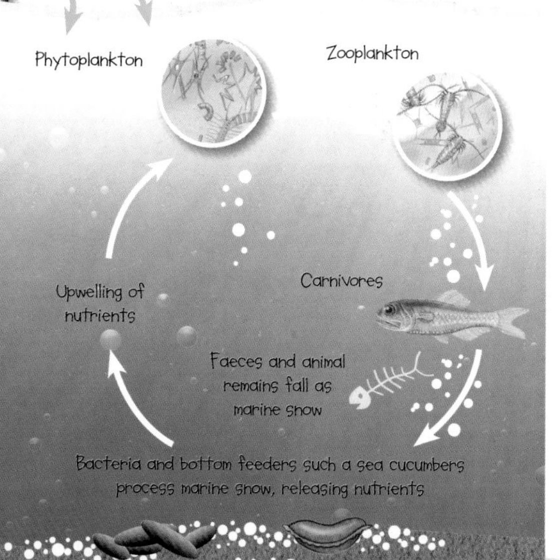

834 Copepods and krill (zooplankton) may be small but they play a big role in the deep-ocean ecosystem. These tiny, plant-eating crustaceans exist in their billions. They swim up to the surface every evening to try to avoid being eaten. In the morning they swim back down into the deep, dark waters. Krill can live to depths of 2000 metres.

I DON'T BELIEVE IT!

One krill is not much bigger than a paperclip, but the total weight of all the krill in the world is greater than the total weight of all the people on the planet!

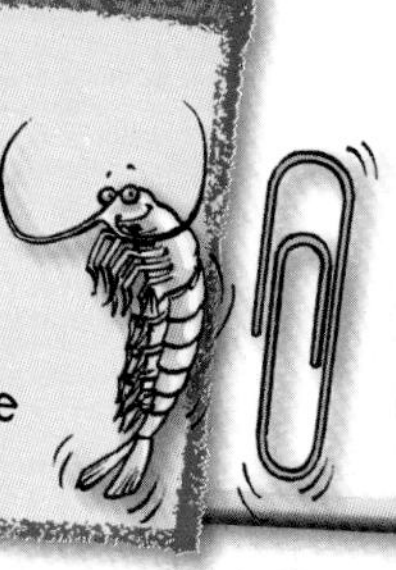

◀ Goblin sharks have soft, flabby bodies and long, strange-looking snouts. They are pinkish white in colour.

835 Large predators, such as sharks, seals and whales, may reach the Dark Zone, but few go deeper. Goblin sharks swim slowly in the Dark Zone and they have snouts that may help them to find food. Their huge jaws can snap forwards to grab prey such as small fish and squid.

▼ Gulper eels can grown to 2 metres in length. They have pink photophores on their tails to attract prey.

836 Gulper eels are all mouth. These predators of the Dark Zone have enormous mouths, but small teeth. It may be that gulper eels use their big mouths for catching lots of small prey at a time, rather than one large, meaty prey.

837 Fangtooth fish are also known as ogrefish. They use their unusually sharp, long teeth to grab hold of squid and fish. Food is scarce in the deep ocean, but with such large jaws, fangtooths attempt to eat almost any prey that comes along, even animals that are larger than themselves.

▶ This soft-bodied animal called a predatory tunicate lives in the Twlight Zone. When an animal swims into its hood-like mouth it closes shut like a Venus flytrap.

Anglerfish

838 If you cannot find food in the dark, make it come to you! Anglerfish have long growths on their heads that work like fishing rods, and the tips are coated in glowing bacteria. Other animals are attracted to the glowing light, called a lure, and are quickly snapped up by the anglerfish.

I DON'T BELIEVE IT!

Pacific blackdragons are dark on the outside, and the inside! Their stomachs are black so when they swallow fish that glow, the light doesn't show and encourage predators to approach!

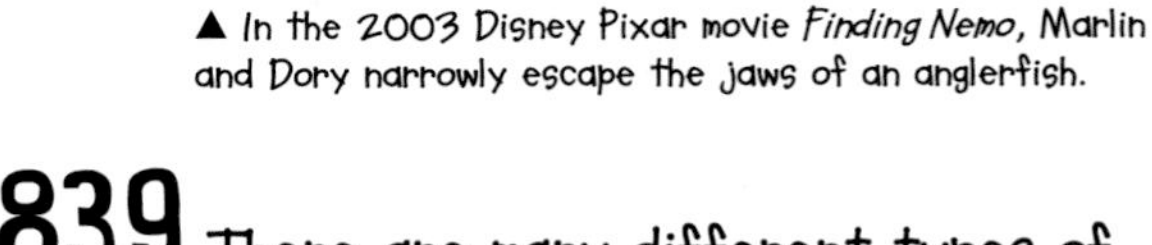

▲ In the 2003 Disney Pixar movie *Finding Nemo*, Marlin and Dory narrowly escape the jaws of an anglerfish.

839 There are many different types of anglerfish and all look very strange. The hairy anglerfish is one of the strangest and it lives at depths of up to 1500 metres. It gets its name from its fins, which have long spikes, and the sensitive hairs that cover its body.

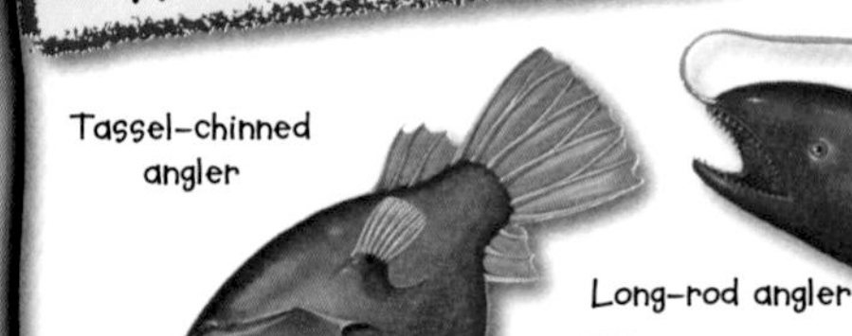

Males

▶ Two tiny males are attached to this female Regan's anglerfish. These anglerfish are sometimes called phantom anglerfish.

840 Finding a mate in the dark can be tough, so some male anglerfish stay attached to a female! The males are much smaller than the females, so they can grab hold and hitch a lift that lasts for life. While scientists have found many types of female anglerfish they are still searching for some of their tiny male relations!

841 Anglers are types of anglerfish that lie on the seafloor. Their wide, flat bodies are covered in soft, fleshy growths that help them to blend in with the mud where they hide. Anglers use their fins to shuffle along, flicking their lures as they go. They are often caught and sold as food, and also better known as monkfish.

842 A dragonfish also lures prey to its death. When a dragonfish spies a shrimp to eat it produces a red spotlight made by photophores below its eyes. The shrimp can't see red, so it is unaware it is being hunted. The dragonfish then snaps up its prey in its large mouth, full of ultra-sharp teeth.

▼ Monkfish are so well camouflaged that they are almost impossible to spot when lying on the ocean floor.

Hide and seek

843 Throughout the animal kingdom, creatures use colours and patterns to hide from predators or prey. In the deep oceans, colours appear different because of the way light is absorbed by water. Colours, other than black and red, are not very useful for camouflage. Deep-sea creatures have developed special ways to avoid being detected.

▲ Deep-sea glass squid are mostly transparent, apart from some brightly coloured polka dots on their bodies.

844 Some deep-sea animals are well adapted for hiding and seeking. Glass squid are almost completely transparent, so light passes through their bodies, helping them go unnoticed. A thin body can help too, because it is hard to see from certain angles. With little light around, enormous eyes are useful. Big eyes can collect more light and turn it into hazy images.

▲ Spookfish have enormous eyes, giving them very good vision.

845 **Silvery scales on a fish's back are perfect for reflecting light and confusing a predator.** When shimmering scales are seen against dim rays of light in the Twilight Zone, the outline of a fish's body becomes less obvious, and it fades into the background or even disappears.

▲ By using their photophores to produce light and their silvery scales to reflect light, hatchet fish become almost invisible to predators.

846 **When there is no light, animals rely on senses other than sight.** Many deep-sea animals can feel vibrations in the water. Shrimp have sensory organs all over their bodies, including their antennae, which can detect movements nearby. Many fish can also sense the small electrical fields generated by other living things.

▶ The snipe eel's jaws curve away from each other so they never fully close.

847 **Snipe eels have long, ribbon-like bodies, and jaws that look like a bird's bill.** They live at depths of up to 1800 metres and can grown to 1.5 metres in length. As males mature their jaws shrink, but their nostrils grow longer. This probably improves their sense of smell and helps them to find females.

ODD ONE OUT

Which of these animals uses colour and pattern to scare other animals, rather than to hide?

Zebra Wasp Tiger
Leaf insect
Arctic fox

Answer:
Wasp

Searching the deep

▼ This timeline shows how technology has developed, improving ways of exploring the deep ocean.

848 Early ocean explorers had to overcome many problems. Divers needed a supply of air and to be able to cope with the water pressure. If divers ascend too quickly, the sudden change in pressure can cause the bends – a life-threatening sickness.

1775 The *Turtle* was an early, one-man submarine

1837 The waterproof Siebe diving suit was developed

1872 HMS *Challenger* set sail for a four-year study of the deep ocean

1882 The USS *Albatross* continued this important research

1925 *Meteor* began mapping the seafloor

849 The first diving suit was invented in the 1830s. It was made of waterproof canvas and rubber, and allowed divers to descend to around 60 metres. About 40 years later a ship called the HMS *Challenger* explored the deeper oceans.

1934 William Beebe and Otis Barton used a bathysphere to make the first deep-ocean dive

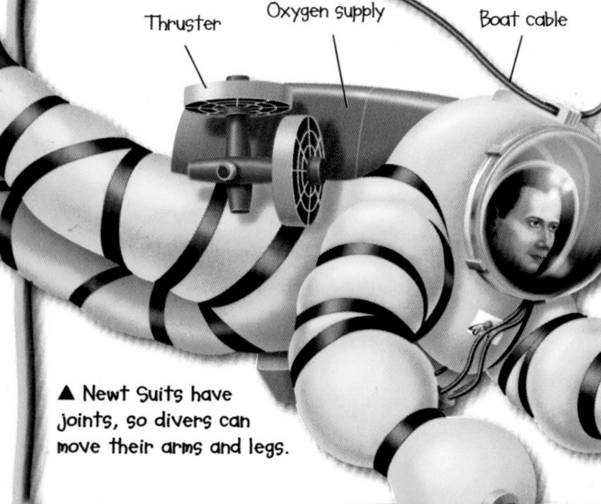

▲ Newt Suits have joints, so divers can move their arms and legs.

850 Today's deep-diving suits are made of metal. These Newt Suits allow divers to work at a depth of 300 metres. Suits have thrusters to help divers move underwater, communication systems to link to the boat at the surface, and video cameras.

851 ***Alvin* was the first submersible that could take explorers deep into the Dark Zone.** It has made more than 4500 dives, and it was on one of these that hydrothermal vents were first discovered. A programme of modernization means *Alvin* will be able to reach depths exceeding 6000 metres.

853 **There are other ways to find out the secrets of the deep, including taking pictures from space.** Satellite images provide information about deep water currents and the undersea landscape. Sonar is a method that maps the ocean floor by bouncing sound signals off the seabed.

1960 *Trieste* dived to the Mariana Trench

1964 Deep-sea submarine *Alvin* was built

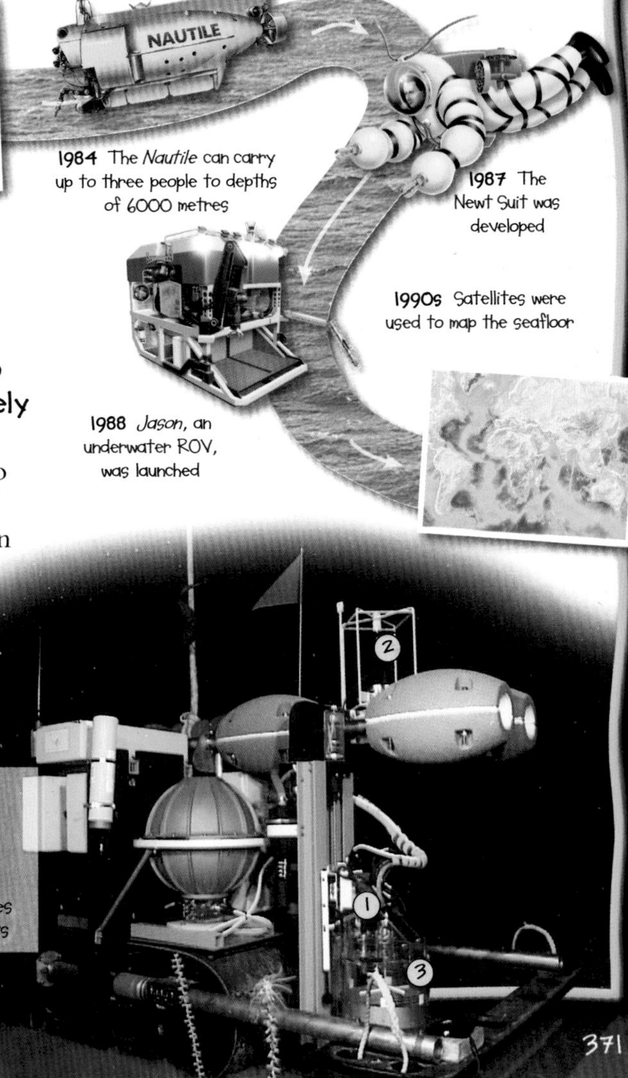

1984 The *Nautile* can carry up to three people to depths of 6000 metres

1987 The Newt Suit was developed

1988 *Jason*, an underwater ROV, was launched

1990s Satellites were used to map the seafloor

852 **One of the safest ways to explore the deep is using a Remotely Operated Vehicle, or ROV.** These unmanned submersibles are lowered to the seabed by cables and are operated by the crew of a ship on the surface. In future, ROVs will be able to operate without cables, so they will be able to move around more freely.

▶ The Monterey Bay Aquarium Research Institute has developed a deep-sea robot called the Benthic Rover. It is helping scientists discover more about the effects of global warming on the oceans.

Sea changes

854 Billions of years ago, life began in the oceans – and this environment is still home to most living things. Every part of the ocean matters, from the shallow seashores to the deepest trenches. It not only provides habitats for marine animals and plants, it also provides us with food and greatly affects our atmosphere and climate.

▶ Robot submersibles are used to gather valuable information about the deep ocean. They can deploy bait cages to attract animals for observation and research, and collect samples to take back to the surface for further study.

855 Overfishing threatens all sea life. Krill, for example, are an important source of energy for billions of ocean creatures, but they are now being harvested in huge amounts, especially in the Antarctic. There is a danger that if too much krill is taken for humans to eat, there will not be enough left to support the ocean ecosystems, including deep-ocean life.

856 **Pollution is a major problem – rubbish is dumped in the oceans, tankers leak oil and the crisis of carbon dioxide pollution looms.** This is caused by burning fossil fuels, which pollutes ocean water and causes the climate to heat up. A new plan is to use the deep oceans to store carbon dioxide. This gas would be collected from power stations and buried deep in the seabed, in a process called carbon capture and storage.

857 **The precious deep-ocean habitat is being destroyed by humans faster than we can uncover its mysteries.** However, in recent times, people have begun to understand how important it is to respect the oceans and protect their wildlife. Hopefully there is time for nations to work together to avoid further damage, and uncover new secrets of the deep.

I DON'T BELIEVE IT!

If you could take all living things on Earth and fill a giant box with them, ocean life would take up 99.5% of it. The leftover space could hold everything that lives on land!

Index

Entries in **bold** refer to main subject entries. Entries in *italics* refer to illustrations.

Index

Index

Index

Index

Acknowledgements

All artworks are from the Miles Kelly Artwork Bank

The publishers would like to thank the following sources for the use of their photographs:

(t = top, b = bottom, l = left, r = right, c = centre)

Front cover Shutterstock.com (tl) Ilya Akinshin, (tr) Enlightened Media, (tr) Sergey Lavrentev, (tr) Michaela Stejskalova (c) NPeter, (br) StanOd, (bl) Ryan M. Bolton; **Back cover** Shutterstock.com (tl) TravelMediaProductions, (bl) Gabriela Insuratelu; **Spine** Shutterstock.com (t) kkaplin

Alamy 162 nagelestock.com; 213 sciencephotos; 262 Bryan & Cherry Alexander Photography; 267(t) Bryan & Cherry Alexander Photography; 316(b) BrazilPhotos.com

Ardea 348–349 Pat Morris

Corbis 24 Gary Braasch; 29 Yann Arthus-Bertrand; 30 David Samuel Robbins; 33(r) Pablo Corral V; 36(t) Robert Dowling; 40 Jeremy Horner; 43(b) Frans Lemmens/Zefa; 44(t) Tim Davis, (b) Rick Price; 47(t) Paul A. Souders; 50 Image Source; 57 Reuters; 58 Eric Nguyen; 60 Warren Faidley; 70 Yann Arthus-Bertrand; 79(t) Jean du Boisberranger/Hemis; 80 Douglas Peebles; 81 Bettmann; 85(t) Michael S. Yamashita, (b) James Andanson/Sygma; 87 Jacques Langevin/Sygma; 93(t) Vittoriano Rastelli, (b) Roger Ressmeyer; 94 Bettmann; 96 Alberto Garcia; 97(b); 99 Bettmann; 106 R.CREATION/ amanaimages; 154–155 Jim Sugar; 155 Micha Pawlitzki/zefa; 156(t) Roger Ressmeyer; 157(t) Reuters; 161 David Muench; 163 Frank Lukasseck; 165 Ric Ergenbright; 171 Paul A. Souders; 180 Michael Yamashita; 183(br) Jason Hawkes; 184 Anthony Bannister, Gallo Images; 188(t) Anthony Bannister, Gallo Images; 189(b) Bettmann; 190 George Steinmetz; 191(t) Roger Ressmeyer, (b)Corbis; 192 Annie Griffiths Belt; 194 Layne Kennedy; 204 Michael Amendolia; 217 Mike Nelson; 218 Martin Schutt; 219(t) Paul A. Souders; 220 Ted Soqui; 221(t) Reuters; 222 Michael S. Yamashita; 224 Bill Varie; 228 Ladislav Janicek/Zefa; 229(t) Louie Psihoyos; 231(c) Bettmann; 232(b) Louie Psihoyos; 238 Rob Howard; 242 Tom Bean; 258 Wolfgang Kaehler; 259(b) Paul A. Souders; 263(t) Jack Jackson/Robert Harding World Imagery, (b) Patrick Robert; 265(t) Galen Rowell; 268 Stapleton Collection; 269 Jason Roberts/Push Pictures/Handout/epa; 271 Van Hasselt John/Sygma; 272 Paul Souders; 280(l) Owen Franken; 281 Frans Lanting, (tr) Demetrio Carrasco/JAI; 295(tr) Martin Harvey; 311(br) George Steinmetz; 314 Frans Lanting; 347 Ralph White

Dreamstime.com 294(t) Sloth92; 311(tc) Braendan; 338(t) Tommy Schultz

Ecoscene 53(l) Nick Hawkes

FLPA 54(t) Jim Reed; 92 S Jonasson; 150 Michael Krabs/Imagebroker/FLPA; 158–159 Tim Fitzharris/Minden Pictures; 170 Tim Fitzharris/Minden Pictures; 214 Martin B Withers; 239 Matthias Breiter/Minden Pictures; 240–241 Michio Hoshino/Minden Pictures; 241(br) Patricio Robles Gil/Sierra Madre/Minden Pictures; 246(t) Michio Hoshino/Minden Pictures; 246–247(b) Jim Brandenburg/Minden Pictures; 249 Michio Hoshino/Minden Pictures; 252(t) Michael Quinton/ Minden Pictures; 252–253(b) Fritz Polking; 256–257 Norbert Wu/Minden Pictures; 274–275 Colin Monteath/Minden Pictures; 289(tr) Mark Moffett/Minden Pictures; 295(b) Frans Lanting; 296(bl) Jeffrey Oonk/Minden Pictures; 310–311 ImageBroker

Fotolia.com 26(r) QiangBa DanZhen; 33(l) Albo; 56(t) flucas; 83 Marko Heuver; 172(t) Cornelius; 176(t) Domen Colja, (cl) Graça Victoria; 219(t) sharply_done, (bl) Mark huls, (r) Bruno Bernier; 182(t) Andreas Meyer; 183 (inset) A Marcynuk; 185(t, l–r) NiDerLander, Maksim Shebeko, (tr) Darren Hester; 186–187(bg) martreya; 280(r) urosr; 282(bl) amaet; 283(r) Impala; 294(b) fivespots; 306(tc) Michael Luckett; 311(tl) Shariff Che'Lah, (tr) Uros Petrovic; 338(c) Tommy Schultz; 339 Desertdiver; 340–341 cornelius; 360(t) zebra0209

Fredrik Fransson 100(b); 101(b)

GeoEye satellite image 95(t); 100

Getty Images 36(b) Stephen Alvarez; 39(b) Paul Chesley; 55 AFP; 56(m) Aurora; 62(b) Mike Goldwater; 86 AFP; 88–89 Philippe Bourseiller; 89 AFP; 91 Philippe Bourseiller; 104 Jonathan S. Blair/National Geographic; 186–187(t); 276–277 Siegfried Layda; 292–293(t) Roy Toft; 316(tr) Matthias Clamer; 346(b) Jean Tresfon; 367(t) Neil Bromhall; 372–373 Emory Kristof/National Geographic

iStockphoto.com 338(b) tswinner; 338–339 MiguelAngeloSilva; 360(b) sethakan

Monterey Bay Aquarium Research Institute 371(b) c. 2007 MBARI

Acknowledgements

NASA 34(b); 41(l), (r); 62(t); 71 NASA; 105 NASA Jet Propulsion Laboratory (NASA-JPL); 101(t) Jacques Descloitres/ MODIS Rapid Response Project at NASA/GSFC; 167 NASA Kennedy Space Center
Naturepl.com 349 Brandon Cole; 361 David Shale
NHPA 264–265(b) Bryan & Cherry Alexander; 266–267 Bryan & Cherry Alexander; 278–279 Nigel J Dennis; 313(tr) Martin Harvey
NOAA 336(l) W. H. F. Smith; 351(c) Archival Photography by Steve Nicklas NOS, NGS; 355 NOAA Office of Ocean Exploration, Dr. Bob Embley, NOAA PMEL; 357 Brooke et al, NOAA-OE, HBOI; 362(l) Edie Widder; 370 USS Albatross Archival Photography by Steve Nicklas, NGS, RSD, Meteor Steve Nicklas, NOS, NGS; 371 Bathysphere US Federal Government (NOAA), map W. H. F. Smith
OceanwideImages.com 368(c) Gary Bell
Photolibrary.com 32 Steve Vidler; 34(t) JTB Photo; 38 Phil Degginger; 39(t) JTB Photo; 47(b) Colin Monteath; 66 Goodshoot; 173 Stephen Barnett; 183(t) Jim Pickerell; 243 Sanford/Agliolo; 250 Noel Hendrickson; 254–255 Juniors Bildarchiv; 260 Tim Davis; 282–283 Nick Gibson; 288–289(t) Wave RF; 289(br) Sergio Pitamitz; 299(tr) Mike Powles; 300(l) David M Dennis, (r) Garcia Garcia; 301(br) David Kirkland; 302–303 Wendy Shattil; 304–305 J & C Sohns; 304(bl) Morales Morales; 315(main) Jacques Jangoux; 317 Berndt Fischer; 363 Reinhard Dirscherl
Reuters 54(b) Denis Balibouse
Rex Features 63(t) Sipa Press; 97(t) Sipa Press; 181 Trent Warner; 188 (br); 189(t) Prudence Cuming/ScienceLtd/ WhiteCube; 229(b) Sipa Press; 234–235 Lehtikuva Oy; 273(t) Toby Zerna/Newspix; 291 Paul Raffaele; 366(c) c.W. Disney/Everett
Science Photo Library 37 Javier Trueba/MSF; 53(r) Peter Menzel; 65(b) NOAA; 84 Bernhard Edmaier; 90(b) NASA/Carnegie Mellon University; 103(t) TAKE 27 LTD/Science Photo Library, (b) NASA/Science Photo Library; 166(bl) Tony and Daphne Hallas; 167(tl) Richard Bizley; 174 Javier Trueba/MSF; 178 Ria Novosti; 182(br) Jean-Claude Revy, ISM;197(b) Sinclair Stammers; 207 Alan Sirulnikoff; 215 Sheila Terry; 219(b) NASA/GSFC/METI/ERSDAC/ JAROS; 223(t) Mauro Fermariello; 232(t) Pascal Goetgheluck; 332–333 Dr Ken Macdonald
Shutterstock.com 2(c) Michaela Stejskalova; 5(tl) Jens Mayer, (tr) pryzmat, (bl) Pantera (br) AlessandroZocc; 6(tr) NPeter; 8(bl); 9(br) Leksele; 10(br) Madlen; 11(tr) Rich Carey; 27 Celso Diniz; 28 beboy; 29 ollirg; 30 Aleix Ventayol Farrés; 236 Snowbelle
Still Pictures 64 C A.Ishokon-UNEP; 259(t) Fred Bruemmer; 275(b) Bruno P. Zehnder
TopFoto.co.uk 26(l) Topham Picturepoint; 270 ©TopFoto
U.S. Geological Survey 94(b) Austin Post, Glaciology

All other photographs are from:
Corel, digitalSTOCK, digitalvision, John Foxx, PhotoAlto, PhotoDisc, PhotoEssentials, PhotoPro, Stockbyte

Every effort has been made to acknowledge the source and copyright holder of each picture.
Miles Kelly Publishing apologises for any unintentional errors or omissions.

The Manager's Guide to Effective Meetings

Other titles in the Briefcase Books series include:

Customer Relationship Management by Kristin Anderson and Carol Kerr

Communicating Effectively by Lani Arredondo

Performance Management by Robert Bacal

Recognizing and Rewarding Employees by R. Brayton Bowen

Motivating Employees by Anne Bruce and James S. Pepitone

Building a High Morale Workplace by Anne Bruce

Six Sigma for Managers by Greg Brue

Leadership Skills for Managers by Marlene Caroselli

Negotiating Skills for Managers by Steven P. Cohen

Effective Coaching by Marshall J. Cook

Conflict Resolution by Daniel Dana

Project Management by Gary R. Heerkens

Managing Teams by Lawrence Holpp

Hiring Great People by Kevin C. Klinvex, Matthew S. O'Connell, and Christopher P. Klinvex

Retaining Top Employees by J. Leslie McKeown

Empowering Employees by Kenneth L. Murrell and Mimi Meredith

Presentation Skills for Managers by Jennifer Rotondo and Mike Rotondo

The Manager's Guide to Business Writing by Suzanne D. Sparks

Skills for New Managers by Morey Stettner

The Manager's Survival Guide by Morey Stettner

Interviewing Techniques for Managers by Carolyn P. Thompson

Managing Multiple Projects by Michael Tobis and Irene P. Tobis

The Manager's Guide to Effective Meetings

Barbara J. Streibel

McGraw-Hill
New York Chicago San Francisco Lisbon London
Madrid Mexico City Milan New Delhi San Juan
Seoul Singapore Sydney Toronto

The **McGraw·Hill** *Companies*

2 3 4 5 6 7 8 9 0 AGM/AGM 0 9 8 7 6 5 4

ISBN 0-07-139134-7

Library of Congress Cataloging-in-Publication Data applied for.

This is a CWL Publishing Enterprises Book, *developed and produced for McGraw-Hill by CWL Publishing Enterprises, Inc., www.cwlpub.com.*

This publication is designed to provide accurate and authoritative information in regard to the subject matter covered. It is sold with the understanding that neither the author nor the publisher is engaged in rendering legal, accounting, or other professional service. If legal advice or other expert assistance is required, the services of a competent professional person should be sought.

—*From a Declaration of Principles jointly adopted by a Committee of the American Bar Association and a Committee of Publishers*

McGraw-Hill books are available at special quantity discounts to use as premiums and sales promotions, or for use in corporate training programs. For more information, please write to the Director of Special Sales, McGraw-Hill, 2 Penn Plaza, New York, NY 10128. Or contact your local bookstore.

This book is printed on recycled, acid-free paper containing a minimum of 50% recycled de-inked fiber.

Contents

Preface

Nobody knows when the first meeting took place or why, but it's a safe bet that the meeting seemed too long to some participants, poorly organized to others, boring to at least a few, and it's likely that some were disappointed with the results.

Every meeting you hold costs time and money—sometimes a lot. Consider this book an investment to improve the return on the time you and your team spend in meetings. Properly planned and conducted meetings can help you and all your employees work together in a more efficent and coordinated fashion.

I believe that if you follow the basic principles and guidelines presented in this book, you'll find it easy to improve your meetings, and you and your people will find them not time-wasters but performance enhancers.

As we use the term "meeting" in this book, it's an event consisting of people, content, and process designed for a purpose. There are many types of meetings that you as a manager might organize and/or facilitate, involving primarily your employees, but perhaps including other employees and managers and even people from outside the organization. With this reality in mind, we frame our discussions in general terms, focusing on what all or most meetings have in common. We also use the word "participants" to refer generally to the people who take part in a meeting. This word suggests an active participation, because we believe that people should be involved in a meeting, not just be there in attendance.

This book will take you step by step through the meeting process. Chapter 1 reviews the factors that cause meetings to be bad, the impact of bad meetings, and the characteristics of good meetings. Chapter 2 outlines and discusses the details of preparing for a meeting. Chapter 3 explains how to start a meeting, including setting rules and assigning roles and responsibilities. Chapter 4 offers suggestions for conducting a meeting. Chapter 5 explains how to close a meeting and follow up on the results. Chapter 6 describes a selection of techniques and tools for helping meeting participants work together more effectively and efficiently. Chapter 7 presents common problems with meetings and ways to deal with them. Chapter 8 discusses the use of technological tools and the issues involved in meeting virtually.

Special Features

The idea behind the books in the Briefcase Series is to give you practical information written in a friendly, person-to-person style. The chapters are short, deal with tactical issues, and include lots of examples. They also feature numerous boxes designed to give you different types of specific information. Here's a description of the boxes you'll find in this book.

These boxes are designed to give you tips and tactics that will help you more effectively implement the methods described in this book.

These boxes provide warnings for where things could go wrong when you're planning and conducting a meeting.

These boxes highlight insider tips for taking advantage of the practices you'll learn about in this book.

Every subject has its special jargon and terms. These boxes provide definitions of these concepts.

It's always important to have examples of what others have done, either well or not so well. Find such stories in these boxes.

This identifies boxes where you'll find specific procedures you can follow to take advantage of the book's advice.

How can you make sure you won't make a mistake when dealing with a problem? You can't, but these boxes will give you practical advice on how to minimize the possibility.

Acknowledgments

I would like to thank first my colleagues at Oriel Incorporated for their help as I have worked on this book, especially Christine Jersild who managed the project in-house and Patricia Klossner, President, who championed the project initially. I also want to thank Bob Magnan of CWL Publishing Enterprises for his great help in developing the manuscript for the book. John Woods of CWL Publishing Enterprises approached us with the idea for this book, and we appreciate the opportunity to create this title for the Briefcase Books series. Thanks also to Nancy Woods for her work in proofreading and helping in the final stages of completion.

About the Author

Barbara J. Streibel is a consultant and manager of intellectual capital at Oriel Incorporated, a consulting and training firm located in Madison, Wisconsin. She is an expert coach of executives, managers, black belts, and teams in decision making, teamwork, Six Sigma problem solving, process management, and process improvement. She is a specialist in guiding development of infrastructures, systems, and processes to support teams and organizational initiatives. She was team leader in the development of the meeting skills training program offered by Oriel, which served as the source of this book. She is co-author of *The Team Handbook, Second Edition* and *Building United Judgment: A Handbook for Consensus Decision Making.* She received her Ph.D. from Pennsylvania State University. Contact her at streibel@orielinc.com and visit Oriel's Web site at www.orielinc.com.

The Manager's Guide to Effective Meetings

Meetings: The Best of Times and the Worst of Times

A meeting is an event consisting of people, content, and process for a purpose—who, what, how, and why. Traditionally, there was also a time and a place—when and where—but as technology allows us to meet virtually (the subject of Chapter 8), these secondary aspects may become less important.

There are many types of meetings, depending on the people, content, process, and purpose. Because a meeting is basically a collaborative work process, the word "meeting" encompasses almost as many possibilities as the word "work" itself. In this book we'll discuss meetings in general terms, focusing on what all or most collaborative meetings have in common.

We'll also use the term "participants" to refer generally to the people who take part in a meeting. A term sometimes used—"attendees"—is not only an incorrect formation (because it would mean "people attended by someone or something") but, more importantly, it suggests a passive presence. We believe that people should be involved in a collaborative meet-

Meeting An event consisting of people, content, and process for a purpose. Because a meeting is basically a collaborative work process, the word "meeting" encompasses almost as many possibilities as the word "work" itself.

ing, not just be there.

"It was the best of times; it was the worst of times."

When Charles Dickens used those words to begin *A Tale of Two Cities*, he wasn't writing about meetings, of course. And yet, it seems appropriate to begin discussing meetings in terms of extremes. We've all attended meetings that were "the best of times," that energized the participants, promoted teamwork, and generated important results. And, unfortunately, we've all attended meetings that were "the worst of times." What makes the difference? That's the focus of this chapter. And the objective of this book is to help you make that difference.

The Worst (of) Meetings

Here's a checklist of some common complaints about meetings. Check each that applies to your meetings:

- ❑ People invited to a meeting don't show up.
- ❑ People arrive late and/or leave early.

Smart Managing

It's Only Words

Does it matter whether you call people who meet "participants" or "attendees" or something else? Yes, according to Lani Arredondo, in *Communicating Effectively* (New York: McGraw-Hill, 2000, p. 151):

> In every type of meeting, think of those present not as employees or attendees, but as *participants*. Doing so encourages you to engage the employees.
>
> It also encourages people to take more seriously their responsibility to contribute to the meeting.
>
> Even if you believe that "it's only words," that what you call people at a meeting is just semantics, it's a no-lose situation to call them *participants*.

- ❑ People doodle, think about things they could be doing, or even doze off.
- ❑ Too many people talk at once.
- ❑ The meeting is dominated by one person or several people.
- ❑ The meeting is dominated by the leader.
- ❑ People get into personal attacks.
- ❑ Nothing gets accomplished.
- ❑ The meeting rehashes topics discussed at previous meetings.
- ❑ Meetings take too long and accomplish too little.
- ❑ People leave expressing relief: "The meeting's finally over. We can finally get back to work."
- ❑ Meetings don't get any better; managers and employees are stuck in a rut of bad meetings.

A meeting can go bad for many reasons. The following lists present many of the general causes for bad meetings. You probably recognize most or even all of these problems—and maybe you could add to these lists.

Sometimes problems start *in advance of a meeting*:

- because it's held for the wrong reason or no reason at all
- because of poor or even no preparation
- because of the people invited—and the people not invited
- because of unclear roles and responsibilities
- because the participants don't know what to expect or how to prepare
- because the manager and/or the participants don't bring necessary resources
- because of the place
- because of the timing

Sometimes problems start *as a meeting begins*:

- because it starts wrong
- because the manager tries to be responsible for everything

- because participants aren't focused on the business of the meeting
- because participants don't get sufficiently and appropriately involved
- because it's not considered to be "real work"
- because of bad attitudes about meetings
- because of low expectations for meetings

Sometimes problems arise *during a meeting*:

- because discussions get off track
- because it takes too much time to do anything
- because of distractions
- because people hesitate to contribute—or they contribute hesitantly
- because people get into conflicts over nothing—or they do nothing in order to avoid conflicts
- because the group can't make decisions

Sometimes problems come *as a meeting ends*:

- because it ends abruptly, with no sense of conclusion or closure
- because the participants are unsure about what the meeting has accomplished
- because it ends without any plans for action
- because nobody knows who's responsible for doing what
- because the participants leave feeling disappointed or frustrated about something that could have gone better
- because participants have contributed without any recognition for their work

Sometimes problems develop *after a meeting*:

- because the effort put into the meeting seems to go nowhere after it ends
- because the people responsible for assignments fail to complete them
- because of all the other bad meetings that preceded it—

people don't take meetings seriously and so don't commit to the outcomes

Whew! With all of those potential problems, it's not really surprising that so many meetings fail in some respects.

The Impact of Bad Meetings

The effects of those problems, the results of those failures, can be serious—for you, your people, and the organization. There are some very good reasons why a smart manager does whatever it takes to make meetings *better.*

Bad Meetings Are Bad for You

When meetings don't work well, you're not maximizing the potential of your people and you're not making the best use of time and energy. That means you've got to work harder to make up for the bad meetings—and you're likely to need more and/or longer meetings in order to produce results.

A meeting is a microcosm of the workplace, a type of project in which you show your ability to manage people, time, and resources—for better or for worse. And as more and more of what organizations do takes place in teams, meetings become the setting in which more of the really important work gets done—or in which more time and energy are wasted.

Bad Meetings Are Bad for Your People

Your employees are negatively affected by bad meetings in many of the same ways you are.

After all, the meetings are wasting their time and energy. Consequently, they have less time to do their other work, which causes frustration—for them and for coworkers who depend on them.

But they also become frustrated by the meetings, because nobody likes to be ineffective and inefficient! (On the other hand, some may decide that if it's acceptable for a group to be ineffective and inefficient, it's OK for individuals, too.) Of course, it's likely that your employees will have concerns about the inability

> MISTAKE PROOFING
>
> **Treat Meetings Like Work!**
>
> Perhaps the single most effective way to improve meetings is to make sure that everyone treats every meeting like any other essential work activity. Every meeting participant should arrive knowing what the group is going to do, aware of what's expected of him or her, and prepared to contribute to the best of his or her ability.

of their manager to improve the meetings.

Bad meetings affect morale. Some of your employees will become frustrated by their coworkers. Collaboration can energize employees—or enervate and annoy them. Some employees may become apathetic and not take meetings seriously; they may miss meetings, arrive late, and spend a lot of time doodling. Others may become negative, pessimistic, skeptical, cynical—and those attitudes are hard to leave behind when the meeting ends.

Bad Meetings Are Bad for the Organization

Now take those bad effects on your employees and on you and multiply them by the number of managers and employees in your organization.

In the short term, bad meetings waste time, talent, and other resources. Inefficient meetings cost organizations billions of dollars each year in lost time and lost opportunities. But those are just the measurable costs.

Bad meetings affect the climate and the culture of an organization as well. And, if word gets outside the walls, there could be damage to the image and the reputation of the organization. After all, bad management is bad management—in meetings and in other areas of a business. (It's that "meeting as microcosm" concept again.)

Bad Meetings Are Bad for Your Career

Beyond the negative effects of meetings outlined above, there's one more that could be huge—the effect on your career. Again, the meeting is a microcosm of the workplace. As we noted earlier, a meeting is a type of project—a project in which you show

Bad Meetings Make Bad Companies

CAUTION!

"Meetings matter because that's where an organization's culture perpetuates itself. Meetings are how an organization says, 'You are a member.' So if every day we go to boring meetings full of boring people, then we can't help but think that this is a boring company. Bad meetings are a source of negative messages about our company and ourselves."

That thought-provoking comment comes from William R. Daniels, senior consultant at American Consulting & Training of San Rafael, California, who has introduced meeting-improvement techniques to companies (quoted by Eric Matson in "The Seven Sins of Deadly Meetings," *Fast Company*, April 1996).

how you manage. If you do meetings well, people recognize your abilities as a manager. If you have problems with meetings, it's generally obvious to your employees—and to others in the organization and maybe beyond.

> The skill to manage a meeting—to develop ideas, to motivate people and to move people and ideas to positive action—is perhaps the most critical asset in any career.... Most professionals have had no real training in devising and managing an effective meeting; in fact, most professionals do not recognize the enormous impact their meetings have on their organizations and their careers.

That's how George David Kieffer summed up the discussions he had with "some of America's most successful and respected leaders in business, labor, industry, education, and government" in *The Strategy of Meetings* (New York: Simon & Schuster, 1988, p. 13).

He devotes 50 pages of his book to the importance of meetings for careers. In brief, to succeed as a manager, you have to manage meetings.

The Best (of) Meetings

Managers often fail to maximize on the potential of meetings. They waste valuable opportunities—for themselves, for their employees, and for the organization. Here are just some of the many possible benefits to be derived through meetings:

- You can share information—and learn from your employees—in a setting that allows and even encourages interaction.
- You can answer questions.
- You can ask questions.
- You can discuss important issues and reach decisions as a group.
- You can direct and coordinate the individual and joint efforts of your employees.
- You can help your employees develop their abilities to think critically.
- You can draw upon the experiences of your employees and others.
- You can get your employees to raise questions and identify problems.
- You can gain perspectives on an issue.
- You can observe how your employees interact.
- You can help your employees work better as a team.
- You can display and develop many of your managerial skills.
- You can promote a sense of community.

Make a Difference

We've briefly considered the differences between bad meetings and good meetings. But the difference that concerns us in the rest of this book is *you*. You can be the difference between bad meetings and good meetings.

You've already committed to improving your meetings by starting to read this book. We hope that you will read it to the end—and make use of it.

This book will take you step by step through the meeting process:

Chapter 2 outlines and discusses the details of preparing for a meeting.

Chapter 3 explains how to start a meeting, including setting rules and assigning roles and responsibilities.

Chapter 4 offers suggestions for conducting a meeting.

Chapter 5 explains how to close a meeting and follow up on the results.

Chapter 6 describes a selection of techniques and tools for helping meeting participants work together more effectively and efficiently.

Chapter 7 presents common problems with meetings and ways to deal with them.

Chapter 8 discusses the use of technological tools and the issues involved in meeting virtually (online).

Manager's Checklist for Chapter 1

- ❑ Meetings can energize the participants, promote teamwork, and generate important results—or waste time and money and cause serious problems. As manager, you make the difference between good meetings and bad.
- ❑ Meetings can go bad for many reasons. Problems can develop in advance of the meeting, as the meeting begins, during the meeting, as the meeting ends, or after the meeting—and virtually all can be prevented.
- ❑ Bad meetings are bad for you as a manager, for your employees, for your organization, and for your career.
- ❑ Good meetings allow you and your employees to discuss important issues and reach decisions together, encourage your employees to develop their abilities to think critically, draw upon the experiences of your employees and others, help your employees work better as a team, and promote a sense of community.

Preparing for a Meeting

Any meeting worth holding is worth planning. The only exception to this rule is impromptu meetings. Although it's sometimes necessary to call a meeting with little or no notice, you should avoid doing so routinely, for the following reasons:

- Such meetings can be an imposition on the people you call together.
- Every impromptu meeting promotes the perception that you don't expect participants to prepare for meetings.
- The results can be be disappointing, because, without a plan, the meeting can veer off track.

We've all attended meetings that seemed to have been "just thrown together"—and the results are often mediocre at best: confusion, frustration, conflicts, disappointment, and time and energy wasted. In the oft-quoted words of Benjamin Franklin, "By failing to prepare, you are preparing to fail."

It's true that sometimes it's impossible to prepare adequately. Sometimes something comes up suddenly that necessitates gath-

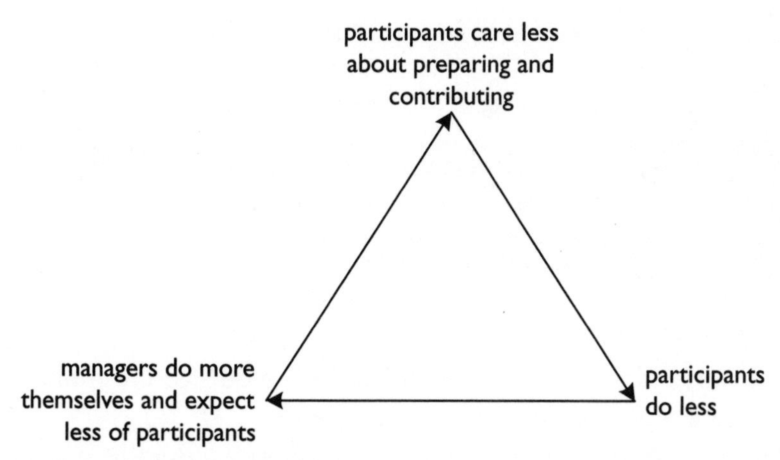

Figure 2-1. Cycle of bad meetings

ering at least briefly. But you've got to avoid allowing one bad meeting to be followed by another. That's because bad meetings usually lead to worse meetings, as shown in Figure 2-1.

The result of this downward cycle is that everybody tends to develop a fatalistic attitude toward meetings—and that can be a tough attitude to break. So, bad meetings usually lead to worse meetings.

The reverse is also true: good meetings often lead to better meetings. And good meetings start in advance—with good preparation.

Develop the Agenda

Whether you've got one purpose for meeting or several, you need to answer the following questions for each purpose in order to develop an agenda:

- What do you want to do?
- How should the pieces of the meeting be sequenced most effectively and efficiently?
- Who should attend? Which parts of the meeting? Why is each person necessary?

Key Term

Agenda A plan for a meeting. We're all familiar with the term and the basic definition. But sometimes managers start off target, by thinking of an agenda simply as "a list of things to cover."

It's useful, then, to keep in mind the origin of this word. It's the plural of the Latin word *agendum,* which means "something to be done," from the verb that gives us our word "act." In other words, an agenda is *a plan consisting of action points.*

Go Solo or as a Team

As you start planning for a meeting, there's a decision to make: do you go it alone or do you involve others?

Many managers prepare for meetings alone, primarily because it's easier—especially if they have only a few minutes here and there to spend on preparing—or because they feel that it's their responsibility as managers.

But it's easy to involve others, even minimally. Toward the end of each meeting, the facilitator can elicit suggestions for the agendas of future meetings.

Preparing as a group presents the following advantages:

- You can take advantage of the creativity and critical thinking of your employees.
- You can encourage your employees to take greater ownership of meetings.
- You can help your employees develop their leadership skills.
- You can delegate some of the preparation.

Working as a group takes more planning and time, but the benefits will be worth the extra investment. If the meeting is to be simple and focused, you can plan with just one or two people.

There are several ways to choose the people to help plan:

- By their strengths: organizational, interpersonal, analytical, creative, logical, etc.
- By their positions within your unit, to represent task areas or functions.

- By their social connections with other employees in your unit and perhaps in other units.

If someone other than yourself will be facilitating the meeting, you should also involve him or her in planning it.

By the way, it's not necessary to invite the planners to the meeting. The people who are best at planning a meeting are not necessarily the ones who should attend the meeting.

Finally, even if you choose to plan the meeting alone, you might benefit from distributing a draft agenda to participants and inviting reactions. Not only will you improve your agenda because of the input, but the participants will have a sense of ownership and will be able to prepare for the meeting.

Determine Your Purpose

Your preparation should start with determining your purpose. What do you want the meeting to do? If you don't have a purpose, don't hold a meeting. It's as simple as this: when it is not necessary to hold a meeting, it is necessary to not hold a meeting.

Determining your purpose involves more than just answering the question, "Why are you meeting?" After all, you could answer that question "Because we always meet on Monday morning" (the "same time, same place" logic) or "Because it's been a month since we had a meeting." Neither of those answers provides a *purpose*—other than that you would be meeting for the purpose of meeting. That line of reasoning leads to mediocre meetings, because it doesn't guide or inspire your preparation.

If meetings are not required by organizational policy or a mandate from the top, set a rule for your-

CAUTION!

Don't Waste Your Time and Energy

If you don't have purpose enough for a meeting, you can never do enough planning to compensate. The result would be only a well-planned waste of time and energy.

As economist John Maynard Keynes noted, "If a thing is not worth doing, it is not worth doing well."

self: justify each and every meeting. Your touchstone should be that basic question—What do you want the meeting to do?

Is a Meeting the Best Way?

The next step is to answer another question: Is a meeting the best way to do what you have to do? Does it require involving other people? If so, in what way(s)?

There are basically two kinds of meetings:

- *Participatory* meetings, which need input from group members
- *Nonparticipatory* meetings, which are mostly one-way communication—*informational* and *motivational*

All meetings would fit somewhere on a continuum, with the extremes being either totally unilateral communication or totally open and active participation. This perspective provides a rough guide to help you decide whether to hold a meeting or to find an alternative:

- If the purpose suggests that it would be a *presented, informational* meeting, then you might want to consider alternatives for getting that information out. At the very least, think about ways to keep it short and/or make it interest-

CAUTION!

Time-Wasters

Management consultant James Champy warns against the following types of meetings that he labels as "time-wasters" ("Wasteful Meetings," *Forbes,* Nov. 2, 1998):

"Progress reports"
"Beauty pageants": Presentations intended to please managers
"Informational meetings"
"Foreign policy meetings": Where people from various units gather "to enact business rituals"
"Planning meetings": Where the planning never ends and turns into action

This warning may be too categorical, since progress reports, informational meetings, and planning meetings can be valuable, even vital. Just don't let them become routine.

ing. A talking head is not a meeting.

- If the purpose suggests that it would be a *presented, motivational* meeting, then start planning—but keep it short. Inspiration is usually best served in smaller doses.
- If the purpose suggests that it would be a *participatory* meeting of any type, then you should schedule the meeting—but think carefully about the methods and the people you invite. (These two dimensions we'll consider a little later in this chapter.)

As a famous person (the comment has been attributed to Mark Twain, George Bernard Shaw, Oliver Wendell Holmes, and Douglas MacArthur) once noted, "No generalization is worth a damn, including this one!" That's only too true: for any generalization, there's at least one exception—and so too for our generalization about informational meetings.

Sometimes a purpose that might not justify a meeting under ordinary circumstances could be sufficient reason in certain situations. Let's take as an example a company with a tradition of applying the "mushroom theory of management" to its employees ("Keep them in the dark, cover them with ____, and, when they raise their heads, cut them off!"). In such an environment, you might be right to hold meetings to provide information and/or hold discussions—to empower your employees and improve morale—although you should limit the length and/or frequency of such meetings.

But every meeting should be special. Every meeting should interest participants by its purpose and the opportunity to make a difference. That's rarely the case for regular meetings, those events that are held at the same time on the same day with (usually) the same people, as much a part of the schedule as lunch, but far less rewarding.

The value of holding meetings regularly may be overrated. Regular meetings tend to become routine. Routine activities tend to become boring, even tedious (it's no coincidence that the word *routine* seems to have derived from the same source as the word *rut*!) or an occasion to socialize. When participants approach a meeting with apathy or even ennui, you'll be working harder and getting less out of your meetings.

Organizations now have more alternatives to face-to-face meetings than ever before. The purpose of many meetings, in whole or in part, is to share information, to make reports, and to provide updates. If possible, try to replace these meetings—or at least reduce the information load—by using e-mail or memos.

Using these other media to share information will save time for everyone and spare those who feel compelled to take copious notes from risking writer's cramp. Also, since few people can take accurate and comprehensive notes or remember every fact in an oral presentation, you're avoiding mistakes and misunderstandings by providing information in writing. (Just be sure to check your facts and your spelling—and make your e-mails or memos easy to read. Long paragraphs consisting of long sentences tend to daunt all but the most enthusiastic.)

Another type of alternative to conventional meetings is *virtual* meetings. We'll discuss these options in Chapter 8.

Set Your Goals

So, you have a purpose for a meeting, one or more things that you cannot do more effectively and efficiently through some other means. Next, you need to decide on your goals, the outcomes toward which the meeting will be directed. That's how you'll measure whether the meeting has succeeded or failed: did you achieve your goals?

Your goals don't need to be fancy. For each thing that you want the meeting to do, you should write a short statement of what you expect to achieve.

For example:

- If your purpose is to discuss expanding your services, your goal might be to create a list of five specific services to study.
- If your purpose is to debate three proposals for cutting

costs, your goal might be to decide on one of the three and develop a policy for implementing it.
- If your purpose is to work on improving workflow, your goal might be to determine the five areas with the most serious problems and to assign people to work to address the causes of each.

Once your purpose is clear, list the *topics* and then the method(s) for handling each topic.

Decide on Your Methods

For each purpose and the goals that you set you should choose an appropriate method. That seems only logical—but the logic is often neglected and misunderstood.

Michael Begeman, manager of the 3M Meeting Network, views meetings in terms of what he calls "conversations" ("You Have to Start Meeting Like This!" Gina Imperato, *Fast Company*, April 1999). He distinguishes three basic conversations:

- "Conversation for possibility"—to maximize creativity and generate ideas
- "Conversation for opportunity"— to narrow down a field of options, through discussing, sharing information, analyzing, taking positions
- "Conversation for action"—to make a decision and commit to taking action

Another way to think about these dynamics is in terms of three stages:

- Open
- Narrow
- Close

Your approach should be appropriate to your "conversation" and your purposes and goals and to the specifics of your circumstances. You should communicate your intent (purpose, goal, and method) in your agenda and then enforce the spirit of that "conversation" during the meeting.

If the participants don't understand the purpose, the goal, and the approach, they will be working in different directions, for different reasons. Here are two scenarios:

- You want to hold a "conversation for possibility" to generate a few ideas, but you don't make that intent clear. You put on the agenda only "discuss ideas." The result: some participants will be brainstorming, others will be shooting down their ideas, and still others may be trying to rush one of those ideas to a vote.
- You want to hold a "conversation for action" to vote on three proposals, but you don't make that intent clear. You put on the agenda only "talk about proposals." The result: a few participants insist on making additional proposals and others suggest forming a task force to gather more information on the proposals—activities that frustrate those who were expecting to reach a decision and then move on it.

We'll consider methods, techniques, and tools for "conversations for possibility" and "conversations for opportunity" in Chapters 4, 5, and 6. In a moment we'll outline ways to reach decisions in "conversations for action."

But first we should touch upon something essential for any of the three "conversations"—*information*. You should frame every discussion in a context of information. That means designating someone to provide information and naming the person(s) responsible on the agenda.

There are various ways to provide information, either in advance (distributed with the agenda) or during the meeting (brief comments, a presentation, questions and answers). How the information is provided depends, of course, on what and how much information the meeting participants will need to know in order to discuss most effectively and efficiently and, if they are entrusted with making a decision, to decide wisely. In other words, the information to be provided should be determined by the purposes, the desired outcomes, and the knowledge and experience of the participants. Later in this chapter, we'll discuss ways of providing information.

Deciding on Decisions

Sometimes *how* you decide may be just as important as *what* you decide. The process used to make a decision affects how people feel about the decision.

If you don't care how your employees feel and if you don't need their support for the decision and their commitment to acting on it, then you don't need to care about how the decision is made. However, if that's not the case, then you should think about how you want to make any decision you put on the agenda.

There are four basic ways to make decisions:

- Managerial—you make the call!
- Vote by majority or plurality—just count the votes
- Consensus—a result that all participants can support
- Delegation—selected members of the group make the decision

Here are some things to keep in mind as you choose and use any of these four methods of making decisions.

Managerial. Managers should not feel compelled to use voting or consensus to make all decisions in meetings. Sometimes it's more appropriate—and certainly more efficient—to exercise your managerial authority. But if an issue is worth considering and discussing in a meeting, be clear about the purpose for discussing it.

Decisions can be placed along a continuum, between totally managerial and totally delegated. In "How to Choose a Leadership Pattern" (*Harvard Business Review,*

Key Term

Consensus The cooperative development of a decision that all members of the group understand and can accept and agree to support. In decision-making by consensus, every member has the power to block any decision until the group has addressed his or her concerns satisfactorily.

March-April 1958, reprinted May-June 1973), Robert Tannenbaum and Warren H. Schmidt present a "continuum of leadership behavior" that outlines seven modes for making decisions. Figure 2-2 shows a version of this continuum.

Mode I	Mode II	Mode III	Mode IV	Mode V	Mode VI	Mode VII
Manager: I make the decision and announce it to you.	Manager: I make the decision and explain it to you.	Manager: I make the decision and discuss implementation issues.	Manager: I make a tentative decision and discuss it with you before implementing.	Manager: We discuss the problem and/or your recommendation first, then I make the decision.	Manager: I delegate the decision to you with limits.	Manager: I delegate the entire decision to the full limits of my authority.

Figure 2-2. Decision-making modes

You should at least consider making a decision yourself, using any discussion as exploratory and advisory, under certain conditions.

Vote by Majority or Plurality. This is the usual concept of voting: one choice receives more votes than any others. (We'll consider another type of voting—multivoting—in Chapter 6.) If there's only one choice (yes or no) or there are only two choices (A or B), then the decision is by majority, since either one or the other—yes or no, A or B—gains more than 50% of the votes cast. If there are three or more choices, then the option gaining more votes than any of the others has the plurality and wins.

Generally, if we consider only the choice that wins, whether it's a *majority* or a *plurality* is merely a technicality. (We've all heard at least once the triumphant cry after children vote on something—"Majority rules!" The fact

TOOLS

You Make the Decision

- When you're meeting with subordinates about budgets, personnel policies, or matters that involve other managers
- When situations involve information that you can't share
- When decisions require information that employees lack and that would take too much time to provide

that it's sometimes "Plurality rules!" wouldn't mean much to those whose choice won—and probably very little to those who voted otherwise.)

Traditionally, many groups have made decisions by voting. This method makes sense under the following conditions:

- The time is limited.
- There are significant differences among the members.
- It's more important to move forward than to resolve differences.
- Sufficient time is allowed for discussion before voting.
- The members consider and evaluate a number of options.
- Members have limited skills in communication and decision-making.
- You don't need the support of all members to implement the decision.
- There are significant differences among the members and it's obvious that consensus in the time allowed is very unlikely.
- It's more important to move forward than to resolve differences.
- Sufficient time is allowed for discussion before voting, so members of the group are all equally informed on the issue and understand each other's perspectives.
- The members consider and evaluate a number of options.
- The members have limited skills in communication and decision-making.
- It seems that the majority can act on the decision without the active involvement or support of the minority and there's a way to keep members of the minority from reacting negatively to the decision.

Consensus. Consensus—the cooperative development of a decision that's acceptable enough for all members of a group to agree to support—is the quintessential team approach to making decisions. Over the last decade or so, the idea of making decisions by consensus has become more established in business.

Participants in consensus own the decision, as opposed to managerial decisions. There are no "winners" and "losers," and no undermining the decision, as opposed to decisions by vote.

The reality is that it can take a long time to achieve consensus. And in practice the process of decision by consensus can fall far short of ideal, because it's often not *true* consensus. When personalities and group dynamics and the pressure to conform come into play, consensus can be harder on some people than either of the other two ways of making a decision.

The goal of consensus is to take multiple perspectives into account and craft a decision robust enough to address concerns. The outcome is that every participant really understands and can explain the decision and support it. Consensus is definitely the best way to go with some decisions. And generally groups become better at the process with experience.

Delegation. A fourth option is to delegate the decision to a subgroup. This is a good option particularly when these are the individuals generally considered best qualified to make the decision or when they're the only people affected by the decision.

TOOLS

Use Consensus ...

- When decisions are important and/or far-reaching in their effects.
- When the exchange of ideas and perspectives would enrich the group.
- When all or most members of the group are equally invested in the decision and are necessary to take action on it.

Adapted from *The Team Handbook*, p. 4-22.

Put It on the Agenda

For each decision on the agenda, indicate "vote" or "consensus" or "managerial" or "delegation." That's a simple way to let participants know in advance what to expect. By being clear and up-front about the method of making a decision, you help focus the conversation.

Allocate Time

The general rule is that "regular" meetings should last no longer than 90 minutes. If possible, you should limit meetings to one hour.

This depends, of course, on the purpose of the meeting. Some meetings are best scheduled for a half day or a full day, such as annual planning, strategic planning, and project reviews.

If you go beyond an hour or 90 minutes, allow breaks—at least five to ten minutes, depending on such practical factors as the number of participants, the capacity of the restrooms, and the distance from the meeting site to the restrooms.

Indicate a length of time for each item on your agenda. There are at least four good reasons to do so:

1. When you think about the time necessary for each item, one by one, you'll estimate the total time more accurately.
2. When participants know how much time you expect to allow for each item, they're likely to be more conscious of the time and more efficient.
3. When you know how long each item should take, you'll proceed through the agenda with more confidence, feeling more in control.
4. When you've allotted a time for each item, it's easier to skip an item if you fall behind schedule—or to allow a little more time for an item if necessary.

> CAUTION!
>
> **Avoid the Tyranny of 12 and 6**
>
> Don't get caught up on halves and wholes. Many managers will automatically allocate either 30 minutes or a full hour when scheduling a meeting, simply because these units of time are common and expected. Schedule a 40-minute meeting if you've got only 40 minutes' worth of work to do. Don't feel pressured to fill an hour. In fact, in some cases, 10 minutes may be all you need—and you can pack a lot of productivity into that time.

For each item, put a start time, a duration, and a stop time. And then break each item into components and indicate start times, durations, and stop times for those components. For example, if the item is "Decide on the best marketing strategy for launching the new and improved Super Widget," you might

> TRICKS OF THE TRADE
>
> **There's Really No Trick**
>
> It's a fact of human nature that people tend to take specifics more serious than generalities.
>
> Why? In part, at least, because specifics show that you've thought more about what you want to accomplish and how. So, let your agenda show what you're thinking—and if the results aren't very specific, maybe you should think some more.

break the item into three components—provide information, discuss options, and vote—and indicate a time allotment for each.

Putting down start and stop times provides structure—and makes the job of the timekeeper easier. Putting down durations allows the timekeeper to adjust the schedule if the group falls behind or goes ahead of the schedule.

Keep in mind that participatory activities, particularly if they involve more creativity and/or more emotional involvement, can vary greatly in time, depending on the following factors:

- Number of people
- Time of day
- Mood (even of only one or a few participants)

Sometimes participants are "in the zone" and contributions come fast and furious; other times, it's like their minds are mired in molasses. You can't predict how people are going to work together: sometimes there's synergy, sometimes lethargy or antagonism.

It's generally best to allow a little extra time for participatory activities, just in case things don't work out as you hope, and allow a lot of time for consensus decisions. Then, if you get lucky, you can do a little more or just end the meeting sooner on a high note.

Finally, if any participants are coming from outside your unit or the organization, you might want to add a little time at the start for introductions—and maybe for any activities where cultural differences may affect interactions.

Sequence the Items

The next decision is how to sequence the pieces of the meeting most effectively and efficiently. It may be that there's a certain natural flow of the items that just makes sense. If not, then you've got choices. You can alternate the agenda items in terms of any or all of these aspects:

- Difficulty: hard vs. easy
- Time: long vs. short
- Energy: intensive vs. light
- Emotions: hot vs. cool

Structure the agenda to keep the meeting from bogging down or diverging and the participants from heating up or burning out. That may not always be possible, of course, but it's worth the effort. When the agenda is structured so the facilitator can vary the pace, it's easier to maintain attention and sustain involvement.

Of course, you're not relying only on the structure of the agenda to keep your meetings in order. You've also got your meeting ground rules to help things run more smoothly. (We'll discuss ground rules in Chapter 3.) If you don't have meeting ground rules, that should be the first item on your agenda. It may take 10 or 15 minutes, perhaps even longer, but the time is definitely well invested in terms of establishing guidelines for interaction and developing a spirit of community.

After you've sequenced your business items, you plan the ending. Shakespeare was stretching a point when he had a character observe (twice) that "all's well that ends well" in his play to which he gave that title. Yet, it's important to end a meeting properly. That means allotting 5 to 10 minutes or so to sum up the main points, the decisions, and the assignments, and to evaluate the meeting.

We'll go into these activities in detail in Chapter 5. Here, we'll just note that you should treat the summary and the evaluation as you would any other items on the agenda. You don't

CAUTION!

Don't Start with Blah, Blah, Blah

Managers often sequence announcements as the first item on their agendas. This is, in general, a bad strategy for at least five reasons:

1. It may lessen the initial feeling of community, unless all of the announcements are relevant to all of the participants.
2. It may distract participants from the purpose(s) of the meeting and the agenda.
3. It sends the message that it's not important to arrive on time.
4. It starts the meeting wrong, with a one-way flow of information. That can make the transition into collaboration more difficult.
5. It suggests that you don't realize there are better ways to make announcements than at a meeting.

need to specify desired outcome(s), but you should indicate a start time, a duration, and a stop time.

Setting a stop time for the meeting encourages the participants to work more efficiently, to not go off on tangents. (It's usually unwise, however, to be rigid about the stop time. We'll consider this issue in Chapter 4.)

MISTAKE PROOFING

Prevent the "Parkinson Puff"

Set a time for the meeting to end.

Do you recognize the name Cyril Northcote Parkinson? Probably not, but you most likely know his law—"Work expands so as to fill the time available for its completion." That's certainly true for meetings.

Set a time for the meeting to end.

Who Should Meet?

We're all familiar with the adage, "The more the merrier." That seems to be the principle by which many managers decide who should attend their meetings. That's great for a party, but not for a business meeting.

It seems to make more sense to follow this principle: "The length of a meeting rises with the square of the number of people present." So, be stingy with your invitations. Invite only those people necessary to achieve the goal(s) of the meeting.

That advice makes sense, but how do you apply it?

Perhaps the best way is by asking one question about everybody you're considering inviting—How do you expect this person to contribute to the meeting? Be specific. Could you explain to this person what you expect from him or her? If you don't know how you expect the person to contribute, maybe you shouldn't include him or her.

If it would make sense to invite some people for only part of the meeting, then do so. If you schedule the items on the agenda with start and stop times and you keep to that schedule, you can have participants show up for one part of the meeting, then leave for the rest. It's generally better to lose a few minutes of meeting time to the disruption of people arriving and leaving than to keep people in the meeting when they are not yet or no longer necessary.

Sure, that may sound harsh. And yes, it's natural to not want to exclude people from a meeting. But it's a balancing act between ensuring a fully democratic process and making the most of the time. Compromise, by appointing or letting employees appoint representatives. You can shorten meetings and reduce the number of participants, so you save time—and money.

You can designate an individual to represent a group of his or her peers. Then, he or she is responsible for discussing the agenda with the others and eliciting comments, suggestions, concerns, and so forth to present at the meeting. (If any employees or other managers question this method of holding meetings, you need only refer them to the U.S. Congress. Certainly nobody would expect 260,000,000 Americans to meet in Washington, D.C. to deliberate and make decisions!)

Maybe you truly believe that more can be better, depending on the purpose of the meeting. There's some truth to that argument—although maybe not enough to prove that you should include everyone in the meeting.

Do you want to share some information? You can often do so at least as effectively and efficiently by another means. It

TRICKS OF THE TRADE

Practice the Project Principle

If you're unsure about whom to invite to a meeting, here's a suggestion. Think of the meeting as a very short-term project. You know the outcome that you expect. Think of your employees as a pool of potential temporary workers. Whom would you hire for the duration of the project?

When you think in terms of a meeting as being real work, a project that will require commitment and collaboration from all, it's easier to select members of the project team.

might make more sense and save time if you provide the information through memos or e-mail. Then your people could read the information, think about it, and attend the meeting only to ask questions and/or discuss the information.

Do you want to motivate? It's true that the direct approach generally works best, rather than trying to motivate through representatives. But if your purpose for meeting is to motivate, keep it short. The best leaders can usually do the most good in the fewest words.

Do you want to make decisions? It depends on the method you choose whether it makes sense to have a lot of people. If you just want a vote, you can do so without a meeting. If you want a discussion, then maybe it's logical to invite everybody—for just the discussion and the vote.

Do you want to gather input and/or generate ideas? You may want all of your people there—or you may want to send

For Example

Voice Mail Replaces Meetings

When the cost of meetings wasn't paying off in results, Kris Kile, CEO of Total Restoration, Inc. in Amherst, NH, replaced them with broadcast voice mail followed up by memos.

"As we added people, our 30-minute sessions started costing us 10 hours of overtime per week," he explained in an interview. "Now I deliver short, focused pep talks by voicemails whenever necessary. I'll describe our current financial picture and remind people of our goals."

Source: "Making Meetings Work," Karen Carney, *Harvard Management Update*, October 1999.

out an e-mail to all and find out who's interested in providing input and/or coming up with ideas.

If you need any more reasons to keep your invitation list short, consider the political: it's easier to justify not inviting *a lot* of individuals than to justify not inviting *a few* individuals. If you invite only the people who are most important, who are essential, there will be enough people who are not invited that none of them should take it personally as a slight. But if you invite any people who are not essential, then you may feel pressure to invite everybody, for fear of offending somebody.

Prepare the People

After you've decided on the people to bring together for the meeting, you should talk with the "special cases"—people to whom you want to assign individual responsibilities and people from outside your unit.

Facilitator, Scribe, Timekeeper, and Note-Taker. Make sure that the people you've chosen to serve as facilitator, scribe, timekeeper, and note-taker understand the responsibilities of the assigned roles and are able to assume them. (We'll describe these roles and responsibilities in Chapter 3. Also, as mentioned earlier in this chapter, you may want to involve the facilitator in planning the meeting.)

You may need to provide some guidelines and offer some suggestions, especially for the facilitator and the scribe, whose roles are demanding. You may want to discuss how to work together during the meeting and what to do if problems arise. You might also show the facilitator Chapter 7 of this book, since many of the problems that could arise during the meeting would be his or her responsibility to help the group resolve.

Go over the items on the agenda. Remind the role players that their responsibilities could inhibit their ability to contribute to discussions and other activities. If any of them want to participate extensively in the activities for a certain agenda item, suggest that they should find someone to take over their roles during those activities, so as to be free to participate fully in the topic. This is especially true for the facilitator, less true for the other roles.

Informants. Make sure that people you've designated to provide information understand what you expect, why the other participants need the information, and how much time they have to provide it. Indicate whether you expect some basic background, a short report, or a full presentation. Emphasize that informants should resist the temptation to be comprehensive: more isn't necessarily better—it's hard to get a drink of water from a fire hose. Suggest that, if possible, they provide the information in writing in advance, so participants get all of the information accurately, have time to read it and think about it, and then can use the meeting to ask questions and discuss the information.

If there are any agenda items for which participants will need information and you don't designate an informant or distribute information in advance, you should prepare a sheet of background information to share at the meeting.

Guests. Beforehand, talk with any guests invited to the meeting. Ask if they have any questions about what you expect to accomplish in the meeting and why you're inviting them. Fill them in on the group's history and meeting ground rules and norms.

CAUTION!

No Dumping

How many meetings have you attended (or conducted) where time was spent presenting information that could have been delivered more efficiently and more effectively in writing? You know the scenario: one person reads the information and the others listen and maybe take notes. Unless they have photographic memories or they've been trained in stenography, they're likely to miss important points or make mistakes in their notes. If there's a discussion, they must rely on their memories and/or their notes. And even if they manage to take in and/or take down all of the information accurately, they may not be able to think about it quickly enough to ask questions or discuss it more than superficially. How *effective* is that? How *efficient* is that?

For Example

Two Different Worlds

In one small publishing company, there were surprising differences among the thirty or so employees, depending on their work activities and their managers. The marketers tended to approach their meetings with anxiety and conduct them in an orderly manner. Each felt under pressure to explain on the spot variances from their predictions and they tended otherwise to contribute only when they felt confident. In contrast, the editors tended to run their meetings a little more freely, interrupting each other, in the same spirit as they edited each other's writing. Two units, separated by less than 20 feet, yet two different worlds in terms of meeting culture and behavior.

What's the People Price?

Before finalizing your "guest list" for a meeting, do a quick calculation: add up the hourly cost (compensation and benefits) of all of the people on your list and multiply the total by the estimated duration in hours.

You can also consider the potential value of that time, the cost of lost opportunities. Every dollar spent on employee time should be returning at least a dollar of value—or you've got more problems than this book can cover.

It's not all about the cost of meetings, of course, since many of the benefits of meetings cannot be reduced to dollars and cents. However, when you know the approximate cost of bringing people together for a meeting, then you appreciate all the more the value of effective and efficient meetings.

When and Where Should You Meet?

Time and place are two issues you need to consider when planning your meeting.

When Should You Meet?

The first part of this question is often not really an issue. Depending on the schedules of the people you're inviting to the meeting, you may have few or no options. You schedule the meeting for a date and a time when all of the people will be free to attend. If that's impossible, you check time with the people who are essential to your meeting and find a date and a time that fits their schedules.

If possible, consider the rhythms of your employees and your workplace. Starting fresh may be smart, but it's not so smart to expect your employees to be ready to meet and to participate actively as soon as they arrive at work on Monday morning. It's also generally unwise to schedule meetings immediately after lunch, when the gathering may seem more like a slumber party.

Some managers prefer to schedule meetings to end at lunch time or at the end of the day, counting on thoughts of eating or going home to motivate participants to keep on track and on time. However, if the activities are such that they let their minds wander, this timing strategy works against you.

You might also consider the circadian rhythms of your employees. You don't have to go scientific over those patterns of physiological and behavioral activity that occur on a 24-hour cycle, more or less. But you probably are aware that some of your people work better in the early morning, some a few hours later, some in the mid-afternoon, and so forth. You've probably noticed your own rhythms: you may handle routine tasks best as soon as you arrive at work, you may be more creative after a few hours, and then you may feel most like making phone calls in the early afternoon.

Arredondo notes (in *Communicating Effectively*, p. 150):

> Typically, we have two "peak" periods when our physical energy and mental alertness are highest. For people who work days, those times are about 9:30-11:30 in the morning and about 3:00-5:00 in the afternoon. Most people experience a "slump" between 1:00 and 3:00 p.m.

If you can't schedule your meetings at a time when all or most of the participants are likely to be at their creative and productive best, maybe you can at least avoid some bad circadian confluence.

Make sure that the room for your meeting is available at the time when you want to schedule the meeting. If you have a choice of locations, you may first want to consider the possibilities outlined in the following section.

Where Should You Meet?

To be realistic, you may not have much choice here. But to the extent that you can choose, here are some quick suggestions.

First, you want a room that will accommodate comfortably the number of people invited. It should also allow space for a facilitator to move around easily and a scribe with a flip chart or whatever type of display you'll be using.

Second, you want a room that allows for the proper atmosphere for your meeting. Seating can make a big difference in the mood and the results.

To promote interaction, the best arrangement is a circle, a square, or a U shape. These configurations give all participants the same status and encourage all to contribute equally.

A rectangular table tends to focus attention toward one end or the other. If you use this configuration, put the scribe at one end (at the front or wherever there's more room). Depending on the circumstances, it may be better for the facilitator to move around the room—to help animate the participants and spare them the neck aches often caused by this seating arrangement—or to sit still—so as not to distract participants from focusing on each other and what the scribe is recording.

(If you're interested in other possibilities, read "10 Layouts for Setting Up a Meeting Room" in *101 Ways to Make Meetings Active* by Mel Silberman, San Francisco: Jossey-Bass/Pfeiffer, 1999.)

Third, make sure that the room has at least adequate lighting, that any windows have blinds or curtains to reduce sunlight and other distractions, that the temperature can be maintained at a comfortable level, and that the room is properly ventilated. It should also have any equipment or other facilities that you need (for slides, video, audio, computers. etc.).

Smart Managing

We're All Only Human

The best meetings may depend, to some extent, on the comfort of the chairs. You might not be able to choose the chairs, but if you can't you should at least keep them in mind when you're thinking about the length of your meetings.

As a fellow manager once pointed out, "You're calling on their brains, but they don't leave their butts behind." To get the most out of the former, you've got to keep the latter comfortable. Be alert for squirming; if it becomes frequent and/or sustained, it's probably time to let the brains go for the sake of the butts.

Finalize and Distribute the Agenda

Now that you've planned and sequenced the items to cover, decided on the people to invite and assigned the meeting responsibilities, set the time, and chosen the room (and reserved it, if necessary), it's time to finalize your agenda. What should it contain?

If the meeting is complex or long, if you expect strong disagreements, and/or if the group has a history of serious problems with meetings, the agenda should contain the following information:

Date and time
Place
Purpose
Start time
Items
    For each item:
        Purpose
        Goals—outcomes
        Methods (activities)
            For each activity:
                Person responsible
                Time allotted
                Start time, duration, stop time
Summary: start time, duration, stop time
Evaluation: start time, duration, stop time

Stop time
List of participants (indicating who's serving as facilitator, scribe, timekeeper, and note-taker and identifying any guests)

For most meetings, this level of detail is unnecessary. A simple list of items may provide enough structure.

What format should you use for your agenda? Figure 2-3 (next page) shows an example of an agenda format.

The format of your agenda doesn't matter much, as long as

- It states the outcome(s) desired
- It is well organized and structured
- The items are outlined concisely, in plain language
- The components of each item are outlined
- The person responsible for providing information or leadership is indicated
- The start and stop times and durations are displayed prominently

You might want to specify the methods to be used. This is particularly important, as we've explained, for making decisions. For discussing options and assigning tasks, you could indicate the methods or leave them to the facilitator and/or the group to choose. As for providing information, it's up to the people designated as informants to choose their methods according to the needs of the participants and the time allotted.

There are no rules for putting an agenda into words—just "serving suggestions." Exercise your best judgment. You know what you want to accomplish. You know the people to whom you'll be distributing the agenda. You'll want the participants to know what you expect to happen at the meeting so they can best prepare to contribute. You'll want other people who might be reading the agenda to know what you're doing—and how you're managing the people and the time so well. The best way for you, in your particular situation, to prepare a particular agenda is not to be found in any book.

Marketing Department
Meeting Agenda

Date: September 4, 2002
Start Time: 10:00 a.m.
Stop Time: 11:04 a.m.
Purpose: Decide on how to use Web to market products; decide on how to market Wonder Widget
Desired Outcome: Strategy for using Web to market products; determine approach for marketing Wonder Widget

10:00–10:02: (2 minutes) Review agenda and any changes
10:02–10:21 (19 minutes)
    10:02–10:08: Information of Web market (Jerry, attached report)
    10:08–10:17: Discussion of options (facilitator)
    10:17–10:19: Decision (vote) (facilitator)
    10:19–10:21: Assignment of tasks (facilitator)
10:21–10:50 (29 minutes)
    10:21–10:28: Outline of three options for marketing Wonder Widget (Alyce, information provided in advance)
    10:28–10:48: Decision (consensus) (facilitator)
    10:48–10:50: Assignment of tasks (facilitator)
10:50–10:56: (6 minutes) Summation of main points, decisions, and assignments (facilitator)
10:56–11:04: (8 minutes) Evaluation (facilitator)
11:04 End

Participants: Anna (facilitator), Same (scribe), Brigitte (timekeeper), Tasha (note-taker), Marisol, Rupert, Martha, Anthony Taylor (Sales Department), Marge Hopkins (R&D)

Figure 2-3. Form for meeting agenda

Get the Agenda Out and About

Get the agenda out to the participants at least 24 hours in advance. Attach any materials for the participants to read or review to prepare for the meeting. Check with any participants responsible for providing information; they may have materials to include. All participants should know what to expect and have time to prepare appropriately for it. A meeting should never be a surprise party.

You might also attach any key questions that will help participants focus their thinking and prepare them for thoughtful and committed interaction.

And then stick to the agenda. That should be obvious—but some managers either shift focus or forget what they intended to do. Tim Paeltz, in his notes for *Circular Management—or How to Run an Organization and Not Go Anywhere*, describes what *not* to do:

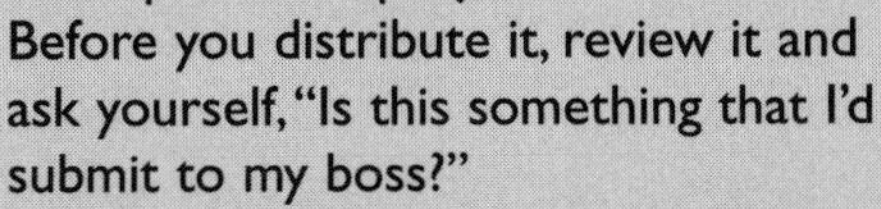

Think "Project Plan"

Think of your agenda as a work plan for a project. Before you distribute it, review it and ask yourself, "Is this something that I'd submit to my boss?"

Remember that paperwork tends to live a long life. As Horace observed of his writing two millennia ago: "I have built a monument more lasting than bronze." Your agenda may not be a work of art, but it should definitely be something that shows your management skills.

> Tell your committee that you will have a meeting in three months to discuss either subject A or subject B. Never state definitely which subject will be discussed. When the meeting starts, announce that you are there to discuss subject C and then ask who is ready to discuss subject C. When no one is ready, state that they had three months to prepare. *You* are ready. Why aren't *they*?

How you distribute the agenda will depend on the culture of your workplace, the participants selected, and the work schedules and habits of the participants. If memos and notices are usually printed and placed in mailboxes, that's probably the best way to go. If memos and notices are generally distributed by e-mail, that's how you should distribute the agenda. It's even better if you use both paper and electrons. Be sure to choose methods appropriate for all of the people you're inviting.

A smart manager allows for individual differences and special situations. If, for example, you know that any of the participants tend to be slow on checking their mailboxes or their e-mail, it's wise to phone those people or even talk to them in person, just to make sure they know about the agenda. Sure, that takes a little extra effort—but it's easier than running a meeting with participants who haven't reviewed the agenda in advance and are not prepared.

It may happen that someone tells you that he or she has nothing to contribute to the meeting or to gain from attending it. If so, take a moment to explain why you're inviting him or her. If you can't, then maybe that person is right and should not be attending.

One final thought about getting the word out about the meeting: it may take more than a sheet of paper. Sure, you're working with adults who can read and can schedule their lives, but they're also busy and not all are as well organized as you. The bottom line is that you're planning the meeting to achieve certain objectives and you're relying on all the people you've invited to contribute toward those outcomes, so you've got good reason to do whatever it takes to make sure they're all there and ready. And with e-mail, voice mail, and cell phones, it's easier than ever to reach out and remind.

Prepare Materials

First, make a list of all of the materials and equipment you'll need. This serves three purposes:

- As you prepare, you'll think more carefully about what you'll need.
- As you're leaving for the meeting, you'll have an easy way to verify that you're bringing all the things that you'll need.
- As you arrive in the room, you'll be able to quickly check the facilities.

Make sure that you have any media you want to use—slides, video, audio, and so on. If you need equipment, check that it will be available for the meeting. How many flipcharts or whiteboards will you need? Your list should include markers (for flipchart or whiteboard) and masking tape to post sheets of flipchart paper on the walls. You might also add to the list a flipchart pad—particularly if discussions tend to keep the scribe busy.

If you prepare informational materials for participants, distribute them in advance, if possible. If you distribute them during the meeting, take the time to review them, explaining and answering any questions. Never hit and run—handing out materials and hoping that participants will read them. Some will dutifully put them away—and most likely forget about them—and others will skim them while you continue—which virtually guarantees that they'll fully understand neither the materials nor whatever the group is doing.

Finally, it may be worth the effort to put the agenda on a flipchart or a transparency, to display during the meeting. The participants will all have copies, of course—if they remember to bring them. (Bring extra copies, just in case.) But with the agenda on display it's easier for the facilitator to keep the meeting on track if he or she can simply gesture toward the agenda item if participants begin to stray from the topic.

The idea is simple—but the effects can be profound. You can print a few questions on a sheet of flipchart paper or have something prepared by a graphic designer. However you put the writing on the wall, it will remind any people who gather in the room that meetings are serious work.

Tricks of the Trade

Lend a Helping Hand

Make life easier for the note-taker. Sure, you can't physically lend a hand to help him or her keep track of the meeting. However, you can provide assistance by investing a few moments in advance.

It's easy with word processing programs to customize the agenda for the note-taker, by inserting a page break after each agenda item, to allow a blank page sufficient to take notes of main points, decisions, and actions on that item.

If he or she will be taking notes on a computer, give him or her the file to serve as a template for taking notes.

For Example

Read the Writing on the Wall

Intel Corporation has been cited as an organization that takes meetings very seriously. On the walls of conference rooms in Intel factories and offices is a poster that lists a few simple questions for the people who meet there:

- Do you know the purpose of this meeting?
- Do you have an agenda?
- Do you know your role?
- Do you follow the rules for good meetings?

Source: "The Seven Sins of Deadly Meetings," Eric Matson, *Fast Company*, April 1996.

Just in Case

In planning the agenda and in preparing materials, your focus is on success. This is preparation to bring about a best-case scenario. However, you should also prepare to deal with a worst-case scenario—or at least problems that are likely to arise. Chapter 7 is devoted to problems, but here are a few that you can usually prevent with a little preparation. So, take a little time to plan and prepare for problems.

Absences. It happens, at least occasionally, that a person designated to be responsible for some aspect of a meeting is unable to make it. You can prepare for this possibility by asking participants assigned to be informants to provide you with a copy in advance of any information.

Personality Conflicts. Problems can arise out of personal conflicts, and such conflicts are only too natural. However, you can reduce the possibility of clashes by talking with potentially contentious individuals prior to the meeting about any concerns. Encourage them to express their perspectives without getting into personal attacks.

Materials and Machines. Arrange your materials so you can quickly find whatever you'll need as you need it. Verify that you've got everything. (This is where a checklist is very valuable.) Practice using any special equipment, such as VCRs, overhead projectors, and so forth.

You can also delegate this responsibility to an administrative assistant, the facilitator, or participants to whom you've assigned special responsibilities. If someone will be using a piece of equipment to make a presentation, for example, he or she should be responsible for ensuring that the equipment is there and working properly and he or she should be familiar with using it.

This chapter has been long, because, as noted at the start, any meeting worth holding is worth planning, and good meetings start with good preparation. It may seem like a lot of work at first, but planning well becomes easier and more natural with time and experience.

Now, on to Chapter 3, where we discuss putting all of this planning into action!

Manager's Checklist for Chapter 2

- ❑ Any meeting worth holding is worth planning. Good meetings start in advance—with good preparation.
- ❑ Before you begin planning a meeting, ask yourself, "Is a meeting the best way to achieve what I want to achieve?"
- ❑ To develop an agenda, you need to answer the following questions:
  - What do you want to do?
  - What outcome(s) do you want?
  - What's the best way to achieve the desired outcome(s)?
  - How much time is required?
  - How should the pieces of the meeting be sequenced most effectively and efficiently?
  - Who is necessary? Why?
- ❑ After you've planned to make your meeting a success, plan for potential problems. Aim at bringing about a best-case scenario, but be ready to deal with any worst-case scenario.

Starting the Meeting

Arrive in the room at least 5 minutes early, 10 if you have materials and equipment to set up, and even a little earlier if you're unfamiliar with the room. You may want to post the agenda—on a flipchart, a transparency, or however appropriate. (It's best if you've prepared in advance some way to display it.) At the very least, put up the goal of the meeting in a prominent place, so it stays foremost in everyone's mind.

If you're not busy setting up materials and equipment, greet the participants as they arrive. This is a sort of natural warm-up, promoting a feeling of community and shared enthusiasm and energy.

3, 2, 1 ... Start!

Start the meeting at the scheduled time. To delay, except under extraordinary circumstances, shows disrespect for those who are there on time and encourages participants to arrive late. Show that you expect all participants to arrive by the scheduled time by starting as planned.

Any missing participants may arrive by the end of the warm-up. In that case, no problem.

If not, then, as the facilitator reviews the agenda, he or she can rearrange the items to work around the absence, if possible. For example, if the missing person was to give a presentation to start the meeting, the meeting can start with another agenda item. (However, if the entire meeting depends on that presentation, you may be forced to wait.)

How long should the group wait for someone essential to the meeting? That depends on the other participants, the ground rules, and the missing person. If the "someone essential" is the CEO of your organization, it's probably wise to wait a little longer than ordinary. If you must call off the meeting, apologize for the inconvenience and thank the participants for understanding the situation.

What if you're running late and can't make the meeting on time?

The facilitator should start the meeting, because, with the agenda and participants who are prepared for the meeting, the group can get started without you. And that's good.

> As a manager the important thing is not what happens when you are there, but what happens when you are not there.
>
> —Kenneth Blanchard, business author

Warm up the Team

As Michael Begeman, manager of the 3M Meeting Network, points out in "You Have to Start Meeting Like This!" (*Fast Company*, April 1999):

> There is a legitimate social component to meetings. Sure, we'd all rather be efficient than sloppy in our work. Sure, we'd all rather spend our time on "real work" than on "idle chitchat." But you should never overlook the social side of work rituals—even in meetings that are "all business."

The usual way to meet the social needs of the participants and transition into the meeting is through *warm-ups*. A warm-up is a quick, round-the-group sharing of ideas, issues, information, or concerns at the beginning of the meeting. A warm-up has several important purposes:

- To break the ice among people who do not know each other.
- To involve all participants from the start of the meeting.
- To generate a team feeling.
- To allow participants to share their concerns, needs, and hopes.
- To focus participants on the meeting purpose and agenda.

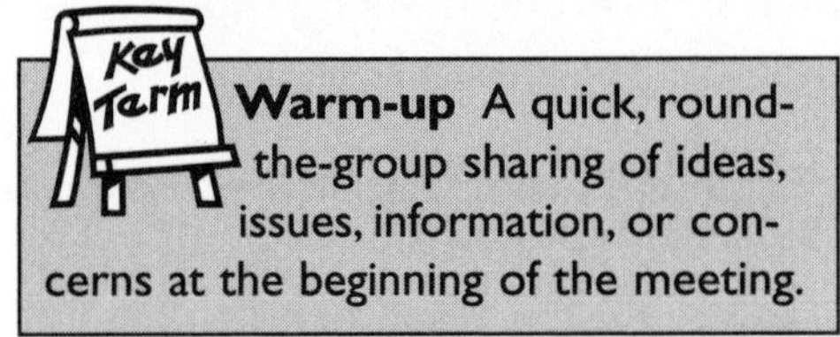

Warm-up A quick, round-the-group sharing of ideas, issues, information, or concerns at the beginning of the meeting.

A simple warm-up consists of giving the participants a sentence starter to finish, such as:

- "Issues and concerns I'm checking at the door are...."
- "What I've been doing prior to this meeting is...."
- "My hopes for this meeting are...."
- "My concerns for this meeting are...."

If any of the participants don't know each other, you might start the warm-up by asking each participant to provide some information about himself or herself, such as the following:

- Name
- Unit
- Job
- Length of time with the unit and/or the organization
- Reason for attending the meeting
- What he or she can contribute to the group

When there are only a few strangers to the group, you might feel tempted to have only those newcomers introduce themselves. That would be a mistake, because it ignores the needs of the new people to also learn something about other participants.

It also creates a gap between "the group" and "the others." Participants in a meeting should feel like peers—a feeling that should start with introductions.

Begeman explains:

> In many of the meetings that I run ... I schedule 5 or 10 minutes of open time, just to encourage people to relate to one another. If you plan for such time, if you put it on your agenda, then you won't feel as if you're not doing what you ought to be doing....
>
> For some meetings, I book a certain amount of time at the beginning to ask, "Is there anything that people need to say in order to be 'present' at this meeting?" ... Just because people walk into a conference room doesn't mean that their mind is on your meeting. If you let people express their frustrations before you get down to business, you allow them to clear their mind and to focus on your meeting.

Set the Tone

Another benefit of a warm-up is that it sets the tone for the meeting. It should be collegial—and the language should be informal. This allows participants to understand each other and to participate more naturally. The language of meetings should be the language that the participants use in their normal workplace interactions.

The success of a meeting depends on participation from every person attending. Meetings are work. You've selected the employees and others who are essential to that work. Now you need to develop the sense of community that will inspire every member of the group to share in the responsibility for making the meeting a success by contributing and collaborating.

Establish the Ground Rules

If the participants have worked together in meetings, the group should already have established ground rules. You may want to

TRICKS OF THE TRADE

All Work and No Play

Michael Begeman reminds us:

"There is much more to people ... than what's above the neck. We are not just intellects that come together to interact with other intellects. The more you involve the whole person in your meetings, the more people will learn, and the more of that learning they will retain. If you want people to work together effectively, let them play together."

Begeman advises having "kinetic stuff" in meeting rooms—squeeze balls, Slinkies, and other toys. He believes that toys help relieve stress and enhance creativity. "I've found that when people have something to play with, when they can get more of their body involved in what they're doing, they become more creative." ("You Have to Start Meeting Like This!" *Fast Company*, April 1999)

review them briefly before getting to the agenda. Get some agreement—verbal or nonverbal—from everyone. It would be good to ask if anyone wants to propose any changes or additions. The ground rules should not be carved in stone: all participants should always feel like the ground rules belong to them and that they can modify them based on their experiences together.

If you haven't established ground rules, then the next logical step would be to do so.

Ground rules are agreements about behaviors: they should promote respect, collaboration, and efficiency without hindering spontaneity and creativity. Most people come to a meeting with some expectations about how participants should act. Establishing a code of conduct is simply about expressing those expectations and reaching agreement on how to regulate behavior to meet them.

So, it's important to set ground rules—and then just as important to make sure that they work.

Developing Ground Rules

As important as the rules themselves is the way in which the rules are developed. Sure, you could just post a list of rules that you personally consider essential to running meetings effectively and efficiently. Then you could just enforce them as you enforce your organization's policies.

But it's better if the participants develop the ground rules themselves, because the rules will be specific to their group, because they'll feel a sense of ownership, and because they'll be more likely to follow the ground rules if they all agree on them.

The facilitator can start the discussion by just asking a question such as "What guidelines should we adopt so that our meetings make the most of what all of us have to offer?" or "What are some principles that we should all keep in mind during our meetings?"

The discussion that generates the meeting rules also serves another important purpose: it reveals values and emotions that can divide the participants or unite them. The way in which participants develop their ground rules shows a lot about how they'll work together.

If participants have trouble starting this discussion, the facilitator can suggest one or two topics for them to consider. He or she might also want to suggest more topics as the discussion wanes.

Once participants start making and discussing suggestions for rules, the facilitator should help them word their proposals and guide them through the decision process. The scribe records the ground rules on a flipchart or whiteboard.

After the meeting, the scribe transfers the ground rules to regular sheets of paper and/or another convenient medium. Then, you can bring the rules to every meeting, to review them for the group and/or display them during the meeting.

Groups typically adopt or at least consider *ground rules* covering the following issues:

- Attendance
- Promptness: procedure for dealing with latecomers—bring them up to speed? sanction?
- Participation
- Meeting role assignments
- Interruptions: pagers and cell phones?
- Respect
- Discussion process

For Example

100 Miles Away

To reduce interruptions, you might adopt the "100-mile rule": no participant should be called from the meeting unless the reason is so important and urgent that the person would be contacted even if the meeting were being held 100 miles from the workplace. This rule would be communicated to secretaries, assistants, and anyone else who might be handling the phones or welcoming visitors. (*The Team Handbook*, p. 4-2)

- Confidentiality: how is it determined what discussions are confidential? What information or comments are not to leave the room?
- Assignments
- Method for evaluating meetings
- Chronic violations of rules

Sometimes groups decide on a penalty for breaking ground rules. For example, the group might decide that any participant who causes an unnecessary interruption must buy coffee, tea, and soft drinks for all of the others during the next break or for the next meeting. Or the group might decide that participants who arrive late are responsible for providing refreshments for the next meeting.

To the extent possible, the group members should be responsible for enforcing their ground rules. The facilitator should be sensitive and as ready to help them with this process as with any other. If somebody breaks a rule and it seems like a serious matter, the facilitator may scan the faces of the other members for any negative reactions and, with a facial expression or gesture, encourage them to react, just as he or she might encourage reactions to a contribution. At times, it may be necessary for him or her to intervene, if a violation of a rule seems serious and the other members of the group aren't reacting to it. And sometimes members of the group may just let violations pass, if they're not serious, but mention them when they evaluate the meeting.

Finally, the simpler the rules, the easier they are to remem-

Smart Managing

Dialogue vs. Debate

Some difficulties cannot easily be avoided through rules. Discussions often cause discords that no amount of rules could prevent. (Consider the discussions in the U.S. Congress, for example!)

It might help prevent problems if you make sure that participants understand the differences between *dialogue* and *debate*:

- In a *debate*, people are driven by their individual interests to advocate for their opinions and positions and to win over other opinions and positions.
- In a *dialogue*, people express their opinions and differences in an effort to arrive at what's better for the group, in a spirit of mutual understanding, a quest for commonalties, and a sense of community.

ber and follow—and for you to review at the start of meetings, as necessary. Also, a group that gets bogged down in legalistic wrangling over rules is setting a dangerous pattern for discussing other matters. In addition, the more involved the discussion becomes, the easier for participants to obsess over rules and neglect the principles behind them—such as respect, collaboration, and efficiency.

The group is responsible for developing and adopting ground rules. In this process, as in all others during a meeting, the members of the group are all equals. The facilitator and the scribe are serving, not governing; they should act as peers. You cannot use your rank as manager to influence anybody; you should act as a peer. Just trust that the participants will decide to modify the rules as they gain a little experience applying them. The ground rules are for the benefit of the group and the members are more likely to adhere to rules that they have generated.

Working with the Rules

Review the rules at the beginning of meetings, at least until it no longer seems necessary. It may be enough to display the rules at every meeting, so everyone can see them. It should be sufficient to post only the essentials, not the details. The essence of most rules can be summed up in just a few words. (If not, then that may indicate that the rule is too complicated.)

Displaying the rules will serve as a reminder. However, if participants start bending or breaking a rule, it's easy for others to call out the rule as a warning. It's generally most effective if participants correct each other, as peers. Just as they took responsibility for developing the rules to guide their community, they should take responsibility for helping each other abide by them.

What if reminders and peer correction aren't effective? Then, it's time to discuss why people are not following the rules.

It may be wise to spend some time occasionally discussing how well the ground rules are working for the group. Are any changes needed? How can the group adapt to issues that arise? You don't want to play the role of police officer, enforcing rules. You want the members of the group to monitor themselves and decide what to do if any ground rules are broken repeatedly.

Assign Roles

"Recognize the principles of shared responsibility," says Eli Mina, author of *The Complete Handbook of Business Meetings* ("Help Make Meetings Productive," by Michele Marrinan, Monster.com). "We need to establish a different kind of culture where it's up to every person at the meeting to pull his or her weight to make it work."

One way to develop the sense of community that will inspire every group member to share in the responsibility for the meeting is through the warm-up. Another great way is to rotate roles for each meeting, so all members of the group share the task of running the meeting and develop their leadership, initiative, collaborative skills, and efficiency. That approach to running meetings may also make life easier for you—but don't count on it, at least not yet.

It's usually most practical to assign four roles, as mentioned briefly in Chapter 2:

- Facilitator

- Scribe
- Timekeeper
- Note-taker

Rotate the roles among the participants as much as possible. It may be easier to ask for volunteers or to assign roles according to the abilities and personalities of the participants. However, you shouldn't assign roles only to the people who seem best qualified: if the spirit of collaboration is strong, every member of the group should be allowed a chance at each role.

Also, it's wiser in the long run to rotate roles, for at least four reasons:

- Rotation provides practical training for each participant in all roles.
- Rotation allows every participant an opportunity to be "just a participant" with no particular responsibilities to restrict his or her freedom to contribute.
- Rotation obviates the possibility that any participants will envy or resent any others for exercising special authority.

Rotation also encourages every participant to be responsible for a successful meeting; people are naturally more likely to behave appropriately when they know that each of them will have a turn at facilitating—and hoping that everybody behaves.

Facilitator

The role of the facilitator is to make the group's work easier. His or her key responsibilities are as follows:

- Coordinate with the scribe, the timekeeper, and the note-taker.
- Maintain an appropriate pace.

> **Change Partners**
>
> MISTAKE PROOFING
>
> Rotate roles to allow each participant an opportunity to handle all delegated meeting responsibilities, if possible. You should at least avoid assigning the same roles to the same people, even if they volunteer for those roles. Rotation ensures each participant a chance to develop skills—and you won't be accused of dumping tougher roles on some employees or playing favorites.

- Cover each of the agenda items, one at a time, in order:
  - Introduce each agenda item.
  - Conduct the discussion of the item.
  - Keep discussions focused on the agenda item.
  - Check for full understanding of any decisions on that item.
  - Close the discussion of the item.
- Encourage full participation by all members.
- Help the participants evaluate the meeting.
- Close the meeting.

Key Term **Facilitator** A person whose meeting role is to make the group's work easier by leading the group through the agenda, systematically and at an appropriate pace, and encouraging full participation by all members.

This role is generally considered to be the most difficult. It requires leadership, quick understanding, tact, sensitivity, good communication skills, and a grasp of psychology. The facilitator needs to be able to anticipate problems and opportunities—and then avoid the problems and take advantage of the opportunities.

Here are some general guidelines for facilitators.

When a participant makes a contribution, the facilitator should:

- Acknowledge it, at least with a nod.
- Check to ensure understanding, if necessary. ("OK, so are you saying that...?")

Smart Managing

Two Heads May Be Better Than One

Some managers might not feel comfortable turning over the meeting to the facilitator. After all, it's a big responsibility that requires skills and sensitivity that not everybody possesses. If you feel that the person you designated to facilitate may not be completely ready and able to handle the role, you may want to work out some way to share the responsibilities. The next time around, both of you may be confident that he or she can go it alone.

- Paraphrase, summarize concisely, if necessary. ("So, what you're saying is that....")
- React positively. ("Good point!" or "That's an important consideration" or "Interesting perspective.")
- Find the best. ("What I find most interesting in your comment is..." or "Your suggestion brings up a perspective that we haven't considered.")
- Question, even challenge. ("Your idea makes sense in a way, but how does it play out with...?" or "We could try the approach you're suggesting, but are there ways to reduce resistance?")
- Show connections. ("That point ties in with what X mentioned earlier, adding the perspective of...)
- Help others develop it. ("That's a good point. Now, what would be related issues?" or "That takes us into new territory. What other aspects should we consider along those lines?")
- Watch for visual clues, such as body language and facial expressions that say, "I've got something to say" or "I like that idea" or "I'm concerned about something" or "I'm bored."
- Remain neutral—or at least objective—and open, however he or she feels personally, and not allow his or her ideas or opinions to inhibit participation.

To bring closure to a discussion, the facilitator should summarize the main points and consolidate related points: "It would seem, then, that we've got four ways that we could go on this issue" and "Several comments show an interest in pursuing this line of investigation."

The facilitator should get all of the participants involved. Here are some situations and ways that the facilitator might deal with them:

- If some participants are quiet, he or she can call on them individually: "Jill, you have some experience in this area. Can you help us out?" or "Tom, you know something about this issue. Would you like to share your insights with us?" He or she can also move around the group for ideas, letting the natural circle invite quiet members to participate.

- If any participants are critical negatively (as opposed to constructively), he or she can try to help them be constructive, by asking questions such as "So, how would we be able to improve that situation?" or "Since we're aware of the problems, could you suggest any solutions?"
- If any comments seem harsh, he or she should try rewording in ways that present the key points without inflammatory language.
- If any comments become personal, he or she should intervene: "Could we get back to the agenda item, please?" or "Could we please focus on the issue that we're considering?"

When a discussion is going well, with contributions coming from around the group, the facilitator must make sure that the scribe and the note-taker are keeping up. If not, then he or she should slow the pace a little and/or help by repeating or summarizing contributions for the two writers.

If a discussion isn't going well, even when the facilitator is

TRICKS OF THE TRADE

Six Killers

The facilitator should be alert to the six "meeting killers" identified by Gregory M. Bounds and John A. Woods in *Supervision* (Cincinnati, OH: South-Western College Publishing, 1998, pp. 89-90):

1. Hogging: too much talking by one person.
2. Bogging: staying on one subject for too long.
3. Fogging: avoiding a topic or being vague or defensive.
4. Frogging: jumping from topic to topic without any closure.
5. Flogging: attacking a person rather than dealing with the person's contribution.
6. Clogging: slowing down the group by failing to accomplish action items.

asking probing and challenging questions, calling on individuals, and offering suggestions, he or she might decide to change the dynamics by dividing the group into twos or threes (dyads or triads, if you prefer fancy terms). He or she should challenge the clusters with one or two questions to consider, allow them a few minutes to discuss the questions, and then bring them together to present the results of their discussions. (If the layout of the room doesn't allow any spatial separation of participants into twos and threes, the facilitator can form pairs—participants seated side by side or across the table—or quartets—both side by side and across the table.)

Scribe

The scribe posts key ideas, points, and comments during discussions on a flipchart, a whiteboard, or other means of display, so that all participants can refer to them. He or she is responsible for displaying a "living record" of the progress of the group. His or her key responsibilities are as follows:

> Key Term
>
> **Scribe** A person whose meeting role is to post key ideas, points, and comments during discussions so that all participants can refer to them. He or she is responsible for displaying a "living record" of the progress of the group.

- Write large and legibly enough so that all can read the notes.
- Check to make sure all ideas, points, and comments are recorded accurately.
- Get input on wording from other participants.
- Summarize all decisions in full sentences.

Keeping a "living record" on display is important because:

- It provides a physical means of keeping the focus on the topic being discussed, which helps prevent tangents.
- It assures participants that their contributions have been recorded, which encourages participation.
- It shows which ideas, points, and comments have been

contributed, which reduces or eliminates repetition.

- It relieves the participants of the burden of taking notes, which allows them to follow the discussion better and contribute more easily.
- It provides a "group memory" so participants can return more easily to a point made earlier, which reduces the urge to jump in immediately, even interrupt, to comment on a point before it's forgotten and left behind.
- It helps keep participants aware of the progress the group is making, which builds morale.

TRICKS OF THE TRADE

Don't Sweat the Small Stuff

What's most important for a scribe is to capture all the contributions and record them accurately and legibly. This means that he or she shouldn't worry about spelling or always using the exact wording (summarize, if possible) or writing in full sentences or even using full words (abbreviate whenever possible).

The roles of the facilitator and the scribe usually require quick comprehension and an ability to follow the pieces of a linear puzzle. For best results, the facilitator and the scribe should work together closely. The facilitator should check to make sure that the scribe is recording the contributions accurately. The scribe should ask for clarification of any ideas, points, or comments that seem unclear, which helps the facilitator guide the discussion.

Timekeeper

The timekeeper helps the group keep on track with the timing of the agenda during the meeting. His or her key responsibilities are as follows:

- Keep track of time during the meeting.
- Warn the group when the time allocated for an agenda item is almost up, by announcing the time remaining. At that point the facilitator can ask the group to decide whether to close the discussion or to continue it and

change other items on the agenda.

- Signal when the time allocated for an agenda item is up.

Key Term

Timekeeper A person whose meeting role is to help the group keep on track with the timing of the agenda.

The purpose of having a timekeeper is not to police time limits rigidly but rather to help the group keep to the timing of the agenda and use its meeting time most efficiently. It's possible to run meetings without this role: the facilitator can keep track of the time or you can do so and use gestures to signal the facilitator.

Also, since very few meetings run exactly by the clock, the timekeeper needs to adjust the stop and start times if the group falls behind or goes ahead of the schedule.

#1 TOOLS

Give the Facilitator a Hand

Lani Arredondo suggests that the timekeeper use simple hand signals (*Commmunicating Effectively*, pp. 152-153): 10 fingers up to show 10 minutes remaining, five fingers for five minutes, and the sports time-out signal when time is up. The timekeeper could also use the show business "slash throat" signal to suggest that the facilitator cut off the activity.

Note-Taker

The note-taker captures and records the basics of the meeting for a permanent record. His or her key responsibilities are as follows:

- Keep the minutes of the meeting using the established format.
- Check with the group for accuracy whenever necessary.
- Finalize the minutes.
- Ensure that copies of the minutes are distributed.

Key Term

Note-taker A person whose meeting role is to capture and record the basics of the meeting for a permanent record.

What should the note-taker record? It's usually

enough just to document the essentials, not to provide the equivalent of a court stenographer's transcript of every word said by anybody. The note-taker should focus on the following four types of information:

- Decisions
- Action items: things that people will do
- Open issues: things to be considered later
- Key discussion points

The note-taker must be accurate, objective, and able to write concisely and in a "reader-friendly" style. He or she is likely to rely on the running record kept by the scribe, but document only the main points. Also, the facilitator may indicate to the note-taker to record a certain idea, point, or comment. It could be suggested that any participant who wishes to make an idea, point, or comment part of the permanent record signal that request to the note-taker.

It usually takes very little time and effort for the note-taker to finalize the minutes after the meeting. (This is particularly true if you provide a laptop computer to whomever you designate for the role.) It's essentially just a matter of transferring to a computer anything written by hand. Then, the agenda can be attached or you can e-mail the note-taker your computer file, which he or she can then insert into the record. If any participants have presented reports, they can e-mail the note-taker files of their reports. Then the note-taker has only to transfer any other information to the computer and print copies. You should keep a copy of the minutes for all meetings in a notebook, for easy reference. You should also get the computer files and archive them, for easier searching and retrieval as necessary (and any later corrections).

Is it necessary to have a formal process for approving the minutes? No, not usually. However, the participants may decide at some point to adopt a rule calling for some approval process. Generally it should be enough to encourage participants to review the distributed copy of the minutes of a meeting and then bring any questions or concerns to the attention of the manager before the next meeting or raise them with the group at the beginning of the next meeting.

As noted above, the note-taker should keep the minutes of the meeting using the established format. This means you should specify the format as soon as possible, so that your meetings will be documented with consistency.

Your organization may have a set format for keeping minutes. On the other hand, you may be free to develop a format, on your own, or with your group. A good format allows anybody to know at a glance what's most important—what was covered in a meeting, what was decided, what actions were planned, what's expected and by when, and who is responsible for those actions.

What should the minutes include?

1. Date, time, and location of the meeting
2. List of participants
3. List of people invited but absent
4. Participants assigned as facilitator, scribe, timekeeper, and note-taker
5. Agenda
6. Main discussion points and outcomes (decisions and action items) for each agenda item, with the names of the participants responsible for the action items and the dates and times for completion
7. Items for consideration at later meetings
8. Meeting evaluation
9. Reports (attached)

To Intervene or Not to Intervene?

You entrust participants with important responsibilities and you should rotate the roles to allow every participant the opportunity to play all of the roles. It's almost inevitable, then, that a role player might not perform up to your expectations—or, perhaps more important, the expectations of the group. So, what do you do?

In general, try to refrain from getting involved. Mistakes are part of the learning process with any responsibility. Against short-term effects, such as confusion and embarrassment and time wasted, weigh the long-term effects of offending the role player, undermining the responsibility of the role, and causing other employees to wonder if you'll intervene when they're playing the role.

You are most likely to be tempted to intervene with the facilitator, because of the importance of the role and the skills it requires. Here are some questions to consider in deciding whether or not to intervene with the facilitator:

- Does the facilitator need help? Is the facilitator asking for help?
- Is the facilitator saying or doing something that you should question or challenge?
- Can you resolve the problem by nodding or shaking your head?
- Is the group planning something that's illegal, unethical, or a violation of policy?
- Do you have any knowledge or experience that is essential in this situation?
- Do you have information that would be beneficial in this situation?

What happens next? It's all outlined in Chapter 4, where your agenda and the facilitator guide the participants through the meeting and into planning for action.

Manager's Checklist for Chapter 3

❑ The group needs ground rules, a code of conduct that promotes respect, collaboration, and efficiency without hindering spontaneity and creativity.

❑ It's essential for participants to share responsibility for running their meetings. They can do this by adopting roles:

- Facilitator, to lead the group through the agenda systematically at an appropriate pace and encourage full participation by all members.

- Scribe, to post key ideas, points, and comments during discussions, as a display of the progress of the group.
- Timekeeper, to help the group keep on track with the timing of the agenda.
- Note-taker, to capture and record the basics of the meeting for a permanent record.

Conducting the Meeting

The facilitator should first make sure that the scribe, the timekeeper, and the note-taker are ready.

He or she should then review the agenda, to make sure that all participants are on the same page—literally. (Sure, you've distributed the agenda early, to allow everyone to read it and prepare for each of the items. But you know that sometimes, even with the best of planning, realities get in the way.) The facilitator should take a minute or two to do the following:

- Explain the purpose of the meeting.
- Check to make sure the participants understand each of the agenda items and the purpose(s).
- Ask if there are any changes to suggest. If so, the group decides whether or not to revise the agenda.The facilitator can ask for a show of hands: "Those who want to make this change to the agenda, raise your hands. Those who prefer to schedule it for the next meeting, raise your hands."

This is also the time for you to make any changes in your plans. But take note of the following recommendations:

> **Ownership Starts with You**
>
> Smart Managing
>
> Why should the group review the agenda, since you distributed it in advance? It allows everyone to accept the agenda or to make suggestions for improving it.
>
> That way, they own the meeting plan and are more committed to following it and participating more fully in the meeting. As Carolyn B. Thompson notes in *Interviewing Skills for Managers* (New York: McGraw-Hill, 2002, p. 14), "A meeting is just a gathering of bodies if there's no meeting of the minds."

- Make only necessary changes.
- Explain why you're making the changes.
- Thank any participants who prepared reports, presentations, or other things for any agenda item affected by your changes. If you're simply postponing an item, tell them so. If you're dropping any items, apologize for the inconvenience.
- Allow any participants to leave whose attendance is now unnecessary.

Follow the Agenda

> **It's Not Carved in Stone**
>
> Smart Managing
>
> "It's a bad plan that can't be changed." Publilius Syrus, an author and social commentator, uttered those words over 2000 years ago. They're still true—and good for you to keep in mind during a meeting.

Here's the starting point for any advice on making meetings more productive: stick to the agenda. You developed the agenda to serve as a map for the group. The facilitator should proceed through the agenda, item by item, unless he or she feels it would be better to modify the order, according to circumstances. (We'll discuss some of these circumstances a little later in this chapter.)

For each item, the facilitator follows the map. The details will vary according to the item, the objectives, and the group,

CAUTION!

Agenda: Handle with Care

Once you've communicated your agenda, it belongs to the group. If you expect people to take agendas and meetings seriously, you should set an example—unlike the manager described by Tim Paeltz in his notes for *Circular Management—or How to Run an Organization and Not Go Anywhere*:

The manager distributed an agenda—and then arrived at the meeting with a new agenda. Several of his employees had spent time and energy preparing reports for the meeting, reports that were not on the new agenda. Then, when the employees who no longer had any reason to attend the meeting asked if they could leave, he made them stay. That decision discouraged the employees from preparing more than minimally for subsequent meetings.

among other factors, but in this chapter we'll consider the following basic responsibilities of the facilitator:

- Share information
- Conduct discussion
- Manage participation
- Get a decision
- Plan action and make assignments

In addition, the facilitator will have to be ready and able to deal with departures from the agenda, notably tangents and delays.

Tangents

The facilitator is responsible for guiding the way and preventing tangents that would delay the journey or digress from the path. But that guidance should not prevent divergent thinking and useful contributions that may not, at first, seem directly relevant to the topic under consideration.

Skillful facilitating allows for flexibility and permits tangents that are beneficial. (Yes, that's a judgment call!)

The facilitator should know that it's OK to depart from the agenda if more important issues arise. He or she should then politely ask the permission of the group to allow the digression.

Doing so shows them that it's *their* meeting, that the process and the outcomes depend on them.

Delays

If it's taking longer to cover the agenda than you'd expected and planned, it might be wise to put some items off for another meeting, in order to end at the scheduled stop time. This is especially true if some of the participants have appointments immediately after the stop time or if the room is scheduled for another activity at that time.

However, if the meeting is going well, if the participants are working together effectively and seem to have the desire and energy to continue, it would make sense to consider going beyond the stop time. If so, then poll the participants: all of them should agree to continue or you should stop and set a date and time for another meeting to continue the agenda.

Set and Maintain an Appropriate Pace

The facilitator should establish an appropriate pace. One of the key characteristics of a successful meeting is productivity or, at least, progress. Conversely, two common complaints about bad meetings are that participants become bored and that participants get confused.

One way to get a group energized is to structure the agenda so that the meeting begins with a few quick items. There could also be an alternation of long and short items, to keep the meeting from bogging down. The facilitator may find it wise to modify the order of items if it seems that the pace of the meeting is slowing down.

The facilitator should always be looking around the room, alert to any signs that he or she should slow things down or speed them up. The facilitator should also be sensitive to any signs of overload, having to hold onto too much information and/or too many ideas and opinions at one time. He or she should also glance at the timekeeper regularly, ready for a signal to move toward a decision or to close the discussion.

The Meter Is Running

We all know that time is money—and that meetings cost a lot of both.

As a very real reminder of this basic fact, you may want to put a kitchen timer where all participants can see it. Then, for each agenda item, the facilitator can set it for the time allowed, as indicated on the agenda, to show that "the meter is running."

The use of a "meter" also makes the job of the timekeeper easier. In fact, if participants share responsibility for keeping the meeting running according to schedule, you may find that the group doesn't even need this role!

Good cooperation between timekeeper and facilitator can help the group avoid what Eli Mina, author of *The Complete Handbook of Business Meetings* (New York: AMACOM, 2000), calls the "rush-hour syndrome"—squeezing too much agenda into too little time at the end of a meeting. With a timed agenda and a diligent timekeeper, the facilitator can lead the group to decide what items to conclude and what items to continue at another meeting.

The facilitator should always keep in mind that *purposes* are more important than *minutes*, that it's more important for the group to be *effective* than *efficient*. After all, what makes more sense—for the group to hurry a discussion to fit the allotted time and make a decision prematurely or to take the time necessary to reach an informed and considered decision?

Don't Let the Clock Run Your Meetings

The group should never allow the clock to limit discussions or drive decisions. Heed the old adage, "If it's worth doing, it's worth doing well." Time is not a valid excuse for avoiding hard work. The agenda schedule is not carved in stone, so don't allow it to be used to justify skimping on discussion or rushing a decision. Do it right—now, or later at another meeting.

Share Information

The facilitator initiates an agenda item by referring to the agenda to state the expected outcomes, explain how the group will deal with the item, and remind participants of the amount of time scheduled for discussion. (We'll describe some methods for discussion in Chapter 6.)

For each agenda item, the facilitator should call for at least a little information. When you develop the agenda, you indicate who is responsible for providing information. It could be the "resident expert" or it could be somebody who's very good at organizing and explaining. It could be you, especially if you're most informed about the item.

As we've cautioned earlier in this book, you should avoid using meetings to provide a lot of information. It's usually expecting too much of participants to absorb and process large amounts of information quickly enough and well enough to discuss an item and reach a decision. (The neologism "infobesity" comes to mind here.) That's why it's wisest to provide information in advance of the meeting, so participants can arrive informed and prepared to discuss and decide.

If you've scheduled a report or a presentation, you should also have given the person responsible a time limit and indicated it on the agenda. The facilitator and the timekeeper must then hold the person to that time limit.

After the informant or the facilitator has provided the information, the facilitator should ask for additional information, concerns, or questions. Any concerns or questions should be about the information and not to express opinions or offer suggestions; opinions and suggestions should be kept for the discussion.

Conduct Discussion

Conducting discussions is often the most demanding of the facilitator's responsibilities. As a friend once noted, "There are two types of conductors: one drives a train down the track and the other manages to get all the instruments in the orchestra to play together." The same is true of conducting a meeting—except that a facilitator is expected to do both, to keep to the schedule and to help all members of the group work together.

To conduct a discussion properly, the facilitator must do the following:

- Open the discussion
- Manage participation
- Keep the discussion focused
- Close the discussion

It's so simple—on paper. However, as mentioned in Chapter 2, the role of facilitator requires many skills.

To Discuss or Not to Discuss?

You've planned the agenda and indicated which items you expect the group will discuss. However, sometimes reality refuses to fit our plans.

There may be issues that don't generate any discussion because of lack of interest or lack of information or for other reasons. Or, more frequently, issues for which you'd planned no discussion seem to be a hot button.

The facilitator is on the spot to make decisions based on "the will of the people" and his or her own judgment. You should refrain from following your instinct to intervene and manage the situation. Allow the group and the facilitator to arrive at a decision—if you want meeting roles to have any authority and responsibility and if you want participation to mean passionate engagement.

However, if the facilitator and other members of the group seem unable to reach an agreement, the facilitator must decide. If he or she seems to be caught, don't prolong the agony: if the facilitator looks to you for help, suggest a decision in as few words as possible—or even a gesture. Then, expect the facilitator to resume control of the meeting and move on.

Open the Discussion

The facilitator then opens the discussion. If the environment feels right and the topic is interesting, that may be all that's necessary to start a discussion. However, if participants are slow to contribute, the facilitator may ask them open-ended questions, so participants cannot answer with just "yes" or "no." He or she may need to keep repeating the main questions, patiently, to draw out contributions.

As mentioned in Chapter 3, if a discussion isn't going well, the facilitator can change the dynamics by dividing the group into dyads or triads. He or she gives the clusters one or two questions and a few minutes to discuss them, then asks each cluster to share the results with the rest of the group.

> **A Little Insurance**
>
> Tricks of the Trade
>
> It can be difficult to start a discussion—and even more difficult if the lack of participation makes the facilitator feel awkward. It's tough in that situation to come up with effective questions.
>
> If you suspect that it might be difficult for the facilitator to get a discussion started, it's a good idea to jot down a few open-ended questions for the facilitator to ask. Just having the questions on hand could give him or her extra confidence.

A good facilitator is someone who can bring out the best in the participants. This happens only if the facilitator shows appreciation and respect for each participant for his or her unique experience, knowledge, and skills. People who feel appreciated and respected tend to contribute.

As participants contribute, the facilitator listens. As necessary, he or she asks for clarification. That may mean asking participants to restate, to define terms, to explain, to provide reasons, to cite facts, to give examples.

The facilitator should encourage involvement, by exploring with queries (e.g., "What else?" and "Any other thoughts?") and asking follow-up questions (e.g., "Why?"). Some people recommend crediting contributors (e.g., "Let's get back to

> **A Discussion Is in the Cards**
>
> Tools
>
> If participants are hesitant to engage in a discussion, here's a trick with cards.
>
> The facilitator distributes index cards and asks participants to note their comments or ideas on the cards. After a few minutes, the facilitator collects the cards, shuffles them, and distributes a few to each participant. Then, in turn, the participants read the cards to the group. The scribe then records the contributions, as usual. That process may generate reactions. If not, you at least have the comments and ideas that a conventional discussion would have generated.

TRICKS OF THE TRADE

It Takes Two (or Three) to Untangle

Sometimes members hesitate to participate because they worry about expressing themselves well. If that's the case with any member of your group, the facilitator can use a variant of the index card technique.

He or she can break the group into twos or threes and give each an index card for recording their thoughts or concerns. This allows the people in each cluster to work together through any difficulties in expressing what's on their minds. Then, after a few minutes, the facilitator collects the cards and reads them aloud. He or she can then resolve any remaining clarity problems while reading them. The scribe then records the contributions.

what Adriana suggested. How could we build on that idea?" and "Sean mentioned something interesting. Who would like to react to his statement?"). However, this may be unnecessary—and even potentially dangerous, because linking people and contributions can draw attention to the people and away from the contributions and the collaboration. If the group builds on a contribution, the participant will feel appreciated—and that's what really matters.

To draw out shy participants, the facilitator can ask them for their thoughts about the item under discussion. Or, better yet, he or she can circle the participants, so the natural dynamics of collaboration induces the quiet participants to join in.

To quiet those who talk too much, offer a thank-you and ask for the comments of those who haven't yet spoken.

At all times, everybody—the facilitator, the other participants, and you—should keep the following questions in mind for guidance:

- "Are we focusing on the issue?"
- "Are we being as productive as possible?"
- "Are we spending our time appropriately at this moment?"

The facilitator should summarize any lengthy contribution—and immediately check on the accuracy of that summary. He or she should also contain digressions, by asking participants to return to the point or by summarizing contributions to guide the group back to the point.

As the facilitator helps the participants express their ideas, concerns, opinions, and reactions, he or she should be scanning the faces of the other participants, attentive to any signs that somebody might not be understanding. If so, then he or she works to clarify.

> **Post and Point**
>
> If discussions often slow down, go off track, or even get derailed, consider this idea. Print the three guiding questions presented here on a sheet of flipchart paper and then post the sheet just before a meeting begins, as you post your agenda and your ground rules (if you do). Then, when a discussion stalls or starts taking a turn, the facilitator (or any other group members) can point to the questions. A word to the wise is sufficient; a gesture is more efficient.

The scribe records the main points of the discussion, on a flip chart or other chosen medium, to allow participants to follow along better and make corrections or request clarification. He or she should try to reduce contributions to their essence, to document the discussion concisely. However, to the extent practical, he or she should use the key words used by the contributor. If a contribution is too long, the scribe should ask the person to summarize it.

As we noted in Chapter 3, grammar and spelling don't matter here. What matters is to maintain a running record of the discussion that all participants can follow.

> **Deal with the Digression**
>
> When the group is digressing, it's generally best for the facilitator to try to bring the group back to the point. But sometimes it's more appropriate to deal with the digression.
>
> The authors of *The Team Handbook* (p. 7-22) suggest that the facilitator comment on the digression: "We've had trouble sticking to this point. Is there something about it that makes it so easy to avoid?"
>
> The answers may be surprising and reveal something worth pursuing. If not, then at least the group has dealt with the digression and can return to the issue at hand.

The scribe should print in large letters (at least an inch high, depending on the size of the room), allowing a lot of space around contributions, to allow other points to be added. It's usually good to use markers of various colors, for easier reading—although too many colors can make the chart busy and confusing. Blue or black are best as main colors; red should be used only to highlight, as it's harder to read from a distance.

The scribe should stand to the side of the chart or board as much as possible, to not obscure the writing. He or she should regularly scan the faces of the group, to check for signs that participants are having trouble reading the writing.

As the scribe fills a sheet of paper, he or she should tear it from the flipchart and tape it to a wall or tack it to a bulletin board, putting the sheets up in order and/or numbering them.

The role of scribe is obviously not just a clerical function. In fact, in meetings with a lot of participation, the scribe takes a more active role to help the facilitator with his or her responsibilities.

As mentioned above, the facilitator should focus on maintaining the pace and the flow of the interaction and ensuring full and productive participation. The scribe can make sure that he or she isn't missing anything in all the activity. This is especially important when there are a lot of participants contributing and when it's necessary to clarify and paraphrase and sum up contributions. The scribe and the facilitator should be constantly checking with each other, to confirm their understanding of contributions and to control the pace and flow of the discussion.

Manage Participation

A primary responsibility of the facilitator is to manage participation. This means that he or she is to make sure that each person is allowed the opportunity to contribute. It's essential to prevent any member from dominating and to engage all members in the discussion.

Every member of the group should understand and accept that he or she shares responsibility for the meeting. One way to

Job Description for Meetings

Make copies of this guide to distribute to people in advance of the meeting, with the agenda.

Responsibilities of Meeting Participants:

- Read the agenda carefully prior to the meeting.
- Prepare to participate in the meeting.
- Arrive on time with your copy of the agenda.
- Contribute—and encourage your fellow participants to contribute.
- Pay attention to what others contribute and respect them.
- Build on others' contributions.
- Work toward the objectives of the meeting.

help ensure that understanding and acceptance of responsibility is by providing every person that you invite to the meeting with a list of responsibilities, as illustrated in the sidebar.

The facilitator should encourage expression of differences of perspective and opinion. The best way to do this is to avoid judging any contributions. In fact, it's the responsibility of the facilitator to help the group get the most out of every contribution. He or she should make sure that all members of the group understand each contribution, asking the contributor to explain or paraphrase if necessary. Then, he or she should accentuate the value in the contribution: e.g., "That's a perspective we've been missing here" or "What's most interesting in your comment is…."

Participants should be encouraged to do the same, to seek out value in every contribution and to respect and appreciate it. A friend once commented, "A relationship is good when two people have the best intentions toward each other and assume that the other also has the best intentions." That truth seems to apply to meetings as well: members of the group should always work for the interests of the group and assume that all share that spirit.

Part of the facilitator's responsibility to manage participation is to direct traffic. What this means and how important it is depend on the group and the purpose of its activity.

"In an orderly meeting, only one member speaks at a time," according to Eli Mina in *The Complete Handbook of Business*

Meetings. You've probably participated in great meetings that were a little less than orderly. That's especially true when the conversation (to use the Michael Begeman term) is a "conversation for possibility," to maximize creativity and generate ideas. And there's a lot of productive territory between *orderly* and *chaotic*.

Sometimes a little disorder is good, allowing enthusiasm and energy to drive the discussion. But there may be times when the facilitator will need to control the flow, using signals like a traffic cop—a hand up or extended palm outward to stop someone from talking and a hand signaling another to continue. (Silent signals are generally better than adding more words to the noise.)

But the advice offered by Mina is sound in principle: "Interruptions are avoided, except when absolutely needed. Regardless of how contentious the issues are, civility and mutual respect are maintained." His basic guideline could be posted at every meeting—"Discussions are 'hard on the issues' but 'soft on the people.'"

The facilitator should help the group handle not only the "hard" but also the "soft."

As we've emphasized from Chapter 1, meetings are work. And you emphasize that fact in your planning, in your agenda, and in all else.

But it's important to keep in mind the words of wisdom quoted at the beginning of Chapter 3: "There is a legitimate social component to meetings.... You should never overlook the social side of work rituals—even in meetings that are 'all business.'" All participants should feel comfortable around each other. A certain amount of conversation and joking is natural and healthy, if it makes the group more productive.

The facilitator should allow and even encourage this social side of the group—but also know when and how to limit the socializing and return to the business of the meeting.

Keep the Discussion Focused and Progressing

The facilitator and the scribe work together to keep the discussion focused on the agenda item at hand and progressing

TRICKS OF THE TRADE

Thumb Time-Saver

If several participants offer contributions that are supportive but do nothing to advance the discussion ("Yeah, I agree with the statement that..."), the facilitator may want to see if the group is close to closure on the item.

A good way to do so is to ask participants to simply give a thumb signal of their position:

- thumbs up: I'm ready for closure
- thumbs down: I still have serious concerns
- thumbs sideways: I'm neutral, I could close or continue

It's a fast way for everyone to know how the others feel about the issue. Of course, if anybody gives thumbs down, then the facilitator should certainly encourage the expression of these concerns.

toward the objective(s).

We often talk about keeping a discussion "on track"—as if it were a train. Well, the problem with that analogy is that it's simplistic. Since trains run on rails, they're either *on track* or *off track*. Discussions, in contrast, can wander all around a subject without truly being "off track"—all the while they're not really "on track." So, it makes more sense to continually monitor the discussion in terms of the results, to keep it focused on the objective(s).

Sometimes a facilitator will be so intent on keeping a discussion focused, however, that the group misses out on valuable opportunities. On occasion, even often, a participant will bring up an idea or make a suggestion that's really good, but not really germane to the discussion. Should the facilitator allow the group to pursue it or does the group continue on track?

There's a third option—run a parking lot. When a participant contributes something that seems to be outside the scope of the discussion, the facilitator can indicate to the scribe to write it down. The facilitator may make that decision or may ask the group, with a simple question—"parking lot?" Also, any participant may propose relegating a contribution to the parking lot, a suggestion that the facilitator and/or the group may then accept or reject.

Key Term **Parking lot** An area—e.g., on a separate page of a flipchart or on a board—where the scribe records any comments, ideas, or suggestions that are off the topic at hand or otherwise outside the scope of the discussion. Also known as an *idea bin,* a *tangent bin*, or an *issues board.*

The parking lot accumulates contributions so they aren't forgotten but don't lead the group off on tangents. Recording contributions that are outside the discussion scope respects concerns of the group and assures participants that the points recorded will be addressed, although not at present.

Make sure to address these points in some way as soon as is practical. Otherwise, participants will perceive that the parking lot is where contributions go to die and they'll be less likely to offer any comments or ideas that are not on the straight and narrow path of the discussion.

It Takes All Kinds: Group Dynamics

Don't expect all participants to contribute equally and in the same ways. They each bring different strengths and weaknesses to the table.

Smart Managing

Drive the Vehicles in Your Parking Lot

The parking lot is a meeting equivalent of the organization's suggestion box: it can generate great opportunities—if the ideas and comments don't just remain there, neglected.

It's a good policy to schedule a discussion in your next meeting whenever there are vehicles in the parking lot. Encourage the participants to "take 'em out for a spin." Some of the contributions won't make it around the block—but you may find one that runs great.

This method of dealing with off-topic contributions, making them the topic of a special discussion, has three advantages:

- It allows you to make the most of the brains and creativity of your employees (twice).
- It shows that you appreciate all contributions.
- It enables your employees to be involved in deciding the fate of their contributions.

A meeting is often the ultimate in teamwork. An effective and efficient meeting depends not only on each of the participants but also on their interpersonal dynamics. The greatest danger is not *conflict*, as many managers believe, but *groupthink*—the tendency of a group of people to seek unanimous agreement in spite of facts that would contradict such agreement.

This phenomenon was identified by Irving L. Janis, author of *Victims of Groupthink* (Boston: Houghton Mifflin, 1972) and *Groupthink: Psychological Studies of Policy Decisions and Fiascos* (Boston: Houghton Mifflin, 2nd edition, 1982). Janis notes in his first study:

> The more amiability and esprit de corps there is among members of a policy-making in-group, the greater is the danger that independent critical thinking will be replaced by groupthink. … The social constraint consists of the members' strong wish to preserve the harmony of the group, which inclines them to avoid creating any discordant arguments or schisms.

Key Term

Groupthink "A mode of thinking that people engage in when they are deeply involved in a cohesive in-group, when the members' strivings for unanimity override their motivation to realistically appraise alternative courses of action," according to Irving Janis, a social psychologist at Yale University who identified and studied this phenomenon.

The following conditions promote groupthink:

- The group is highly cohesive.
- The group members have worked together for a long time.
- The group values harmony above all else.
- The group members are under considerable pressure to make a quality decision.

How can you recognize groupthink? These are some signs that you might notice in meetings:

- Whenever a member with authority, power, or perceived expertise expresses a position, the others support that position.
- Members consider the risks and weaknesses of a position insufficiently or not at all.
- Members rationalize group views, including poor decisions.
- Unanimity is very important.
- Members seem reluctant to express their feelings.
- The group examines few or no alternatives.
- Members are quick to dismiss different perspectives.
- Members tend not to be critical of each other's ideas.
- The group doesn't seek the opinion of experts (especially from the outside).
- Members try to keep out information that conflicts with the group perspective.
- Members exert pressure on fellow members who question or disagree.
- The group doesn't make contingency plans.

If you suspect a tendency toward groupthink, how do you deal with it? Better yet, how do you prevent that tendency? Here are some general suggestions, for you and for the facilitator:

- Encourage members to raise objections and concerns.
- Assign one or more members to play the role of critical evaluator or devil's advocate.
- Promote an environment open to questions and alternative perspectives.
- Divide the group into smaller groups to discuss, then compare the results.
- Get input from experts outside the group.
- Require the group to develop a certain number of options before moving toward a decision.
- Instruct the group to first develop a list of criteria for evaluating options—and then ensure that the members use those criteria.

Groupthink vs. Consensus

MISTAKE PROOFING

Groupthink and consensus may seem similar, but there's a key distinction. It's *groupthink* when all the members of a group seem to agree on a decision, but there are some who are censoring themselves and not expressing concerns or who have not resolved some differences they consider important and who are "just going along with the crowd" because they feel pressure to agree and to avoid disrupting the unity. It's *consensus* when all members of the group have thoroughly explored a range of choices, considered the risks and weaknesses of each option, and resolved all important differences.

One general way to counter any tendency to groupthink is by helping participants understand and appreciate the value of critical thinking, disagreement, and diversity of thinking. Encourage facilitators to elicit a variety of contributions, encourage thoughtful consideration of all suggestions, and praise members who show the courage to think independently.

Another way is to avoid expressing your opinions and offering suggestions until the other participants have contributed and to encourage and welcome critical reactions to those opinions and suggestions—not always easy, but definitely necessary.

Close the Discussion

The facilitator brings the discussion to a close when the timekeeper indicates only a few minutes remain of the allotted time or when interest either wanes or waxes too hot to be productive.

As the timekeeper signals, the facilitator might say simply, "OK, we have three minutes left. Are there any points we haven't considered?" Then, in the last minute or so, he or she can recap the main points of the discussion by referring to the notes kept on display by the scribe.

It's a little more involved if the facilitator decides to end a discussion early, for any reason. If it's because participation has slowed, he or she should ask the members to indicate by a show of hands if they feel ready to reach a decision or (if you've specified a managerial decision) to turn the meeting over to you. If, in contrast, the discussion has gotten too hot, the facilitator can propose a choice, if a decision is not urgent: to table the discussion until the next meeting or to move on to a decision.

It's generally not the responsibility of the facilitator to determine what should be done, but rather to recognize that it may be time for the group to decide on the next steps.

Get a Decision

For most agenda items, the purpose of a discussion is to arrive at some decision—if only to consider the items further at another time. In fact, it could be argued that no meeting should end without a decision. (And no, the decision to adjourn doesn't count!)

Types of Decisions

As suggested in Chapter 2, you should let participants know in advance, on the agenda, how a decision will be made:

- Managerial—you make the call!
- Vote by majority or plurality—just count the votes.
- Consensus—cooperative development of a decision that's acceptable enough for all members of a group to agree to support.
- Delegation—selected members of the group make the decision.

Managerial Decision. (Because you may be meeting with other managers or with people from outside your unit or the organization, you may not be the top dog. However, because most meetings for which you're responsible will be with your employees, we'll word this section accordingly.)

Before the discussion starts, clarify the purpose. If you'd like the group to explore options for you to consider when you make the decision, make that clear, so they will understand your expectations and their responsibilities. If you've reached a tentative decision that you want to "try out" with the group, make that clear, so they know that you're inviting their perspectives and help in identifying aspects that you may have missed.

Generally, you will probably want to make your decision later, after the meeting. But if the discussion has allowed you to reach a decision and you want to announce it, proceed with care. After a group discussion of an issue, a managerial decision may seem abrupt and autocratic. So, you should take a few minutes to frame your decision and promote closure.

First, thank the participants for helping you explore the issue from all perspectives. Then, sum up the best points raised during the discussion and how you've considered each of them. Next, announce your decision and outline the actions you're planning based on that decision. You don't need to be specific about your plans, but just show that you've thought things out beyond your decision.

As shown in the continuum in Chapter 2 (Figure 2-2), there are various modes of making managerial decisions:

- The manager makes the decision and announces it.
- The manager makes the decision and explains it.
- The manager makes the decision and discusses implementation issues.
- The manager makes a tentative decision and discusses it before finalizing it.
- The manager and the group discuss the issue and then the manager makes the decision.
- The manager delegates the decision to the group, with limits.
- The manager delegates the decision to the group, to the full limit of his or her authority.

These more moderate approaches may be a good way to share managerial authority with the group—if you have a very good rapport with your employees, if they understand the continuum, and if they know your reasons for taking the approach that you've chosen. Otherwise, be careful, as members of the group may view these approaches as paternalistic, as being only the semblance of shared governance, as conciliatory—or even as a sign of weakness.

If you choose to make a decision in a meeting, you should have strong reasons to do so and you should handle them in the following way:

- Give your reasons for making the decision yourself.
- Express your appreciation for the assistance and support of the group.
- Cite the good points raised in the discussion.
- Present your decision.
- Outline the actions you plan or ask the group to discuss possible actions.
- Move on to the next item on the agenda.

If you indicate on the agenda that the group will be responsible for making a decision, you may decide to change your mind. You have that right, of course, particularly if circumstances change. But that reversal—which is essentially revoking a delegated responsibility—would require the utmost of sensitivity and tact.

Signal the facilitator that you would like the floor. Then, proceed in the manner outlined above, but with even greater care.

Decision by Vote. Perhaps the biggest disadvantage of voting is that it leads to an all-or-nothing perspective: every choice wins or loses. Sure, the result is a decision—and if what matters most is reaching a decision quickly, then voting works well.

When there are "winners" and "losers," there's a risk of psychological and emotional effects that may undermine the effects of the result. Those who did not vote for the winning choice may not be very committed to supporting the outcome. They may even resist implementation of the decision, openly or covertly, actively or passively. Factions may form.

Another disadvantage with voting is that the group may not address all concerns and answer all questions. It should be remembered that the purpose of a discussion is not only to help the group reach a decision but also to make participants aware of potential problems with that decision. That awareness helps the group plan more effectively to act on the decision.

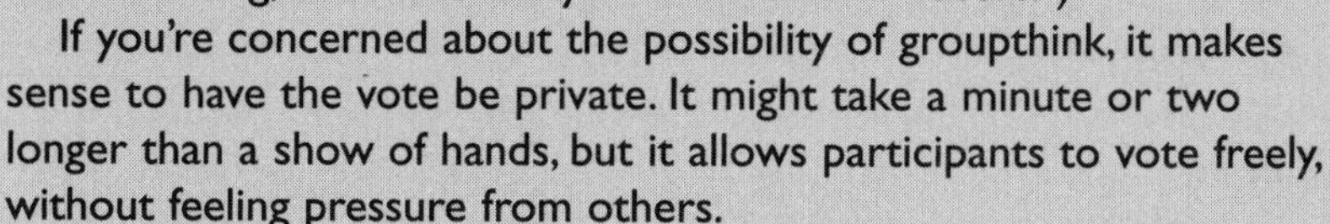

Why Take Chances?

If you want to avoid a "winners-losers" split in the group, it's best to use consensus to reach a decision. (With any kind of voting, there are always "winners" and "losers.")

If you're concerned about the possibility of groupthink, it makes sense to have the vote be private. It might take a minute or two longer than a show of hands, but it allows participants to vote freely, without feeling pressure from others.

It's simple to do. The facilitator distributes an index card to each participant. The participants write their vote on the card, fold it, and toss it into the middle of the table. The facilitator collects the cards and then reads each one and the scribe tallies the vote on the flipchart, whiteboard, or blackboard.

If the decision is to be put to a vote, you can reduce the disadvantages by allowing and promoting extensive discussion, so all participants have the opportunity to present their perspectives and raise questions. If it seems that a vote could divide the group and yet reaching consensus would be difficult or even impossible, the facilitator should encourage the participants to propose compromises.

As a last resort, you or the top authority could intervene and make the decision. Even if the decision is no different from what would have resulted from a vote, a managerial decision allows the opportunity to sum up all of the good points raised in the discussion and to thank the participants for their efforts. The facilitator then resumes leadership of the meeting, so he or she can guide the group in planning to act on the decision.

Decision by Consensus. Consensus is the quintessential team approach to making decisions. The idea of making decisions by consensus has become more popular in recent years. But how that idea plays out in practice shows some misconceptions.

As defined above, consensus is the cooperative development of a decision that's acceptable enough for all members of a group to agree to support. Since any decision must be acceptable to all, every member has veto power.

In theory at least, that means that every member knows that

the group cannot reach a decision without his or her approval. As a result, everyone can focus on contributing to the discussion without worrying about any rush to decision that might run over or around any issues.

In some groups, however, consensus can cause negative feelings, as some members may exert pressure on others to "fall in line" and "go with the flow" and "not make waves." In other words, the feeling of unity that is the strength of this approach to making decisions may be used to circumvent the spirit of consensus. This is what Eli Mina, in *The Complete Handbook of Business Meetings*, calls "the tyranny of the minority." The facilitator and you should be alert to any signs of pressure within the group.

Sometimes the problem with consensus is quite the opposite. Consensus can take a lot of time—especially when there are serious concerns to be addressed.

The facilitator must guide the participants to make a decision. He or she should focus on identifying the areas of disagreement, with probing questions: "What aspect of this issue is keeping us from moving forward? What can we not support at this point?"

Consensus does not mean there's no conflict. But it requires that the members of the group be committed to putting the time and energy into working through any conflict. It requires considering all perspectives and concerns while trying to arrive at a decision that all members can support. Consensus decisions are in the spirit of participants working together toward a common goal, not two or more groups of adversaries pursuing different objectives.

If you've indicated "vote" or "consensus" for an agenda item, but you don't feel strongly about your choice, or if you haven't indicated an approach, you can get guidance on how to make the decision on the item from the following quick check. The facilitator asks the participants to raise their hands if the decision matters to them. If no hands go up, it's probably OK to vote on it. If there are a few hands, then it's probably better to use consensus to make the decision.

The key value of consensus is that the group works to incorporate members' reservations and concerns into the proposal under consideration. The result is that consensus can produce more creative and more robust decisions than voting, where members often compromise to gain votes for a proposal. Compromise is a process of "giving up": I'll give up X if you give up Y. Consensus is a "both-and" process: How can the group both support X and address Y concerns?

It takes particular skill to facilitate consensus decision-making. Here are some simple techniques:

- Frame the issue so all participants can understand it and the importance of making a decision. This is crucial because it determines or at least greatly influences the orientation of the discussion.
- As the participants discuss the issue, help them shape any option into words that express it adequately, clearly, succinctly, and fairly.
- Sum up any agreements, to mark and maintain progress toward a decision. For example, "So now we agree that ________."
- Establish a "balance sheet" from time to time, especially when the discussion lags or stalls: "OK, so we agree on ________, but we're still not together on ________. What concerns do we need to settle?"
- If it seems that the group may not achieve consensus, ask, "What will happen if all of us can't agree on this issue?" or "Should we abandon consensus and put it to a vote or turn the decision over to our manager?"

Delegation. This way of handling a decision is relatively simple, at least in concept. A number of participants are given the authority and responsibility for making a decision. As mentioned in Chapter 2, this is a good option particularly when certain members of the group are generally considered best qualified to make the decision or when they're the only people affected by the decision.

Check the Decision

If the participants are to make a decision (by vote or by consensus), the facilitator must first check the decision. This is a simple action that, if neglected, can bog down a meeting and frustrate the participants. To check a decision means that the facilitator states the decision in full sentences and makes sure that all participants interpret the sentences in the same way.

Of course, if you as the manager are to make the decision, there's no need to check it, at least not for the usual reason. However, because communication is essential, it's still a good idea to express your decision in terms that all of the participants can understand. Also, since the note-taker will be recording the decision for the minutes, this is your opportunity to word your decision as you would want anybody in the organization to understand it.

We've all been in meetings where people were unsure about the options even as they were making their decision. The facilitator should make sure that all members of the group understand exactly what they're doing.

What if the group can't reach a decision? That depends on the situation. If the group has thoroughly considered all of the aspects of the issue and especially if time is short, it may be up to you or the top authority to make the decision, to exercise your managerial responsibility. However, if you believe that the group would benefit from further consideration of the issue, it may be advisable to postpone the decision and schedule another discussion.

But, in that event, the facilitator should assign to the participants the task of gathering information and/or input from others outside the group. Depending on the areas that seem to have been insufficiently explored (e.g., finances, time, logistics, resources, expertise and skills, psychological impact, or whatever), the facilitator might divide the participants into teams and assign a specific responsibility to each. Another possibility is to assign a team to each of the options among which the group is unable to decide, to prepare the best and most compelling case for the next meeting.

Plan Action and Make Assignments

When a decision is made, through whatever process, it means little if it doesn't result in action. So, the next step after making a decision is planning to act on that decision.

The facilitator should do the following:

- Help the group determine what action(s) to take on the decision and, if necessary, the approach(es).
- Establish, through consensus, if possible, the time by which to take the action(s).
- Assign a person or people to be responsible for the action(s). It's best to assign a specific task to a specific person, not an area of responsibility to a team.
- Specify what's expected as a result of the action(s).

Then, after the scribe and the note-keeper have recorded the actions, approaches, deadlines, assignments, and expectations, the facilitator moves on to the next item on the agenda.

Maybe the group has finished all of the items on the agenda, made decisions, and planned actions. If so, congratulations! Or maybe the time scheduled for the agenda items is almost over. (That happens to the best of groups with the best of managers—and it's not necessarily a sign of failure.) In either case, the facilitator should bring the meeting to a close. To do so properly takes a little time, some planning, and a little guidance. The next chapter can't provide any time, but it can help you plan and it can provide guidance for the facilitator.

Manager's Checklist for Chapter 4

- ❑ The group should review the agenda at the start of the meeting, to link it to decisions and assignments from the previous meeting, for continuity, and revision as necessary.

- ❏ Trust the facilitator, the scribe, the timekeeper, and the note-keeper to run the meeting and trust the other participants to work with them.
- ❏ The facilitator should follow the agenda, as you've mapped out the meeting, keeping to the schedule, if possible, but understanding that a meeting is a journey, not just a destination with a deadline.
- ❏ To conduct a discussion properly, the facilitator opens the discussion, keeps the discussion focused, manages participation, and closes the discussion. It's a simple process, but it requires great skill.
- ❏ Every item on the agenda should lead to some action. The facilitator should lead the group through the following steps:
    - Determine the action(s) to take and, if necessary, the approach(es).
    - Establish the time by which to take the action(s).
    - Assign a person or people to be responsible for the action(s).
    - Specify what's expected as a result of the action(s).

Closing the Meeting and Following Up

Although it may not be true that "all's well that ends well," it's important to close a meeting properly. That's why we've devoted about three-fourths of this chapter to closing the meeting.

Final Matters

You've developed a strong agenda and invited the right people to the meeting. Your facilitator has helped all of the participants contribute to productive discussions, supported by the scribe, the timekeeper, and the note-taker. It's been a great meeting—so far.

But the outcome might be disappointing if it doesn't end right. That's the focus of this chapter, to help you turn all of that preparation and those contributions into results.

End on Time

End your meeting on time—even if it starts late. You can't

always control the beginning of the time frame, but you should try to control the end.

There are at least four good reasons to end your meeting at the scheduled time:

1. It shows respect for the participants, who have schedules to keep and other work to do.
2. It encourages participants to work efficiently—and rewards them for doing so.
3. It helps avoid ending meetings on a frustrating or disappointing note, as most meetings that run over the set time tend to prove the law of diminishing returns: it takes more time and energy to accomplish anything.
4. It's a symptom of poor management if you can't plan either to achieve your objectives within the allotted time or to allow enough time to achieve your objectives.

The timekeeper should signal the facilitator that the time to conclude is approaching, just as he or she does toward the end of each part of the agenda. In fact, as noted in Chapter 2, the time to begin the conclusion should be indicated on the agenda.

The facilitator then begins concluding the meeting. An appropriate conclusion consists of four points:

- Summarize the main points, decisions, actions, and assignments.
- Sketch the agenda for the next meeting—if any.
- Express appreciation.
- Evaluate the meeting.

In this chapter we'll proceed through this five-part conclusion point by point. As elsewhere, we'll outline general principles and offer some specific recommendations. But, as we've emphasized, you should bear in mind that meetings are microcosms of the culture and spirit of the workplace and they should be structured and conducted according to their specific purposes. Logically, then, a meeting should conclude in a way that's consistent with how it began and how it progressed until the end.

Keeping Them Updated

For Example

A TV drama of the early 1980s, *Hill Street Blues*, began every episode in the first four seasons with a meeting of the police officers before they began their shift. It was purely informational, as the desk sergeant updated them on the situation in their precinct.

Then, he generally ended in a way that was most appropriate for the culture (action in a tough environment) and his personality (gruff but affectionate), with a few words to motivate them—"Let's roll!"—and to remind them of the dangers—"And hey, let's be careful out there." It was a perfect way to end meetings in the spirit of that workplace.

Summarize the Main Points, Decisions, Actions, and Assignments

One of the biggest problems with meetings is that there's a lot of talk but not much action afterwards or even too much action and too few results. The results of discussions can be so vague that participants don't know who's to do what and when. Sometimes two or more people take on the same task while other tasks go undone.

To avoid this unfortunate situation, you should build your agenda around decisions and actions, as discussed in Chapter 2, and, as discussed in Chapter 4 the group should understand every decision and determine what action(s) to take on those decisions and who will be responsible for the action(s).

Then the facilitator should briefly sum up the meeting. The summary should relate directly to the purpose(s) of the meeting, to answer the following basic questions:

- Why did we meet?
- Did we achieve our objectives?
- What are we going to do next?

When a meeting ends with a summation of progress and an outline of future actions, there's a feeling of closure and of accomplishment. That's important: people who participate in a meeting must feel that they've done something. That will encourage a greater commitment to taking action on those decisions.

The facilitator should briefly outline:

- The main points of the meeting
- Any agreements and decisions
- Any tasks assigned, including the people responsible for them, the time by which they are to complete their assignments, and what's expected of them

Sketch the Agenda for the Next Meeting—if Any

The assignments will naturally go onto your agenda for the next meeting: You'll be following up on those that are scheduled to be accomplished by then and you may be discussing those that are still in progress. The facilitator also asks the note-taker to jot down any unfinished business that you might want to include on the agenda.

Some meetings experts recommend that the facilitator also set a time and place for the next meeting. In certain situations, especially with a project team or a task force that is working toward long-term goals, this might be a good idea. On the other hand, to conclude a meeting by scheduling the next meeting can easily develop into a routine of meetings for the sake of meetings and/or for the purpose of motivating employees to complete their assignments. Sure, a meeting can provide extra incentive—but that's a bad habit, since it's an expensive incentive. Would you schedule meetings to motivate performance in any other areas of work activities?

It would generally make more sense for the facilitator to ask the participants when they expect to have their assignments completed. That way, the group schedules its next meeting based on reasons to meet.

It may not be possible to schedule during the meeting. There may be people who will be essential for the next meeting but who are not present to check their schedules. Some participants may have potential conflicts that they need to check before committing to a date and time. It may be hard to schedule a room. But at least the group will arrive at a general time frame for the next meeting, so you can work out the scheduling details.

Express Appreciation

How do you feel when you've done your best, when you've put your heart and mind into a team effort, and it just ends abruptly? Well, do you want the participants of a meeting to feel the same way?

When a meeting ends, the facilitator should thank the participants:

1. Thank (again) any participants who made presentations, gave reports, or contributed in any other way that required preparation.
2. Thank the scribe, the timekeeper, and the note-taker.
3. Thank anyone assigned to a task, especially those who volunteered.
4. Thank the rest of the participants.

It's always good to show that you genuinely appreciate what members of the group contributed to the meeting. After all, those who've done their best deserve to know that you appreciate their efforts—and those who haven't contributed their all to the team effort may feel a little embarrassed and may resolve to do better the next time.

Evaluate the Meeting

The authors of *The Team Handbook* put it simply (p. 4-9): "Evaluating every meeting is key to having effective meetings." That's why we're devoting so many pages in this chapter to evaluations.

There are various methods for evaluating a meeting. In this section we'll consider a range of possibilities.

Which way is best? That depends on your situation, the people, the preparation, and other factors. You may want to experiment a little or to alternate among the methods.

By the Participants, Unwritten

The most common way of evaluating meetings is to have the participants do it. There are dozens of options.

The simplest method of evaluation is a round of feedback at the end of the meeting. You can prepare one or more simple questions for the group.

For example:

- Did you read the agenda in advance and prepare to discuss the items?
- Did you contribute to the meeting to the best of your ability?
- Do you know what you are responsible for doing as a result of this meeting?
- How could we improve the next meeting?

Another simple way to evaluate a meeting is through gestures. This method is described briefly in *The Team Handbook* (p. 4-10). The facilitator asks how participants would rate the meeting and they signal their overall evaluation with thumbs up (good), thumbs sideways (neither good nor bad), or thumbs down (bad). Then each in turn explains his or her reasons.

A variant of this method would be to have the facilitator read a list of specific items, one by one. Another variant would be to use either of these approaches, but ask for reasons only from participants who gave a thumbs-down to the meeting. The facilitator could also follow up on the reactions by

For Example

Success Starts in the Mind

Intel Corporation, as mentioned in Chapter 2, has been cited as an organization that takes meetings very seriously. A poster on the walls of conference rooms in Intel factories and offices lists simple questions: "Do you know the purpose of this meeting? Do you have an agenda? Do you know your role?"

At the close of meetings, participants are encouraged to mentally answer questions posted on conference room walls: Why was I here? What was my role? Was I well prepared? What was resolved?

asking for any suggestions for improvement.

A more open method of eliciting feedback is round-robin comments. The facilitator asks each participant in turn to share his or her reactions with the others. This method is especially good when participation has been uneven, because it encourages more reserved members of the group to contribute, providing perspectives that otherwise might not come forth.

A less structured method is a general discussion: just ask for reactions and participants volunteer their comments. This works well if other general discussions have been balanced and at least moderately orderly.

The facilitator can also provide some focus for the round-robin or general discussion by asking questions. They can be comprehensive—What did we do that worked well? What could we have done better?—or specific—How could the agenda have been improved? What could we do to promote more participation?

When participants share their reactions, the facilitator should guide the discussion just as he or she would guide discussion of agenda items. By probing for clarification, by paraphrasing, and by following up with questions, the facilitator should try to elicit suggestions for improving meetings.

Whatever method of oral evaluation you use, the facilitator should ask the scribe to record all comments and suggestions. It might also be good for the note-taker to keep track as well, since participants can become quite animated when sharing their reactions.

All of these methods should end with agreement on at least one thing to do to improve the next meeting.

By the Participants, in Writing

Evaluations in writing offer several advantages over the methods described previously:

- Participants may express things in writing that they would not mention in a group.
- Participants may express themselves better and more

completely in writing than orally.

- Writing provides direct documentation of reactions, not captured and summarized by the scribe and/or the note-taker.
- You can usually cover more items in written form than in a discussion.
- You can better direct the input you want through the format you choose.

And no, written evaluations don't necessarily take a lot of time, either to prepare or to conduct.

However, there are disadvantages. One is that many written comments are difficult to understand and/or don't provide sufficient basis for taking action. Another is that it's more difficult to share the information with the group and it takes someone time and effort to analyze the evaluations and present the essence. Finally, most groups strongly prefer evaluating orally.

For these reasons, it's probably best to use written evaluations only if verbal methods won't work for some reason, such as if some participants won't speak out frankly. You should also decide who will read and analyze the evaluations and how you and the group will work with the results.

Multiple-Choice. A format that usually takes little time and provides very specific input asks participants to indicate their reaction to a statement with yes or no and/or on a Likert scale (usually three, four, or five points). The facilitator distributes a form and asks participants to rate the meeting on criteria

Key Term

Likert scale An assessment method in which respondents indicate their degree of agreement or disagreement with a series of statements. A Likert scale may present options such as "strongly agree," "agree," "disagree," and "strongly disagree" or "always," "almost always," "sometimes," "rarely," and "never." Five-point scales are most common.

The scale was developed by Rensis Likert, a professor of psychology who worked in business and government before founding and directing the Institute for Social Research at the University of Michigan.

important to the group. They each complete the forms, individually and silently, and then return them to the facilitator.

Figure 5-1 shows a simple form for evaluating meetings, taken from *Communicating Effectively*, by Lani Arredondo (p. 164). The author used it for evaluating meetings in general

CAUTION!

Plot, Don't Average

When analyzing the results of evaluations that use a Likert scale, it may be tempting to calculate an average for each item. Don't do it! Averages can minimize or conceal some important differences.

Instead, for each item show a dot plot. That way it's easy for anyone to see at a glance any significant differences among members of the group or any extremes that an average would not show.

Meeting Evaluation Form

Circle the number of the adverb that most often applies.	**Yes 1**	**Somewhat 2**	**No 3**
The meeting started on time.	1	2	3
The meeting followed the agenda.	1	2	3
Everyone observed the ground rules.	1	2	3
Everyone came prepared.	1	2	3
Everyone participated.	1	2	3
Communication was courteous and constructive.	1	2	3
The meeting followed a process for solving problems.	1	2	3
The meeting accomplished the purpose.	1	2	3
Follow-up actions were done and reported on time.	1	2	3
Leadership was effective.	1	2	3
The meeting ended on time.	1	2	3

Figure 5-1. A sample meeting evaluation form

(with a scale of "usually—sometimes—rarely"), and modified it slightly to focus on a specific meeting.

You can mix rating scales, as shown (Figure 5-2) in this short evaluation form presented as an example in *The Team Handbook* (p. 4-10), which uses three-point and six-point Likert scales:

Our meeting today was:	Focused 1 2 3 4 Rambling
The pace was:	Too fast Just right Too slow
Everyone got a chance to participate:	Yes Somewhat No
Our purpose was:	Clear 1 2 3 4 Confused
We made good progress on our plan:	Yes Somewhat No
We followed our ground rules:	Yes Somewhat No

Figure 5-2. Meeting evaluation form with mixed rating scales

If you mix rating scales, be careful not to make the form too complex. Also, you could space the statements to allow for comments to be added after any or all of them.

Any evaluation form that you take from a book—even the best form, even the best book—should be modified to fit your situation and your culture. For example, you might include statements about the rules the group has set for meetings (see Chapter 3).

Here are some statements to get you started in developing your evaluation form:

- Members were notified enough in advance.
- There was an appropriate and well-organized agenda.
- The agenda was distributed in advance.
- The meeting room was scheduled and set up properly.
- The meeting was well organized.
- Everyone invited attended.
- Everyone who attended arrived on time.
- The meeting started on time.
- The manager and/or facilitator made clear the purpose(s) for the meeting.

- There was a transition from the last meeting.
- One topic was discussed at a time.
- All members participated in the discussions.
- One person had the floor at a time.
- There was an atmosphere of free expression.
- Participants showed respect for each other.
- The facilitator made good use of questions.
- The facilitator summarized the main points of each discussion.
- The discussion was relevant.
- The group considered the pros and cons of all issues.
- Decisions were made fairly.
- The meeting proceeded at an appropriate pace.
- The meeting covered the entire agenda, as planned.
- The group achieved the purpose(s) of the meeting.
- Assignments were complete and clear.
- Responsibilities were evenly distributed.
- Plans for the next meeting were announced.
- The atmosphere of the meeting was good.
- The meeting ended on time.

Remember: you should develop the evaluation to fit your people and your meetings. If you simply borrow a form, participants may feel that it's not worth it for them to put much time and thought into using it. Invite the group to modify the form so it addresses the issues that are important to them.

Open. Open-ended questions require more time and energy from participants, but they also usually provide more information. Make them as specific or as general as you like, but try to word them to be as neutral as possible, so as not to influence the participants. For example, "the agenda was appropriate" would be a better statement than "your manager created a great agenda."

One method is for the facilitator to pass around 3 x 5 or 4 x 6 index cards at the end of the meeting and ask three basic questions:

1. What did you like most about this meeting?
2. What did you like least about this meeting?
3. How could we improve the next meeting?

For a more focused assessment, you could print evaluations with more specific open-ended questions, such as those listed in *The Team Handbook* (p. 4-9):

- How did this meeting go?
- How were the pace, flow, and tone of the meeting?
- Did we handle items in a reasonable sequence? Did we get stuck?
- How well did we stay on the topic?
- How well did we discuss the information? How clearly? How accurately?
- How well did we respond to each other's questions?
- What might we do differently? What should we do that we didn't do? Do more of? Do less of? Not do at all?
- What was just right and should continue as is?
- Any other comments, observations, recommendations?

Notice that the final question shifts the series of questions from focused to totally open. It's usually good to allow at least one such question, so you don't miss anything that any member of the group might consider important—and to allow members the freedom to take the evaluation in any direction.

You may want to open up the evaluation even further, by moving from the written form into a discussion. At this point, however, time becomes an issue. It could take participants five minutes to write out their comments and any discussion would likely take at least 10 minutes more. That's a big chunk of a meeting that runs only one or two hours. That's why long written evaluations are appropriate only after meetings that take one or two days, not for shorter meetings. One exception would be if you're consistently having problems with your meetings and decide to devote a meeting to evaluating the process and group dynamics.

If you decide to follow a written evaluation with a discussion, here are some suggestions.

The facilitator should first make sure that all of the participants have finished completing their forms. He or she should watch for signs that most have stopped writing and are looking up from the forms, then ask if anybody needs more time.

The discussion should be based on several selected questions, not all of them, or just start with a totally open question. If you want to discuss several questions, the facilitator should instruct the timekeeper to allow a certain amount of time for each question.

When the time for discussion expires, the facilitator should ask for the evaluation forms. Don't be surprised if some members of the group start writing again; discussions can stimulate thinking and help people remember comments that they wanted to make.

Role Players

You can also do evaluations of the facilitator, the scribe, and the timekeeper the first few times that you use these roles, to help the group understand the process better and to help everyone be more aware of the responsibilities and challenges of each role.

In *Running Effective Meetings* (p. 42), the authors suggest asking the following questions of these role players:

Facilitator

- What was it like to facilitate?
- What did you try to do to help?
- What was frustrating or challenging?

Scribe

- What was it like to be the scribe?
- What was frustrating or challenging?

Timekeeper

- What was it like to help the group deal with time issues?
- What was frustrating or challenging?

Because these individuals have special perspectives of the meeting process, you should follow up the comments on frustrations and challenges by probing for reasons and for suggestions on how to improve. Then, open up the discussion to the rest of the group for further comments.

Another way to have the role players evaluate the meeting is to have them gather afterwards to discuss the meeting. Ask each to write down any advice that he or she would offer other people chosen for that particular role. You can then share that advice with the individuals to whom you assign those roles for the next meeting and with the group at the start of the meeting.

General Guidelines

Allow appropriate time to evaluate the meeting. How long? The answer to that question is...it depends on the following factors:

- How well your meetings have gone, in general. But be careful: don't use evaluations only when there are problems. Evaluations can help good meetings become even better.
- How well the members of the group know each other.
- How much time can reasonably be allotted for the evaluation.
- The points that you want to cover in your evaluation. A lot or a few? General areas or specific items?
- The method of evaluation.

The last two points are choices that depend on the first three points.

A good rule of thumb might be to allow a maximum of 10 minutes for evaluating a meeting of two hours or longer. For a written evaluation, 10 minutes should be enough. For a discussion, you might allow a little longer. For a written evaluation followed by discussion, 15 minutes might be adequate.

Whatever method(s) you use to evaluate your meetings, emphasize that participants should focus on problems with the process and not judge or blame the people. If they comment on

No Time to Evaluate

MISTAKE PROOFING

What if you just run out of time before you can do any evaluation? Distribute a written evaluation to all the participants, as an e-mail or a memo, immediately after the meeting. It's generally not advisable to hand out forms as they leave the meeting: if you're running so late that you can't squeeze in an evaluation, participants are likely to be thinking about what they're doing next, so they tuck away the form and may forget about it. But if the form comes to them as part of their normal business activity, they're probably going to give it some time and attention.

the facilitator, the scribe, or the timekeeper, they should note what they did that was helpful and offer one suggestion for improvement. Also, evaluations should elicit positive comments as well as negative, because knowing what works can help you identify what to keep doing to be effective.

How you evaluate a meeting depends on the purpose(s) of the meeting, the people who participated, the culture of your unit, and the problems that you've noted and want to resolve.

Write and Distribute the Minutes

The minutes of a meeting are essential to following up on the decisions and the assignments. Good minutes docu-

In Like a Lion, Out Like a Lamb

Smart Managing

Many meetings are like the month of March: they begin like a lion, with a warm-up and socializing and a review of the agenda by the manager, and end like a lamb, as participants collect their things and file out of the room.

One way to end with energy is to simply stand up at the end, before anybody leaves the room, and close with a few words of appreciation and/or inspiration. You don't need to say much or be eloquent: be sincere and be specific. For example, if there was a major conflict, thank them for working through their differences, or if some of the action plans are ambitious, offer a few words of encouragement.

Another way to provide closure is to thank participants and encourage those with assignments to feel free to come and talk with you about them. Be sincere, enthusiastic, and positive.

ment not only what happened during the meeting but also what is scheduled to happen as a result of the meeting.

Write 'Em Right

Traditionally, the minutes of most meetings are prose narratives that tend to be dull and just go on and on or else are so brief that they don't provide a fair sense of what happened in the meeting.

Minutes can more effectively capture the essence of a meeting and show what the participants have accomplished and will accomplish when they focus on *action.* Action minutes are basically lists, rather than narratives—easy to read and understand.

It should be noted here that good narrative minutes may be more appropriate, even necessary, for some meetings. If the group moves fast, if a meeting covers multiple projects, and/or if discussion is involved, the minutes should capture the main lines of thinking, the discussion threads, the issues raised, and how the group addressed them. As we've emphasized throughout this book, you should always consider your situation, the people, the culture, and the purposes of your meeting. If you decide that a narrative—"intelligent minutes"—would be more appropriate, you should probably ask the note-taker to prepare action minutes as well, as a summary to accompany the narrative.

As outlined in Chapter 3, the minutes should include the following:

1. Date, time, and location of the meeting
2. List of participants
3. List of people invited but absent
4. Participants assigned as facilitator, scribe, timekeeper, and note-taker
5. Agenda
6. For each agenda item:
   - Main discussion points and outcomes (decisions and action items)
   - Names of the participants responsible for the action items and the dates and times for completion
   - Result(s) expected

7. Items for consideration at later meetings
8. Meeting evaluation
9. Reports (attached)

The minutes should be easy to scan: a simple structure helps the facts stand out—decisions and actions are put in boldface or all caps.

If you've created a form for the minutes, as suggested in Chapter 3, it should be easy for anyone to know what's most important about a meeting at a glance—what was covered, what was decided, what actions were planned, what's expected and by when, and who is responsible for those actions.

Get Out the Word

How soon should the note-taker distribute the minutes? Experts disagree on this question—within three or four days, no later than two days after the meeting, in 24 hours.

The best answer to this question would be *as soon as possible*. You should set a deadline based on the means of distribution and the content and format of the minutes. The shorter the deadline, the more you emphasize the importance of the meeting.

Sure, the note-taker has other work to do, but if you want everybody to recognize that meetings matter, you should expect the note-taker to make the minutes a top priority. That sense of immediacy also sends the message that the assignments outlined in those minutes should also be a priority for the participants to whom they're assigned.

Finally, the faster you get out the minutes, the less time the participants have to rely on their perceptions and memory of the decisions and assignments. They'll soon have it all in black and white.

It's really not a complicated job. The note-keeper can record the essentials listed above in very few words. Since the note-keeper was jotting down the main points during the meeting, often marked as important by the facilitator in his or her summaries and/or by the scribe in his or her running record on display, the minutes are almost done by the close of the meeting.

There's just the task of adding context so the notes make sense to anyone who was not present at the meeting. Then, it's basically a matter of typing up the minutes, printing them out, getting any reports presented at the meeting, and making copies.

Who should receive a copy of those minutes? All of the meeting participants, of course, and any other interested parties. Who are the "interested parties"?

- Anybody who received a copy of the agenda.
- The supervisors of any participants, because the minutes are a record of the work they did. At the very least, the supervisors of any participants who are responsible for assignments from the meeting, because those assignments will take time and effort away from their other work.
- Any manager or other employee who will be involved in the assignments in some way. For example, if an assignment involves getting information from another unit, the head of that unit should know about the decision to seek that information. If an assignment is to survey employees outside your department, a copy of the minutes should go not only to the supervisor of those employees but also to the employees themselves.

Here's another advantage in keeping the minutes succinct and structured: the success of the assignments depends to some extent on making it easy for people to read them!

How should the note-taker distribute the minutes? That depends on your organization, on the culture, on the channels for distributing information, and on the recipients.

The conventional method is by memos. That method has largely been replaced by e-mail. However, for recipients who don't have ready access to a printer or who don't read their e-mails regularly, a memo may still be a good method—at least for anyone who will be involved in any of the assignments from the meeting.

Smart Managing

Just in Case

Because the minutes are so important, not only as a record of the meeting but also as documentation of action plans, you may not want to risk inaccurate or incomplete information. It's not necessarily a question of not trusting the note-taker, but an acknowledgment of the importance of the minutes.

You might want to establish a policy of having the note-taker pass the minutes to you to review before he or she distributes them. It should take you just a few minutes to skim the minutes—and it's time well spent. Just think of it as taking a precaution and providing a safety net to avoid problems and save the note-taker from embarrassment or worse.

Another conventional method of publicizing minutes is by posting them on a bulletin board or other permanent, visible location. Technology has provided the next generation of bulletin boards: minutes can also be posted on internal Web pages. This is a good way of reaching people who were not participants but who are on your list of "interested parties." But don't count on the bulletin board or Web pages to get the minutes to those involved in any of the assignments.

The note-taker should be responsible for distributing and otherwise publicizing the minutes. Make sure that you let him or her know who should receive a copy and how.

File the Agenda, the Minutes, and Other Key Documents

This is the easy part, the last thing on the note-taker's list—and perhaps too easy to neglect. Make sure that he or she knows where and how to file the agenda, the minutes, and any other related documents, such as reports and information presented during the meeting.

If the depository for paperwork from meetings is outside your department, it's a good idea to keep a second file. You want to document work done in meetings and as a result of meetings in the same way you would document any other work activities in your department. It's an easy and effective way to show the importance of meetings.

Work the Assignments

At this point, the meeting is officially ended. Now, it's up to participants with assignments to work those assignments.

With some groups, such as project teams and ongoing teams, most of the work happens outside of meetings. Consequently, assignments (such as collecting and analyzing information and preparing reports) may require considerable time and effort. It may be necessary to ask other members of the group to lend a hand, as needed, to complete the assignment by the set date.

The point here is to keep the people who participated in the meeting collaborating with each other. This is a team effort, in a way—and ongoing support can make a big difference in what they accomplish.

Communicate, Communicate, Communicate

Part of that ongoing support is through continued communication—about the meeting, about decisions, about actions, about accomplishments. After all, if you expect your employees and others in the organization to consider meetings to be "real work," you should communicate about them as you would about other work activities.

Keep all stakeholders informed of progress on the action plan through memos, e-mail, bulletin boards, and so on. Then, when those action plans produce results, get a summary report out to all stakeholders. It should include recognition of the individuals responsible for the actions and express thanks to all the participants of the meetings that developed those action plans.

Improve Your Meetings

Although we've put improvement last in this chapter, it's really the most important single activity in the long run. Do you remember all the problems with meetings that we discussed in Chapter 1? Well, this book is dedicated to the proposition that you can resolve all of those problems.

Unfortunately, we can't prescribe remedies, because only you know the problems. But we can propose some general actions to take.

First, the group should discuss any concerns and suggestions expressed in the evaluations. If doing so takes more time than the group can commit, it may be useful to form a task force to review the evaluations and come up with some ideas for improvement. You may also want to develop a special evaluation to focus on certain key areas and elicit suggestions for improvement from the participants of your next meeting.

What if problems can be attributed to the agendas and other preparation? If that's your responsibility, here are three suggestions. You could distribute copies of a recent agenda to members of the group and ask them to mark it up with comments, anonymously, and put it in your box or slip it under your door. You should probably also read this book again. You may also want to involve other members of the group when you develop the next few agendas, to get feedback before you finalize and distribute them.

If comments are aimed at how members of the group fulfill the roles of facilitator, scribe, timekeeper, and note-taker, you may decide to provide training sessions. You might also work with the people who have those roles, in advance of the meeting, to better prepare them. Then, during the meeting, you could help them by sending signals—giving a "thumbs up" or nodding, shaking your head, making gestures to slow down or pick up the pace, clarify, or ask questions. (Some of these signals are almost universal; the others you should discuss in advance.) Think of it as coaching inexperienced athletes to help them make the most of their abilities.

If there are problems with behavior, meet with the individuals, just as you would if they behaved inappropriately elsewhere in the workplace. By doing this, you improve your meetings in two ways: the individuals in question behave better and your intervention shows that you consider meetings to be as important as other work activities.

When you deal with behavior problems, be careful, as advised in Chapter 3, not to do anything that might be perceived as an attempt to suppress individual freedom of expression or to require "attitude adjustments." Focus on helping individuals understand that everyone benefits when they show respect for others, when they follow the rules, and when they express their differences in a civil manner.

Chapter 7 will discuss various problems with meetings and suggest ways to deal with them. But first, we will focus on the positive, considering some tools and techniques for more effective discussions, problem solving, and decision making.

Manager's Checklist for Chapter 5

- ❑ You've developed a strong agenda and invited the right people to the meeting. The facilitator, the scribe, the timekeeper, and the note-taker have handled their responsibilities. The participants have contributed and collaborated well. But the outcome might be disappointing if it doesn't end right, if all of that preparation and those contributions don't turn into results.
- ❑ The facilitator should summarize the main points, the decisions, actions, and assignments.
- ❑ The facilitator should thank the participants, especially those with special responsibilities for the meeting and those assigned to tasks.
- ❑ The key to effective meetings is evaluating every meeting—and working to improve them.
- ❑ The minutes of a meeting are essential to following up on the decisions and the assignments. The note-taker should finalize and distribute the minutes as quickly as possible.
- ❑ Keep the people who participated in the meeting collaborating after the meeting.

Techniques and Tools

The subject of this chapter actually merits an entire book by itself. In fact, there are dozens of books with techniques and tools for meetings. This chapter can't possibly present all the techniques and tools found in those books and others. But you'll find here some of the basic and best.

The techniques and tools presented in this chapter can be very useful—or a waste of time and effort. That depends on the extent to which the tool or technique you choose to use fits your need as well as on how you use it.

- Know which techniques and tools work for what purposes in what situations.
- Understand how and why the techniques and tools work.
- Use the techniques and tools appropriately.

Discussions tend to follow a basic pattern:

- Open: produce a lot of ideas, questions, information, or options
- Narrow the focus: reduce the list of ideas, questions, factors, or options to a prime few

CAUTION!

Think Environment

It's not enough to choose techniques and tools appropriate to your purposes. You also need a suitable environment. Participants should feel comfortable with each other and with the techniques and tools.

Don't assume that group members know about even the more common activities—especially because many techniques and tools have variations. The facilitator should explain the rules at the start.

Even more important, especially for activities that involve creativity or critical thinking, members should feel at ease to make suggestions and express their opinions. The facilitator should be sensitive to any discomfort.

- Decide: apply criteria to those ideas, questions, factors, or options, and select one or prioritize.

Here's a guide to selecting and using some of the most effective techniques and tools for groups:

To identify the Cause(s) of a Problem:
- Repetitive why analysis
- Cause-and-effect analysis

To Generate Ideas:
- Brainstorming
- Mind-mapping
- Displayed thinking

To Organize, Analyze, and Prioritize Ideas:
- Affinity diagram
- PMI
- Six thinking hats
- Effort-impact matrix

To Make Choices Involving Multiple Factors:
- Paired comparison analysis
- Grid analysis
- Multivoting
- Nominal group technique

To Implement the Decision:
- Force-field analysis

Identify the Cause(s) of a Problem

Let's look at the different methods and tools you can use in a meeting to identify problem causes.

Repetitive Why Analysis

The repetitive why is a very simple technique. It consists of asking "Why?" about a problem, then asking "Why?" about the answer, then asking "Why?" about the next answer, then asking "Why?" ... Well, you get the idea.

Here's an example:

Q—"Why was the report late?"

A—"I had trouble using the software."

Q—"Why did you have trouble using the software?"

A—"I couldn't find the manual."

Q—"Why couldn't you find the manual?"

A—"It floats from office to office."

Q—"Why does it float from office to office?"

A—"There's no central place to keep manuals."

Depending on the situation—and the persistence and patience of the team—the repetitive why could continue for a while. In this example, the team could continue, getting into matters of budget or lack of interest or other possible causes of the problem.

A version of this technique is the *five whys*—asking the probing question to five levels, as if there's something magical about five, rather than four or six. The use of this technique in business originated with Taiichi Ohno of Toyota Motor Company. However, any parent would attest that kids seem to use the technique quite naturally.

Cause-and-Effect Analysis

The cause-and-effect analysis is a relative of the repetitive why analysis. Perhaps the biggest difference is that the cause-and-effect analysis builds on a diagram (Figure 6-1) that structures it more than the repetitive why analysis, so it's better for problems with many interrelated causes.

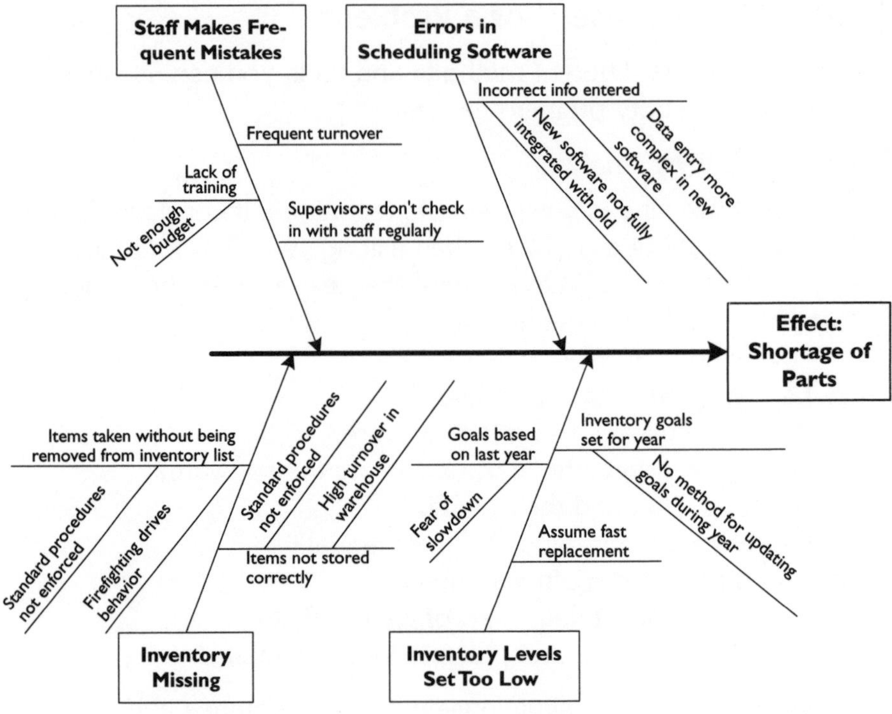

Figure 6-1. Example of a cause-and-effect diagram

You begin by defining the problem, the effect in the cause-and-effect analysis. Then, you consider all of the possible causes of that effect. Group these factors into primary categories, secondary categories, tertiary categories, quaternary categories—until you run out of Latinate adjectives.

For working with a cause-and-effect diagram, it's better to use a blackboard or a whiteboard than a flip chart, so you can erase a factor here to move it there. If you use a flipchart, using self-adhesive notes to put factors on the chart allows similar flexibility.

Write the primary factors at the end of the diagonal lines that branch out from the horizontal line. When brainstorming possible causal factors for the diagram, people often use one of the following organizational schemes to help them think of all the causes:

- Methods, materials, machines, manpower (the "m" word for people) (4 M's)
- Procedures, policies, equipment, and people
- Place(s), procedure(s), people, policies (4 P's)
- Surroundings, suppliers, system(s), skills (4 S's)

You don't use these factors on the diagram itself because the diagram lists specific factors. For example the cause-and-effect diagram might have "leaking seals" as a cause of some problem, but would not have "equipment" because that is not specific enough.

Write the secondary factors alongside the diagonal lines to which they're most logically related. From those secondary factors, draw branches for the tertiary factors that relate to them. The practical maximum depth of a cause-and-effect diagram is usually four or five levels.

Once you've put all of the possible causes on the chart, you should be ready to verify which factors are actually causing the problem.

Because of the appearance of the diagram, it's also called a *fishbone diagram*. A third name is the *Ishikawa diagram*, named for Kaoru Ishikawa, a Japanese professor (not of ichthyology, but of engineering) who first used the diagram in 1943.

Generate Ideas

To deal with a problem, you need to come up with possible ideas and solutions. There are a variety of ways to do this. Let's look at them.

Brainstorming

You certainly recognize this technique—or at least the name. It seems that people are using the term "brainstorming" to refer to any type of discussion. ("Stop by my office and we'll brainstorm a little." "We had a few minutes left, so we brainstormed about that suggestion.") As a result, we all know about brainstorming, in a way, but what we know may not actually be brainstorming.

The term and the technique we owe to Alex F. Osborn, an advertising executive. In the late 1930s or early 1940s, he was challenging his team to think creatively. According to Osborn, "Brainstorm means using the *brain* to *storm* a creative problem ... in commando fashion."

The strategy was to be totally free—uninhibited, unrestricted. As Osborn explained the logic behind being crazy, "It is easier to tone down a wild idea than to think up a new one."

The Basics. The purpose of brainstorming is to encourage creative thinking and generate a large number of ideas. These can be concepts, solutions, or whatever thoughts arise along the direction you set for the brainstorming session—a project, a problem, an opportunity, a program. Brainstorming works, when done properly, because it allows participants to separate two thinking processes—generation and judgment—into two phases.

The goal is to generate as many ideas as possible, because the essence of brainstorming is the belief that the more ideas, the greater the chance of coming up with good ones. The facilitator should encourage creativity, involve all participants, and work to generate energy and excitement.

Brainstorming works best with a about a half-dozen people, but it can work with a dozen or more or with only three. To begin, the facilitator reviews the topic, so that all the participants understand it, and writes it on a board or a flipchart to keep it on display during the session. Then, the participants take a few minutes to think quietly. Next, the facilitator invites ideas.

There are two common methods for eliciting the contributions: round-robin and popcorn. In the first, the participants take turns contributing an idea, going around the group one by one, passing if they have nothing to contribute, until everyone passes for a round. In popcorn, participants call out their ideas in no order, until they have nothing left to contribute. (You can also set a time limit.) Round-robin is a better way for people who are less aggressive and/or more methodical. With the popcorn method, it may be harder for quiet people to participate; it can also become very active—which makes it a greater challenge to capture all of the contributions.

Depending on the size of the group, the topic, the creativity, the environment, and the method (round-robin or popcorn), the contributions can overwhelm the scribe. Consequently, it's probably wise to have two or three people to record the ideas, with the facilitator orchestrating the recording so the scribes don't miss any ideas or duplicate their efforts.

Here's a variation that is more efficient if the group will later be using an affinity diagram. As each participant makes a contribution, he or she then writes it on a large self-adhesive note sheet and hands it to the scribe, who places it on the flipchart.

Principles. In setting up a brainstorming session, here are some principles that the facilitator should explain to the group:

- Don't react to any ideas—there should be no criticism or other judgments.
- Treat everyone with respect.
- Make all comments to the group—no side discussions.
- One person speaks at a time: don't interrupt.
- Build on ideas (hitchhike or piggyback)—add, shift, combine.
- Don't get caught up in details or differences.
- Feel totally free to offer any ideas.
- Keep focused on a specific topic.

To Time or Not to Time? Some guides to brainstorming recommend setting a time limit. Others do not. What is more important is the pace of the brainstorming. It's critical that the participants understand that they have to think and contribute quickly. A quicker pace will generally encourage more effective and exciting brainstorming. If you decide to set a time limit on the duration of the brainstorm, but then the ideas are still coming as the allotted time dwindles, don't hesitate to extend the time.

Variants. If some or many members of the group tend not to be assertive, you can start with "quiet brainstorming." The facilitator asks the participants to take five minutes to jot down as many

Key Term **Hitchhike** To build on the idea of another participant, to contribute an idea that's only slightly different from another. Also known as *piggyback*.

ideas as possible. Each person then shares his or her ideas, which allows the group to move into spontaneous brainstorming.

The biggest obstacle to brainstorming is reactions—smirks, grimaces, raised eyebrows, sighs, and comments or questions. If you feel a need to more actively discourage reactions, pass around red cards or cards marked "Stop!" for participants to hold up if there are any reactions to contributions.

What Next? After a brainstorming session, take a short break to allow participants to recover energy and change their perspective from creative to analytical. Then they can use a tool like the affinity diagram to organize the ideas into clusters.

Mind-Mapping

Mind-mapping (or mindmapping) is a technique developed in the late 1960s by Tony Buzan, who called it *radiant thinking*. He wanted a method for releasing the full power of the brain, for using the whole brain, not just the left half or the right half.

Mind-mapping helps a group capture complex ideas quickly, easily, and visually, to see the big picture and identify relationships among ideas and processes. As with brainstorming, no judgments are allowed and analysis comes later, after the group has finished mapping. Also, as with brainstorming, the facilitator should encourage participants to experiment and to show respect for each other. There are at least two major differences between mind-mapping and brainstorming: in mind-mapping the contributions are connected, to develop a structure (the map) and contributions and associations are represented graphically, using designs and shapes and colors whenever possible, rather than words.

Here's how it works:

1. Choose a central idea or concept to explore. The key is to choose a starting point that is clear and focused, yet

Questions to Pry, Prod, and Provoke

If the group is slow to get into brainstorming, toss out an old idea (current product, service, process—whatever the topic for brainstorming) and apply SCAMPER, a technique created by Michael Michalko in his book, *Thinkertoys: A Handbook of Business Creativity* (Berkeley, CA: Ten Speed Press, 1991). SCAMPER is an acronym for nine techniques for transforming products, services, or processes into something new:

Substitute
- What can be substituted? How?

Combine
- What can be combined? With what? How?

Adapt
- What else is similar?
- What idea could be incorporated?
- Who could be emulated?

Magnify
- What could be made larger, increased, expanded, extended?

Modify
- What could be altered?

Put to other uses
- What else could this be used for? As is? If modified?
- Other purposes? Other markets?

Eliminate or Minimize
- What could be made smaller, decreased, dropped?
- What could be divided into parts?
- What's not necessary?

Rearrange
- What other arrangement, layout, sequence, schedule might work better?

Reverse
- What could be turned around, upside down?
- What would be the opposite?

broad enough to stimulate divergent thinking.

2. The scribe writes this central idea down in the middle of flip chart or white board.
3. Set a time limit. (Buzan maintains that the mind works best in bursts of five to seven minutes.)

4. The facilitator elicits contributions inspired by the central focus.
5. The scribe captures the contributions, drawing lines branching out from the central focus and recording each contribution in one or two words or abbreviations or a sketch of an image or a code—whatever captures the contribution quickly and appropriately. A contribution that relates to another contribution on the chart or board, rather than the central focus, is recorded on a branch from that contribution.
6. If any area of the map becomes too dense, the scribe can start a map on another sheet or board for that particular area.

Those are the basic steps. There are many guidelines, of which these are the most important:

- Print words, using small or capital letters.
- Use bright colors.
- Draw—symbols, codes, shapes, etc.—rather than write whenever possible.
- Connect words and drawings with lines and arrows of varying colors and thicknesses and design.
- Show relationships and order with numbers, if helpful.
- Emphasize words or other representations by bolding and/or underlining.
- Use organized and appropriate spacing.

What the group does with its mind map depends to a great extent on what the map reveals. It's an exploratory tool, rather than analytical, and obviously spatial rather than linear.

Displayed Thinking

This is a technique similar to mind-mapping that allows a group to organize and logically display the results of both creative and analytical thinking. Also known as a form of storyboarding, it can be used to generate, sort, and develop ideas and to organize and/or plan. It creates a logical, visual structure to show interconnections among the ideas and how all the pieces fit together.

As with brainstorming and mind-mapping, participants are encouraged to contribute ideas and build the display. Anything goes, in a spirit of positive and creative thinking. The results are submitted to critical thinking later.

Displayed thinking requires a large surface: a corkboard or a blackboard or an empty wall. (It can take a lot of space.) To write out the ideas, use index cards (3 x 5 or 4 x 6 work best) or self-adhesive note paper. To attach the cards to the surface, use pushpins (on corkboard) or masking tape (on a wall).

Then, follow these steps:

1. At the top of the board, the facilitator puts a topic (e.g., a problem, an opportunity, or a process to be improved).
2. Under the topic, the facilitator and the group put headings (e.g., categories, main directions, general points, primary considerations, or divisions of the organization).
3. The facilitator spreads out on the table markers, cards or paper pads, and pushpins or tape (if necessary).
4. The facilitator instructs the participants to write down their ideas, one per card or note—a statement on the front and, if necessary, an explanation or description on the back. Then, the facilitator explains that they are to post each idea on the board where it belongs logically.
5. After the participants have posted their ideas, the facilitator leads them in grouping like ideas and reorganizing any ideas as the group finds appropriate.
6. Then the participants fill out the board with ideas and details, as necessary.

The result is a large, visual representation of ideas in a logical structure.

Organize, Analyze, and Prioritize Ideas

How do you organize and prioritize ideas? Let's look at some widely-used methods for doing that.

Affinity Diagram

An affinity diagram is a technique for reducing a large number of ideas, opinions, concepts, issues, and so forth—such as after brainstorming—by sorting them into clusters. The group can use a blackboard, a big whiteboard, a wall, or a large table for sorting.

If the contributions are already on self-adhesive note sheets or on cards, the group is ready to begin. If not, the facilitator distributes the flipchart sheets from the brainstorming session to the participants, who divide into as many groups as there are sheets, and then passes out index cards and masking tape or self-adhesive note pads and asks the groups to record the ideas from their sheets onto the cards or notes.

The procedure is simple.

1. The facilitator asks the participants to take their cards or notes to the sorting area and silently put them in logical clusters. They can move around the cards or notes as they want, without talking. After they all arrive at a consensus, they return to their seats. If a card or note seems to fit into more than one cluster, a participant can make a duplicate card or note so the contribution can be put into both clusters.
2. The facilitator takes one cluster of cards or notes at a time. He or she reads the contributions in that cluster and asks the group to come up with a heading or title or label (usually three to five words) that best describes or encompasses the contributions in that cluster. The group may agree at this point to combine similar clusters or to split large clusters.
3. The group then discusses the clusters and how they interrelate.

PMI

PMI ("Plus/Minus/Interesting") is a simple but important tool for making decisions. It's used to weigh the pros and cons of alternatives, particularly actions.

The scribe draws on the flipchart or whiteboard three columns, headed "Plus," "Minus," and "Interesting." Across the top, he or she writes the alternative or action under consideration.

Then the facilitator asks the group to come up with points about the alternative or potential results of the action. If a point is good or a result is positive, the scribe records it in the Plus column. If a point is bad or a result is negative, the scribe records it in the Minus column. Points or results that fit into neither the scribe puts into the Interesting (Implications) column.

If the issue under consideration is an *action*, it may be very obvious by the end of the discussion whether or not the action makes sense: either the Plus column or the Minus column dominates. Of course, it's not a matter of quantity of entries, but quality: one major factor can outweigh a long list of minor factors. If the decision is not obvious from the discussion, the group should consider each of the items in the Plus and Minus columns and assign a numerical score (e.g., +2, -4, +3) for its importance, by consensus. The group should consider the items in the "Interesting" column, which may tilt the balance one way or the other. Only as a last resort, if the discussion does not lead to a decision, comparing the totals for Plus and Minus can help the group reach a decision.

If the issue under consideration is an *alternative*, the group should do a PMI for both or all of the alternatives, following the procedure described above.

Six Thinking Hats

Six thinking hats is a technique for considering an issue (a decision, a problem, an opportunity) from all important perspectives. It forces participants to move beyond their usual thinking styles and helps them form a more complete picture of the situation.

This tool was created by Edward de Bono, who presents it in full detail in his book, *Six Thinking Hats*. He developed this technique as a process for using lateral thinking in problem solving, particularly in groups.

The technique is simple in concept. When the group is considering an issue, the members all wear one hat at a time, figu-

Key Term **Lateral thinking** A set of systematic techniques for using multiple perspectives and approaches for exploring an issue. Edward de Bono divides thinking into two styles—*vertical thinking*, the traditional method that uses the processes of logic, and *lateral thinking*, which involves breaking from routine thinking to consider issues from other angles.

ratively. (Of course, if your budget can cover six hats for each participant, they can wear the thinking hats literally and dress for success.) The facilitator indicates which hat to wear and when to switch hats. Some approaches will be more important than others, depending on whether the issue is a decision, a problem, an opportunity, or whatever else.

So, what are these hats and what perspectives do they represent?

White Hat: Participants focus on the information available and see what they can learn from it. They also look for gaps in their knowledge and they either try to fill them or take them into account. "I think we need to do some white hat thinking: what facts are we lacking to make this decision?"

Red Hat: Participants consider the issue using their emotions, intuition, and gut reactions. They also try to feel how other people will react emotionally to the issue, especially those who don't fully know the reasoning of the group. The red hat allows participants to express reactions without any need to justify them. "If I can put on my red hat at this point, I think this proposal would be a mistake."

Black Hat: Participants identify and examine all of the potential negatives of the issue. They should be critical, cautious, and defensive. This perspective is important—and often neglected because people usually want to be positive and optimistic. But if you're aware of the potential negatives of an issue, you can work to reduce or eliminate them and/or to plan appropriately. "We need to wear our black hats for a while, because we're getting caught up in our enthusiasm over this idea."

Yellow Hat: Participants think positively. They take an optimistic perspective to consider all of the good points involved in an issue. This perspective is especially important when dealing with a problem or considering a decision that's an uneasy compromise or necessitated by circumstances. "It seems that we're going to need to make this change whether we like it or not, so maybe we should put on the yellow hats for a moment and find the silver lining in this cloud."

Green Hat: Participants allow their creativity to play freely. The emphasis is on imagination—possibilities, alternatives, and new ideas; critical analysis is suspended. "OK, now, we've been going around in circles with this problem. It's time to try our green hats."

Blue Hat: Participants are thinking about the process, not the issue. This is the hat that decides which hat might be best to wear next. "I'm putting on my blue hat and deciding that we should do some more red hat thinking here."

So, in summary, the six thinking hats technique consists of five focused perspectives or approaches and a hat that serves as the fashion sense, to decide which hat would be most appropriate at any given point.

TRICKS OF THE TRADE

Develop Differences

Perhaps the most neglected yet important aspect of promoting better interaction for discussing, generating ideas, solving problems, and making decisions is to invite to the meeting individuals with diverse perspectives, a range of experiences, and different thinking styles.

To get new perspectives on your employees, read any article or book on thinking or collaborating styles—such as *Team Players and Teamwork: The New Competitive Business Strategy* by Glenn M. Parker (San Francisco: Jossey-Bass, 1996)—and then try to analyze each of your people in terms of those styles. That new perspective could enable you to ensure diversity of thinking in your meetings.

Effort-Impact Matrix

This tool, also known as the *effort-impact grid,* is used in effort/impact analysis. This type of analysis is appropriate when the top criteria for decisions are the effort (time, money, difficulty) needed to implement them and the impact (effectiveness) expected from them, and the number of items to consider is small. The effort-impact matrix can also be used to choose which project among many to undertake first.

The group plots each choice along gradients of effort and impact, such that the choices fall somewhere within one of four quadrants (Figure 6-2). The group should decide in advance how it will prioritize the quadrants, according to the situation.

In general, low-effort, high-impact choices are best and high-effort, low-impact choices would come last. But then, which quadrant rates higher: high-effort, high-impact or low-effort, low-impact? The group may decide to act on choices that are low-effort and low-impact as resources allow and to study choices that are high-effort and high-impact. However, a group that wants to focus on a single choice that will make the biggest difference would want the choice with the greatest impact, regardless of the effort involved.

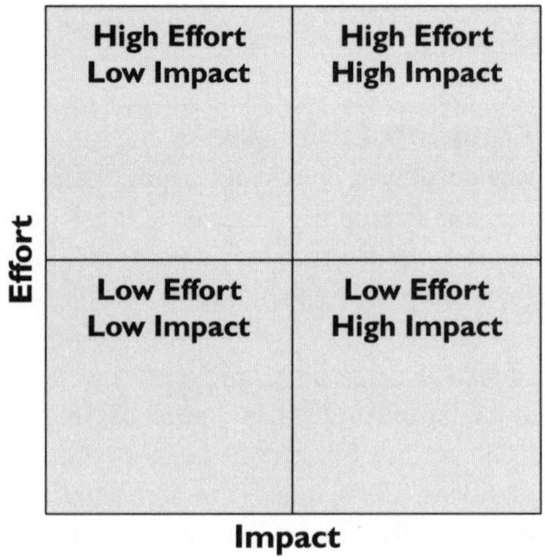

Effort	**High Effort Low Impact**	**High Effort High Impact**
	Low Effort Low Impact	**Low Effort High Impact**
	Impact	

Figure 6-2. Effort-impact matrix

If the members reach agreement on priorities before analyzing each of the choices, the group can avoid the time and energy that might be spent after the choices are plotted in the matrix, as some members advocate for specific pet projects.

Make Choices Involving Multiple Factors

Making a group decision that everyone accepts and works to implement can be tricky, but there are some useful methods you can use to do this. Let's look at some of these.

Paired Comparison Analysis

Paired comparison analysis, also known as comparative valuation, is used to work out the importance of a number of options relative to each other, to set priorities. It makes it easier for the group to decide, for example, which problem to solve or which solution to implement. The tool—a priority grid—provides a structure for comparing each option against each of the others.

Here's how to use paired comparison analysis:

1. The scribe lists all of the options and gives each a simple label (one or two words or a number or letter).
2. The scribe draws up a priority grid with enough rows and columns to allow for the options.
3. The scribe enters each option as both a row header and a column header. (See Figure 6-3.)

	Option A	Option B	Option C	Option D
Option A	—			
Option B		—		
Option C			—	
Option D				—

Figure 6-3. Priority grid for paired comparison analysis

4. The facilitator leads the group in comparing each option with each other option, one by one. The group decides which of the two options is more important and the scribe marks the cell where the row and column intersect with the label assigned to that option. The group can also rate the difference in importance by assigning a score, such as 1 (little difference) to 3 (big difference); the scribe puts the score in the cell.

   (Of course, cells remain empty where the group would be comparing an option with itself—normally along the diagonal running from top left to bottom right of the grid. Also, the group will not be duplicating any comparisons—normally all cells below the diagonal. The scribe can block out all the superfluous cells.)
5. The facilitator adds up the cells marked for each option and, if there are scores, the scores for each option. Often this is followed by discussion of the choices as a check to make sure that the option with the highest total score really makes sense as the best choice.

Grid Analysis

Grid analysis is effective for making a decision, especially when there are a number of alternatives and many factors to consider.

Here are the steps for using a grid (also known as a *decision table*):

1. The group lists the options.
2. The group lists the factors that are important for making the decision.
3. The scribe makes a grid, listing the options as rows and the factors as columns.
4. For each factor, the group assigns a weight to show its importance. (If the group is unable to agree on weights, it can use paired comparison analysis to determine relative importance.) The scribe marks the weight on the grid beneath the factor heading.

5. The group rates each option in terms of each factor, from 0 (poor) to 3 (very good). The scribe puts the rating in the cell.
6. After the group has rated all of the options in terms of each of the factors, the scribe multiplies each rating by the weight of the factor, to arrive at a score in each cell of the grid.
7. The scribe adds up the scores for each option. The option with the highest score is the best.

Figure 6-4 shows an example of a completed grid.

Options	Time 3	Cost 8	Other Resources 6	Negative Effects on Division 3	Negative Effects on Customers 8	Total Scores
	Factors and Weights					
Launch new product	1=3	1=8	1=6	2=6	3=24	**47**
Expand current product market	2=6	1=8	2=12	1=3	3=24	**53**
Raise price of current product	3=9	3=24	3=18	0=0	1=8	**59**

Figure 6-4. Grid analysis

Again, this is usually followed by some discussion to make sure the option with the highest point score makes sense as the first choice. In general, grids are useful structures to ensure systematic discussion, but it's not wise to let the math alone make the decision.

Multivoting

Multivoting is effective when the group needs to prioritize a lot of ideas.

1. The scribe lists and numbers the ideas to be considered on a flip chart, a blackboard, a whiteboard, or other display area.

2. The facilitator determines the number of votes to allow the participants. It's generally a third of the number of choices. So, for example, if there are 25 choices, allow nine votes.
3. Ask the participants to each write down their selections silently.
4. The participants then register their votes. There are several ways of doing this. The facilitator may go down the list and ask for a show of hands (votes) for each choice. The facilitator may distribute sticky dots or colored markers to all participants and ask them to place one dot or a mark (a vote) next to each of their choices.
5. The facilitator counts the votes for each choice and the scribe records the tallies. The top choices are then prioritized in the order of the number of votes received. It may be necessary to have a second round of voting; if so, the group can drop from contention ideas receiving the fewest votes.

> **Stock Your Tool Box**
>
> Smart Managing
>
> We're all familiar with the saying, "If all you have is a hammer, everything looks like a nail." If you're using only one tool or technique, the odds are pretty good you're using it wrong sometimes. Unfortunately, sometimes a technique or a tool works well enough that managers don't explore other options and thus limit the possibilities for their groups.

As mentioned at the beginning of this chapter, there are many techniques and tools for meetings, presented in more complete detail in other books. With a little experience, you'll find which of the ones presented in this chapter and which you find elsewhere work best for your purposes and the culture and spirit of your group.

Nominal Group Technique

This technique is used to obtain many contributions on an issue in a structured brainstorming format and then to prioritize the ideas, factors, or solutions. It's a good way to get many ideas from a group, especially for identifying causes and solving problems and for planning.

Nominal group technique was developed to eliminate the social and psychological dynamics of group behavior that tend to inhibit individual creativity and participation. The process is a structured variation of conventional group discussion methods, with some significant advantages:

- It allows every member of the group an equal opportunity to contribute.
- It prevents individuals from dominating the discussion.
- It encourages more passive members to participate in the discussion.
- It allows the group to reach agreement faster.
- It uses different processes for different phases of decision-making.

Here's how nominal group technique works:

1. The facilitator states the problem, question, or task and the scribe writes it on the flipchart, blackboard, or whiteboard.
2. Each member of the group spends several minutes silently thinking about the issue and writing down on a sheet of paper as many ideas as possible.
3. The facilitator asks each participant, in turn, to share one idea from his or her list. No discussion is allowed, although members may ask the contributor to clarify. The scribe records the ideas on the flip chart or board.
4. This process continues until all ideas have been contributed and recorded. Participants may pass if they run out of ideas. They may also build upon ideas suggested.
5. The facilitator reads each idea listed and asks for any questions, clarifications, or interpretations. The facilitator should not allow comments to turn into arguments. The group can combine similar ideas or drop repetitive ideas, if all participants agree. The scribe should number (consecutively) each idea that the group discusses and keeps. (Up to this point, the method has been a highly structured version of brainstorming.)

6. The facilitator gives each participant the same number of blank index cards (between three and seven, usually five). We'll assume five here, for the sake of simplicity; the pattern would be expanded for six or seven and reduced for three or four. Then the group prioritizes the ideas in the last two groups.
7. Each participant writes down, one per card, the five ideas on the list that he or she feels are the most important, with the number. Then he or she rates each idea selected, in the following way:
   - Choose the most important and write a 5 in a circle in the lower right corner of the card.
   - Choose the least important and write a 1 in a circle in the lower right corner of the card.
   - Choose the most important of the remaining three cards and write a 4 in a circle in the lower right corner of the card.
   - Choose the least important of the remaining two cards and write a 2 in a circle in the lower right corner of the card.
   - On the remaining card write a 3 in a circle in the lower right corner of the card.
8. The facilitator collects all of the cards and shuffles them. He or she then reads from each card the idea and the points. On the flip chart, the scribe marks the points next to the idea.
9. After reading all of the cards, the facilitator adds up the points for each idea and the scribe records the total.

Implementing the Decision

Once the group has made a decision, it's useful to explore what's involved in its implementation, including potential problems. Force field analysis is a method for doing that.

Force Field Analysis

Force field analysis is a technique for considering what a group needs to do to successfully implement a decision. Once a decision has been made, a force field analysis can help the group identify actions to take to improve the chances of success.

The analysis shows the forces that the group could or should work to strengthen and the forces that the group could or should try to remove or weaken.

The technique of force field analysis was developed by Kurt Lewin, a pioneer in the social sciences, who assumed that in any situation there are forces that influence any change that may occur. He labeled them "driving forces" and "restraining forces."

To carry out a force field analysis:

- The scribe draws a T chart and labels one side "driving forces" or "pros" and the other side "restraining forces" or "cons."
- The facilitator asks the group to identify forces either driving or restraining the decision. As suggestions come forth, the group assigns to each force a score from 1 (weak) to 5 (strong). The scribe records the force and its score in the appropriate column.
- As the group lists restraining forces, it may also think of driving forces that counterbalance them. On the other hand, sometimes listing a driving force can cause the group to come up with one or more restraining forces.

The point is to identify as many forces as possible on each side, to have the most complete picture of the context of the decision under consideration. Then the group can discuss the restraining forces and propose ways to remove or weaken them and/or discuss the driving forces to find ways of maximizing them.

Manager's Checklist for Chapter 6

- ❑ There are many techniques and tools for discussions, generating ideas, solving problems, and making decisions. It's essential to know which techniques and tools work for what purposes and in what situations, in order to understand how and why the techniques and tools succeed, and then to use the techniques and tools appropriately.

- ❑ Whether you want the group to make a decision, solve a problem, or come up with ideas, you must break the process down into steps in order to choose and use any technique or tool properly.
- ❑ To identify the cause(s) of a problem, repetitive why analysis or a cause-and-effect diagram (fishbone analysis) is effective.
- ❑ To generate ideas, many people use brainstorming (in some form), but mind-mapping and displayed thinking can also help. Following that, an affinity diagram is a good way to organize ideas, to discover key themes and issues.
- ❑ To analyze alternatives, there's the simplicity of PMI and the fun focus of the six thinking hats.
- ❑ To make choices involving multiple factors, the effort-impact matrix is good for possible actions, while paired comparison analysis and grid analysis allow a group to make a choice when there are many factors to consider.
- ❑ To prioritize a list of items or choose among issues under consideration, two standard approaches are the nominal group technique and multivoting.
- ❑ To understand what actions are needed to successfully implement a choice, use force field analysis.

Uh-Oh ... Now What? Problems and Possibilities

The possibility of problems always exists when you bring people together in any situation, including meetings. So in this chapter we'll discuss some of the more common and/or serious problems that occur in meetings that were first listed in Chapter 1. Keep in mind, however, that no book can offer solutions for every situation—nor can any solution work in all instances of a situation.

We hope that you'll never need this chapter—but we know that you will, unfortunately. We recommend that you pass along this book to each person that you select to serve as facilitator, when you give him or her the "good news," and suggest reading this chapter.

An Ounce of Prevention

Dealing with problems during a meeting is most difficult—not necessarily because of the nature or severity of the problems, but because problems during a meeting are generally not your responsibility, but the responsibility of the facilitator and the other members of the group.

But you can take some preventive measures to reduce the chances of major problems. Chapter 2 recommended talking with participants one on one in advance of the meeting to reduce the possibility of problems resulting from personality conflicts.

If you suspect problems are likely or even possible, you can suggest in advance that the facilitator begin the meeting by setting a constructive tone. He or she can mention that there are items on the agenda that could bring out differences of opinion and reinforce that these differences are useful and often lead to better discussions and decisions—as long as the focus is on the issues, not the people. The facilitator should express trust that the participants will keep in mind the purposes of the meeting and act responsibly in the best interests of the group.

Then, later in the meeting, if unproductive conflicts break out, the facilitator can remind the clashing participants and others of the importance of constructive disagreement.

Better Than Any Suggestions

For many situations that may arise during a meeting, the first and generally best remedy are the ground rules your group has set for its meetings. (Those ground rules should also help prevent problems or at least limit their severity.)

They're probably better than any suggestions this chapter could offer, for two reasons:

- Your group developed them, by consensus.
- They're appropriate to your environment and culture.

If no ground rules govern the situation, then the suggestions offered in this chapter might help. If your situation is not covered here, then maybe a suggestion for a similar circumstance might apply.

If you find that you and your facilitators are improvising remedies more than occasionally, it might be time to review the rules and revise them to better fit your needs.

Getting Started

Let's look at some of the problems that might occur just as meetings are getting started.

> **Don't Rush to Rule**
>
> CAUTION!
>
> Be wary about feeling that for every problem there should be a ground rule. Keep these rules as simple as possible. The more rules you have, the easier it is for participants to neglect the principles behind them—such as respect, collaboration, and efficiency.

Late Arrivals and No-Shows

A person arrives late. The facilitator should ignore the arrival and simply continue. This reaction minimizes the effects of the interruption and doesn't shift the attention from the agenda to the individual. You could follow up by talking with the person after the meeting, if you're curious about his or her reason(s) for arriving late.

Late arrivals become common. If it's the same person or several people arriving late, you should meet with them one on one and discuss the importance of starting meetings as scheduled. Find out why they are arriving late and work to address the causes.

> **Don't Punish with Work**
>
> CAUTION!
>
> Avoid assigning tasks as punishments. That sends the message that contributing to the group effort is something bad, rather than a normal responsibility.

If arriving late is a widespread problem, you might consider whether it would help to establish a ground rule about arriving late. However, since some delays are inevitable, you would be placing the facilitator or yourself in the uncomfortable position of deciding whether a reason is acceptable or not—which may make members of the group feel as if they're back in school—not a good thing.

It seems wiser to give participants more reason to arrive on time. How are you beginning meetings? Do you get to essential agenda items immediately or do you spend time on matters that are less important? If participants feel that the first few minutes don't mean much, you're actually encouraging them to arrive late.

You could also consider scheduling meetings for "first thing," so participants are less likely to be delayed, at least not by work matters. But if the beginning of meetings is not interesting to participants, this approach is unlikely to work.

People invited to a meeting don't show up. You should talk one to one with anybody who misses a meeting. There may be a valid explanation—or it may reveal a problem with the meetings. If it's a chronic problem with one or several individuals, you should assign some responsibility, to give the individuals a more compelling reason to attend the meetings. You might make them informants, responsible for providing information about an agenda item.

Group Interaction

Problems that occur in the interaction between people at the meeting are common and can be quite vexing and an important reason people don't like meetings. Here's how to anticipate and deal with some of the problems you'll likely encounter.

Confusion

Participants seem to be confused. The facilitator should ask them why they're confused.

If it's because they don't understand the purpose of the meeting and/or the agenda, the facilitator should review the purpose and the agenda.

If it's because they haven't read the agenda in advance and are not prepared, take note and make a point of providing more details in your agendas and even indicating how you expect participants to prepare for the meetings.

Weak Participation

Participants are apparently thinking about other things or even dozing off. This is a tough situation, because there could be various reasons. Are they disinterested in the agenda? Do they feel that the meeting isn't challenging them? Are they just bored with the pace and/or the tone?

If they're disinterested, it may be because they feel there's little or no need for them to be attending the meeting or at least all of it. Find out. If so and they're right, then think more carefully about the people you're including in meetings.

If they're not interested because the meeting isn't addressing any issues that matter to them, at the end of the meeting the facilitator should encourage them to suggest items for the agendas of upcoming meetings.

If the meeting isn't challenging them, there's a remedy for the moment and a remedy for later. The facilitator can involve them with questions, calling on them by name. If this problem develops over more than one meeting, you can try another tactic: assign the individuals responsibility for providing information or even leading the discussion of an agenda item. This approach has two major benefits:

- The individuals will not be inattentive for the entire meeting, because they will be in the spotlight for at least a little while.
- The individuals will better appreciate the greater difficulty of conducting a meeting when members of the group don't get involved.

If they're bored, find out why. Meetings should inspire participants with a sense of purpose, with enthusiasm about achieving goals. The problem could be, in part, with the agenda—the items and/or the format. How did the meeting begin? There should be positive energy from the start: participants should feel that they are gathered to collaborate and accomplish. How is the facilitator conducting the meeting? As mentioned in Chapter 4, the facilitator should set and maintain an appropriate pace. If you suspect that the problem may be, to some extent, with the facilitator, you may want to prepare the facilitator a little better. You might also think more carefully about the time allocations on the agenda.

TRICKS OF THE TRADE

Lend a Hand

If a facilitator is not maintaining a suitable pace and participants are showing signs of boredom or impatience, you might want to help him or her by sending a subtle signal to pick up the pace.

If the facilitator is moving too quickly, so participants are having trouble contributing or maybe even following, a signal should make him or her aware of the problem.

If pacing is a consistent problem and involves more than one or two facilitators, the problem could be in the agenda. It may be that you need to allocate time more appropriately.

There's another tactic when participants aren't paying attention or getting involved, but it's risky. Bring "toys" to the meeting. Some people listen better when they have something like play dough to work with during the meeting. However, if the lack of attention and involvement is because the meeting doesn't seem important to those members of the group, then you need to address the purpose of the meeting.

Some participants remain silent. This problem may be similar to the preceding problem of participants being inattentive and uninvolved, depending on the cause(s). That's a judgment call for the facilitator and for you. Is the meeting uninteresting? Is it unchallenging? Is it boring? If it seems that the silence is due to any of these factors, the facilitator should try the recommendations above.

However, participants may remain silent because they haven't prepared sufficiently for the meeting. If the facilitator suspects that this is the reason, he or she should ask them questions that don't require any preparation, just thinking, such as to comment on contributions by others. In other words, don't punish them or exclude them, but find ways for them to contribute.

Maybe, on the other hand, the silence is due to personality and/or group dynamics: some people are usually quiet around others, while some are quiet only in certain situations. An instinctive reaction for the facilitator might be to call on a quiet person to contribute. That tactic is often not very effective—and it can cause other quiet members of the group to resent the facilitator. A more effective tactic might be to circle the group for comments, allowing individuals to pass when it's their turn. It's about opportunities, not obligations.

This tactic can be particularly effective if the facilitator can select individuals because of their special expertise, experience, or interests; e.g., "Adriana, I believe that you've worked with this issue in the past. Would you like to share anything you've learned from that?"

> **Responsibility Through Advocacy**
>
> MISTAKE PROOFING
>
> To encourage participation at meetings, a colleague recommended this approach, borrowed from Native American tribes. When people would gather to discuss and make decisions, each person would be assigned the responsibility of representing a constituency, including entities such as nature. The person would be expected to participate from the perspective of his or her assigned constituency and to serve as advocate.

Finally, if there's enough time and space, the facilitator could also break the group into twos and threes to discuss the issue and report back to the group.

The group is generally not participating much. The facilitator could either try to guess at the reason(s) for the lack of involvement—or just ask! There may be an issue that the group should address before continuing. It could take a change in the agenda or a short break.

But what if there are no specific reasons or, at least, no reasons that the group can address? Then, the facilitator could break the group into twos and threes and give them some challenging questions, to provoke them to think, or try one of the techniques described in Chapter 6.

You should also analyze the situation. Maybe the time is wrong, such as immediately after lunch, first thing Monday morning, or late on a Friday afternoon. If you're providing refreshments, maybe that's part of the problem: rich foods can undermine participation, so fruits and vegetables might improve participation for future meetings. Again, rather than just guess, you might try asking; when the members of the group do their evaluation at the end of the meeting, add a question or two about why there's so little participation and what could be done to increase it.

Too Much Talk, Not Enough Action

Too many people are talking at once. The facilitator should thank them for their enthusiasm, but then remind them that good contributions can be lost if more than one person is talking at any one time and that the confusion can keep some people out of the discussion.

If appropriate, the facilitator can direct traffic, by pointing to individuals, one at a time, to give them the floor. The facilitator can also suggest going around the group for comments, to establish a "natural" sequence of contributions. There's no reason to go formal—"The chair recognizes ..."—but just to direct the vehicles of thought a little to avoid traffic jams.

> Tricks of the Trade
>
> **Keep on the Ball**
>
> If participants talk over each other, here's a gimmick that should help maintain order. Provide the facilitator with a foam ball. When a discussion opens, the facilitator tosses the ball to the first member of the group who signals that he or she wants to contribute. Then, that participant tosses the ball to the next member who signals. The facilitator may occasionally have to direct a toss, but at least everybody will know at any moment which person has the floor.

Someone keeps bringing up the same point. Often, what motivates people to repeat a point is that they think others don't understand them. The facilitator should summarize the person's statement to make sure that all understand.

If the person continues to repeat the point, the facilitator can indicate the flipchart or other display where the scribe has already recorded that idea: "We've already got that point here. Are you offering any additional support for it or any new perspectives?" He or she then invites others to contribute, to assume responsibility for the meeting. This tactic encourages contributions from the other members and emphasizes that all members of the group are responsible for the meeting—and conveys the message that nobody should monopolize the discussion.

The group is stuck on the same point, repeating comments, not coming up with anything new. This situation is just like the preceding, except in quantity—unless there's not a single member to call on to break the group out of the rut. In that case, to dislodge participants from their positions, the facilitator should change the discussion activity. It might help, for example, to have the scribe list the positions and then go into the technique of the six thinking hats, described in Chapter 6—especially the black hat (to identify potential negatives), the red hat (to react emotionally), and the white hat (to look for gaps in knowledge).

A participant continues on an issue, but the others are not contributing. Before reacting to this situation, the facilitator should try to figure out why only one person is participating in the discussion.

- Is he or she the resident expert on the issue under discussion?
- Is he or she popular, charismatic, a natural leader to whom others naturally defer?
- Is he or she the only member of the group interested in the issue?
- Is he or she boring or annoying the others?

Diagnosis: the soloist is the resident expert on the issue under discussion. Maybe the group is ready to make a decision, since it seems that the members have reached consensus. The facilitator should ask them if it's time to decide.

Diagnosis: the soloist is popular, charismatic, a natural leader. It can be difficult to work around an aura, but here's an idea that might work. The facilitator can distribute index cards, one to a person, and leave extras in the middle of the table, just in case. Then, he or she asks the members of the group to each write down three concerns that somebody outside this group, who would be affected by this decision, might have. This approach of shifting the context of the discussion to the perspectives of outsiders may shake the influence of the thought leader. Then the facilitator collects and reads the cards and the scribe records the concerns. This technique allows members of the group to express their own concerns anonymously, and you may find that others share these concerns.

Diagnosis: the soloist is the only member of the group interested in the issue. If the facilitator suspects that disinterest is the restraining force, he or she should ask the group if they want to move to make a decision.

Diagnosis: the soloist is boring or annoying the others. The facilitator can use the approach suggested above when some participants remain silent: "Now we know how Terry feels. Who else is willing to share some thoughts?"

Conversations on the Side

Participants are talking among themselves. Not all side conversations are bad. Sometimes they can serve the same purpose as breaking up the group into twos and threes: they allow members of the group to express themselves less publicly. If there are several side conversations going, the facilitator could suggest that the other members form clusters, too. Then he or she should put a question or two on display for the clusters to discuss. If the facilitator asks each cluster to sum up its discussion and conclusions on a sheet of paper or index card, it should help focus chatters on the agenda item.

OK, that's how side conversations can be good. In general, however, they're distracting and annoying. There are some things that the facilitator can do to discourage chats:

- If seated, stand.
- Try to create eye contact with the chatters.
- Walk around the room, slowly, and then stand near the chatters, for as long as it takes.
- Talk louder.

- Tap on the table to call for order.
- Say that you are distracted by multiple conversations and ask to limit talking to the discussion.
- Call on the chatters by name to invite them to contribute.

It Takes All Kinds

Smart Managing

It's important for a manager or a facilitator to keep in mind that a meeting is work and that people work in various ways. The facilitator should exercise judgment and discretion in governing this micro society. The sidebar, "The Psychological Dynamics of Teamwork," presents one way to better understand the members of your group.

The Psychological Dynamics of Teamwork

Problems with participation may be a factor of personality types. To facilitate interactions more effectively and efficiently, the facilitator should understand the basics of *team player styles.*

Glenn M. Parker explored this aspect of personality in his book, *Team Players and Teamwork: The New Competitive Business Strategy* (San Francisco: Jossey-Bass, 1996). His research revealed that there are four team player styles that are essential to the success of any team. We all have characteristics of each style, to a greater or lesser extent, but each of us has a dominant style.

Contributor: Provides information and focuses the group on the task at hand.

Positive characteristics: dependable, responsible, organized, efficient, logical, clear, relevant, pragmatic, systematic

Negative characteristics: shortsighted, compulsive, hung up on facts, uncreative, perfectionist

Collaborator: Provides a sense of direction, gets the group to set goals, and emphasizes overall purpose.

Positive characteristics: cooperative, flexible, confident, focused on the future, conceptual, accommodating, generous, open, visionary, imaginative

Negative characteristics: overly committed, overly involved, too global, overly ambitious, insensitive

Communicator: Attends to "people issues" and helps the group address matters of process.

Positive characteristics: supportive, encouraging, relaxed, informal, spontaneous, helpful, friendly, patient, considerate, tactful

Negative characteristics: aimless, foolish, placating, impractical, manipulative

Challenger: Encourages the group to question its methods and goals, asks tough questions, and pushes the team to take reasonable risks.

Positive characteristics: candid, questioning, outspoken, straightforward, ethical, honest, truthful, principled, adventurous, brave

Negative characteristics: rigid, arrogant, self-righteous, contentious, quibbling

Focus

Not focusing appropriately on the issues can be another reason people tend to avoid meetings. Let's look at some of the problems in this area and what to do about them.

Too Little Focus

A participant is talking around the issue, not making his or her point. The facilitator should not single out any particular participant: that reaction could embarrass the person in question and have a chilling effect on participation by others in the group.

The facilitator should wait until he or she is opening the next discussion, and then request that participants try to communicate concisely. He or she should remind them of the time allotted to the discussion and suggest that each contribution be limited to about two minutes.

That doesn't mean that the timekeeper will necessarily need to clock the contributions, but the facil-

TRICKS OF THE TRADE

Styles and Strengths

A facilitator who can identify the characteristics of team player styles can build on the positive.

To help the group get out of problem situations, the facilitator can encourage participants whose styles are most beneficial. Here are some general situations and the style that might be most appropriate:

- If the group is getting caught up in digressions—Collaborators
- If a discussion seems to be too soft, not probing and questioning—Challengers
- If emotions are rising and straining collaboration—Communicators
- If the discussion is becoming abstract—Contributors

itator should signal—tactfully—any participant who obviously exceeds the limit.

A participant starts getting into another, unrelated issue. The easiest way for the facilitator to handle the situation is simply to say, "We're getting away from the agenda now. Maybe this issue should be set aside for another meeting." Then the group can decide later whether or not to put the issue on an agenda in the future.

The facilitator could also turn the digression over to the group, by asking for reactions: "Who would like to relate these comments to our discussion?" If others can find connections, then the comments may not be really a digression. If not, then at least the digressive party has had a chance to shift the discussion, although not gaining support from the rest of the group.

If the discussion doesn't shift, the facilitator should return to the agenda item. If the digression has taken the group away from the agenda for a while, he or she should summarize the discussion or at least the most recent contributions in order to get the group back on track.

If the facilitator can't remember where the discussion was going before it veered off the track, he or she should ask members of the group to reconstruct the discussion. This approach can be a good way to encourage participation and recover momentum.

Participants are all going off on a tangent together. The facilitator should gesture toward the agenda (if displayed) or otherwise remind the group of the agenda item under consideration. He or she could then ask if there would be enough interest in the tangent to put it on the agenda for another meeting. If a show of hands indicates sufficient interest, consider scheduling it for an upcoming meeting. If you're unsure that it merits any consideration, you can e-mail participants and solicit their thoughts on the topic. It may be that you're missing something—or it may be that a lack of response will show that the tangent was interesting only at the moment and not worth any meeting time.

Participants are all going off in different directions at the same time. Here again, the facilitator should point to the agenda (if displayed) or otherwise remind the group of the agenda item under consideration. He or she should then invite the participants to submit their tangents to you for possible inclusion in a future meeting.

Then the facilitator should direct the discussion back on track, by reminding the group about the agenda item and the purpose: "We've strayed off the track a little from discussing ____ and trying to reach a decision about ____." Then he or she should turn to the notes kept on display by the scribe and review the last few relevant points.

Another possibility is for the facilitator to explore the reasons for the tangents: "It's been difficult for us to discuss this issue. Why?"

Too Much Focus

The group seems too focused on reaching a decision. It might not seem like it's really a problem for a group to be too focused on pursuing decisions. However, whether the impetus is general impatience, or a dominant participant, or a feeling of pressure to "just do something," this focus on making a decision usually causes tunnel vision.

If the facilitator senses that the group is feeling "action attraction," he or she should emphasize the process, that the group should discuss issues thoroughly before moving into a decision.

There are other suggestions below, for groupthink and for dealing with dominant personalities.

Group Dynamics and Individual Personalities

Group dynamics, the term itself conjures up problems for some people. Let's examine some group dynamics issues that get in the way of effective meetings.

Groupthink

As explained in Chapter 4, *groupthink* is the tendency of a group of people to seek unanimous agreement in spite of facts that would contradict such agreement. To help keep discussions healthy and worthwhile, here are some things you can do in advance:

- Assign one or more members to play the role of critical evaluator or devil's advocate.
- Invite outside experts to provide information and perspectives.
- Require the development of a certain number of options before moving toward a decision.
- Instruct the group to first develop a list of evaluation criteria before coming up with any ideas—and then ensure that the members use those criteria.

During a meeting, the facilitator can take any of the following actions:

- Elicit contributions from every member of the group.
- Encourage members to raise objections and concerns.
- Encourage the group to consider all contributions carefully.
- Praise members who show the courage to think independently.
- Challenge comments: "Is that a fact or an opinion?" or "Do we have any information to support the point that you're making?"
- Divide the group into smaller groups to discuss, then compare the results.

Dominant Participants

What types of participants might dominate a meeting?

- People who are experts—or are accepted as such by others in the group.
- People who are respected, admired, and followed by others in the group.

- People who are eloquent, who express their perspectives so well that others refrain from contributing.
- People who have strong personalities.

A participant is dominating by expertise. The facilitator should acknowledge the contribution and thank the participant for sharing his or her expertise. Then the facilitator might ask a question or two to redirect the discussion, so the others don't have to feel like contributing would be competing with the expert in that particular area.

If the participant won't stop, the facilitator should interrupt—tactfully, of course: "Thanks, Bob. You obviously know a lot about this issue and we probably should have scheduled you to do a little presentation. However, we have only X minutes left for this item and we should allow everybody a chance to contribute."

A participant is dominating by status. This situation is similar to the first. It may be prudent for the facilitator to pause slightly after the participant finishes, acknowledge the contribution, and then ask a question that shifts the direction of the discussion slightly, so that other members of the group don't feel obligated to follow up on that contribution. Otherwise, you can expect silence or comments in agreement.

A participant is dominating by eloquence. The facilitator should acknowledge the person—"Thank you for expressing your opinions/concerns so eloquently"—and then sum up the points. This straightforward summation breaks from the eloquence and may make the others feel less inadequate about joining the discussion. The facilitator may also want to ask a very specific question, to channel the flow of contributions.

A participant is dominating by personality. The facilitator can try reminding the participant that he or she should allow others to contribute. If a reminder isn't enough, the facilitator should circle the group, going around to each member in turn.

As a last resort, the facilitator should take personality out of the equation. A good way to do this is by having a "silent discussion." He or she should hand out index cards to the members of the group and ask them to write their comments on the issue or answers to a specific question that the facilitator puts on the flipchart. Then, the facilitator collects the cards and reads them aloud; the scribe takes notes. In this way, every member of the group gets an equal opportunity to participate. No index card ever dominated by personality.

Disruptive Behavior

A few members of the group are goofing around. The facilitator can ignore the behavior and assume that those involved will stop on their own or under pressure from their peers. He or she can also try asking them to settle down, in a kind, lighthearted way. The focus should be on what's better for the group, not on what the facilitator wants or what the rules specify—unless the "fun bunch" fails to respect the request. If there are a lot of people goofing around, it may be more effective to suggest a five-minute break, since it's likely that they're feeling overloaded or worn out.

Someone is telling jokes or otherwise trying to entertain. The facilitator should try something like "We appreciate a little humor, but we need all the time we have for the agenda."

Someone who's disruptive won't calm down. As a last resort, the facilitator can call for a five-minute break. Then he or she should take the person aside, where they can talk one on one about what's behind the problem.

Negativity

A participant is critical about ideas and opinions expressed by other participants. The facilitator should deal with the negative comments, but frame them constructively, using affirmative language to phrase them as questions or suggestions. If, for example, the person complains about wasting time on a certain issue, the facilitator might say, "You seem to be wondering if we could deal with this issue more efficiently. Do you have any suggestions for doing this?" The tone should be positive and inviting, not challenging. The opportunity to offer suggestions may put an end to the negativity—or some good ideas may come of it.

A participant makes a contribution that the other members of the group dismiss or ignore. This reaction is what the authors of *The Team Handbook* label "discounts and flops" (p. 7-21).

They recommend that the facilitator support the participant and encourage discussion: e.g., "Anna, it seems like this point is important to you and we should give it some consideration" or "I believe that what Kati just said brings a new perspective that we should discuss."

Emotions

Participants are becoming very emotional in their discussion. It's good for members of a group to be passionate about their work; most managers complain about the opposite, apathy. However, emotions can easily get out of control and destroy the spirit of collaboration.

If the facilitator believes that emotions are running too high, he or she should propose a five-minute break. (It's better to lose a little time than to lose any chance of accomplishing anything for the rest of the meeting.) Then, after the break, he or she should reconstruct the content of the heated exchanges as dispassionately as possible.

If it seems that the participants are still feeling too emotional about the issue, the facilitator should propose continuing the discussion at the next meeting. If a majority of the members agree, it's settled.

If not, then it might be a wise tactic to move to a round robin discussion, where each member of the group gets a chance to state his or her view and give two key reasons in support. Nobody comments on any of the opinions and nobody argues. After the circle, the facilitator summarizes areas of agreement and disagreement and asks for ideas to address and reconcile the disagreements.

Conflict

Any activity involving a group of people may produce conflict. That's natural. The facilitator should not assume that conflict in

Bill of Rights—and Responsibilities

You may want to copy and distribute the following to all members of the group:

Rights and Responsibilities of Meeting Participants

I have the right to feel respected—and the responsibility to help ensure that all members respect each other and feel respected.

I have the right to feel comfortable—and the responsibility to help ensure that all members feel comfortable.

I have the right to feel a sense of collaboration and cooperation—and the responsibility to help ensure that all members collaborate and cooperate.

a discussion is necessarily a negative consequence. Social scientists make a distinction between *objective* conflicts and *subjective* conflicts:

- *Objective* conflicts are over ideas and problems and suggestions for solutions.
- *Subjective* conflicts center on the people rather than the issues.

A conflict arises because of differences in opinion over an issue. It's probably an objective conflict, so it can be healthy for the group, which benefits from diverse perspectives. It may make the facilitator uncomfortable, but he or she should not try to end an objective conflict.

Objective conflict Discord over ideas and problems and suggestions for solutions, potentially healthy for the group.

Subjective conflict Discord centered on the people rather than the issues, potentially harmful for the group.

The danger of an objective conflict is that it could develop into a subjective conflict. So the facilitator should focus on keeping the conflict constructive and not allowing it to become personal. The facilitator should make sure that any conflict remains centered on the issue. If necessary, he or she should intervene to frame the conflict in objective, neutral, unemotional terms.

When a conflict arises, people outside the conflict generally tend to withdraw. That means that there might be less participation in general, as the protagonists in the conflict take over the meeting by their intense interaction. The facilitator should continue to encourage other members of the group to participate constructively. He or she should keep rephrasing "hot" comments in neutral, constructive terms and help all participants focus on the useful points raised.

Of course, if the facilitator senses that people are becoming uneasy about the conflict, he or she should intervene. Perhaps the most prudent course would be to hold up a hand toward each party in the universal "Stop!" gesture and then to sum up the positions—again, in objective, neutral, unemotional terms. An alternative—if the squabble has not gone too far—is to invite each party to phrase his or her position in 25 words.

When differences in opinion cause objective conflicts to become subjective, it often involves differences in values and/or preferences. The facilitator should try to keep the discussion focused on the issue, to minimize these differences.

It's possible to persuade conflicting participants

TOOLS

Timeout

When a conflict arises, participants who are not involved can feel uncomfortable, in large part because it may seem like the situation is out of control. It makes sense, then, to allow every member of the group a chance to exert control, just in case.

Explain at the first meeting, when the group sets its rules, and then repeat regularly at subsequent meetings, that any member of the group who feels at any time that a situation is getting out of control can call for a timeout. The signal is the two-handed signal used in sporting events, with hands open and flat, touching perpendicularly to form a T. Every meeting participant should know that it's his or her obligation to call a timeout, when necessary to help keep the meeting under control. When a timeout is called, the facilitator should announce a two-minute break. (It can be more or less, of course, at the discretion of the facilitator, according to the situation and the feelings of the group.)

to agree (either implicitly or explicitly) to work around their differences. It may be a matter of helping them to realize that those differences in values and/or preferences need not prevent them from working together. Or the facilitator can help them understand that for the good of the group they should put their energy into working together rather than fighting. When participants come together frequently for a significant purpose and experience success on joint goals, often relationships improve.

A conflict arises because of personality differences. The facilitator can attempt to cool the conflict by intervening decisively, saying something like "Could we all focus on the issues and not each other?"

Don't expect your facilitator to deal with these subjective conflicts. If there are feuds among your employees, it's your responsibility as manager to end them or at least to limit the effects they have on others and on meetings.

As mentioned toward the end of Chapter 2, you can reduce the potential for clashes caused by personality differences by talking with potentially contentious individuals prior to the meeting. And, as mentioned at the beginning of this chapter, the facilitator can begin the meeting by setting a constructive tone, if he or she suspects that personality conflicts are likely or even possible.

In short, it's up to the facilitator to deal with any problems that arise during the meeting, but it's your job to manage any ongoing conflicts that members of the group bring to the meeting. At the very least, you should help the group set rules to prohibit personal attacks, so that your facilitator has some means of dealing with situations that arise from relationship problems that you cannot resolve.

People are quibbling about trivial matters. The facilitator should help the group let go of the details and focus on the big picture, on the objective for that agenda item. It probably won't help to reprimand the group about wasting time, unless the facilitator is sure the participants are arguing about trivialities intentionally.

As mentioned at the start of this chapter, no book can cover

Modes of Conflict

To help members of the group feel less discomfort when conflicts arise, you might share with them the following. (In addition, you could also have them take the inventory.)

How do we handle conflict? The Thomas-Kilmann Conflict Mode Inventory can help us better understand ways of dealing with conflict.

In the mid-1970s, Kenneth W. Thomas and Ralph H. Kilmann devised a system that plotted a matrix of five conflict modes, in terms of two axes: unassertive-assertive (our desire to satisfy our own concerns) and uncooperative-cooperative (our desire to satisfy others' concerns).

Their model shows that conflict-handling behaviors are neither good nor bad. We improve our ability to resolve conflicts when we understand our reactions and can choose the most effective behaviors for a particular situation.

Here, in brief, are the five modes plotted by Thomas and Kilmann:

- ***Competing***: High assertive and low cooperative. The goal is to *win.*
- ***Avoiding***: Low assertive and low cooperative. The goal is to *delay or avoid altogether.*
- ***Compromising***: Moderate assertive and moderate cooperative. The goal is to *find a middle ground.*
- ***Collaborating***: High assertive and high cooperative. The goal is to *find a win-win situation.*
- ***Accommodating***: Low assertive and high cooperative. The goal is to *yield or go along.*

For information about this instrument, visit the Consulting Psychologists Press, Inc. Web site, www.cpp-db.com, or contact the company: 3803 East Bayshore Road, Palo Alto, CA 94303, phone: (800) 624-1765 or (650) 969-8901, fax: (650) 969-8608, e-mail: custserv@cpp-db.com.

all problem situations and no tactic can work every time. But the principles applied in this chapter should guide you in dealing with any other problems that arise.

And now, all that remains is to do a quick overview of how technology is changing the ways in which we meet.

Manager's Checklist for Chapter 7

- ❑ Dealing with problems during a meeting is difficult—not necessarily because of the nature or severity of the problem, but because problems during a meeting are generally not your responsibility, but the responsibility of the facilitator. You should recommend that any person you select to be a facilitator read this chapter.
- ❑ Take preventive measures to reduce the chances of major problems. To reduce the possibility of problems resulting from personality conflicts, talk with participants one on one in advance of the meeting and then begin the meeting by reminding everyone to focus on the purposes of the meeting and act responsibly in the best interests of the group.
- ❑ For many situations that may arise during a meeting, the first and generally best remedy is the rules your group has set for its meetings, because your group developed them, by consensus, and they're appropriate to your environment and culture. The rules should specify how to deal with any violations.
- ❑ No book can cover all troublesome situations and no tactic can work every time. But the principles applied in this chapter should guide you in dealing with most problems.

Technological Tools and Meeting Virtually

This chapter is *about* technology—but it's not really *on* technology.

It won't tell you all about the specific technological tools you can use to meet in ways other than face to face, same time, same place. The tools change too quickly for any book to cover them at all adequately. In the weeks that it takes this chapter to go from my computer to the bookstores, the technological tools discussed here will change, perhaps significantly, or even dramatically.

Besides, there are thousands of sales reps who will be more than happy to tell you all about what their products and services can help you do. And, as you explore the possibilities of those technologies, a technician in your organization will be able to advise you on the technical requirements of any of these possibilities.

This chapter is about what you could be missing with those tools and how you can compensate.

What Makes a Meeting?

Technology is extending the concept of meetings as it expands the possibilities for communicating and collaborating. So, to start this final chapter, we return to the beginning of this book, to our definition of "meeting": *an event consisting of people, content, and process for a purpose.*

A systematic way to approach an overview of meeting technology is by considering the concept of meetings through the five W's and one H: who? what? when? where? why? and how?

In our simple definition of "meeting," the *people* are the *who,* the *content* is the *what,* and the *purpose* is the *why.* Those three dimensions are basic to any meeting. The remaining dimensions vary:

- The *where* is the location, an either/or situation: either one place or different places.
- The *when* is the time, another either/or: either one time or different times.
- The *how* is the methods and media (words and objects) used to communicate and collaborate, and the senses. (Technology is limited—so far!—to the eyes and the ears, so we talk in terms of *visual* and *aural.*)

The virtual meetings that technology allows still fit the basic definition of *meeting* as an event consisting of people, content, and process for a purpose. (At least the common definition of *event* as "an occurrence, a social occasion or activity," although not the more specific and scientific definition in Merriam-Webster—"the fundamental entity of observed physical reality represented by a point designated by three coordinates of place and one of time in the space-time continuum postulated by the theory of relativity." Whew!) But by changing the dimensions of the events, the technology challenges us to think differently about our meetings.

Technology frees us from the necessity of meeting in one place. It can also free us from the necessity of meeting at one

Key Term **Virtual** "Being in essence or effect but not in fact," according to dictionaries published before the cyber boom. A virtual meeting is communication and collaboration involving two or more people who are not present in the same physical place and/or at the same time.

time. It allows visual communication and collaboration, through text and through images (still and moving). It allows aural communication and collaboration, through words and through sounds. So we'll discuss technologies in terms of visual and/or aural and in terms of synchronous or asynchronous.

Some technologies can be used either synchronously or asynchronously, while others are either the former or the latter. (A funny thing about time: since it's a continuum of moments, there's not necessarily a real delineation between *synchronous* and *asynchronous*. If I send you an e-mail message and you reply within minutes of receiving it, our exchange is not synchronous, yet it's practically so. If we're using instant messaging and I step away from my computer to use the rest room, get a cup of coffee, check my mail, and chat for a few moments with a colleague in the hallway, by the time I get back to you, is our messaging still instant—synchronous?)

Key Term **Synchronous** Pertaining to interactions that happen more or less simultaneously, in real time.

"Real time" has become a buzzword of uncertain but positive meaning. (Who wouldn't want the real thing, rather than ... what? Fake time? Unreal time?) For example, there's now a sports utility vehicle that features "real-time" four-wheel drive.

Asynchronous Pertaining to interactions that happen at different times. An asynchronous system does not place time constraints on its users. It allows "serial meetings."

In any discussion of technology, you can be overwhelmed by all of the features and the promises. To understand what all of it means and, much more important, what it can mean to *you*, think in terms of the following three factors:

- What freedom the tools bring
- What you sacrifice for that freedom
- How you can compensate for those sacrifices

You're probably already using technology for virtual meetings, in some way. A phone conversation—one on one or conference call—can be a virtual meeting (aural, synchronous, and at a distance). An exchange of faxes can be a virtual meeting (visual, synchronous or asynchronous, and at a distance).

Virtual Meetings

The Internet and information technology facilitate people meeting when they're physically in different places.

Advantages

You're probably familiar with the advantages of virtual meetings, because the companies that produce and promote the many tools used for virtual meetings vie with each other to tout those advantages.

A major advantage—often cited first, at least by marketers and sales reps—is money. Virtual meetings are usually less expensive than face-to-face meetings:

- They eliminate the costs of travel, accommodations, and meals.
- They minimize the inconvenience of interrupting work.
- They reduce the loss of time and thus productivity.

Another major advantage is that virtual meetings can bring together people who are separated by space or time, such as employees who work in several locations and/or at different times.

There are also advantages that are harder to quantify or even to prove. Some claim that virtual meetings sharpen the sense of purpose, because they generally require more focus and more discipline. It could be argued that they do so to the extent that they reduce the opportunity for socializing. It's also

MISTAKE PROOFING

First, Come to Terms with the Terms

When discussing any technology with colleagues, your organization's tech staff, or vendors, make sure from the start that you're all understanding the terms in the same way. You may feel confused, but even the experts don't agree on what all of the terms mean specifically.

As we'll discuss later, terms like *teleconference*, *e-conference*, *Web conference*, and *multimedia conference* can have various meanings. Make sure you're not discussing apples and oranges or you may end up with a high-tech version of fruit salad.

claimed that virtual meetings can increase objectivity, because each participant feels the presence of others in the group less than in a face-to-face meeting. That benefit would be greatest with technologies that connect with words and asynchronously and least with video conferencing.

Disadvantages

On the other hand, you may not be aware of the disadvantages of virtual meetings. The most obvious disadvantage of virtual meetings is that they're not face-to-face: there's something missing or at least different in any technology, which means that both the possibilities, and the group, and individual dynamics are different.

Virtual meetings can work well for smaller groups, but they're more difficult if there are more participants. What size is optimal? What size is the maximum? That depends on the technology, of course, but also on the culture of the work environment and the dynamics of the participants. The greatest difficulty is using interactive techniques in a virtual meeting—the techniques presented in Chapter 6, and breaking into groups of two or three, for example.

Each technology presents different challenges, many of which we'll discuss in the following sections, as we outline the basic technologies for meeting virtually.

Audio Conferencing

Also known as a *conference call*, an audio conference connects three or more people by telephone or through the Internet.

The primary advantages of an audio conference are that it saves time and money, it's relatively simple to set up, and it's easy for people unfamiliar and/or uncomfortable with newer technology. It's an effective way to meet when there's no need to share visual materials or when the materials have already been shared through some other means, such as by e-mail, fax, or delivery service.

Preparation

E-mail or fax the agenda and send any other materials in advance.

Emphasize the importance of preparing. Pauses that would seem natural and normal in a face-to-face meeting can seem very long when the interaction of participants is aural only.

Emphasize that all participants must be ready to begin the conference on time. Ask remote participants to connect five minutes before the scheduled start time. If any participants are in different time zones, state the start time in all the relevant time zones, so there are no misunderstandings.

Allow in your agenda for a possible late start and delays due to technological problems as well as for a different "feeling of community" among participants.

Take precautions to keep your location quiet and free from distractions and interruptions. Remind all remote participants to do the same. Noises can divert attention and even be confusing when your only contact is aural. Side conversations can disrupt any meeting, but they're definitely to be discouraged when audio conferencing.

If any site is using a speakerphone, test the acoustics of the room to make sure that all participants are coming through loud and clear and that there are no echoes or other disruptive sounds.

Meeting

Start by asking each participant to identify himself or herself and—if any of the participants do not know each other—to explain briefly why he or she is involved in the meeting. This helps create a feeling of community and sets the tone for the meeting. It's also a good way to test the quality of the audio—far better than repeating, "Testing, 1, 2, 3" again and again, because it invites the participants to think about the people, rather than focus on the technology.

It's a good idea to post the names of all participants and their locations on a flipchart at each location, to create a "map" of the group. People who will be meeting together over a period of time can send photos of themselves, so there's also a visual sense.

After you review the agenda and objectives, establish guidelines for audio conferencing, such as the following:

- Identify yourself when you start to speak; e.g., "Pat Ohura, from Production, in Kalamazoo"—whatever it takes so that participants at other sites know who's talking.
- Pause from time to time to allow questions or other reactions—or just so others can take notes.
- Keep your contributions brief. If others want to know more, they'll ask.
- If you point to something on any materials, such as charts or handouts, specify what you're indicating.
- Imagine that the room is totally dark or your eyes are closed. That's how you're coming through to remote participants: if they can't hear it, you're not communicating it.

The facilitator should try to involve all participants and make it clear who should contribute when. It may be necessary to direct questions and comments to specific individuals or at least specific locations, for two reasons. First, without any visual cues, participants are likely to hesitate to contribute. Second, without visual cues, it's more likely that more than one participant at a time will start talking.

Somebody at each site should explain any actions or silence

at that location: e.g., "Pam is writing the ideas on a flipchart and Todd is taking notes, which he'll fax to you during the break," or "The silence here is all of us pondering that question."

At the end of the meeting, the participants should evaluate it. What worked? How could the meeting process be improved?

Why Meet?

Smart Managing

The Wharton Center for Applied Research reported in *The Wall Street Journal* that senior and middle managers said only 56% of meetings were productive and that phone calls, memos, e-mails, or voice mails could have replaced over 25% of the meetings. What would the percentage be in your organization, in your unit?

Follow-up

After the audio conference, use e-mail or fax to distribute the minutes and to encourage participants to ask any questions or share any concerns. If not all members of the group have access to computers, use alternative channels for communication.

Make available (on the organization's intranet or in the library) any records of the meeting—any presentations, audiotapes, videotapes, and so forth.

Set up a discussion list to allow further exploration of issues raised during the audio conference.

E-mail

Electronic mail is ideal for making announcements, sharing information, and eliciting opinions. It's also practical for serial meetings, in which participants can exchange information, opinions, suggestions, and so forth over a period of time. In fact, for some topics a discussion by e-mail might be more appropriate than a brief one-hour meeting, because an e-mail discussion allows participants more time to think and to consult resources.

An e-mail message will usually consist primarily of text, but it's possible to attach files to the messages, allowing participants to share documents, images, graphics, audio, and video—if each has the software to open the files.

E-mail is fast—sometimes almost synchronous. It's convenient. It's inexpensive. The technology is almost universal and simple to use. Also, e-mail may encourage people to be more candid, because they can't see the others to whom they're sending their messages.

Unlike synchronous means of communication, it allows people time to think. This may be an advantage particularly for people who are introverts or who are less at ease when they feel pressured to act quickly.

Each participant has a copy of every contribution—although sometimes messages can become so long and involved with replies that it's difficult to sort out the pieces. That's why it's useful to establish a protocol, such as the following:

- Keep contributions short, focused on one issue at a time.
- Identify the issue in your subject line.
- Begin each e-mail with your name, so it's easy to know immediately who's saying what.
- Put your contribution at the top of your e-mail, not inserted into previous texts.
- Make contributions easy to read: short sentences, short paragraphs.

Since e-mail has become so essential to most people in business, there's generally no need to explain how to use this technology. However, even experienced users will occasionally make mistakes, such as using "Reply" rather than "Reply All" or neglecting to identify the subject appropriately.

There are other potential problems. Do all members of the group have access to computers? If not, then make sure that you're also using alternative channels for communication. Technology should help us expand opportunities for collaboration, not exclude people or make them feel marginalized.

Bear in mind, too, that not all people who have e-mail accounts check their e-mail regularly. Because the technology allows almost instantaneous exchanges, that's what we expect, so it can be frustrating meeting by e-mail with people who check their inboxes only a few times during the day or who take a long time to reply. It's important, then, to start serial meetings by expressing expectations, e.g., "Since we'd like to take care of this issue within the next day or two, please check your e-mail every hour or so and reply to messages as quickly as possible."

E-mail discussions also make it easier for members of the group to participate passively: they may read every e-mail they receive, but send out few or none. The facilitator may want to send out occasional reminders to encourage the quiet members to get involved in the exchange.

Of course, there will also be members who will be very active, pouncing on the keyboard to reply to every e-mail received. Here again, the facilitator may want to remind the group about the need to allow all members to participate.

Emphasize that participants should make their messages short and to the point, so it shouldn't take long to read messages or to reply to them. They should also refrain from trying to deal with a lot of points in a single e-mail, just as they would refrain from doing so in a conventional meeting. And they should specify the subject of each e-mail they send—and adjust the subject as the discussion changes direction.

Point out that participants who don't check their inboxes frequently may suddenly find themselves overwhelmed by messages if a discussion generates a lot of interest. Arrange e-mail meetings by phone, if you suspect that any participants might not be checking their e-mail inboxes frequently and so might miss a meeting entirely.

Another disadvantage of e-mail is that it depends on words and files to communicate: we cannot convey or support our messages with voice tones and inflections, facial expressions, or body language. You could compensate somewhat for this disadvantage by encouraging participants to use *emoticons* and acronyms to supplement their words. But avoid complicating communication with an abundance of these artificial conventions. Suggest that participants use capital letters to emphasize words or phrases—but no more than that or it's interpreted as shouting.

Key Term

Emoticon Any of a variety of little faces formed from combinations of characters. The faces are created horizontally, to be appreciated by tilting your head to the left. Emoticons—the word is short for "emotional icons"—developed as a means of making text more expressive. They are sometimes called *smileys*, because the most basic is a smiling face: :) or :-)

Here are some common emoticons:

:) I'm smiling
:D I've got a big smile
:(I'm sad
:|| I'm angry
:/ or :\ I'm perplexed
:O I'm surprised
;) I'm winking at you (joking)
:P I'm sticking out my tongue at you

Some people have trouble expressing themselves in writing, especially with the concession that we expect in e-mail. This may cause participants to take longer to reply to messages or they may even refrain from contributing. If you suspect that this could be a problem for any member of the group, you should emphasize that what matters is *substance*, not *style*.

E-mail provides a great way to follow up after meetings. If handouts are distributed at a meeting, participants can ask any questions or express other reaction by e-mail. Answer their questions as soon as possible and take note of any concerns, for the next meeting.

TOOLS

Keeping It Short

E-mail has developed a vocabulary of acronyms, some of which can sometimes puzzle even the experienced e-mailer. Here are some you might encounter in business e-mail (in caps or, often, in lower case):

BTW: by the way
IMHO: in my humble opinion
F2F: face to face
TIA: thanks in advance
BG: big grin
LOL: laughing out loud

It's generally best to avoid using acronyms, since the recipient may not understand and/or may consider them unprofessional.

Discussion Lists

A discussion list is a community connected by a program that distributes every e-mail from any subscriber (member of the group) to every other subscriber, automatically. This is a convenient way of creating a forum for meetings, with two advantages over e-mail:

- It allows for archiving all messages automatically, which can be useful for later reference.
- It allows for adding people to the group at any time, because they can catch up on what has happened earlier.

As with e-mail, discussion groups can make it easier for meeting participants to contribute because they have time to organize their thoughts and express them more carefully. This is usually an advantage, especially for people who have trouble with language or who are not native users of English.

It takes a little effort to set up a discussion list, so it makes sense primarily for ongoing project work. If your organization is networked, your tech expert can set up a list with the appropriate software and ensure protection against viruses. If not, there are numerous Web sites through which you can create discussions lists.

Smart Managing

To Moderate or Not to Moderate?

Discussion lists can be set up as either *moderated* or *unmoderated.* A moderated list requires human intervention for every e-mail, to allow it to be posted as sent, to modify and then post it, or to delete it. That intervention can keep the discussion focused and prevent it from digressing or becoming too heated and/or too personal. Moderation obviously can require a lot of time—and it should not be necessary if you trust the members of the group to be responsible. If the group sets some ground rules, which can be appended automatically to every e-mail as a reminder, or posted regularly, there should be no need to moderate the discussion. If there are problems, you should be able to intervene with a post to remind participants of the focus of the discussion and the ground rules. In other words, moderate only as needed.

Still Images and Documents: Faxes and Files

Fax is still the most widely preferred way to send images. The major disadvantage in terms of meetings, at least for collaboration, is that outputs from fax machines cannot be modified. Also, the quality is often very poor.

If you want recipients to be able to modify still images, the best bet is to send graphic files as e-mail attachments. Of course, it's necessary to send it in a format that can be altered and to make sure that any recipients have the appropriate software to alter the files.

Also, make sure that all recipients can receive attachments—and that they know the maximum size allowed. If your files are too big, a compression program (such as WinZip) may reduce them to an acceptable size. Of course, your recipients need to have the same program or one that's compatible to restore the files to their original format.

As a last resort, you may need to save the files to a CD and send it by mail—which can take a lot of time and effort, especially if there are more than a few people collaborating and/or they're spread out across borders.

There are other disadvantages to collaborating through e-mail attachments:

- Sending large attachments can take a long time, especially with dialup connections.
- When any member of the group modifies a document, that version needs to be sent to all members.
- If two or more members of the group modify the same document at the same time, somebody must merge the changes into a single version manually.

If your meetings involve much modification of files, data conferencing would be a better way.

Teleconferencing

Teleconferencing is distance conferencing, interactive communi-

Beware of Teleconference

Teleconference is another term for which you need to establish a common understanding before you discuss teleconferencing with anyone.

Some people use the term to mean a conference call or an audio conference. Others understand it as a general term for distance conferencing, encompassing video conferencing, audio conferencing, and data conferencing.

In the latter sense, some people will also use the terms *Web conferencing* and *e-conferencing* as roughly synonymous with teleconferencing—although *Web conferencing* is also used as synonymous with *data conferencing*.

Confusing?

cation among three or more people who are separated geographically. It's a generic term that encompasses various technologies and applications, primarily the following:

- Audio conferencing
- Data conferencing
- Video conferencing

We've already discussed audio conferencing. We'll cover data conferencing next and then video conferencing. But first, we should mention two points.

The term *multimedia conferencing* is also used when a teleconference involves three or more types of technologies. This term, however, is more promotional than descriptive.

There's yet another term that's used for some forms of teleconferencing—*Web conferencing*. This term, as you would assume, refers to any type of conferencing—audio, data, video—over the Web. Here again, the use of this term is not universal, so don't discuss Web conferencing with anybody without first reaching agreement on what you'll mean by it.

Data Conferencing

Data conferencing allows participants to share applications. This means that they can collaborate on whiteboards, spreadsheets, word processing programs, graphics programs, and other tools to work on projections, budgets, reports, diagrams, designs, and so forth. These applications are generally supplemented by at least an audio connection, whether by phone or more advanced technology.

Preparation

Understand the collaboration package and applications. That just seems like common sense. But whoever will be running the meeting—you, a facilitator, a resident expert on the specific applications—should get enough training and guidance to not only know the ins and outs of the application but also feel confident using them. It's one thing to use an applications by yourself in your office and quite another to use it in data conferencing.

Determine who will control the technology. It's possible to set up a data conference so that more than one participant can use an application at one time. However, it can easily get confusing for the participants and challenging for the facilitator if several people are contributing simultaneously—drawing on a whiteboard, changing figures in a spreadsheet, or editing a document. It may work better, at least until the group becomes familiar with data conferencing, for one person to control the application and for participants to make suggestions. Another possibility, particularly when graphics are involved and it's more difficult for participants to explain suggestions than to simply show what they mean, is for the facilitator to direct traffic, indicating which participant will control the application at any point in the meeting.

As the host, the facilitator has ultimate control over how and when the application is shared. He or she should know which key allows participants to access an application and which key restricts access.

As with audio conferencing, emphasize that all participants must be ready to begin on time. Because the technology is more involved, you may want remote participants to connect 10 minutes before the scheduled start time. (There may be some challenges dealing with firewalls, for example.)

Have a technician on hand, at least for your first few data conferences. At the least, have the names and phone and pager numbers of people to contact in the event of technical problems.

> Key Term
>
> **Firewall** A system—hardware, software, or a combination—designed to prevent unauthorized access to or from a private network. All messages entering or leaving the network pass through the firewall, which screens them according to specified security criteria and blocks those that do not meet the criteria.

Save meeting time by loading the application and the appropriate file(s) before making the connection. This shows that you're prepared to start the meeting immediately.

Meeting

The best way to ensure a successful, productive data conference is for the facilitator to be familiar and comfortable with the applications that the group is using.

The facilitator should make it clear from the start how the group will use the application(s), as determined above, under "Preparation." He or she should explain how members are to participate—by using keyboard or mouse or by guiding the facilitator. If participants are allowed to control an application, the facilitator should not hesitate to take control if collaboration becomes chaotic.

Anybody who works with an application should move a little more slowly than usual, make gestures that are more deliberate, and explain carefully what he or she is doing. Allow time for remote participants to ask questions or make suggestions. Unless all locations involved in the conference have very high-bandwidth Internet connections, response time can be slow.

At the end of the data conference, the participants should evaluate the meeting. What worked, in terms of the process? What suggestions would they make to improve data conferences?

Key Term **Bandwidth** A measure of the transmission capacity of a communications channel. The higher the bandwidth, the more information the channel can carry. Bandwidth is most accurately measured in cycles per second (hertz or Hz), but it's also common to use bits per second (bps) or bytes per second instead. High bandwidth means faster and higher-quality teleconferencing.

Follow-up

Follow up the data conference by making available the final version of any files created or modified during the conference. The collaboration software should have file transfer capabilities. If not, you can e-mail the files.

Encourage participants to ask any questions or share any concerns (especially if any members of the group were unable or unwilling to participate actively). Use alternative channels for communication if any participants don't have easy access to a computer.

Consider setting up a discussion list so participants can continue to ask questions and make suggestions asynchronously.

Video Conferencing

In its simplest form, video conferencing is the synchronous connection of people in two or more locations using some combination of video, audio, and often data to communicate.

Preparation

Video conferencing brings you the closest to the experience of a conventional meeting. However, because of the technology and because participants may not be familiar and comfortable with using it, video conferences require more planning and preparation than other types of meetings discussed so far. (You should review the earlier suggestions on preparing for audio conferences.) Also, the closer the capabilities of any virtual meeting to the look and feel of a same-place, same-time meeting, the easier it is to forget about compensating for the differences—however slight.

It's even more important with video conferences than with conventional meetings to minimize the number of participants. One suggestion is to limit the number at any location to eight, unless the video conference consists solely of a presentation. It's also generally wise to keep video conferences narrower in scope and shorter than conventional meetings because of the greater difficulty of maintaining attention, keeping up energy, and staying focused.

Prepare the participants by distributing the agenda and any materials far in advance and providing instructions in writing. Share with participants the tips listed below, under "Performance."

Have a technician on hand, at least for your first few video conferences. If that's not possible, have the names and phone and pager numbers of people to contact in the event of technical problems.

It's important to prepare the room for a conventional meeting. For a video conference, it's even more important—and obviously involves more thought and effort.

First, position the camera. Generally it's best to put it close to the monitor, either on top or directly to the side, so it appears as if participants on site are looking directly at remote participants. Don't point the camera toward the door or any window where there might be movements that could be distracting to the viewers.

Next, set the camera to output to the monitor. That will allow you to view your site from the perspective of remote participants.

Make sure that lighting is at least adequate, especially between the camera and the participants' faces. If overhead lighting is insufficient or unbalanced, it may help to place a desk lamp near the monitor to compensate. Turn off any bright lights in the background, close the blinds or curtains on any outside windows if it's sunny, and cover any reflective surfaces.

Clean up the site. Get rid of any items within camera range that might make the site seem cluttered. Remove anything that could distract or offend.

Arrange seating so that all participants can be seen easily by remote viewers and can feel comfortable working together.

Use individual microphones, if possible, for equal sound quality. If you use a table mike, position it the optimal distance from all, according to the manufacturer's instructions, so participants don't have to move to speak.

Hold up any visuals (charts, graphs, etc.) in front of the camera, so you know how to position them to allow remote participants to see them clearly and easily.

Finally, after you've arranged lighting, background, seating, audio equipment, and positioning of any visuals, set the monitor so participants on site can see their remote co-participants.

Now you're ready!

Meeting

Here are some suggestions for making your video conference as much like a "normal" meeting as possible.

- Address the screen as if it were another participant seated in the room. Don't stare. Make eye contact with participants on site, not just remote participants.
- Speak in a normal volume, a little more slowly, and as clearly as possible.
- Avoid making any noises that the microphone(s) might pick up. If you're using table mikes, refrain from rustling papers, tapping your pen, and other unnecessary sounds. What if you have to cough, sneeze, or burp? If you have a table mike, lean away from it. If you have a lapel, lavalier, or headset mike, cover it up.

At the end of the video conference, the participants should evaluate the meeting. What worked? How could the meeting process be improved?

Follow-up

Follow up the video conference by e-mailing or faxing the meeting notes and action items. Encourage participants to ask any questions or share any concerns (especially participants who were inhibited by the technology). If not all members of the

Smart Managing

No Panacea

Marty Morrow, CEO of Quovix, a company that "builds networked collaborative communities," summed up the technology science concisely (*Darwin* magazine, November 16, 2001):

> There must be over 1000 software vendors selling "collaboration tools" at this point. Everything including email, Instant Messaging, VideoConferencing, Virtual Whiteboarding, Project Rooms, Portal Strategies—all selling themselves as *the* solution to a company's collaboration needs.... The tools are 20% (or less) of the problem you're trying to solve.

Keep that final thought in mind as you explore technology for meetings.

group have access to computers, use alternative channels for communication.

Make available (on the organization's intranet or in the library) any records of the meeting—any presentations, audiotapes, videotapes, and so forth.

Consider setting up a discussion list so participants can continue to ask questions and make suggestions asynchronously.

Conclusion

This chapter could be much longer and provide much more detail about these technologies. But what matters most at this point you won't find in a book.

You need to consider your employees and any others you would involve in virtual meetings. Are they ready? Do they have enough experience and confidence with technology that they could soon be using it as easily and comfortably as they now use flipcharts and tangible whiteboards? Sales reps and technicians will talk about *requirements* for an application or a system, but the requirements that you should consider above all are the psychological, emotional, and social requirements of your employees. What do they need in order to meet virtually? The answers to these questions are not on a Web site or in a brochure or manual. They're in what you know about your employees and the culture of your workplace. They're in the potential that you recognize in your employees and in yourself.

Before you start exploring technology for virtual meetings, you should at least skim *CyberMeetings: How to Link People and Technology in Your Organization* by James L. Creighton and James W. R. Adams (New York: AMACOM, 1998), probably the one best book on the subject of this chapter.

Then, to find out more about any of the technologies mentioned in this chapter, just enter the name into your favorite search engine and check out the sites it finds. If any of the technologies appeals to you, talk with some sales reps. But be prepared to be overwhelmed by the possibilities—and keep in mind that no technology will guarantee better meetings—or even meetings that are as good.

Manager's Checklist for Chapter 8

- ❑ Our definition of "meeting" is *an event consisting of people, content, and process for a purpose.* Technology is extending the concept of meetings as it expands the possibilities for communicating and collaborating.
- ❑ Virtual meetings are usually less expensive than face-to-face meetings: they eliminate the costs of travel, accommodations, and meals; they minimize the inconvenience of interrupting work; and they reduce the loss of time and thus productivity. In addition, they can bring together people who are separated by space or time.
- ❑ Virtual meetings have various disadvantages, depending on the technology and the specific situation. The most obvious disadvantage is that they're not face-to-face: there's something missing or at least different in any technology, so group and individual dynamics are different.
- ❑ Sales reps and technicians will talk about *requirements* for an application or a system, but the requirements that you should consider above all are the psychological, emotional, and social requirements of your employees.

Index